Nevada-California-Lake Tahoe Region, Circa 1947

Flanigan

Pyramid Lake

Doyle

⑤

④ Sutcliffe

S.P. RR

Nixon

95

40

Wadsworth

Fernley

95

S i e r r a

California

Nevada

395

W.P. RR

40

Truckee River

Sparks

ALT 95

③

Reno

395

Verdi

V&T RR

50

Lake Lahontan

Truckee

40

Donner Lake

Mt. Rose

27

Virginia City

50

Carson River

Five Lakes Country

Squaw Valley

Deer Park

Truckee River

N e v a d a

Crystal Bay

Little Valley

Washoe Valley

① Franktown

② Washoe Lake

Dayton

ALT 95

Wabuska

Tahoe City

Tahoe Tavern

V&T RR

Lake

Carson City

River

Bliss State Park

Glenbrook

50

Genoa

395

Minden

ALT 95

Tahoe

Stateline

Nevada

California

Carson River

Gardnerville

Yerington

Major Dude-Divorce Ranches

① Flying M E Ranch
② Washoe Pines Ranch
③ Donner Trail Ranch
④ Pyramid Lake Ranch
⑤ TH Ranch

Source: Nevada State Highway Map, 1947, adapted by PAUL CIRAC

The DIVORCE SEEKERS

On Nevada dude ranches, the talents required for operating successfully were similar to those on other dude ranches: the men had to know horses and sometimes cattle, while the women had to manage food, entertainment, and other details. But an additional burden that the Nevada hostesses had to shoulder was the need to be a mother confessor to women and men with shattered marriages and broken lives.

—Lawrence R. Borne,
Dude Ranching, A Complete History

Books by William L. McGee

Bluejacket Odyssey 1942-1946, Guadalcanal to Bikini, Naval Armed Guard in the Pacific

Amphibious Operations in the South Pacific in WWII series:
   The Amphibians Are Coming! Emergence of the 'Gator Navy and its Revolutionary Landing Craft. Volume 1

   The Solomons Campaigns 1942-1943, From Guadalcanal to Bougainville—Pacific War Turning Point. Volume 2

About the Authors

William L. McGee was born in 1925 on a ranch in Montana. At seventeen, he enlisted in the United States Navy and served in the Pacific Theater from 1943 to 1945. Following World War II, he spent several years cowboying in Wyoming, California and Nevada. Later, he made a successful transition into the business

world, with an import-export company, followed by a thirty-two year career in radio and TV broadcasting, during which he authored nine guidebooks on broadcast advertising sales.

Sandra V. McGee was born in Southern California. She studied ballet and piano and performed with various chamber groups in the San Francisco Bay Area. Later, her focus shifted to the business world. She opened her own company managing and designing commercial real estate and owned and operated several retail shops in major shopping complexes in Northern California. She currently is Director of Marketing for BMC Publications.

(Photo Joanne A. Calitri)

The DIVORCE SEEKERS

A Photo Memoir of a Nevada Dude Wrangler

To Jackie —

Happy Trails Ahead

WILLIAM L. McGEE AND SANDRA V. McGEE

Bill McGee   *Sandra McGee*

WITH A FOREWORD BY WILLIAM W. BLISS

BMC PUBLICATIONS

ST. HELENA, CALIFORNIA

2004

The DIVORCE SEEKERS

A Photo Memoir of a
Nevada Dude Wrangler

BMC Publications, St. Helena 94574
© Copyright 2004 by BMC Publications

Library of Congress Control Number: 2003097644
McGee, William L., and Sandra V. McGee
    The Divorce Seekers: A Photo Memoir of a Nevada Dude Wrangler
    by William L. McGee and Sandra V. McGee
    Includes bibliographical references, notes and index.
  ISBN 0-9701678-1-4
1. Nevada divorce trade (1930-1970)—United States—History
2. Dude-divorce ranches—Nevada—History
3. Migratory divorce and the Nevada legal practice—History
4. Divorcés—socialites and celebrity profiles—History
5. Lake Tahoe Region of California and Nevada—History
I. Title

Printed in the United States of America on acid-free paper

FIRST PRINTING

Designed and produced at WHITE SAGE STUDIOS
Virginia City, Nevada   whitesage@gbis.com

Published by BMC Publications—
(A BMC Communications Company)
    1397 St. James Drive
    St. Helena, CA 94574
    Tel: (707) 967-8322

    E-mail: BMCpublications@aol.com
    Website: www.BMCpublications.com

Cover design by Paul Cirac

The west is dead my Friend

But writers hold the seed

And what they saw

Will live and grow

Again to those who read

—Charles M. Russell, 1917

More than one person urged Emmy to write her memoirs, but her response was always the same and would go something like this—"Dear, I wouldn't dare. There are only so many types of guests. No matter what I would write, someone would think I was writing about them."

IN MEMORY OF

Emily Pentz Wood
1895 – 1966

*A truly great lady who brought elegance
and compassion to the Nevada dude ranch business*

Contents

Foreword

Bill and Sandra McGee, co-authors of this photo memoir, are well-qualified to chronicle this true story of a special period in Nevada history.

Bill, as young Montana cowboy, worked his way to Nevada in 1947, via Wyoming, and is one of the few dude wranglers "still above ground" (as he puts it) who lived and worked on a leading Nevada dude ranch during the post-World War II era.

Sandra, a native of Southern California, has an enthusiasm for Nevada's history that is catching. The mammoth photo-research and information-gathering from dude ranch guests and their offspring would have been impossible had it not been for Sandra's tenacity to follow any and all leads relative to this time—a rather colorful time—in my State's history.

Aside from exhaustive research, Bill and Sandra have added the words of some old-timers still with us—from dude ranchers and ranch guests to divorce attorneys—who lived and worked in the era. The end result: *The Divorce Seekers: A Photo Memoir of a Nevada Dude Wrangler.*

The book is Bill's tribute to Emily Pentz Wood and is well-deserved and long overdue. As the proprietor of the famous Flying M E guest ranch in Washoe Valley, Emmy brought a touch of class to the Nevada dude ranch business. She was loved by locals and guests alike. She introduced an element of "sophistication to the sagebrush," if you will.

In 1931, the Nevada State Legislature reduced residency requirements for divorce in Nevada to six weeks. The grounds for divorce were "mental cruelty," which conveniently covered every stretch of the imagination. With such reduced residency requirements and lenient grounds for divorce, compared to other states at the time, Nevada, in a sense, became the only choice. But by the early 1960s, changing attitudes about divorce and, in turn, increasingly more liberal divorce laws in other states put an end to the need for a migratory Nevada "six week cure."

During the heyday, most divorce attorneys recommended top guest ranches to their more affluent clientele, generally located within twenty to thirty-five miles of Reno, and providing a free and easy lifestyle with a maximum of privacy from the press. Other options included Reno's better hotels—the Riverside or the Mapes. At nearby Lake Tahoe, the Cal-Neva Lodge and Skywater Lodge catered to the six week guest. Even the established, staid, family-oriented Glenbrook Inn accommodated an occasional guest for a similar period and purpose.

Interesting, glamorous, intriguing, outrageous, sometimes scandalous stories of divorcés and the dude ranches patronized by the rich, the famous, the colorful, the others—divorce seekers all—persist today. Some in legend, some in myth, most in fact.

I have encouraged Bill and Sandra to create this "memoir within a pictorial" as have several other old-time Nevadans. Those of us who lived through the brief but fascinating, often raucous, period of migratory divorce want to be sure it is preserved for future generations and, as far as I know, this is the first book on the subject written *from a dude wrangler's perspective.*

This pictorial will add to our lore and entertainment and will be consulted by historians, students, and history buffs of the West who want to know how we lived, how we spoke, what our attitudes were—and how we lived through it all. The authors' dedicated work will surely help keep the day-to-day history of this period from being lost.

Bill McGee, as I have come to know him, tells it like it really was on a dude ranch when Reno was the "divorce capital of the world."

I'm confident that this photo memoir by one of Nevada's dude wranglers will help preserve this brief, but special, time in the history of our great Silver State.

—WILLIAM W. BLISS

GLENBROOK, NEVADA

Preface

I had several reasons for writing this book. First, I wanted to produce a lasting tribute to a truly great friend and lady, Emily Pentz Wood, owner of the Flying M E, the most famous dude ranch in northern Nevada. We first met in 1947 in Reno at the Riverside Hotel Corner Bar, when she hired me as the head dude wrangler. The "M E"—which stood for "Emmy"—was located in Washoe Valley, twenty-one miles south of Reno, on the site of the historic Franktown Hotel. I would soon come to learn firsthand why this petite lady was loved by so many, and how she came to epitomize the hospitality for which the West was noted in her time.

Nevada journalist and author Basil Woon summed up Emmy's character in these words:

> Emmy was the same to everyone. She met cowboy, divorcée, servant, lawyer, merchant, or the casual friend on a night out, on terms of a completely natural equality.
>
> Besides her resident guests (during most of the year almost every guest room was taken)—highway cops, judges, fellow ranchers, gamblers, and other locals dropped in. Eleanor Roosevelt and Clark Gable stayed there merely because they loved Emmy.
>
> Neither money nor social position meant much to her—manners, however, meant a lot. Of a celebrated and wealthy writer she said, "He's a boor, my dear. I don't think I shall have him here again." Of a gnarled and sun-blackened rancher, whose only school had been nature itself, she said, "He's a gentleman. He's always welcome here."

Emily Wood brought elegance to the dude ranch business. But more than that she brought a quality of human understanding. Many of the divorcées came to the ranch shattered, despairing. Before many days, Emmy had given them hope and a new outlook on life. That was Emily Wood's real gift—giving hope and understanding.

The second reason for writing this book was to dispel a number of myths about the divorce business in Reno, "Divorce Capital of the World," during the 1930s to 1960s era.

Third, I had been promising friends and family I would write this memoir about my cowboy and wrangler days, and finally decided it was now or never. I still had my journal and, with the help of a small network of Nevadans, the research got underway. (Had I started twenty years earlier, I would have had many more interview opportunities.)

Fourth, I was encouraged to write this book by the Nevada Historical Society's Eric Moody, Curator of Manuscripts, and Phillip Earl, former Curator of History (retired), "since there has never been a book published on the subject from a dude wrangler's perspective."

This book is primarily about the more affluent divorce seekers who could afford to stay at one of the top dude ranches or best hotels in northern Nevada in the 1930s to 1960s era. When these people arrived to begin their six weeks' residency to get a divorce, their East Coast attorney had invariably made all the arrangements for a local attorney and a place to stay.

A lot of "hard-working modest folk," as one lawyer called them, would arrive in Nevada without a referral from their home state attorney, or a place to stay. They just showed up unannounced in a lawyer's office or sought out one of a handful of "discount" lawyers. They found housing options in second- or third-rate motels, private homes, boarding houses, rooming houses, apartment houses, duplexes, auto courts, campgrounds, and even the YMCA.

However, my time as a dude wrangler was with the affluent divorce seekers—those who spent their six weeks' residency "out West" on a Nevada dude ranch.

• • •

They say there's a story behind every story. My beautiful wife, Sandra, an accomplished publicist, offered to help me with research for this book. Her enthusiasm for the history of Nevada dude ranches and migratory divorce was immediately obvious. Within six months she knew almost as much as I did, even though I was wranglin' dudes when she was still a Southern California toddler. So I promised her *with* billing on the cover—meaning "by William L. McGee with Sandra V. McGee." Next thing you know, she was not only offering suggestions but editing my work to reflect a woman's point of view, when appropriate. Furthermore, she initiated the first draft writing on several of her favorite chapters. Result: She has earned co-author billing on the cover, and I couldn't be more proud of her.

Sandra was also able to track down an amazing number of family members and descendants of divorce seekers via the Internet. The result was hundreds of never-before-published photographs for this book. In some cases, the quality of the image may have been marginal, but if the photo enhanced the story, we used it, and were grateful for the contribution.

There is another special lady I must single out, Valerie Vondermuhll, an editor at *Life* magazine. As the reader will soon learn, this book contains dozens of Valerie's excellent photographs documenting life at the Flying M E during the late 1940s. Thanks to Valerie's brother, George A. Vondermuhll Jr., who uncovered Val's photo album, this book was transformed from a simple cowboy memoir into a photo memoir with more than 500 images.

—WILLIAM L. MCGEE
ST. HELENA, CALIFORNIA

Acknowledgments

We are deeply grateful to the following individuals and families for taking their time to search through attics and basements to find almost-forgotten images of another era so they could be shared in this photo memoir: George A. Vondermuhll Jr., Norman and Rhonda Azevedo, Bernadette "Bernie" Bechdolt, William W. "Bill" Bliss, Julie Bechdolt Contri, Susan Countner, Patricia Cramer, Nikki M. Demas-Butz, Richard C. Greenleaf, Gail Greenleaf Hencken, Janice Goodhue, Dirck L. Hinton, Kit Hinton, Ann Clegg Holloway, Jack and Grace Horgan and their grand-daughter Christine Carter, Noreen I. K. Humphreys, Barry and Jan Hundemer, Tina Bundy Nappe, Harry Parker, Nadine Prior, Deborah Tokar Schneider, and Ethel Hall.

We are equally grateful to the following professionals and associations for permission to use their photos: Neal Cobb; Barbara Van Cleve, Lazy K Bar Ranch; Jeff Way, general manager, Eatons' Ranch; Charles Henry, executive director, and Junelle Pringle, historian, Colorado Dude & Guest Ranch Association; author Joel H. Bernstein; The Dude Ranchers' Association; photographer Larry Prosor; and Magnum Photographers.

We are also grateful to the following for their contributions "above and beyond." These individuals have generously shared their memories and provided many leads that kept the research trail alive: Bill and Bernie Bechdolt, Bill Bliss, Janice Goodhue, Dirck Hinton, Kit Hinton, Gail Hinton Payette, Jack and Grace Horgan, David Myrick, Tina Bundy Nappe, David P. Sinai, Esq., Harry B. Swanson, Esq., Carol Van Etten, and Neill E. West.

A special acknowledgment goes to talented artist, Joan Allison McGee Wagner, for allowing us to reproduce her caricatures of some of the more colorful guests who stayed at the Flying M E in the 1940s.

We also wish to thank the McGee clan for the loan of Flying M E photos from their personal albums: Lucy McGee Haynes, Betsy McGee Clarke, Billy McGee, and Kathy McGee.

Thanks also go to John Parker of Parker Graphic Design in Ventura, California and Edward Salas of Timecast in Carson City, Nevada for their help in scanning close to 1,000 images for possible use in the book.

Collectively, the images from the above individuals represent the vast majority of illustrations in this book. However, we also owe our thanks to the following organizations and their staffs for allowing us to selectively augment our collection from their archives and special collections: Nevada Historical Society, Special Collections Department at University of Nevada at Reno, Nevada State Museum, Nevada State Railroad Museum, Northern Lake Tahoe Historical Society, Jackson Hole Historical Society & Museum, and Yellowstone National Park.

Many of the following individuals have made their own creative contribution to recording Nevada's colorful history and have allowed us to draw on their wealth of knowledge: Gwendolyn Clancy, Clancy Video Productions; author Andria Daley-Taylor; Kelli Du Fresne, *Nevada Appeal*; Les Groth, Chief (retired), Warren Engine Company No. 1; Penny McClary, Washoe Pines; Mark McLaughlin, MicMacMedia; author Marilyn Melton; Maya Miller, Washoe Pines; Dr. Richard Miller, Washoe Pines; Sue Morrow, *Nevada Appeal* (retired); Gerri Murphy; Paul Webster, Vice President and Trustee, Warren Engine Company No. 1; and Kay and JohnD Winters, Winters Ranch. Many others have assisted us with information and suggestions, and they are acknowledged in the notes at the points at which their specific help was particularly useful.

Among the archives, libraries, and publications who generously shared their knowledge and answered our endless questions, a few deserve special mention: Eric Moody, Curator of Manuscripts, and Lee Philip Brumbaugh, Curator of Photography, Nevada Historical Society; Robert E. Blesse, Director of Special Collections Department, University of Nevada, Reno; Guy Louis Rocha, Assistant Administrator for Archives and Records, Nevada State Library and Archives; Joyce Cox, Head of Reference, and the staff at Nevada State Library and Archives; Baylen B. Limasa and Rick Rasmussen, Nevada State Library and Archives, Micrographics and Imaging Program; Bob Nylen, Curator of History, Nevada State Museum; David Moore, Editor, Nevada Magazine; Marie Crusinberry, Interlibrary Loan Department, Santa Barbara Public Library; and Carol-Ann Swatling, University of Nevada Las Vegas, Lied Library.

The following select list of authors and publishers have generously granted us permission to quote from their previously published works, thereby enriching our efforts immensely: Lawrence R. Borne for *Dude Ranching: A Complete History*; Carol Van Etten for *Tahoe City Yesterdays*; Myra Sauer Ratay for *Pioneers of the Ponderosa: How Washoe Valley Rescued the Comstock*; and William W. Bliss for *Tahoe Heritage: The Bliss Family of Glenbrook, Nevada*.

Finally, we wish to thank the following for their critique of specific chapters and/or the manuscript in its final phase: Phillip Earl, former Curator of History, Nevada Historical Society; Lee Whittlesey, National Park Service, Yellowstone National Park; and author Joel H. Bernstein. And no work would be complete without the hundreds of hours of proofreading for which we thank fifth generation Nevadan Donald Dickerson, Flying M E "graduate" Joan Allison McGee Wagner, technical writer Lee Mourad, and grammarian Spencer Boise.

We are especially grateful to our designer, Paul Cirac of White Sage Studios in Virginia City, Nevada. As a fifth generation Nevadan, Paul brought his knowledge of Nevada history as well as his passion for the project to every work session we spent at his studios in the historic mining town of Virginia City.

It is the authors' intention to contribute the McGee Collection of photos to a repository in northern Nevada upon completion of the book. Mr. George A. Vondermuhll Jr., a true gentleman of the old school, has also agreed to contribute his sister Valerie's collection of more than 200 images taken at the Flying M E and its environs during her visits to the ranch in the late 1940s. Together these two collections will provide future generations with a visual record of a brief but unforgettable era in Nevada's history.

Introduction

I've always had a love affair with the American cowboy. You know, the tall, silent guy who prefers the company of his horse to people. Owen Wister is said to have created the first romantic cowboy in 1902 with his best-selling novel *The Virginian*. The hero was brave and honorable, tough but soft-spoken, and was later portrayed on the screen by Gary Cooper—a mighty attractive combination to a lady dude.

If you've read the book-jacket copy, you know that my husband is a former real American cowboy from Montana and that I am a dude from the sunny beaches of Southern California. My husband knew the West as a cowboy and dude wrangler in the decades of the 1930s and 1940s—by his account a purer and more authentic period. Imagine—cowboy-and-the-lady romances on rustic dude ranches "out West." Imagine —Eastern Social Register types, drenched in full-length mink, and way too many monogrammed trunks, being met at the Reno train depot by the likes of a tall, silent and

(Illustration: B. Kliban)

handsome cowboy—a description which many think fit Bill, by the way. That's the stuff of romance and a good film noir.

Please write your memoirs about your time as a cowboy and a dude wrangler, Bill was urged on many occasions.

The memoirs got off the ground—more or less—in 1991, when Bill drove solo across the country for three months, on a "roots quest" to find and interview all his living relatives. However, researching his years in the U. S. Navy during World War II kept him occupied for a decade, and produced four scholarly military histories set in the South Pacific during WWII.

Then, in the spring of 2001, we were invited to sign books at a military reunion in Reno. With time to kill before checking into our hotel, I suggested we drive by the site of the former Flying M E, where Bill "wrangled dudes" in the late 1940s. Located in Franktown, on the old Highway 395, most of the main ranch building had burned down in 1963—yet I wanted to see where Bill had worked as a dude wrangler in northern Nevada. I began asking questions: What were the accommodations like? What were the guests like? What was a dude? What was a dude wrangler? And how could a Social Register-type from the East, used to having a bedroom suite with a personal maid or valet, share a room and a bath with a stranger for six weeks, just to get a divorce?

My curiosity about this period of my husband's life was mounting. Bill simply had to write about this. After all, how many former dude wranglers from the 1940s were still alive to tell the story? You can count me in to help, I said. Who could resist being drawn into a project whose characters and places had names like Chaska West, Utah Bob, Allie Okie, the Cowboy Bar, and the Newman brothers—Hoot, Holler and Yell? (I hear they had a sister named Whisper).

• • •

My part in this book consisted of doing research of the usual sort—hundreds of hours looking through newspapers and magazines from the 1940s and 1950s (on microfilm) for divorce stories and related items; locating photographs and pouring through file boxes in historical societies and library archives; doing a fair amount of editing, as well as contributing some original writing when the text beckoned a woman's view point; and searching for divorcés and other guests (or their offspring) who had stayed at the divorce ranches.

However, the best moments of research were, without a doubt, the interviews with survivors from this cast of characters—a remarkable breed of men and women who survived the Great Depression, the Second World War, and every amazing change that has occurred since then, and managed along the way to fall in love, out of love, and change partners with a degree of grace and style that seems to be lacking today.

My research also changed my perception of Reno. When some people hear the name "Reno," they think of what was once known to the locals as the "Red Line" area—the gaudy neon lights, the bars and the hotels and casinos that surround the train depot. They think of a town shoddy by day and tawdry by night. But looking at the rest of the city is another story. Perched at an elevation of 4,500 feet, the town is at the feet of the majestic Sierra Nevada mountains. The Truckee River races through the center of town on its way from Lake Tahoe to Pyramid Lake. On a high bluff of the south bank of the river are big handsome mansions and beautiful, tree-lined neighborhoods. There's the University of Nevada and, within a few miles, the historic mining town of Virginia City and the pristine Lake Tahoe. There's a segment of the population that the casual tourist never meets: the writers, artists and historians who make their homes in Reno, Virginia City, Carson City, or Lake Tahoe. The intellectual and cultural life is there—though not visible at first glimpse.

This may explain why so many Eastern blue bloods, Social Register types, titled Europeans and others to the manor born, came to Nevada to get a divorce, fell in love with the scenery, the climate and the people, and remained in the Silver State.

And—of course—there were those cowboys!

—SANDRA V. MCGEE
ST. HELENA, CALIFORNIA

Reno Divorce Glossary

Publicity about the "Reno Divorce Colony" generated its own terminology.

A Spare	The euphemistic name for the man or woman the plaintiff brought with them to Reno for six weeks, and whom the plaintiff intended to marry when the divorce decree was granted.
Alimony Park	The park across the street from the Washoe County Courthouse.
Biggest Little City	Reno
Bridge of Sighs	Truckee River Bridge, Virginia Street
Divorce	From the Latin *divortium*, to turn different ways, to separate
Divorce Colony	Reno
Divorcé	A man divorced
Divorcée or Divorcee	A woman divorced
Divorcés	Men and women divorced
Divorcement	Dissolution of the marriage tie
Divorcer	One who procures or produces a divorce

(Postcard courtesy Nevada Historical Society)

Divorceuse	A woman who is divorcing her husband
Divorcive	Causing or tending to divorce
Divorce Capital of the World	Reno
Divorce Mecca	Reno
Divorce Mill	Reno
Divorce Trade	Nevada
Divorce Ranch	A uniquely Nevada term used by the national media during the "Quickie Divorce" era.
Divorcée Special	Any train bringing clients to Reno
Divorce seekers	Males or females
Going Reno	A generic term for divorcés on the loose
Golden Age of Divorce	1930 – 1960
Heyday of Divorce	1930 – 1960
Quickie Divorce	Six weeks in Nevada
"Reno"	A type of bra that both "separates and supports." The idea is attributed to Ruth Lusch, a colorful Reno publicist in the late 1940s.
Reno Cure	Six weeks' residency in Reno to get a divorce.
Reno Colony	Reno social set composed of locals and visiting divorce seekers.
Reno-vation	A term coined by Walter Winchell for the change that despondent spouses went through in Reno. Also: "Reno-vated" and "Get Reno-vated."
Separation Center of the West	Reno
Severance Stay	Six weeks in Reno
Sin City	Reno, or so they say.
Six-weekers	Divorce seekers
State of Easy Divorce	Nevada
Take the Cure	Get a divorce
The Separator	Washoe County Courthouse
Widow's Corner	Corner Bar at the Riverside Hotel virtually next door to the Washoe County Courthouse; a meeting place for locals and the Reno Divorce Colony.

Jane Something-Somebody

A profile by Basil Woon

In the year 1931, or it may have been '32 or '33 or '34 or even later, Jane Something-Somebody felt she just had to get a divorce. All her friends were doing it, and anyway her husband was unfaithful, or she was. Jane lived in New York or Boston or maybe on Philadelphia's Main Line. She had a home and a "place" in the country. She was 27 or 37 or thereabouts. She had never cooked a meal in her life or made a bed, or washed anything but herself. Since she was a small girl, money had been something she or her husband or her dad signed a check for. And she had never lacked for anything in the world, except perhaps a perpetual *je ne sais quoi* which disturbed her dreams and that she knew money couldn't buy.

Jane had been a deb at the Ritz (or the Bellevue-Stratford). She had been to Bermuda, to Paris (of course), to Rome, to Greece, and to London. She had golfed in the Highlands and dared the Cresta Run of St. Moritz. But she had never been west of the Alleghenies, and her only contact with the Wild West had been at Smith (or Vassar or Wellesley or Bryn Mawr) where she had a girlfriend from San Francisco who strangely was neither Indian nor Chinese.

Our girl had charge accounts at the Ritz and the Plaza and the better restaurants and stores, and drew a warm welcome at Tiffany's (or Cartier's or Black, Starr & Frost). She had been sheltered and paid for all her life and was, to cut it short, a beautiful, but spoiled baby.

One day, Jane whispered to a friend that she thought she'd like a divorce, and her friend replied, "My dear, there's absolutely only *one* place to go—Reno. It's at the other end of the world, of course, but wait until you see those cowboys!"

Around midnight a few weeks later, while Reno's Commercial Row was roaring and the bars were lined by picturesque gentlemen in cowboots and bent sombreros, the Overland Limited deposited Jane at a small yellow station labelled RENO, where two persons awaited her arrival. One was distinguished by the fact that he wore a tie, so you were pretty sure he was a lawyer. The other was "Slats." Slats had no stomach, wore a huge hat, fancy carved boots, sheepskin coat and jeans. He was Jane's very first wrangler. He was very polite, called her "Ma'am," and was so absolutely outside her experience that, a few weeks later, she almost married him. Slats fastened her five suitcases (she had been warned to bring only necessities) in the rumble seat of his Model A, saying that he would fetch the trunks tomorrow. The lawyer said that perhaps Jane would like a drink but, after a nervous look at the reeling customers outside the Palace Club, she thought she'd better not.

Sitting besides Slats in the Model A, Jane saw the lights of Reno disappear in a few minutes. Thereafter for thirty-five miles or so, there were no more lights, not even of other cars, only the misty shapes of naked mountains, and occasionally of a steer as it lumbered along the narrow washboard highway, turning to regard them placidly as Slats braked and honked. Finally the car turned on a side road, the sagebrush scraping its sides as it turned and twisted upward toward a star-studded sky. Twice Slats stopped to unpadlock and open a gate, which he carefully closed afterward. The jolting woke Jane up and, at last, there were lights ahead. Slats honked, the car came to rest, and a door opened. A hearty female voice shouted, "Hi! Welcome to the X-Bar-Y!" (A brand invented by the writer.)

The voice belonged to a comely, motherly young woman who wielded a steaming pot of coffee. "You like yours straight?" she asked Jane, waving a bottle in the other hand. "Slats likes a slug in his." She poured two fingers of bourbon in Slats' mug. "Number Four," she said, and Slats began to unload the suitcases.

Then, to Jane, "Sit down and rest. Slats'll take your bags over. We're kind of rough and ready here. But," she smiled, "the boys'll see you have a good time. Do you ride?"

Jane said she did, and that she had brought her habit (made for her by O'Rossen of the Place Vendôme—she had cut a figure in it along the allées of the Bois). Back home, she had a hunter; in Virginia she rode to the hounds. Her English saddle was handmade to measure in Jermyn Street. She was never once to use the saddle nor the costume in Nevada.

"Number Four" was some distance across the yard, a 12'x 8' cabin with an iron bed, an armchair made of rawhide, a small writing desk and table and, behind a screen, a washbasin with a jug of water on the floor beside. The floor was carpeted with a colorful rattan rug. There were two small windows, out of one of which Jane stared appre-

hensively into the mysterious night. Slats appeared with a jug of hot water. "Bathroom's in the house," he told her, "but this'll do you for now. Someone'll bring you another jug in the morning'. Breakfast's at seven or when you git up." He pointed casually into the darkness, now beginning to be illuminated by a tardy but brilliant moon. "Toilet's in that li'l shack over there—you follow this path. There's a lamp lit inside." The discerning host, he took a quick look around. "Guess you're O.K.," he said. "Sweet dreams!" He opened the door to a prolonged wail sounding from a nearby canyon. Jane, startled, said, "What in the world…?" Slats, laughing, said, "Kyote. Sounds kinda lonesome, don't he?" He went out, the door shut, and Jane returned nervously to the window.

Dogs barked, coyotes yelped, a stallion in a pasture whinnied. The X-Bar-Y was now bathed in the purest moonlight Jane had ever seen. There was a subtle smell of sage permeating the cabin. Into a patch of moonlight leaped effortlessly a buck deer, nostrils twitching; another graceful leap and he was gone into the shadows. Jane came from the window and collapsed on the bed, looking at the suitcase that for the first time in her life she would have to unpack. She wondered where her maid had put things.

Two weeks later…in jeans and astride a Western saddle, tanned, healthy, and with at least two cowboys mad about her…Jane was learning to rope a calf.

—From Basil Woon's
None of the Comforts of Home:
But Oh, Those Cowboys!
The Saga of the Nevada Dude Ranches

Bill McGee, 1947

Yellowstone National Park

CHAPTER 1

Wyoming Horse Wranglin'

Yellowstone National Park

I stepped aboard the bay gelding and was waiting for the rest of the wranglers to mount up. All of a sudden, my horse jerked his head down, exploded beneath me with lightning-fast power, and tossed me over his head. I wasn't hurt but I was sure as hell embarrassed. I'll never know for sure, but I think Jim Brayton, my newfound Montana cowboy buddy, goosed that horse when I wasn't looking—especially since Ed Taylor had told me earlier, "This bay is a little high-strung now but he's one of our better dude horses."

All of us were thrown a time or two in spite of Ed's tips. It was part of the job. Each morning and again after noon chow—especially during the first couple of weeks—seemed more like a rodeo saddle bronc event. No matter how hard we tried to keep them from bucking, some horses succeeded. Many of these early mounts were unknown to Ed since they had been acquired by Harry Jackson over the winter as new or replacement mounts for his dude string.

One night, after hitting the sack, I reflected back on my first day on the job. Harry Jackson's ranch hand picked me up the morning of May 1, 1947 in Bozeman, Montana and we headed for this horse camp in east Yellowstone Park, Wyoming. We made one stop in Livingston, about twenty miles east of Bozeman where I was born in 1925, and picked up Jim Brayton, another cowboy. Turns out he's a former Marine and Montana State dropout. But here's the kicker: his family has a ranch in Shields River Valley some twenty miles north of Livingston, where my dad proved up a homestead in 1913. Talk about a small world.

After we entered Yellowstone Park, we passed through Norris Junction and Hayden Valley—the latter once a prehistoric lake and now a favorite turf for bull moose. Then we crossed the Yellowstone River by way of Fishing Bridge and turned up a gravel road for maybe fifteen miles to our camp.

Our camp consisted of a good-sized, rustic log cabin nestled in a grove of lodgepole pines on a knoll overlooking two corrals and a lean-to shed some twenty yards down a draw. The corrals were filled with horses.

Harry Jackson was here to greet us and introduce us to the other cowboys who had arrived earlier. Then he was all business. His little talk went something like this:

"Okay, men, listen up. I've been doing this for a good many years and have learned a thing or two along the way. By tonight, we'll have twelve wrang-

Hayden Valley—once a prehistoric lake—and the Yellowstone River (Courtesy Yellowstone National Park Wyoming)

lers in camp, plus the cook. A few of you are new; others have been with me for several summers. There's room for all of you to bed down in the cabin, but feel free to sleep under the stars, weather permitting. Remember to stash your bedroll in the cabin, during the day.

"Another thing," he went on, "don't ever leave any food outside the cabin because there are plenty of bears around here. The cook will prepare hot meals at breakfast and supper and pack each of you a midday snack of some kind. Any questions so far?"

No one spoke up, so Jackson continued. "Great. Now I want to briefly recap why we're all here and what we have to accomplish over the next six weeks. For you college boys," he added with a smile, "call it your 'job description.'

"By tomorrow night we'll have about one hundred-seventy head of horses here, give or take a few, all fresh off the winter range. Your job is to top them off. In other words, gentle them down, so

that, come June 15, park guests can safely ride them."

"How do we know when a horse meets your definition of gentle?" one of the wranglers asked.

"I'll explain that in a few minutes," Jackson said. "In the meantime, hold your questions. Now let's discuss a typical day here at the camp.

"On average, you'll ride two horses a day. Ed Taylor," he said pointing to Ed, "is my senior wrangler and foreman. He remembers the behavior of most of the horses we've used in previous years. So he'll help you select your mounts, track when they've been ridden and by whom, and then, with your help, note how they behaved. By the end of the month, we'll have culled out all potential troublemakers—meaning horses that buck too readily or act too high-strung for whatever reason. Our insurance coverage requires we do this. If we lose our insurance coverage, we're out of business.

"Now back to our typical day, if there is such a

thing: after everyone is mounted—and this can take time, believe me—we open the gate and turn the rest of the horses out to graze. At this point, you become wranglers, as there are no fences around here.

"The horses will be hungry because we don't feed them in the corrals, but the range grass is good, so they won't run far before they settle down to graze. But we still need to keep an eye on them at all times. At this point, you will be doing double-duty by working out your mount as you wrangle the herd.

"Some of these horses, especially the young ones, will buck like they've never had a saddle on before. Others might crow hop a little. Even some of our best older dude horses will do this after running free all winter.

"Well," Jackson continued, "you get my drift. That's why Ed here keeps what we call a 'Tip Sheet' on each horse. He can usually give you this information on your next mount before you saddle up.

"Now, let's get something straight. I don't want to see you practicing your rodeo skills on this job. Anyone caught encouraging his horse to buck will be dismissed on the spot. Is that clear?"

All appeared to nod in the affirmative, so Jackson continued. "I'll be honest with you. Some joker breaks this rule most every year and, as a result, gets his walking papers. That said, be prepared for some rough rides because some of the horses will really test you. We don't want any broken bones. We need all of you to wrangle dudes this summer. That's about it. Any questions?"

Someone wondered where the nearest phone was. Another wanted to know how far it was to the nearest bar, but no one had questions about the "job description."

"Okay," Jackson said, "Bob Jennings, better known as 'Cookie,' has made you a bunch of sandwiches. After you eat, it'll be time to go to work. You're in Ed's hands now. Good luck. I've got to get back to the home ranch north of Gardiner, Montana. I'll see you later."

The next few weeks seemed to fly by. The job was just what this cowboy needed. I'd been aboard ships instead of horses for the last four years. Of course, I wasn't the only one who had been away. We rode from sunup to sundown, and sometimes later, every day. We hit the sack early, all tired out most nights, but happy to be doing what we were doing.

The cowboys turned out to be a great group of guys. Average age, maybe twenty-six; mostly single (two were already divorced); about half were vets from WWII; and all but two hailed from nearby Rocky Mountain states (one was a Texan, the other from Kentucky). All had stories to tell, mostly funny, but a few sad. Of course, there were many about girls and sexual conquests. All reminded me of navy sea stories, tall and enhanced with age. The camaraderie that developed among the

Wranglers bring in the horses
(Courtesy Joel H. Bernstein Collection)

group was also reminiscent of the military.

The chow was better than we expected. "Cookie," a mustachioed-and-goateed old-timer, had worked for Jackson for many years. Every morning he served up a choice of ham, bacon or sausage with eggs and hash browns. Supper was the usual meat and potatoes fare plus one of Cookie's special pies or cakes. No one went hungry, that's for sure.

One camp chore, rotated among the wranglers, was to get up about 4:30 a.m. and fire up Cookie's kitchen stove and the potbellied stove used to heat the cabin. The first time I pulled this duty, I had a little brush with a bear on the back stoop of the cabin. Here's what happened: Cookie kept a stack of firewood along the wall outside the back door. As I opened the door one morning to bring in an armload of wood, holding a lantern in one hand and a hatchet in the other, much to my surprise, I was eye to eye with a bear up on his hind legs. I don't know which one of us was the more surprised, but I do remember striking out with the hatchet and slamming the door in quick succession.

I don't think he or she was big enough to be a grizzly; no doubt it was a black bear. In any case, it was too close for comfort! All hands were up earlier than usual that morning and enjoyed a good laugh over my little escapade.

The most satisfying part of this job was wrangling the horses each day on the open range. Typically, half of the wranglers controlled the herd while they grazed and the rest of the men worked out their

mounts nearby. The workouts varied considerably from horse to horse, as you can imagine. Return horses that had already proven themselves in previous years required very little work. The new horses were another matter. Ed Taylor was counting on us to gentle them down, which took time. At the end of six weeks, all but fourteen out of one hundred-seventy had received satisfactory marks in Ed's Tip Sheet notebook. The fourteen "failures" would be sold.

About June 10, Ed Taylor informed us over breakfast that we would be "trailing the horses

Grizzly bears at Yellowstone. The grizzly is much larger than the black bear and can be recognized by the pronounced hump at the shoulders and the very long front claws. (Courtesy Yellowstone National Park Wyoming)

Black bear at Yellowstone
(Drackert Collection, Special Collections Department, University of Nevada, Reno Library)

Grand Canyon, Lower Falls, from Artist Point— one of the most popular visitor attractions.

(Courtesy Yellowstone National Park Wyoming)

cross-country tomorrow to the Canyon Hotel some twenty miles away. Harry Jackson will meet us there and we'll decide on your summer positions. The horses will be hauled to the various park stables by horse trailer from the Canyon Hotel corrals."

Ed's announcement was my cue to request a meeting with him later that day. I reluctantly described my first malaria flare up in two-and-a-half months, then said, "Ed, I'm sorry, but the last couple of days I've been having some symptoms and it looks like I'm going to have to check into a damn hospital again. The V. A. doctor told me this could recur."

Ed was as disappointed as I was, but, at the same time, seemed to understand my dilemma. "When we get to the Canyon Hotel, we'll pay you off so you can go do what you have to do," he said. "You're not the first war veteran and cowboy with that problem and you sure as hell won't be the last."

Early the next morning, we packed up our belongings and piled them by the door before breakfast. Harry Jackson would pick them up on his way to meet us at the Canyon Hotel later on.

With Ed Taylor leading, we pulled out of camp, as the sun peeked over the mountains, with one hundred-seventy head of horses accompanied by twelve happy wranglers. We took a shortcut across the Park's open Mirror Plateau range and headed in a southwesterly direction for the Canyon Hotel.

It was a memorable ride in many ways. The grandeur of America's first national park was on full display, from rugged mountain terrain to gentle meadows and meandering streams. Wild game sightings along the way included mule deer, elk, pronghorn antelope, and bison, plus bears and coyotes. It was some ride!

We arrived at Canyon around four p.m., herded the horses into a fenced pasture near the highway, unsaddled our mounts, and waited for the boss to show up. He arrived about thirty minutes later. After conferring with Ed for a few minutes, he called us together for new instructions.

"Okay, now listen up," he said. "Ed tells me you've done a good job since we last got together. I made up this list," pointing to the pages in his hand, "with each of your assignments for the season ahead. Feel free to request a switch in assignments August 1 if you like.

"As you know," Jackson continued, "the Park season runs from June 16 through Labor Day. So the next three days are yours to do as you please, but please be sure you're back at your assigned stations by June 15. The list includes the name of the wrangler in charge for each station. You'll report to

Yellowstone Wildlife

Mule Deer

Bull Moose

Bighorn Sheep

Pronghorn Antelope

Western Elk

(Courtesy Yellowstone National Park Wyoming)

Right, *Mt. Washburn is one of several peaks over 10,000 feet in Yellowstone National Park.*

Below, *Yellowstone Lake*
(Photos Courtesy Yellowstone
National Park Wyoming)

him. That's all for now. Stay out of trouble, and I'll see you soon. Ed has your paychecks in case you need a few bucks."

Then it was Ed's turn. "If you need to call home, you'll find pay phones at the Visitor Center. Public transportation is very limited until the Park is fully open. Your best bet is to carpool to Jackson, about eighty-five miles south of here, for a good time. How many of you have your own car or truck here?" Larry and Tex raised their hands. "Good," Ed said. "Looks like you have rides. I'll let you work it out."

Ed then motioned me to follow him, and we walked over to Harry's truck. Ed summarized my condition for Harry and explained why I couldn't stay on for the summer. Harry couldn't have been nicer about it. He was very understanding and asked

me if I would be returning to the V.A. hospital in Helena.

"I'm not sure," I said. "I'm going into Jackson with some of the guys for a couple of days, then decide."

Seven of us voted to head straight to Jackson that night in two pickup trucks. I went with Larry "Spud" Henderson from Pocatello, Idaho, along with Ray Weathers and Bob Vorhees—two good ole' Wyoming cowboys. We tossed a coin to see who got to sit in back with our saddles and bedrolls, and Weathers "won." Two other wranglers rode with E.Z. "Tex" Marvin, who hailed from Amarillo, Texas.

We were a happy-go-lucky bunch that night as we headed south on Highway 89, singing along to country music on the radio.

Elk arriving at the National Elk Refuge, Jackson Hole, Wyoming.

(Courtesy Collection of the Jackson Hole Historical Society & Museum)

Jackson

We pulled into Jackson about nine p.m. and headed straight for the Cowboy Bar. It was everything we'd heard it was and more. It was a great place to stop for a brew and dance to live country western music. It was full of memorabilia and murals depicting the Old West. The long bar was fully occupied, but there was plenty of standing room for seven thirsty cowboys. In 1947, the Cowboy Bar also had wide-open gambling—much to my regret later on—similar to the casinos in Reno, although gambling was supposedly illegal in Wyoming.

After a couple of rounds of beer, we moved to the lower level for some chow, followed by a search for a motel. Thanks to the bartender, we found a good place at the right price on our first stop. After checking in and depositing our gear in the rooms, we decided we better check out the Silver Dollar Bar and Lounge at the world-famous Wort Hotel in the heart of downtown Jackson. This bar also lived up to its reputation, but it was too expensive for the likes of us, so we only had one round and headed

Cowboy Bar, on the Square in Jackson, Wyoming. Although gambling was illegal in Wyoming, the Cowboy Bar had its share of roulette wheels, gambling tables and one-armed machines.

(Courtesy Collection of the Jackson Hole Historical Society & Museum)

OWBOY BAR
JACKSON, WYO.

The interior of the Cowboy Bar in the 1940s. The classic burled pine woodwork and painted murals arrived during one of the many early remodels and remain a trademark today. The stools have been replaced with saddles.
(Neal Rafferty Album, Courtesy Collection of the Jackson Hole Historical Society & Museum)

back to our motel. It was after midnight and pretty late for a bunch of tired ole' country boys who had been up since dawn.

The next morning after chow, we played tourist. First stop, the Visitor Information Center with its museum-like collection of artifacts and topographical mock-ups of the entire Jackson Hole valley. As the information lady said, "It's to help put the proper perspective on our history and places. Probably the most frequently asked question we get from visitors is what is the difference between Jackson and Jackson Hole? The answer: Jackson Hole is the valley, about forty-nine miles long and varying in width up to about eight miles. Jackson is our town

here at the southern end of the valley."

As we strolled around town with its board sidewalks, elk horn arches, hitching posts, and western architecture, it was easy to imagine we were back in the Old West. I particularly enjoyed the Jackson Hole Museum which portrays the history of the valley in artifacts, implements, weapons, clothing, and old photos collected and donated by descendents of the earliest settlers.

After a bite of lunch, all seven of us decided to tour the Teton Park and Jackson Hole country we had passed through the previous night. It was a beautiful, late spring day, so we decided to all go in Spud Henderson's pickup, three in the front and

The Tetons from Deadman's Bar on the Snake River. Les Trois Tetons—the three breasts—served as landmarks to guide early trappers.

Opposite, *Jackson Lake*

(Photos courtesy Collection of the Jackson Hole Historical Society & Museum)

four in the back sitting on saddle blankets. We agreed to swap places at each stop.

First stop. The Park Headquarters Visitor Center at Moose Junction where we picked up magazines and pamphlets on park history, geology, wildlife, and flora. The helpful rangers answered our many questions and suggested a few must-see stops for the afternoon.

Second stop. Jackson Lake Lodge near Moran village about seventeen miles to the north. As we continued north in this sky-high valley, we were inspired by the open meadows carpeted with mountain spring flowers. The Lodge, situated on a bluff, overlooked Jackson Lake, with a breathtaking view of Mount Moran. It was not yet open for the season, but the friendly help invited us in to look around. Later, as I gazed at Jackson Lake in the shadow of the mountains, from the large viewing deck of the Lodge, I promised myself a return trip someday for some fabulous fishing and hunting.

Third stop. Jenny Lake Lodge some ten miles back toward Jackson on a Park road with signs warning "Closed in Winter." The Lodge was actually a bunch of log cabins surrounding a central building, located in an alpine meadow in the shadow of the spectacular Grand Teton mountains at 13,766 feet. One of the employees raved about the excellent hiking trails, fine fishing nearby, and the horses for Lodge guests.

As we headed back to Jackson, we were in agreement: Jackson Hole deserves every accolade it receives at the Visitors' Center. I was particularly impressed with how the lakes mirror the nearby peaks, whose pointed summits rise a mile or more above them.

Final stop. Wilson, Wyoming, about five miles west of Jackson on Highway 22, to check out the Stagecoach Bar, billed as "one of the last of the Old West's watering holes." We had also been told they serve great hamburgers at modest prices, had a couple of pool tables, and country western music with lots of dancing. The Old West ambiance in the bar was something else.

We summed up the day's observations over man-sized hamburgers and beers. Noted trappers and mountain men like Old John Colter (who accompanied Lewis and Clark on their exploring expedition, 1803-06), Davey Jackson (after whom the valley was named), and James Bridger (a famous guide and trapper who was also known for his tall tales) recognized Mother Nature at her very best when they came upon the sky-high Grand Tetons, with the crystal clear lakes and river below and the vast valley providing sanctuary for large and small animals from moose to marmot.

We also agreed that Jackson Hole would be a perfect place to own and operate a first-class dude ranch, because one could offer a great choice of guided horseback rides through some of the most beautiful country in the world, guided fishing and big game hunting trips, boat excursions on the lakes, as well as float trips on the Snake River. Horseback riding could also include a variety of breakfast rides, evening steak fry rides, and an occasional covered wagon cookout. Now, if we just had the money!

After chow, we shot a couple of games of pool, then high-tailed it back to Jackson with high hopes of finding some "action" at the Cowboy Bar.

That night I got my feet wet at the blackjack table, while the others hung around the bar hoping to meet the lady of their dreams. Turned out I was the only lucky one. I won almost $100, while my compatriots failed to score anything.

The next day, I invested most of my winnings in a Navajo saddle blanket and a footlocker to hold my cowboy gear—lariat, bridle, spurs and chaps—plus my sleeping bag and extra clothing. Turns out it was a wise investment, because, before the day was done, I lost all but two twenty-dollar bills I had tucked in my boot earlier just in case. Later that same night, one of the bartenders leaned over the

bar and whispered, "Be careful, the guy who controls the tables is rumored to be crooked." "Fine time to tell me," I said, "but thanks anyway."

That night I explained to the guys why I would not be returning to Yellowstone Park with them. The next morning I called the new V.A. hospital in Reno, Nevada, that the doc in Helena had told me about.

"Come on down," an admitting nurse said. "We have plenty of beds. Sounds like you need more treatment. That happens sometimes."

Everyone checked out the next day before nine. I had just enough money to cover my share of the bill. Then I was "taxied" to Jackson's railway express office, where I shipped my saddle and footlocker, safely locked with a heavy-duty padlock, to Reno, freight collect. Then the guys insisted on caravanning me to the west end of Wilson. "You'll have a better chance of catching a ride over the pass and into Idaho Falls," Spud insisted. I was sure he was right, so I accepted.

Finally, it was time to say goodbye. We had only been together for six weeks but had become good friends. It reminded me of the sad and somewhat depressed feelings I felt in the Navy when being detached from a ship. We waved goodbye when the two pickups turned back, and I started walking west down the side of the highway, wondering if I would ever see them again.

About five minutes later, a Chevy bobtail truck loaded with hay slowed to a stop, and the driver, a man around fifty in a tan Stetson, called out, "Hey, cowboy, you're headed the wrong way if you're lookin' for work. I sure could use another hand on my guest ranch in Jackson Hole this summer. Interested?"

"Sorry," I replied, "but I have a date with a doctor in Reno. I'll be out of commission for the summer."

We exchanged names for future reference, and then he headed for his ranch.

Looking south at the Reno Arch, Virginia Street, in the 1940s (Courtesy Neal Cobb Collection)

Reno or Bust!

As it turned out, Spud was only half-right. My first ride came along ten minutes later, an old-timer who took me to Swan Valley, a little more than halfway to Idaho Falls. My second ride, a fourth generation Idaho farmer, took me to the Chubbuck junction, just north of Pocatello. "You'll have a much better chance of hitching a ride to Twin Falls here," he said. One look at the map quickly confirmed this.

I was tempted to spend one of my last dollars on a sandwich but thought better of it. It was a good thing, too, because the next ride not only took me all the way to Twin Falls, one hundred-plus miles closer to Reno, but he went out of his way to drop me off south of town on U.S. 93. Lady Luck may have deserted me at the Cowboy Bar, but she was back now.

The sun was low on the horizon, and I was beginning to wonder where I would spend the night, when a car pulled over and the driver called out, "How far you going, cowboy?"

"Reno," I replied. "How about you?"

"Wells, Nevada, about 120 miles south," he said. "Hop in."

He talked almost non-stop. He was married with three kids, represented some kind of manufacturer in three states, and had a stop in Wells tomorrow before heading home to Salt Lake City. I fell asleep at some point, and the next thing I knew he shook me awake and said, "Here's Wells. Where do you want me to let you out?"

"Near the center of town, please. Not sure, but don't think I'll try to go any further tonight," I replied.

I strolled along Main Street for a while, then decided on a plan. It was almost ten p.m. by now. Since I was close to flat broke and couldn't afford a motel room, I asked myself, "Why not try to keep moving on?" So I followed the main drag to a truck stop on the west end of Wells. Then Lady Luck smiled on me again.

I had a cup of coffee and went outside and watched for truck drivers coming out the door, heading for their trucks. I asked each one where they were headed. If they said west, I would ask for a ride. I knew that a lot of the bigger companies

Harolds Club in the 1940s, dealing blackjack (Courtesy Nevada Historical Society)

didn't allow their drivers to pick up hitch-hikers. But about thirty minutes later, the owner-driver of a big eighteen-wheeler asked me two questions.

"How far you goin'?"

"Reno."

"Can you drive one of these things?"

"You bet."

"Get in."

He didn't offer me the wheel right away. I could tell he was sounding me out. He was deadheading back to Reno to get another load of appliances for his Utah and eastern Nevada retail customers. His trailer looked old and tired, but the Mack tractor sounded fine. The two-speed rear end called for double-clutching, but I knew how to do that from my grain-hauling days in Montana.

We probably covered thirty miles before he decided I qualified as a relief driver. Then he pulled over and I got behind the wheel. He watched me drive for maybe ten minutes, then relaxed and fell into a sound sleep. I can't remember his name but he was a Utah native, about thirty-five, an Army vet, and owned his own rig.

I drove nonstop to Winnemucca, Nevada, a distance of about 175 miles, before "Utah" sat up wide awake and suggested we stop for coffee. After a pit stop, coffee and donuts, and a fill-up at the pump, Utah took over and drove straight through to Reno. After the usual thank-yous and goodbyes, he dropped me off on North Virginia Street, four blocks north of the "Biggest Little City" arch.

The sun rose to greet me as I strolled down Virginia Street, the main drag of the "city that never sleeps." The town didn't look much different from when I first saw it, five-plus years earlier during my "wanderlust years." The casinos are never closed and, I'm sure, still feature beautiful showgirls and lavish bars and restaurants. But all of that will have to wait for now. Malaria comes first.

After counting my folding money and pocket change, I came up with a total of $7.45. That should be more than enough for some breakfast and cab fare out to the V.A. hospital. So I splurged on an order of bacon and eggs at a coffee shop next to Harrah's Club. Then, after watching some weary, all-night crap shooters for an hour or so, I took a cab out to the hospital on the eastside of town.

CHAPTER 2

Reno–Timeout

I checked into the hospital the morning of June 16, 1947, four years to the day after my indoctrination under fire off Guadalcanal—a date I will always remember.

Unlike the historic facility at Fort Harrison, Montana, the V.A. hospital in Reno was brand new. The first-day drill was much the same; admission in the morning, examination in the afternoon by a doctor.

Malaria Flares Up

"How have you been feeling? Can you describe your symptoms?"

"Well, I think I've been running a fever, just like I did last winter in Montana, with much the same symptoms I had in the South Pacific in 1945. I get the chills, then feel feverish."

"You have a textbook case of *plasmodium vivax*, a benign form of malaria. You can expect the cycle of chills followed by fever to repeat itself every day or so until the medication kicks in. We'll

have you back in the saddle in six to eight weeks."

During my hospitalization, I had time to reflect on my life, especially the last nine months while in transition from sailor to student to cowboy.

Veteran's Hospital, Reno, 1962 (Nevada Historical Society)

Looking back, I was discharged from the Navy in August 1946, after four years of service. I visited my family in Seattle. During the war, they moved there from Montana, so they could take jobs that aided the war effort.[1]

After three days in Seattle, I drove to Bozeman, Montana, in my newly-acquired '36 Ford coupe to see if I could qualify for Montana State College on the G.I. Bill without a high school diploma (I had dropped out of high school to work in Kaiser's shipyards, until I turned seventeen in September 1942, when I would be old enough to join the U.S. Navy). The college entrance exam was so easy that I wondered if they ever rejected a veteran.

My long-term goal was to have my own ranch somewhere in the West. It could be a working cattle ranch with around 400 mother cows or a combination cattle and dude ranch. I'd been reading up on dude ranches, and liked the diversification of cattle and dudes. Another possibility, assuming I completed my undergraduate work, was to go to veterinarian school.

Bill McGee in Montana State days, 1946-47.
(Authors' Collection)

The first semester in the fall was a real challenge to this high school dropout. Mustering up the discipline to study subjects of little interest to me, such as chemistry, was a real problem. On the other hand, livestock judging was a breeze. But I recognized the need to know about other subjects. My grades ranged from D's to A's.

I landed a good part-time job at the Bridger Club, a dinner nightclub on the edge of town, washing dishes Tuesday through Sunday from six to ten p.m. It was a fun place to work but not conducive to good study habits. To further complicate matters, I started dating the cocktail waitress.

When the second semester (winter) was almost over, despite my distractions, I was keeping up my grades. Then I came down with an attack of malaria, my first relapse since my original bout in New Guinea in early 1945. I might be studying or "pearl diving," when all of a sudden I would get incredibly cold, even on a warm day. Then I would start to shake and break out in a sweat from a fever which might last several hours.

I skipped class the next morning and called the V.A. hospital at Fort Harrison in Helena. I recapped my South Pacific malaria experience for

Bridger Club trio on a day off, Livingston, Montana, 1946-47. Left to right: "pearl diver" Bill; cook Ruth; and George the piano player. (Authors' Collection)

an admitting nurse who said, "Come right over, we've plenty of beds." I packed my bag and drove straight to Helena, about a two hour drive.

The next three weeks were spent in the V.A. hospital, several days in bed as they observed and recorded the frequency of attacks and temperature spikes, and the rest as an up-patient wandering around the halls and grounds. By mid-March I was back on campus trying desperately to catch up. Semester finals were coming up and I was far from prepared. On the other hand, my night job washing dishes was a breeze.

With each passing day, I realized I was spending more time with my friends at the Bridger Club and less time with my college classmates and books. My study habits suffered and so did my winter semester finals. At the time, I blamed my poor grades on the malaria flare-up and hospital stay, but that was only part of the reason. I realize now that I enjoyed working and found studying a bore unless it was a subject that interested me.

Sometime around mid-April, I was having a drink at the Bridger Club bar. It was after ten p.m. and the kitchen was closed. An old-timer wearing a Stockman hat sat down next to me.

"You're Bill McGee, right?"

"Yes, sir. What can I do for you?"

"My name is Harry Jackson. I hear you might be lookin' for a cowboy job."

"Could be. What did you have in mind?"

"I'm looking for six young cowboys to work in Yellowstone Park this summer. I'm a park contractor and we furnish the horses for the stables in the park, as well as mules and horses to some of the independent outfits. The summer work is pretty much wranglin' dudes on trail rides, but I also need men who can ride a buckin' horse. We have to first top off all of the horses in about six weeks so they'll be gentle enough for the park guests to

ride by mid-June when the park opens. Sound okay, so far?"

"Yes, it does. What's it pay?"

"Fifty dollars a week plus room and board."

"When would I start and when do you need my answer? If I seem hesitant, Mr. Jackson, it's because, if I accept your job offer. I'll be making a major change in my plans."

"I understand, young man. I'm guessing your decision involves college and it's an important one. If you sign on with me, I'll need you to start in early May and would like your answer by this Friday, three days from now. Think you can do that?"

"Yes, sir. I'll call you by Friday."

"Oh, one more thing," Jackson added, "if you decide to join us, and I hope you do, I'll have someone pick you up. Our horse camp in Yellowstone is hard to find."

Needless to say, that night was a sleepless one, and as I weighed my decision, pro and con, I asked myself and answered a lot of questions.

If I leave college now, will I ever return? Answer: Probably not.

If I stay in college now, am I prepared to commit to six long years in order to become a vet? Answer: I don't think so.

Is college really necessary in order to acquire and run a successful ranch operation? Answer: No.

Well, you can see where I was headed. Looking back, I probably rationalized my answers to some degree, but by morning my mind was made up. I would join Harry Jackson and get back in the saddle again.

I called Jackson next morning with my answer and then, over coffee, made a list of things to do before the first of May.

The Bridger Club crew seemed pleased for me, and I stayed with them until they found my replacement. My days were now free to take care of matters like selling my car and picking up the new custom roping saddle I had ordered earlier—kind of a luxury, but cowboyin' is not unlike many other jobs where it helps to own your own gear.

In retrospect, it's clear I made two life and career changes as a result of the malaria attacks. One, I dropped out of college. The other, I decided to pursue work on a dude ranch instead of cowboyin' on a working cattle ranch. I have no regrets on either decision.

Now, here I am in Reno, finally being discharged from the V.A. hospital with the proviso that I report daily to the out-patient department for check-ups and medication.

Thanks to a fellow out-patient and new friend, Bob "Utah" Hatch, a former marine and cowpuncher from Emery County, Utah, I had a ride downtown the day I was discharged. Utah was full of helpful information on Reno acquired while recuperating from war-related corrective surgery. For starters, he introduced me to the Round Up Bar at 114 West Second Street and its proprietor, Lena Geiser, widow of a famous cowboy artist. Geiser prints hung on the walls alongside those by Charlie Russell, and woodcarvings of rodeo cowboy action decorated the back bar. The Round Up, as I soon learned, was Reno's leading cowboy hangout and unofficial "hiring hall."

Lena was one of those special people you never forget. She loved ranchers and cowboys of all ages and could have been a mother to most of us. Her heart was as big as all outdoors and she backed up this love with her checkbook on many occasions.

Round Up Bar and Newman's Silver Shop on W. Second Street, Reno (Courtesy Neal Cobb Collection, Nevada Historical Society)

Nevada Hotel, next to the Cal-Neva, on E. Second Street, Reno (Courtesy Neal Cobb Collection)

For example, when she learned my saddle and foot-locker were at the Railway Express office, she not only insisted on loaning me the funds to pick them up, but also provided me with free storage in the bar's basement.

Lena and Utah recommended I check into the Nevada Hotel at 26 East Second Street, a small, clean hotel with reasonable rates, about two blocks east of the Round Up. It was even better than their description.

The next day, Utah and I went to work as "shills" at Harolds Club. Shills get paid an hourly wage to gamble with house money, giving the appearance the tables are busy because many gamblers, especially high rollers, won't play at slow tables. As I recall, I made two dollars an hour, plus the occasional tip from a high roller (high stakes gambler) who would bet with me at the crap table when I had the dice. Each time I won, he or she would toss me one or two five-dollar chips. They could really add up if I made my point several times in a row.

The job was perfect for me because I could work the swing shift, allowing me to check in with the out-patient clinic on a daily basis.

My routine for the better part of a month was

Shooting craps in Reno (Nevada Historical Society)

kind of boring. Sleep in, or try to, until about eight a.m.; hang out at the Round Up until it was time to check in at the V.A. hospital; show up for my Harolds Club shill job from four p.m. 'til midnight; and then maybe stop in at the Round Up again to check out the action. The one consolation, according to my doctor, "You're coming along fine. Just be patient."

The Reno Rodeo was held every Fourth of July, and provided a great change of pace. In 1947, there were more than one hundred entries in the rodeo events, competing for $11,000 in prize money—a lot of money in those days. The

rodeo attracted capacity crowds each day.

The *Nevada State Journal* reported on July 4, 1947:

Reno is cracking at the seams with visitors who have come from all parts of the nation. Hotels and auto courts have been sold out for a week.

Big names in the rodeo riding world who will be out to collect their share of prize money today include Bert Clennan, Norman Reisons, Bill Ward, Buster Ivory, Red Kelly, Mitch Owens, Levi Frazer, Jackie Cooper,

Reno Rodeo parade, circa 1940s (Courtesy Neal Cobb Collection, Ernie Mack Photos)

Above and below, *Reno Rodeo parade, circa 1940s*
(Courtesy Neal Cobb Collection)

Reno Rodeo (Courtesy Neal Cobb Collection)

Ride 'em cowboy
(Courtesy Neal Cobb Collection,
Nevada Historical Society)

Gardner Sheehan, Bud Lindermann, Wallace Brooks, Glen Tyler and George Yardley.

In addition to the riding, roping and bulldogging events, there will be antics of rodeo-land's most famous clowns to amuse the spectators. These include Elmer Holcomb, Slim Pickens and Jess Krell.

Some of the top rope artists on hand are Homer Pettigrew, Buckshot Sorrels and Clay Carr.

Most of these professional rodeo cowboys made one or more nighttime appearances at the Round Up. Many knew Lena Geiser from previous years. The only one I had met before was Bud Lindermann from Red Lodge, Montana. I had competed with him once—if you can call it that—on the Montana County Fair circuit as a high-school teenager. But he was way out of my league even then.

Utah and I spent most of our time around the bronc and bull riding chutes each day along with a new cowboy friend, Frank Burrows, who had recently moved to Reno from Arizona. But what I've remembered most about that rodeo weekend was bailing Bud Lindermann out of jail Saturday night, with some key financial help from Lena Geiser. As we would learn later, Bud got into a fist-fight with some local joker while under the influence of Wild Turkey whiskey and was arrested for disturbing the peace, charges that were dropped later. He went on to repeat as all-around Reno champion cowboy in 1947 in spite of that late Saturday night mishap.

I met many interesting people at the Round Up Bar, a popular watering hole not just for cowboys but for all types, from casino dealers to divorcées and their lawyers. One of my favorites was a Boston transplant, Dick Sylvester. We had absolutely nothing in common, his being from the Eastern upper crust and all that, but he was enam-

ored with my life as a cowboy. In no time, Utah, Frank Burrows and I had become his best friends. When he was sober, he was full of questions and had a great sense of humor. When he was drunk, he was very quiet and sullen. In short, Dick was an alcoholic. He was a remittance kid, a black sheep of a well-to-do Eastern family who shipped him out west to avoid embarrassment and un-favorable publicity.

Dick lived in Pleasant Valley, about eight miles south of Reno. He had several acres, as I recall, but his "ranch house," as he called it, was modest in size. There was no barn or livestock on his "spread," but to Dick, it was the "Sylvester Ranch," nevertheless. We used to kid him about this, and he seemed to enjoy the ribbing.

One night following the rodeo, a newspaper story on Bugsy Siegel's death triggered a lively debate at the Round Up. The key questions were who ordered Siegel's murder and how much influence did the Mafia exert on Nevada gaming? According to the newspaper story:

Benjamin (Bugsy) Siegel may have paid a staggering $1,500,000 debt with his life.

H. Leo Stanley of the Los Angeles district attorney's office said the gang chief told a friend a week before his death that he had to raise the money or go into hiding.

"But I wouldn't know where to hide," Siegel said.

(Siegel was shot dead on June 20, 1947 at the Beverly Hills mansion of his girlfriend, Virginia Hill, apparently at the order of mob associates.)

Siegel's vast debts, many of them incurred to build his luxurious Flamingo Hotel and casino in Las Vegas, Nev., were uncovered fol-lowing disclosure that he wrote two bad checks, totalling $150,000, to Del Webb, owner of the New York Yankees baseball club and Del F. Webb Construction Company which built the Flamingo.

Webb denied he ever saw the checks.

"As far as I know, the company doesn't have the checks," he said. "I did not receive the checks and I know nothing of them."

The Flamingo club cost around $5,000,000 and Webb was said to hold liens on it totaling $1,500,000.

Special Agent Walter Lentz of the attorney general's office said he believed still more of Siegel's bad checks were out.

"We believe these are not the only checks on which he stopped payment," he said. "We think his primary purpose in coming to Los Angeles the day of his murder was to raise money to cover those checks."[2]

In the final analysis, there was wide agreement that night that the Mafia probably had too much influence on the Nevada gaming industry. But there was no agreement as to who shot Siegel.

The debate prompted Sylvester to propose an overnight visit to Las Vegas and the Flamingo Hotel via Bonanza Airlines to his three cowboy friends "all expenses paid, of course." When we hesitated to accept his offer, he said, "Look, I wouldn't have offered to host the trip if I didn't want to." That was Dick for you.

The next day we took a Bonanza Airlines C-47 to Las Vegas to check out the infamous, new Flamingo Hotel and casino.

At first sight, it appeared to be situated in the middle of a desert oasis. (The now world-famous "Strip" was still in its infancy.) The hotel casino was not exactly jammed with patrons, in spite of its early notoriety, but it was still impressive.

Both star-studded shows in the beautiful theater-restaurant were sold out, so we spent most of our time in the casino bar and lounge. As I recall, the stand-up comedian was very funny, but the

Bonanza Air Service, circa 1940s (Nevada Historical Society)

vocalist and her backup pianist were quite forgettable.

We must have talked to a dozen pretty ladies that night, ranging from club dealers on their breaks, to tourists and call girls, but only Frank Burrows scored—or so he said anyway. Dick was out of it by midnight, so Utah and I helped him to his room.

We all had one thing in common before the night was over: bad hangovers in the morning.

We returned to Reno the next day convinced that northern Nevada was the better place to work and play. Work-wise, the economy was much more diversified. And, as for play, what in southern Nevada can compare with the outdoor magic of the High Sierra mountains and Lake Tahoe?

Dick Sylvester became a good friend to the three of us, in spite of his alcohol problems. We, in turn, looked out for him. One or another of us drove him home in his car on many occasions when he'd had too much to drink. That usually meant spending the night until he sobered up so he could drive us back to town. At other times, if we weren't around, Lena would call a cab to take him home.

Dick was equally popular with men and women, but we never saw him "date" a woman per se. Oh sure, he would take them to dinner, but that was the end of it. On more than one occasion,

Utah, Frank and I wondered if he might be a closet homosexual, but he never once made a pass at any of us.

Frank Burrows was the Round Up's "lady killer." Women gravitated to him like bears to honey. It was understandable, because he was tall, with the good looks of a Hollywood movie star. Unfortunately, he had a tendency to get mean and slap his date around when he had one too many.

Utah, on the other hand, was always good-natured. He was built like a steer wrestler, about five foot ten, barrel-chested and muscular, with a big, gravelly voice, and was quick to laugh, even at lousy jokes.

The four of us became good friends that summer in spite of our differences and, to Lena, we could do no wrong.

Another one of my Round Up favorites was Frank Polk. Frank was about my father's age and was a real hero figure to us younger cowboys. He was a cowboy artist of the first order, and could carve a bucking horse or anything of that nature out of wood as well as a Charles Russell, thus earning Frank the nickname "Reno's whittlin' cowboy." He was a regular at the Round Up, always attracting a friendly group around him. Oddly, when he was sober, he stuttered, but when he got a few drinks in him, he didn't. Lena and everyone around the bar loved him.

Stories abounded in Reno about cowboys and wealthy ladies, and Frank had a story of his own to tell on this particular subject. It's not only colorful, but it's absolutely true. (The full story appears in Chapter 5.)

As I said, the Round Up was an unofficial hiring hall for cowboys, and Lena Geiser made a point of helping her unemployed customers, especially ranch hands, find work. Ranchers from as far away as Elko would call her if they needed a hired hand. They knew they could count on her to spread the word.

One day in mid-July I asked her to name the leading dude ranches in Washoe County. Without hesitation she answered, "The Flying M E in Washoe Valley, the Pyramid Lake, the Washoe Pines, also in Washoe Valley, and the Donner Trail near Verdi. Why do you ask?"

"Because I've about decided to give dude wrangling a shot when the V.A. doc gives me the green light. I've been reading up on several successful operations in *Dude Rancher* magazine this summer and kind of like the diversification a combination cattle and dude ranch provides. I know a little something about the hospitality business, too."

"I'll keep my ears open," Lena said. "The better places seldom have an opening."

Donner Trail Ranch Fiasco, Or I Don't Milk Cows

Two days later, Lena introduced me to John "Jack" Fugitt, owner of the Donner Trail Guest Ranch located near Verdi about ten miles west of Reno. Talk about timing. We hit it off pretty good. Fugitt described the ranch and the duties of the wrangler. He also explained how the ranch got its name from the Donner Party that was stranded in the Sierras one hundred years ago. Forty-two of the eighty-nine members died, some resorting to cannibalism.

He then explained that Jake, his current wrangler, was leaving in two weeks to return to New Mexico. "But you can start tomorrow if you like. That way, Jake can show you around before he leaves. I'll have him pick you up here at the Round Up tomorrow morning about ten, if that's okay with you."

As the saying goes, some things sound too good to be true. As it turned out, Jake was leaving because he was fed up with milking six cows twice

Jack Fugitt's outhouse humor, Donner Trail Ranch, 1947 (Drackert Collection, Special Collections Department, University of Nevada, Reno Library)

a day, a chore I also hated and one Fugitt conveniently "forgot" to tell me about. So when Jake pulled into the ranch and Fugitt came out to greet us, I resigned on the spot.

Fugitt's reaction was predictable: first surprise, then anger, but I held firm. He then did an about-face and apologized for "inadvertently" misleading me and told Jake to take me back to town.

I've never forgotten that brief encounter nor have I ever regretted my decision. I had to milk two or three cows as a kid early every morning and again in the evening. When you have milk cows,

whether it's only one or a hundred, you are tied down seven days a week, as the cows have to be milked more or less on time or they will dry up (stop giving milk).

According to Jake, Fugitt had six purebred black and white Holsteins and a modern milking barn with enough stanchions for a dozen cows. "What he really needs is a combination field hand-milker in addition to a wrangler, as I see it," Jake said.

Sometime later, I heard that Fugitt made his fortune in San Francisco in penny arcades and back-of-the-house gambling. Not sure it was true but Lena had heard the same story. She did tell me a year or so later that Jack sold off his milk cows as "too much trouble" and started buying his dairy products in Verdi.

Driving for Star Taxi

On July 23, 1947, according to my journal, I started driving a cab in Reno for Star Taxi. I hadn't planned to, it just sort of happened. I heard they had an opening and thought, hey, I can do that, so I went in for an interview and started work the next day. I took the job for several reasons, and, as it turned out, was glad I did. For starters, standing at a crap table night after night was getting old. Cab driving gave me flexibility time-wise and the opportunity to meet many interesting people. It also paid more. In fact, counting tips and "kickbacks," far more. (More on kickbacks to follow.)

My malaria was much better according to the V.A. doctor, but he cautioned me to continue taking the medication to avoid a setback.

I continued to work the swing shift so my days were free to see the doctor, scheduled now for three times a week. At the start of my first shift, Laurie Fisher, the dispatcher, an attractive thirty-something lady, handed me a Reno-Sparks map marked up by cab zone areas. "All you have to do," she said," is note your pick-up and drop-off zones, then check the rate grid for the customer's fare. It's really very simple," she assured me. "In a town this size, meters are really not necessary."

It didn't take long to learn the town's main streets thanks to some very understanding customers, a friendly dispatcher, and a good map. For the lesser-known streets, I referred to the map's street index unless the rider knew the way.

Laurie Fisher (not her real name) was waiting out her time for a divorce. She and several of the other drivers were very helpful. It wasn't long before I knew which cabstands generated the most frequent fares, resulted in the most airport runs, produced the most time calls, and, most importantly, offered the greatest potential for wedding party arrivals and divorcés in need of a six-week residence.

It soon became obvious: the good money was made by the driver who was always on the lookout for a "live one," the big spender or high roller who might hire the cab by the hour (time call) to stay with him as he moved from casino to casino. Or he might want to hire the cab for a trip to Truckee, California, some twenty miles west, to visit the pay-for-play ladies—the nearest whorehouse since the Army "coerced" Reno's city authorities into closing down "The Stockade" in 1942.[3]

Here's an example of how kickbacks work and how they can add up: A young couple from California arrives by Greyhound. The driver on the cabstand spots them as they come out of the depot. Their facial expressions and body language give them away. The following conversation is representative of what happens once this couple is in the cab.

Driver: "Looks like you folks plan to get married. Am I right?"

Young couple: "How did you know? Is it that obvious?"

"Just practice, I guess. People in love have a special way of showing it. May I offer some suggestions that will save you time and money?"

"Of course."

"I can take you to the marriage license bureau, arrange for a judge or minister to marry you, and can even be your witness if you didn't bring your own."

"What does it cost for all that? What's your charge?"

"My cab fare is five dollars an hour and it shouldn't take more than two hours. Your only other costs are five dollars for the license and twenty dollars for the judge."

"Let's do it. Can you recommend a flower shop?"

"Sure, we can stop on the way to the courthouse if you like. Do you folks have a room reservation?"

"No, but I bet you're going to help us there, too, right?"

"Of course, that's what I do."

In a typical wedding scenario everything is completed in less than two hours for a total out-of-pocket cost of $35 (cab fare $10, marriage license $5, judge $20), plus any extras like flowers or a ring.

The cab driver earns his usual 50 percent of the cab fare plus a five dollar kickback (also known as a "witness fee") from the judge.

Should the groom purchase a wedding bouquet or a corsage for the bride for, say, five dollars, the driver can drop back later and collect his one dollar kickback from the florist.

Finally, if the couple accepts the driver's recommendation for one of "his hotels" (for example, the El Cortez Hotel at Second and Arlington), he will receive a special ten dollar kickback later, regardless of how many nights the couple stays.

The main reason for the influx to Reno of wedding parties is because there was no wait for a license under Nevada's marriage laws. Based on figures assembled by the Washoe County Clerk, 28,874 couples took out marriage licenses in 1946 —an average of 79 per day. As you can see, it really pays off for a cab driver to be on the lookout for Reno's "special business opportunities." (For information on Nevada's divorce and marriage trade, see Part III, "Gettin' Untied.")

As for accommodations, the more affluent candidates for divorce arrived by train or plane having made prior arrangements for a Reno lawyer and their six-week residence. However, a surprising number of people arrived by bus or train without any reservations: read, another "special business opportunity."

One of the drivers for Whittlesea Taxi, Star's main competitor, gave me a few tips over a cup of coffee one day as to where and how to spot these people. "Simply stated," he said, "you have to try to meet the planes, trains and transcontinental buses arriving from the East, and as many "hounds" [Greyhound buses] as you can from California. I'll leave the rest up to you." I thanked him and said I would put his counsel to work on my next day shift.

According to Laurie, our dispatcher, four close-in, modestly-priced, so-called guest ranches, the Alamo, Biltmore, Del Monte, and Whitneys, offer a kickback equal to a one week's stay on a six week reservation which is equal to the 15 percent a week most travel agents get. However, you have to wait until the six weeks are up to collect. Laurie went on, "I believe their weekly rates now run about $75 for a single room and meals plus horseback riding and daily transportation to and from town. So it pays to try to help them. But you need to work days to get in on most of this action."

One evening around the middle of August, just as I was getting to know my way around Reno and Sparks and make some decent tips and kickbacks, Laurie called to say, "You've got a 'personal' at the

Round Up. Lena didn't say who it was." (A "personal" in the taxi business meant the customer specifically asked for you.)

As I walked into the bar, I spotted Lena at the far end of the bar talking to a man I'd never met. "Bill McGee," Lena said, "say hello to Bob Scates." Bob and I shook hands and, as I pulled up a stool, Lena added, "Bob is looking for a wrangler for his outfit at Lake Tahoe. Sounds like something you would be interested in, Bill. I'll leave you two to talk it over."

I knew Lena liked Scates when she introduced us, and no wonder. He was a fifty-something cowboy dressed in boots, Levis and a white Stetson, with the tanned good looks chiseled by years of sun and wind.

We hit it off right from the start. Scates opened with, "Lena tells me you're from Montana. I could have guessed by the shape of your hat.[4] She also filled me in on your interests in the dude ranching business. Well, Bill, I don't have a dude ranch, but we do wrangle dudes."

He went on to describe his summer operation on the north shore of Lake Tahoe as "summer trail rides and backcountry fishing trips and fall deer hunting pack trips. What do you think?" he asked.

"Sounds like a great way to spend a couple of months. You know, I spent two days at Tahoe three years ago while on navy leave and fell in love with the area. I promised myself a return trip, but didn't think it would be this soon. What's it pay, Mr. Scates, and how soon would I start?"

"I can start you at $60 a week plus room and board. During hunting season, I'll bump you up to $75 a week. You'll also get some generous tokes (tips) from the hunters. I'd like you to start tomorrow, if you can, but no later than Labor Day weekend as two of my wranglers have to leave for college. How does that sound?"

"You've got a deal, sir," I replied. "Let me call Star Taxi, then I can give you a start date."

As it turned out, Star had a standby driver in the wings, so I was able to meet Scates at the Round Up the next morning, August 21, to pick up my gear for the ride to Tahoe City.

I had an impromptu drink with Laurie, my favorite dispatcher, and two other swing shift drivers that night after work at the Round Up. After the two drivers called it a night, Laurie and I strolled down to the Roaring Camp on Lake Street for a bowl of Ramona's chili and a margarita nightcap.

Roaring Camp back bar (Courtesy Neal Cobb Collection)

We left Roaring Camp a little after one a.m. and headed back to the Round Up. In front of my hotel, we paused, trying to read each other's mind. I wasn't sure Laurie would join me in my room, but I figured, why not ask?

"Laurie, would you like to come up?"

She looked at me with a smile. "Of course, silly."

As we entered Room 232, I reached for Laurie and she came to me eagerly. Her lips, slightly parted, were warm, moist and sensual, as if a foretaste of sweeter things to come. Her tongue danced and excited me. Holding her, I could hear her breathing quicken and felt her slim body quiver with pent-up passion, responding fiercely to my own.

As we drew closer, my hands began exploring. Laurie sighed deeply, savoring waves of pleasure now, anticipating ecstasy ahead. It had been too long since she had been with a man and she was excited, urgent, waiting. Impatiently, we moved to the bed.

Then, tenderly and lovingly, I undressed her.

Then myself. Then I kissed, embraced and gently mounted her, thrusting strongly forward, gloriously inward, while Laurie seized and clasped me, and cried aloud with joy.

"I love you, Bill! I love you!"

At last, exhausted, happy, and fulfilled, we had a cigarette, made love again, then slept through what was left of Reno's colorfully lit up night, the neon lights twinkling and flashing from the nearby casinos.

As we dressed that morning, I called Star for a taxi for Laurie. We waited together on Second Street. When the cab arrived, we embraced and kissed. Laurie whispered, "Good luck with your new job, Bill. Call me when you get back in town. I'll still be here."

"I will," I promised her.

I returned to my room, put in a request for a wakeup call, and grabbed a little more shuteye before it was time to meet my ride to the Scates stables in Tahoe.

CHAPTER 3

Tahoe Dude Wrangler

Later that morning, Bob Scates was briefing me on his outfit during our ride to Tahoe via U.S. 40 and Truckee. His stable operation is on the north shore of the lake on the west end of Tahoe City. He caters to the affluent clientele at the world famous Tahoe Tavern, the Lake's leading hotel.

Scates got his start in the 1930s as a wrangler at the Tavern when it still had its own stables. In the late 1930s, he joined Bob Souther's stable in the bottomland next to the Truckee River, first as a wrangler, later as a partner, and finally as sole owner. Along the way he married Janet, rumored to be a wealthy San Franciscan. The stable acreage, originally owned by the Tavern, was sold to Scates by Carl Andrew Bechdolt, owner of the Tahoe Inn in Tahoe City.

Then Scates went into more detail on my new job. "For the first two or three weeks, you'll be leading trail rides along with two other wranglers and my foreman, Pete Tracey. Then we'll move the horses, tack and camping gear to Deer Park about five miles down river. It's just an old run-down barn with corrals but it works as our pack station. Deer season opens on October 5, but most of our customers want to be packed in before then.

"Chaska West, an old-time Nevada cowboy who runs his own summer stable operation at Brockway on the north shore, will join forces with us for the deer season. By the third week in September, our combined outfit will number some forty head of horses and seven wranglers plus Pete Tracey, Chaska West and me.

"It's a lot of hard work," he added, "but well worth it and everybody has a really good time. That's about it. Any questions?"

"Sounds great," I said. "What do you do when deer season ends?"

"My wife and I move down to the foothills for the winter, near Auburn, about thirty miles this side of Sacramento. We have the horses trucked down there, too. My wife doesn't like the cold or the icy roads in winter."

As we pulled into Truckee, Scates suggested we stop for a cup of coffee before heading south for the Lake.

The first time I saw Truckee was when I took a Star Taxi fare to visit one of its infamous "houses of ill repute" (and received a kickback). While waiting in the living room, the Madame summarized the town's colorful past with these words, "Truckee was named for Washoe Indian Chief Trokay. The town was once a lawless lumber and railroad town."

From what I could see, much of its Old West charm still remained, including its nineteenth century false-front buildings and a train that still ran through the middle of town.

Over coffee, Scates briefed me on his longtime friend and foreman, Pete Tracey. "Pete and I were both wranglers at the Tavern stables. He joined me when I started my own outfit. He's from Kingman, Arizona, has been single all his life, and still goes south to his winter grazing ground, the Arizona Biltmore or Castle Hot Springs. He's one hell of a packer as you'll soon see, and one of the last of the 'gentlemen cowboys.'"

For the last fourteen miles of our trip, we followed the winding Truckee River through some mighty fine country. I was pleased with my decision to join Scates. Should be an enjoyable experience, I thought, as Tahoe City came into view.

As we approached town, the first commercial property on the left was the Lake Inn. Scates' stables were across the highway along the river.

When we pulled in and parked near a building with green-stained, shingle siding, a young cowboy came out and asked, "Need a hand, boss?"

"Sure enough, Charlie. Say hello to Bill McGee. He's joining us for the rest of the season. Give him a hand with his gear, then show him around."

After we stashed my footlocker and saddle, Charlie "Red" Ulrich played tour guide. The stable operation consisted of a fairly long bunkhouse toward the back of the property with a kitchen area at one end, plus a combination tack room and blacksmith shop next to the main corral. There were two smaller corrals, too. "The Scates' summer residence," as Red called it, "sits over there adjacent to the stable property, fronting on the Truckee River."

Red was raised on a ranch in Modoc County near the California-Oregon state line and started working for Scates in June "so I could see the other side of the mountains and get out from under my old man's control." Going on he added, "Come on, Bill, let's go say hello to Pete Tracey."

I could hear the familiar sound of a hot horseshoe being hammered into shape before we rounded the corner of the blacksmith's shop and spotted Pete hard at work. He looked up as we approached, turned and put the shoe back in the fire, and said, "You must be the new wrangler."

"That's right, Pete," Red said. "Meet Bill McGee."

"Welcome aboard," said Pete, as we shook hands. "We'll talk later. Got to finish shoein' this horse while the coals are hot."

We watched him finish shaping the shoe and nail it in place on the front left hoof of a sorrel mare.

Tracey had to be pushing sixty. He had the craggy, weather-beaten look of a man who had always been a cowboy. His tan Stetson, shaped with an Arizona crease, and his denim shirt were both stained with sweat. The unruly salt-and-pepper mass of bristle over his upper lip belied his soft-spoken manner.

Red and I were looking over the horses in the far corral when several riders came into view making their way through the river. "That's Bud Crane in the lead, one of our wranglers," Red said. "He's been guiding that group of Tavern ladies on a trail ride all morning. Must be gettin' close to chow time. Let's give Bud a hand with the horses."

As the ladies dismounted, we unsaddled their horses and turned them loose in the big corral. Then Red introduced us.

"Bill McGee, meet Bud Crane, the youngest wrangler in this outfit. But don't let his baby face fool you. He's a good hand with a horse."

As we shook hands, Red added, "Bill's from Montana. He'll be with us through deer season. Bud's just finished high school in San Francisco and is supposed to go to college this fall."

Bud is a tall, nice looking kid who looks right at home on a horse. His dad is a successful doctor in the Bay Area. The Crane family spend their summers at the Lake and the doctor comes up most weekends. Turns out, Bud and his dad, along with some of their Bay Area friends, have been Scates' deer hunting customers for several seasons. But this would be Bud's first season to work as a paid guide.

Lunch consists of delicious BLT (bacon, lettuce and tomato) sandwiches and homemade potato salad prepared by Juanita, a middle-aged Mexican lady, who doubles as the Scates' housekeeper. We ate at a redwood picnic table under a big weeping willow tree near the river.

"It doesn't get much better than this, does it, Bill?"

"Right you are, Bud," I said.

Tahoe Trail Guide

After lunch, Pete and I took the next customers, two young married couples from the Midwest, on a two-hour ride which allowed Pete to show me some of the more popular trails. During the ride, he reviewed "Scates' Sacred Rules for Riders":

No rides without a wrangler—an insurance requirement.

No horsing around on the trail.

Lope or canter horses on meadow trails only.

Violators will be banned from future rides.

Pete also emphasized the importance of matching a horse to a rider's experience. "Half the city dudes think they can ride, but most can't. So we like to give them the ole' Missouri 'show me' test, meaning, give all new customers a real gentle horse the first time out. If they pass the test, give them a more spirited horse on their next ride."

"Scates' Rider Rules and the 'show me' test make sense to me, Pete," I said. "He knows his business."

Both Red and Bud were out with customers when we got back to the stables, but about thirty minutes later, two teenage sisters showed up to ride. "They're 'regulars,' staying at the Tavern with their parents," Pete said. He introduced us and jokingly added, "Bill will be your guide today. He's new, so go easy on him."

After a brief discussion on choice of mounts, we saddle two of the horses they liked from previous rides and are on our way. After crossing the Truckee, we head for the Tavern—the girls were hoping someone would see them—then we lope the horses across a small meadow to Ward Creek.

We follow the creek up a draw for almost two miles, then traverse the slope to what the girls said was Page Meadows where we let the horses run for maybe a half mile. Then we stretch our legs while the horses have a breather, before heading back to the stables. It's almost six p.m. by now. I probably enjoyed the ride more than the girls did. It's a memorable day for me because I was back in the saddle again. And who could ask for a more beautiful place to work? Lady Luck was still with me!

Later that evening we trail eighteen stable horses through the middle of town, past the landmark "Big Tree," and on to some fenced, bottom-land pasture in Lake Forest with an excellent crop of timothy hay. Total ride is about three miles. When we get back to the stable, we grain our mounts and feed them some baled hay, then wash up for supper.

In the morning, usually on the early side, we would reverse the process and trail the stable horses from Lake Forest to the stables. The townspeople, especially the children, waved and smiled as we passed by and, of course, we reciprocated. This daily ritual is still one of my fondest memories of wrangling dudes for Bob Scates.

The land surrounding Tahoe City's Big Tree is special. The earliest structures on the site were two livery barns built for the Truckee-to-Tahoe stagecoach line. After 1900, Tahoe Tavern took over these barns and continued to use them for carriage house and livery stables until the increasing prevalence of horseless carriages gradually changed their respective functions to riding stables and auto storage. In 1932, a fire destroyed both barns and, since the growth of the town was not compatible with stables in its midst, the Tavern relocated its horses to a site across the highway from the resort's main entrance.[1]

The Scates' wrangler job for the next four weeks was pretty routine, but the clientele was anything but. We discussed customer types over a couple of beers at the Lake Inn across the road later that night.

Bud: "Some of the younger gals come by every day, but not always to ride. Maybe they can't afford it, or they just want to flirt with us."

Red: "Be careful, Bill, some of them are jailbait," he warned as he tried to keep a straight face. "And then there's ole' Pete there. He's still waiting and hoping one of those rich Tavern women will propose to him!"

Pete: "Yup, that's right, Red, and I'm prepared to wait, too. Our customers are all over the lot, from grade school to college graduates and well beyond. Some are wealthy; others can only afford to ride for one hour. Lots of the locals have their kids take lessons at the Scates stables, too."

Then we discussed backcountry pack trips.

Pete: "Scates guides most of the fishing trips each summer himself. In fact, he leaves tomorrow with three members of the Towne family—you know, the Blake, Moffitt & Towne paper people. They pack in for a week of fishing every August. They'll come out at Emerald Bay and two of us will go get them with the horse trailers."

Pete went on, "Two of the Hills Brothers Coffee sisters also pack in with Scates each year. You'll probably meet them, Bill, because they live on the river upstream from Scates and come here to ride quite a bit."

The Lake Inn has a colorful past. Early on, the cabins that were uphill from the restaurant were reportedly used by ladies of the night. In the '30s and '40s, gambling on Tahoe's north and west shores was commonplace and the Lake Inn offered slots, "21," craps, and roulette—all reputed to be unfairly adjusted in favor of the house. The year 1947 marked the beginning of the

Tahoe City, Big Tree, 1940-1950 (Images of Lake Tahoe, Special Collections Department, University of Nevada, Reno Library)

While fishing is an enjoyable pursuit in itself, just being in a beautiful spot at sunrise can be as rewarding as landing a trout. (Photo Larry Prosor)

Bob Scates and Helen Towne (Courtesy Bechdolt Collection)

end for many gaming operations on the California side of the Lake. Fred Ichelson, owner of the Tahoe Tavern, pleaded guilty to the charge of possession of gambling machines, and in a few years the Lake Inn and other businesses which owed their success to the income generated by gambling closed their doors. (Today the popular Pfeifer House sits on the site of the former Lake Inn.)

Tahoe's long summer days were as good as it gets, interrupted on occasion by a passing thundershower. They were also long, albeit satisfying, workdays starting around six a.m. and ending about seven p.m., seven days a week.

We had a good choice of off-duty hangouts ranging from the Lake Inn, Tahoe Inn or Tahoe Tavern, to the action in Truckee about fourteen miles north. Bud had the loan of one of his dad's "Tahoe cars," so we had wheels, which was nice.

Tahoe City, 1945-1955   (Images of Lake Tahoe, Special Collections Department, University of Nevada, Reno Library)

Tahoe Tavern Tryst

As you might imagine, we wranglers had our share of action after work in a resort area like Tahoe. Most of the women riders were on the younger side and many were jailbait. One woman in particular stands out from all the rest for me.

I'll call her Mrs. Jane Arrowsmith (not her real name), a descendant of a Big Four railroad family. (The Big Four of Railroads, Collis P. Huntington, Mark Hopkins, Leland Stanford, and Charles Crocker, organized the Central Pacific Railroad in the 1860s and reaped a big bonanza in millions of dollars.) Jane was married to a San Francisco investment broker. The Arrowsmiths spent their Augusts at the Tahoe Tavern. He would spend the weekdays in the Bay Area, leaving her free to indulge in her love of riding, a sport he did not enjoy.

Lady Luck was smiling on me, because my first week on the job Pete Tracey appointed me as Mrs. Arrowsmith's guide for her afternoon trail rides. She was an all-American beauty—a tall, striking brunette, with long, shapely legs, a trim figure, and a tanned, healthy complexion probably acquired through leisure hours spent outdoors golfing, skiing, riding, and playing tennis. Her voice was soft and seductive, like Rita Hayworth or Ava Gardner.

After our second ride, she invited me for cocktails at the Tavern after work. Bob Scates and Pete Tracey warned, "Be careful, young Bill. You're not her first cowboy in these parts."

We were meeting in her suite instead of the bar which triggered a nervous feeling in me. As I knocked on her door around six, my impulse was to skip this tryst and hightail it back to the Scates camp for a safe evening of beer and tall tales with the guys. Before I could act, the door opened and there she stood, one gorgeous brunette with shiny red lips, a golden tan, and simple white slacks and sweater that showed off her shapely figure.

"Come in, Bill. What would you like to drink?"

"Bourbon and water, please. That's some view of the Lake."

"Yes, we reserve this suite every year."

"I have to tell you, I'm not sure I should be here. What if Mr. Arrowsmith walks in?"

She smiled and held up her drink. "Cheers, Bill. Mr. Arrowsmith won't be here until Friday."

We finished our first drink and she fixed another. We finished that and I fixed the next round. Things were starting to heat up, and then she came on strong. I still didn't think this was such a good idea, but by now we were both too excited to turn back.

In bed, she whispered things to me in that Rita-Ava seductive voice. "Oh, Bill, you're so big and strong. Go slow, cowboy, make this last. Almost there, Billy. You tell me when. Yes, darling! Oh yes, now!"

Well, Jane's passion might have been an act, but, heck, it was a good one. Her cries and moans sounded real to me and I'm sure to the people in the next room. My brain was calculating the number of trysts we could fit in based on Mr. Arrowsmith's work schedule. But there were other things to consider. This was my first week here. Did I want to tie down all my free time to one woman? Shouldn't I stay loose?

There was a knock on the door, and room service entered with club sandwiches and a bottle of champagne.

I'd have to work out my new-found dilemma later because soon we were in each other's arms again. We were getting better and better.

Later, when I was leaving, Jane kissed me at the door. "Bill, can we do this again?" in that Rita-Ava voice.

I smiled. "Damn you, Mrs. Arrowsmith. What do you think!"

Tahoe Inn, summer scene, 1940-1950 (Images of Lake Tahoe, Special Collections Department, University of Nevada, Reno Library)

The following has been excerpted and condensed with permission from Carol Van Etten's *Tahoe City Yesterdays*.

Lake Tahoe Mini-Histories

Tahoe City. Tahoe City's settlement was initially agrarian. A meadow (part of which became the town's golf course) extended from the Lake Outlet northeast for about four miles, and from this fertile cropland, in the summer of 1862, a concern comprised of Fish, Ferguson, Coggins, and Smith reportedly harvested a shoulder-high crop of wild timothy hay.

But Tahoe City was destined for grander purposes than to be the producer of animal fodder. Situated at the mouth of the Truckee River Canyon, it was ideally suited to become a hub of activity within the Basin. Access to the outside world by way of the canyon gave the location an advantage over neighboring sites, making it the first settled and later the most heavily populated community for many miles in each direction.

Among the town's first actual residents was William

Tahoe Inn, winter scene (Courtesy Bechdolt Collection)

Pomin(e) who, in 1864, completed a two-story frame structure with lean-to, most likely near the later site of Tahoe Inn.

The Pomin brothers were destined to play important roles in the town's—and the Basin's—history. Fredric, Ernest and Joseph were also among the area's first residents, engaging initially in commercial fishing. Ernest and Joseph later saw service as captains of several of the Lake's steamers, while Fredric provided a taxi service by rowboat to all points on the Lake.

Owing to the difficulty of overland travel, the use of boats became a critical factor in the development of the region. In the spring of 1864, Captain Augustus Pray (one of Glenbrook's first residents) had launched his forty-two foot *Governor Blaisdel*, the first of the Lake's steamers, and with it was launched the future of the town as well.

By July of 1864, the newly-completed King's Hotel (also known as the Tahoe City Hotel or King's Castle) was hosting a gala celebration of the opening of steam navigation on Lake Tahoe, with tickets priced at a whopping $7 each (including round-trip fare on the *Blaisdel*, which supplied the transportation for guests scattered around the perimeter of the Lake.)

The freight business was growing, and Pray's flat-decked side-wheeler was soon joined by a number of other steamers, employed not only in transporting passengers and freight, but in towing log booms to the mills of Glenbrook. The demand for timber continued to increase as the Central Pacific Railroad progressed eastward over Donner Summit and down the eastern slope of the Sierras.

By the late 1860s, the local lumber industry was well established, and a growing visitor population was increasing the demand for overnight accommodations. In 1867, William Pomin added onto his original residence and opened his doors to the public, calling the enterprise Tahoe House. Pomin's hostelry and saloon accommodated the weary traveler and resident boarder alike, offering more modestly-priced fare than King's Grand Central Hotel.

In spite of an increasing summer population, the other nine months of the year remained quite a different matter. Historians logged fifteen residents during the winter of 1873-74. This number doubled by the early 1880s, but there was no significant increase until the late 1890s.

Lumbering remained the chief activity of the small town's residents, with commercial fishing providing a livelihood for a dozen or so locally-based anglers. Tourism would have its day, but the 1895 fire which brought an end to King's Grand Central demonstrated how limited this industry still was. In the three years which followed, life in Tahoe City must have been exceedingly quiet, for without the magnetic charm of the Grand Central, the town had little more to offer the visitor than a drink to cut the dust of the toll road and access to the steamer (by which one could reach one of several lakeshore resorts or connect with the Glenbrook-Carson City stage). But the winds of change were blowing a gale, and Tahoe City lay directly in its path.

Tahoe Inn. The Tahoe Inn was practically synonymous with Tahoe City, in spite of several ownership changes over the decades. The origins of the Tahoe Inn date back to about 1876. It was built with no setback from the street, and its ground-level porch, open on three sides, served as a boardwalk for pedestrian travel. A second floor veranda running the length of the building afforded a sweeping view of the street and the Lake beyond.

Although the Inn was ostensibly a hotel and restaurant-bar, it was also a meeting place for service organizations, an answering service and message center, a place to conduct business or drown sorrows with sympathetic friends, and a home away from home to all who passed through its doors.

In 1923, the partnership of Carl Andrew Bechdolt, Harry Cullyford and Jack Mathews bought the Inn. All three men were associated with the Tahoe Tavern, and Bechdolt and Mathews continued to work there while Cullyford managed the Inn.

In 1930, Bechdolt bought out his partners and assumed control of the Inn. From that point on, the Inn stayed open year-round, catering to the visiting public while serving the community as an unofficial Town Hall.

The original Inn was built without particular concern for the future. It contained no fireproofing, and so when a blaze broke out in the kitchen on April 24, 1934, the fate of the entire building was sealed.

The blaze also destroyed the nearby dance hall, the original Log Cabin saloon, and a number of smaller outbuildings. The results of the blaze were devastating, but Bechdolt's determination overcame this setback, and carpenters working around the clock managed to complete a larger and grander Tahoe Inn for a gala reopening on July 3 of the same year.

Stories and legends associated with the Inn and its colorful owner are an integral part of Tahoe City's history. Bechdolt, familiarly known as "Pop," was imbued with a rugged individualism which won him many friends and some enemies during his years as proprietor of the Inn.

Tahoe's wilderness setting made it a popular location for films of the backcountry, and brought scores of Hollywood luminaries to town for a number of productions. In 1935, MGM brought their crews to Tahoe for the filming of *Rose Marie*, and Bechdolt was given the job of feeding several hundred Indian extras who had been trucked in for the occasion.

Following World War II, a new feature of the Inn

"Pop" Bechdolt (Courtesy Bechdolt Collection)

developed under the guidance of "Pop's" younger son, Bill. At Bill's direction, a private dining room freshly painted powder blue was dubbed "The Blue Room," and soon became the new unofficial "Town Hall" of Tahoe City.

The Blue Room operation began each morning when the kitchen opened for breakfast, and often continued into the wee hours. As seating was limited to one large table and about a dozen chairs, standing room only was often the rule. The Blue Room adjoined the Inn's kitchen, allowing the cook to double as a waiter most of the time.

Dinners in the Blue Room were priced at thirty-seven cents. However, it was Pop Bechdolt's unwritten policy that those who could not afford to pay were assessed what they could afford, or allowed to work off the expense of their meal. This gesture provided sustenance for many temporarily-down-and-out souls and kept the Inn's dishes washed, and plumbing repaired.

Although it became the town's soup-kitchen, the Blue Room also catered to the local elite, providing the setting for the financial transactions of such prominent wheelers and dealers as Henry J. Kaiser, Stanley Dollar and the W. W. Meins. When Squaw Valley Corporation was being organized in 1947, Bill Bechdolt offered Alex Cushing the use of the Blue Room.

One of the Tahoe Inn's original outbuildings was the Log Cabin, a saloon on Front Street, one door east of the Inn proper. The rough and ready activities common to barrooms of the day were not considered a proper atmosphere for ladies, and the old Inn did not

Bechdolt Family, 1999. Standing in back row: Cheryl Balbuena, Aaron Partelow, Julia Partelow, Denise Bechdolt, Michael Bechdolt, Julie Contri, Eric Partelow, Bernadette Bechdolt, Phillip Balbuena, William Bechdolt, Luke Bechdolt, Lyle Job, Joshua McKernan, Mary Bechdolt, Ronald Partelow; kneeling in middle row: Mark Bechdolt, Carrie McKernan, Aleja Balbuena, Andrea Job, Erica Job, Rosalie Contri, Laura Job, Joshua Balbuena, Lynnel Job; front row: Ashley Job, David Partelow (groom), Sherri Partelow (bride), Michael Bancroft, Daniel Job, Clint Bechdolt, Justin Bancroft. Not pictured: Caleb Balbuena, Jean Bechdolt, Ben Bechdolt, Jim Bechdolt, Josh McKernan, Jace McKernan.
(Courtesy Bechdolt Collection)

include a bar—thus the separate structure.

The Log Cabin's popularity continued undiminished through the years of Prohibition, perhaps even enjoying enhanced success by virtue of its isolation and lack of interference from representatives of the law. Local enforcement of legislation governing alcohol and gambling was notoriously lax, and the Log Cabin was able to maintain an open-door policy with impunity, relying on tip-offs from well-placed sources to prevent surprise visits from Federal officers.

The opportunity to challenge Lady Luck was just as readily available on the premises. The Log Cabin offered slot machines, poker tables, and wheels of fortune, equaling the variety—if not the volume—of Nevada's gaming houses. (Gambling was legalized in that state in 1931.)

By the mid-1930s, the repeal of Prohibition had eased any concerns over alcohol-related raids, but gambling continued to play a major role in the recreational offerings of the establishment until 1948, when Edmund G. "Pat" Brown took over the California governorship. Soon thereafter, local gambling operations which had thrived when he was Attorney General were forced to shut down.

Tahoe Tavern. To its patrons, the Tavern was a grand hotel—the showplace of Tahoe. Yet to the community which was its neighbor, the Tavern was also a force which provided recreational and social opportunities, trained its leaders and inspired a sense of self.

By the 1890s, the decline of the Basin's lumber industry was closing Glenbrook's mills, and a mass relocation of the once-bustling Nevada east shore community began. Basin slopes had been almost totally denuded of timber. However, the Bliss family, whose extensive interests had dominated the Glenbrook (and the Basin) economy, had wisely spared the magnificent stand of trees around the Lake Outlet at Tahoe City, and it was to this location that they began to move the structures and materials which would be the basis of their new operations.

This new endeavor would be in the realm of tourism. The Bliss family's plans called for the construction of a hotel to rival any in the country, but preparations necessary to the success of such a grand undertaking would require the establishment of several key services previously unknown in Tahoe City. Most basic of these would be a comfortable and dependable system of transportation.

Prior to 1900, a jostling fifteen mile stagecoach ride from Truckee was the last leg of a trip to Tahoe—a certain impediment to visitor travel. During the summer of 1898, architect William Seth Bliss, the oldest son of D. L. Bliss, was chosen by the newly-formed Lake Tahoe Rail-way and Transportation Company (LTRT), a Bliss-owned venture, to survey the route for the narrow gauge railroad.

By the fall of 1898, all the rolling stock for the new railroad had been barged over to Tahoe City from abandoned lines in Glenbrook and Bijou. The laying of track on the new fifteen mile roadbed continued through the summer of 1899, and in the spring of 1900, the line was put into tentative operation.

With the new rail system in place, sightseers could

Casino at Tahoe Tavern, 1920
(Images of Lake Tahoe, Special Collections Department, University of Nevada, Reno Library)

Autos at Tahoe Tavern (Images of Lake Tahoe, Special Collections Department, University of Nevada, Reno Library)

travel all the way to the lakeshore by rail. But of more immediate importance to the company, the materials necessary for implementing the second phase of their grandiose plans could now be efficiently transported to the site of operations.

By mid-July 1901, all was in readiness for the announcement of the company's grand new undertaking. "D.L. Bliss was here yesterday," reported the July 13 issue of the Auburn Republican, "and he is going to build a hotel at Tahoe City. It is said its construction will cost $150,000, which means a fine hotel." Time was of the essence, and by late September, construction of the new hotel was well underway.

When the Tahoe Tavern opened for business in 1902, the diversity and durability of its success could not have been estimated by its founders—nor could they have foreseen the difficulties ahead for an easily-accessible, self-contained resort, miles from the nearest civic center.

Transportation to the isolated resort had been assured by the completion of a railway system linking it with the Central Pacific at Truckee. Yet, there were other, equally challenging construction problems to be dealt with, including water, power and communication systems.

A water system was crucial to the supply and maintenance of the grand resort. Water from the distant Burton Creek was delivered to the Tavern via two reservoirs and several miles of connecting pipeline. Steam-powered generators proved the solution to the Tavern's energy needs until the late 1920s, when Sierra-Pacific Power brought the lakeside communities into the electric age. In addition to a telegraph office, the Tavern could boast of one telephone party line by 1900.

With these systems in place, the High Sierra hostelry was ready for business for the 1902 summer season. For the sixty-two summers which followed, the Tavern held undisputed sway as "the place" to go at Tahoe (although the rivalry of Tallac and, later, Glenbrook, Brockway, and Chinquapin would give it competition).

The quality of the Tavern's clientele was maintained by decidedly steep prices, though guests were inclined to overlook the expense in view of the sumptuous hospitality. A two-week stay was minimum, and many guests considered the Tavern their personal summer residence. Over the years, the hostelry hosted an impressive list of visitors. Numerous statesmen on holiday and globe-trotting celebrities signed the guest register, as well as many from the entertainment world, including Will Rogers, Jeanette MacDonald and Nelson Eddy, Charles Laughton, Bing Crosby, and the Marx Brothers.

And no wonder. The Tavern's facilities were second to none in the region—or elsewhere, for that matter. Such cosmopolitan amenities as a ballroom, barbershop, bowling alley, theatre, and riding stables were all part of the Tavern facilities, and a manicurist, beautician and physician were always in residence.

In April of 1925, the Linnard Hotel interests approached the Bliss family regarding their willingness to sell the Tavern property, including its railroad and steamers. Acquisition of the transportation system was considered crucial by the Linnard interests, as their affiliation with Southern Pacific Railroad figured in their plans for the property. The sale was consummated in 1926, and included a ninety-nine year lease agreement with William Seth Bliss which gave Southern Pacific use of the railroad right-of-way for the sum of $1 per year.

Following the conversion to standard gauge track, completed in 1926, visitors arriving by train could be delivered directly to the Tavern's doorstep without changing trains.

The Tavern did not change hands again until about 1940, when it was purchased by Matt Green. As a young carpenter, Green had been on the crew which built the Tavern, and over the years he gradually acquired stock in the company. His successful contracting business eventually allowed him to purchase the hotel outright. His ownership continued until the spring of 1946.

In 1946, the resort proper and its many outlying parcels were sold to a large partnership which in turn sold the Tavern to Albert Ichelson and his son, Fred, and distributed the other parcels among its partners. The Ichelsons operated the Tavern until 1963, when they sold it to the Moana Corporation.[2]

—Excerpted and condensed from
Carol Van Etten's *Tahoe City Yesterdays*.

Jimmy Norman (left) *and Bob Scates*
(Courtesy Bechdolt Collection)

Postscript

In the fall of 2002, thanks to a lead from Julie Bechdolt Contri, the authors met up with Paul Scates Patton, the son of Bob and Janet Scates. Paul and his wife, Judy, invited us out to the family compound on the Truckee River in Tahoe City, the same site where Bob and Janet Scates lived when I worked for Bob in the summer of '47.

It was remarkable how little the property had changed. Janet took us on a tour of the main house and guest houses. She was proud that their rustic character had been maintained over the years.

We sat outside in the grassy area near the river where we wranglers used to have our meals, and reminisced about Paul's father—Bob Scates, the good-lookin', charismatic cowboy who was well-liked by everyone around the Lake. Bob also enjoyed a reputation as quite a hell-raiser. I learned that Bob and Janet split blankets sometime after I left in '47. Janet remarried, and Paul was adopted by his stepfather.

I recalled my first lunch at the Scates' compound and stables—Juanita's delicious BLT's served at a redwood table under a weeping willow tree near the river. I could almost hear young Bud Crane saying, "It doesn't get much better than this, does it, Bill?"

Heading out for a morning ride in the Sierras. (Authors' Collection)

CHAPTER 4

Tahoe Hunting Guide

About two weeks after Labor Day weekend, Pete Tracey and we wranglers began preparing to move lock, stock and barrel downstream to the pack station. Deer Park, about a quarter mile up an old dirt road off Highway 89, served as the gateway to Five Lakes, Upper and Lower Hell Hole, and the Granite Chief-Rubicon Wilderness country.

The morning of our scheduled move, Chaska West and three of his wranglers showed up with eighteen head of horses from West's Brockway stables. That was our cue to mount up and join them with Scates' string of horses for the short, four-mile ride to Deer Park. Scates, West, and Tracey brought up the rear in the truck and horse trailers loaded with tack, packing, and camping gear.

Tahoe Inn, hunters
(Courtesy Bechdolt Collection)

Red Ulrich and I rode point (the lead position) about a quarter mile ahead of the string so we could give oncoming drivers plenty of time to slow down and stop if necessary. The move came off without a hitch. After unloading and storing all the gear, Pete broke out the sandwiches and soft drinks, and while we ate he filled us in on the plans for the next few weeks.

"Okay, men, listen up. Some of what I'm about to say may seem like old stuff to y'all who've been with us before, but pay attention anyway 'cause there's always something new. All told, we've got eight wranglers for guides this year, plus Bob and Chaska. As of today, we have sixty-seven different hunting party reservations who want to be in their backcountry camps before opening day, October 5. But we face the same old logistical nightmare. They all want to show up one or two days before opening day.

"The reservations average three hunters per party. So if they all show up, we'll have about two hundred hunters in the backcountry for opening day. Now here's a potential sticky point. We only have five established campsites: Cranes Camp, Shanks Cove, Bear Camp, Big Springs, and Whiskey Creek. That's an average of forty men per camp if I've counted right. That's more than we like to see in any one camp. We can always set up one or two temporary campsites if necessary, but let's cross that bridge when we come to it.

"Scates, or in his absence, West, will settle any undecided issues or complaints. Most of our customers are old friends by now, but there are always one or two disgruntled people to contend with. Now here's some more math for you mental geniuses," Pete said, with just a hint of a smile. "All told, we now have forty-seven head here at the Park: thirty-eight dude horses we can use as saddle horses or as pack horses, plus our own personal mounts. They will all get plenty of work before we're through.

Bill McGee at Deer Park, Fall 1947 (Authors' Collection)

"Any questions, so far?" Pete asked. Since no one raised a hand, Pete continued. "Good, let's move on. We shoot for an average of six hunters per guide for each backcountry trip. In terms of horseflesh, that's six saddle horses and three pack horses, not counting the guide's mount. We figure two hunters per pack horse unless they're a heavy drinking bunch in which case we add another pack horse just for the booze and charge extra to boot. So it can take ten horses just to pack in a party of six hunters for a stay of about a week."

Now it was Bob Scates' turn. "Good goin', Pete," he said. "You've covered most of the bases.

Allow me to add my two cents worth. In the early going over the next few days, Pete will try to schedule each of you for one backcountry trip a day. When we get closer to opening day, you'll need to figure on two trips a day. When this happens, you'll leave before dawn on the first trip and probably get back after dark on the second trip. Depending on the length of your morning trip, you will change mounts before going back in on a round trip. Then once the pressure is off, it's Katie, bar the door, and we'll all have a ball. I promise.

"One more thing," Scates added. "You new men will be accompanied on your first trip or two by an experienced guide who knows the trails and where the camps are located. If need be, Chaska and I will probably be available.

"Pete is our packer extraordinaire. He does all the packing of provisions into the panniers," he said, referring to the pairs of box-like compartments joined together with straps, then draped over the packsaddle with one compartment on each side for a balanced load.[1]

"By October 4, we should have all hunting parties ensconced in their backcountry camps. Now here's where it can get political. Each camp is assigned one wrangler with his mount, plus one pack horse, in case your hunters need to pack their bucks back to camp. That's part of our deal when we take their reservations. If you are one of the five wranglers assigned to a camp, you are to help out with the camp chores, including the cooking.

"Your mount is for your exclusive use in case of emergencies, so don't let someone talk you into borrowing it. That leads me to my next point. We always get requests to leave more saddle horses in camp. You have to hang tough here because we have to keep them down here at the park for late arrivals. Not all hunters can make opening day. Besides, there isn't enough grazing around the camps this time of year for more horses.

"How many of you brought your own rifle and hunting license?" Scates asked. Most of us raised our hands. "Good. Now here's another potential sticky wicket. If you brought your own rifle, license and deer tag, you can go hunting as time permits.

"If you don't have a license but want to hunt, be sure, let me repeat, be sure you hunt with someone close by who has a tag he is willing to swap for the buck you shoot. We don't want any game warden problems. That said, you can be sure more than one hunter in each camp will be quite happy to make a swap."

Deer Park history goes back to the late 1880s, when John Brown Scott and his wife built the Deer

Park Springs Inn, a three-story, twenty-room hotel. Scott drove a stagecoach to Truckee to meet guests arriving on the railroad from San Francisco and the valley towns. In the twentieth century, particularly the decades of the 1930s and 1940s, Deer Park gradually reverted to its primitive state. (Today an old barn and a corral are all that are left of Deer Park Springs Inn.)

The next two or three days were pretty quiet, then all hell broke loose. Hunters started arriving from all over. To avoid confusion, each hunting party had been pre-assigned to a backcountry camp by Bob Scates. Furthermore, Pete Tracey had staked out assembly points outside the main Deer Park corral for each backcountry camp—somewhat reminiscent of the organized confusion of a military operation.

Packin' In

Tracey and Scates had scheduled departures to the five backcountry camps based on reservation dates and arrivals at Deer Park. From past experience, they had ready answers to most questions. Of course, the return hunters knew the drill, so there was less confusion than one might expect.

I'll never forget my first trip up the mountains with Bob Scates leading off, followed by four hunters, then me with four pack horses tied head to tail, then three more hunters. I'd packed in before in Montana, but with only three or four people at a time. This was a big-time operation and I was proud to be a part of it.

The trail followed Bear Creek up Bear Valley for about a mile (site of the future Alpine Meadows Ski Resort). Then the trail zigzagged up a steep grade with a 1,200-foot gain in less than a mile. As we rounded the sharp bend of the second switchback, half of our strung-out party were temporarily out of sight.

I caught a glimpse of the High Sierras' Mount Watson and Mount Pluto over my shoulder through a cloud bank, both at 8,000 feet-plus elevation, as we reached the crest of the ridge before descending through a Jeffrey pine forest that soon gave way to a wide meadow. Squaw Peak, nearly 9,000 feet, was off to the right with Granite Chief Wilderness straight ahead.

As the trail leveled off, Scates dropped back to ride alongside me.

"How you doin' ?" he asked.

"Great," I replied. "It's beautiful country and the hunters seem like good people."

Then he reached into his saddlebag and handed me a folded map. "This topo (topography) map details the configuration of the Five Lakes terrain ahead and the location of each of our hunting camps. You'll need it until you get to know the lay of the land, so guard it with your life." Then he added, "Shanks Cove is about ten miles from here. Can you find it?"

"Sure enough," I replied and proceeded to find it on the map.

Then Scates added a sobering note. "Our camps are spread out, about three miles apart in a rectangular area roughly five miles wide by fifteen miles long. Each camp has a lake, stream, and/or spring nearby. But we still have to guard against trigger-happy hunters shooting each other. So be sure they always leave camp in a loud-colored shirt or jacket."

Scates then returned to his up-front point position. From time to time, for the next couple of hours, the forest opened into meadows allowing a clear view of the High Sierras around us.

We arrived at Shanks Cove a little after high noon. Bob Scates and I unloaded the pack horses, while the seven hunters removed their rifles plus the sleeping bags lashed behind their saddles, and started setting up camp. I transferred the provisions to some old Army-surplus duffel bags, so we could take the empty panniers back with us.

These were experienced hunters, but Scates still reminded them that the black bears of the Sierras—which can be anywhere from pure black to brown, cinnamon, or blonde—are always hungry and will go to almost any length to get a good meal.

Scates then warned the hunters to take precautions with their provisions. "Bacon, cheese and other strong smelling foods should be packed in airtight containers, then stuffed into duffel bags or some other large container. Then hang the bags from a heavy duty line tightly strung between two trees, ten feet off the ground, well above any bear's reach and well away from the tents. That's a must for all backcountry campers. Follow these rules and you won't have trouble; but woe to the person who disregards them."

Scates also reminded them of where and how to set up the camp "outhouse." "I suggest you dig a human waste trench at least one hundred feet from your water source, campsite and trail. Then cover up and add to the trench length each day as needed."

The hunters were busy setting up their tents and gathering firewood as Scates and I pulled out for Deer Park with the seven saddle horses and four pack horses in tow. The return trip was uneventful except for a brief shower. But the rain, which quickly settled the dust, passed and the sky cleared.

We had skipped noon chow to save time, so the

Hunters arrive at Deer Park (Courtesy Bechdolt Collection)

trail mix of dried fruits and nuts I kept in my jacket pocket hit the spot. The sun had set about a half-hour before the pack station came into view, but no problem. The moon was on the rise and shining its warm yellow light on the trail.

"Well done, Bill," Scates said as we unsaddled the horses. "You're a welcome addition to this outfit. Will you see that our horses are grained and get some alfalfa in the small corral. They earned it today."

"Sure thing, boss," I replied, "and thanks for the vote of confidence. It means a lot to me." And to think I get paid for this, I thought.

The next morning, Pete Tracey asked me to give Scates, West and him a hand with his packer chores. It was also my first chance to get to know West, something of an original. He was born and raised in Reno. He looks like an old black-and-white photo of Wyatt Earp come to life. He's five-foot-six, about a hundred-thirty pounds, and sixty-two years young. His graying hair is thinning; a thick handlebar moustache, sometimes straight, sometimes curled up, covers his lip. His face is wrinkled and expressionless; weathered like a piece of cracked rawhide after decades in the relentless Nevada wind and sun.

In some ways, West and Tracey look like brothers and soon became two of my favorite people. Both wear faded Levis, cowboy boots, yoked denim shirts and cowboy hats creased down the middle Southwestern style. They're both quiet and no doubt still tip their hats to the ladies. Both are articulate in an Old West kind of way. They say things like, "We're fixin' to get some hellacious weather tonight when them ole' thunderheads come a poundin' over the ridge" and "Looks like it's goin' on fall. It can start snowin' at Tahoe this time of year."

Prior to starting up his stable business, Chaska West had been a cow-poke and dude wrangler. He had also been a top-notch bronc rider and calf-roper on the rodeo circuit in his younger years. In the 1923 reenactment of the Pony Express run for Wells Fargo, Chaska won the gold medal for fastest time.

Pete used the old barn and the area around it as his packer base. Packing gear was neatly stacked, piled or hung everywhere. "Come on, Bill, let me show you what we have to work with," Pete said. "First, we have three dozen packsaddles and a like number of panniers, meaning we can pack in seventy-two hunters at any one time since we try to limit each hunter to one pannier compartment. In

Chaska West as a young cowboy at the TH Ranch near Pyramid Lake, riding the corral fence while waiting his turn at bronc riding, circa 1930s. (Courtesy Nevada Historical Society)

other words, two hunters per pack horse. Of course, they can have more pack horses if need be, but we charge extra to discourage that.

"Over here," Pete said as he pointed toward the side of the old barn, "I try to keep the hackamores, halters and bridles hung up. Now here's where you come in, Bill. We want to do all of the packin' here at the barn. But here's the rub: the newer customers always want to help out and they only screw things up. We've learned that the hard way. That's why we load the panniers ourselves to keep the loads from shifting on the trail, which can really delay things.

"Scates tells me you've done some packin' in Montana, so here's what I want you to do. Make sure the next hunter up is goin' to the camp we're packin' for. Then sort his gear into piles. Be sure he knows that his rifle, scabbard, and sleepin' bag or bedroll will be carried by his saddle horse and that it's his responsibility to see that it happens.

"Chaska or I will take it from there, so you can check out the next hunter in line. You'll get a chance to do some packin' later on when things slow down some."

I was impressed by Pete's packing skills. I watched him every chance I got and soon realized I was far from an expert. I learned that loading a pack horse right can be a painstaking job. As I watched, Pete gauged the weight of each pannier compartment with the delicacy of a man assaying gold dust. For example, on one occasion he transferred a box of pancake mix from the right side to the left before hoisting the pannier onto the pack horse.

"See this little spot in between the crosstrees, Bill. It's the most protected place on the pack. It's the best spot for any breakables."

He would then top off each load with tents, cooking equipment, an ax and any other gear, then cover the load with a large piece of canvas carefully lashed down with rope.

Camp cooking (Courtesy Bechdolt Collection)

We loaded the pack horses based on each hunting party's camp destination and scheduled departure. Eight early bird hunters were first up that morning: destination, Cranes Camp; departure time, right after breakfast.

By the time the hunters had chowed down, Bob Scates had picked out eight saddle horses and four pack horses for wrangler John McGinn, one of Chaska's men, to saddle up and bring around to the barn. While doing that, I sorted each hunter's gear, then watched as Pete and Chaska loaded the pack horses. Meanwhile, McGinn saddled their mounts and helped them attach their rifle scabbards and sleeping bags to their saddles. As they headed out, the next group of hunters lined up: destination, Whiskey Creek.

For the next few days, I alternated between hunting guide and packer. I had learned a lot from both Pete and Chaska. I preferred the guide role and looked forward to escorting hunting parties to Big Spring, Whiskey Creek and Bear Camp. Along the way, we had one black bear and numerous mule deer (named for their large mule-like ears) sightings.

On October 4, 1947, Red Ulrich and I took the last six hunters into Shanks Cove that were scheduled to be there for opening day. I was assigned to the Cove for the next six days as hunting guide. Red took all the horses except my mount, Buck, a big singlefoot buckskin gelding, and one pack horse back to Deer Park.

Red Ulrich, Chaska West, Neill West (Chaska's fourteen year old son), Pete Tracey, and Bob Scates were to man Deer Park and pack in any late arrivals. The other camp guides were Bud Crane, for his dad's group at Cranes Camp, plus John McGinn and Jim Thayer, another West wrangler.

By the time we stowed the gear and pitched tents for the new arrivals who didn't want to sleep under the stars, it was close to suppertime. I had one last chore before I could relax: hobble the two horses so they would graze nearby.

Many of the hunters at Shanks Cove, like Bill Bechdolt, Jay Shontz, Bob Pomin, and Bill Conners, were Tahoe locals, had been packing in with Scates for years and were very familiar with the area—bound to make my job easier. They liked to fish and hunt, but mostly they just liked to camp out in the High Sierras for a couple of weeks and enjoy the camaraderie with good friends.

Two of the men had cooked up a giant pot of beef stew, so after washing up, there was nothing to do but sit around the campfire, down tequila shooters with a beer chaser, and chow down.

"It sure doesn't get much better than this," I said, repeating young Bud Crane's comment to me my first day on the job. A dozen or more men within earshot agreed.

It's a fine warm evening. I sit near the fire with my back to a tree. The moon climbs out of the evergreens and pours its calm and generous light across the meadow. Everyone is eager to get an early start in the morning. A few men cleaning their guns trigger a debate over the best deer rifle. The two most popular rifles in this group are both Winchesters: the Model 70 bolt-action 30-06 and the Model 94 lever-action 30-30. My personal favorite is the old 30-06 my dad gave me many years ago.

Opening Day

Opening day arrived and Shanks Cove slowly came alive an hour before sunup. I broke the crust of ice in the water bucket and started brewing coffee. We were camped at about 7,200 feet. Today's volunteer cooks have already lowered the provision containers and pulled out the breakfast makings. In a few minutes, the aromas of bacon and coffee will be wafting through camp, a sure call to hungry campers to come and get it.

By seven a.m., seven 5-man hunting parties

Pack train outgoing (Courtesy Bechdolt Collection)

have assembled and agreed to fan out from camp in a giant circle. An unspoken competition develops: Who will bag the first buck?

I decided to stay near camp in case one of our hunters gets lucky. So I helped the cooks clean up after breakfast, then strolled toward the stream about one hundred yards from camp. I heard the cries of waterfowl and looked up to see several dozen mallard ducks wending their way south.

I looked down and saw animal droppings on the trail, brown pellets the size of marbles. Mule deer, I decided, as they were bigger than a rabbit's.

These piles, known to game managers as scat, can be used to estimate the mule deer population on the range. It seems that each deer, by the peculiar mathematics of nature, defecates thirteen times a day. By counting the piles of scat in a certain area and applying some arithmetic, a ranger can determine the number of deer per acre. However, for an accurate count he must be careful not to include last year's scat.

Some trees show bare patches that from a distance resemble the ax cuts used to blaze a trail. Closer inspection shows them to have been caused by deer rubbing against the trunks to clean the velvet from their year's new growth of antlers.

Every year a buck drops his antlers in late winter and then must grow a whole new set. The growth process takes most of the summer and is painful, in the way that an infant feels pain when cutting new teeth. New antlers are soft and sensitive, covered by a layer of velvety skin that is full of nerves and blood vessels. By August the antlers have hardened into bone and the velvet can be scuffed off. The animals pick young saplings which have a bit of give to them to rub against.

A buck's antlers have only one use: to battle other males during the autumn rut—the recurring sexual excitement of split-hoofed male mammals. The males that have spent most of their time running together in amicable bachelor groups now turn mean. Their neck muscles swell, they forget to eat, and they start tearing up the sod with their hoofs and antlers. Whomping and stomping, they get mad enough to fight snakes. Bucks send war cries to each other, a melancholy, high-pitched bugle that sounds like a jazz cornet in the upper registers. Then the battles begin. All this to see which buck mates with which female.

Further down the trail, I see signs of other animals. One set of claw marks, deep parallel gouges in a tree trunk, is bear, for sure. As I was studying the bear sign, two shots from the north rang out. They were followed a minute later by another shot. Maybe we'll have venison steak for supper I said to myself as I headed back to camp.

I spotted my horse, Buck, and the pack horse grazing in some timothy grass about a hundred yards off the trail. I was about to go get them when Eldon Campbell, one of Scates' best customers, showed up with a big grin on his face. "Hey, Bill, I just bagged my buck. Will you help me bring him in and butcher him?"

"Glad to," I replied. "That's what I'm here for."

Hunters dressing the kill (Courtesy Bechdolt Collection)

Eldon figured it was a good mile to his buck, so we caught up and saddled the horses and were on our way in nothing flat. The packsaddle is not configured for riders, but Eldon didn't seem to mind the discomfort on the short ride to his buck.

During our short ride to his bag, I explained to Eldon how I had learned to butcher beef as a Montana country boy, then added, "Sure hope I haven't forgotten how, as it's been more than seven years since I last dressed a steer." I went on to say that sooner or later every hunter should learn how to clean, cut and store his bag, as more and more states forbid meat markets and packing plants to do it, for control purposes, or so they say.

Eldon had dropped his four point buck on a slope near a stand of Western hemlocks. We managed to reposition him with his head at the lowest point, then I cut the jugular vein at the base of the neck to let the blood flow freely.

After he was fully bled, we dragged him over to the nearest fir tree. Then—and here's where my Montana training kicked in—I retrieved an old-fashioned set of wire stretchers from my saddlebag and we strung him up to a tree by his hind legs. Then I slit the skin for a few inches at the breastbone with my hunting knife and cut to the end of the cavity where the hindquarter meat begins, in order to remove the innards and intestines. I'll skip the remaining "gut and cut" detail for the benefit of any queasy readers and refer interested hunters to their favorite bookseller for books on preparing game.[2]

Next, we hoisted the carcass aboard the pack-saddle and secured it with heavy-duty twine. Then we headed for camp, with Eldon leading the pack horse with proof positive of his hunting skill.

Before opening day was over, Shanks Cove hunters had bagged three more bucks—and a doe, shot by mistake. Fortunately for me, the hunters already knew how to dress their kill, so I only had to haul the carcasses back to camp.

We feasted on venison steak that night. Not just any old venison steak—Bill McGee's sautéed venison steak.

One of the other cooks prepared a big pot of cabbage, turnips, chestnuts, and mushrooms—"classic game accompaniment," according to his wife—but a lot of it was still there the next morning. Sounds kind of good now, but at the time, between the steaks and our friends, Wild Turkey, Jack Daniels and Budweiser, no one in camp had much desire for vegetables. I'll bet there wasn't a vegetarian anywhere near Shanks Cove that night.

The next day after lunch, Buck and I were exploring the country southwest of Shanks Cove on horseback in the direction of Grayhorse Valley. I was following a creek. Ahead, the creek winds between low hills and gentle meadows and the pines. At the edge of a glade, Buck and I flush two does and their fawns grazing in the tall grass. With supreme nonchalance, they wander back into the cover of the trees and turn to stare at us as I ride past.

> ### Bill McGee's
> ### Sautéed Venison Steaks
> Have ready ½-inch young venison steaks. Before cooking, rub with garlic. To keep them crisp and brown on the outside, rare and juicy inside, first sauté them in 1 tablespoon of butter and 2 tablespoons of vegetable oil for 5 to 6 minutes to the side. Serve with Hot Cumberland Sauce: ½ cup currant jelly, 2 tablespoons horseradish, and ½ teaspoon dry mustard. Makes about ½ cup.

Signs of other animals fill the woods. Then I spot a six point buck eyeing me from about a hundred yards through some tall underbrush. I stare at the buck as I rein in Buck, and he at me, for sixty seconds, hardly breathing. Then he trots off into the trees. Then I decided, what the hell, I'll shoot first and then decide what to do if I knock him down. So I tether Buck to the nearest tree and set out on foot after the buck.

Then I got lucky. He stopped, as if to reconnoiter the situation—a big mistake, as it allowed me time to point and shoot through a small opening in the trees. He dropped in his tracks. My shot also spooked the two does, who left in a hurry with their fawns following close behind in leaps and bounds.

After I bled and gutted the buck, I decided to hoist it aboard Buck, with a big assist from the pulley action of my wire stretchers, and walk back to camp, a distance of about three miles as the crow flies.

By the time I made it back, I knew exactly who I was going to give my buck to: Joe Alderson, a very nice Marin County doctor, an experienced backpacker and rock climber, but a novice hunter.

Joe accepted the buck with the enthusiasm of a kid at Christmas, then watched and listened intently as I showed him how to skin the carcass and quarter the two sides of venison. He then attached his deer tag to the antlers and said, "Thanks, Bill. I am now a full-fledged deer hunter."

Looking back, my favorite memory of Shanks Cove is the camaraderie of the group around the campfire each evening. Lots of stories, of course.

Pack train returning (Courtesy Bechdolt Collection)

Some serious, but mostly humorous: war stories, enhanced with age, no doubt; bear stories, of course; jokes, both clean and dirty; and for sure, sexual conquests, both actual and imaginary. We even had sing-along sessions, thanks to Bobby Burton and his guitar, packed in with no little trepidation.

The night before our group broke camp, we had some "hellacious weather" as Chaska West would call it, as one thunderhead after another rolled through, delivering brilliant lightning strikes followed by rolling claps of thunder, but, as sometimes happens, with very little precipitation, to the relief of those of us who chose to sleep under the stars. As I gazed at the heavens, my thoughts turned to our group. Just one week in the back-country can change one's whole perspective. The wilderness somehow gives us back a sense of wonder and chips away at the insulation of civilization with surprising alacrity. That's enough wilderness philosophy, I said to myself. Now go to sleep!

Packin' Out

By sunup October 12, there wasn't a cloud in the sky. All you could see was the big bright blue Sierra sky. Good weather for our return ride to Deer Park, I thought. Everyone in camp scheduled for departure today was ready and waiting long before Red Ulrich arrived with the pack train. It was now time to reverse the process and start packing hunters out.

The group of seven "early birds" Bob Scates and I packed into Shanks Cove on September 27 will be the first out. We headed for Deer Park about eleven a.m. with Red mounted on his black, high-stepping gelding, Midnight, leading the pack animals. The rest of us fell in behind in single file.

A little later, as the trail widened through the meadow, I moved up beside Red.

"What's happening, Red?" I asked. "Have you been busy?"

"You bet your boots," he answered. "Chaska and I have been making round trips everyday, sometimes two times, with smaller groups who didn't make it for opening day. We took all of them to Bear Camp or Whiskey Creek, because they were closer. That's why you haven't seen me."

"So you haven't got in any hunting yet?" I asked.

"Hell, no, but I still hope to," he replied.

When I told him about my good luck, he yelled, "Hot damn! You lucky so and so. And a six pointer to boot."

Deer trophies at Tahoe Inn (Courtesy Bechdolt Collection)

"I'm sure glad Scates sent you in with extra pack horses. The Shanks Cove group has already bagged eleven bucks and one slightly illegal doe, but she sure was good eating," I added.

The ride out seemed long and dusty due to the recent heavy horse traffic on the trail. To ease the pain, we rotated positions every hour so everyone got a shot at the lead and drag positions of the train.

I took the point as we started our descent down the steep slope with its many switchbacks to the park. Going downhill on a horse makes you much more aware of the danger when the trail narrows and the drop off is steep. They are definite reminders of the increased risk of a serious accident; e.g., a horse stumbles and falls taking the rider over the down slope with him. Guide responsibilities can be awesome at times—that's a fact.

We pulled into Deer Park around six p.m. It must have taken two hours to get everyone unpacked and squared away. Some of the group were going to head straight for the Bay Area without so much as a beer. Others were going to spend the night in Tahoe City or Truckee before heading home.

Scates and Tracey had Red and me scheduled to go back in early the next morning to retrieve more hunters, but until then we had the night off, if you can call it that. We were so pooped all we could do was go into Tahoe City with Tracey for a hamburger and a couple of beers at the Tahoe Inn, then back to the park for some shut eye.

The next thing I knew, Tracey was shaking me by lantern light. It was only four a.m.

"Come on, Bill, rise and shine," he said. "As we told you last night, you and Red are gonna take a string of eleven saddle horses and eight pack horses up to Whiskey Creek today to retrieve ten hunters. I'll saddle your string while you get some coffee and doughnuts."

Well, you get the picture. We went full bore until October 20, Scates' self-imposed deadline to have everyone out of the backcountry. Hunting season lasted longer, but due to the crush of hunters during the first two weeks, the deer had gone over the hill until the first big snow.

On October 21, it was a treat to wake up to warm sunshine and spend a lazy morning over Pete Tracey's breakfast of sausage and eggs, hash browns, and buttermilk biscuits with some good, piping hot coffee.

About ten a.m., we—meaning Bud Crane, Red Ulrich, John McGinn, Chaska West, and yours truly—broke camp at Deer Park and trailed the horses back to the familiar Lake Forest pasture. Meanwhile, Scates and Tracey loaded the truck and pickups with the tack and camp gear and made the short haul to Scates' stables in Tahoe City.

Later, all eight of us, plus Scates' wife, Janet, met for a late lunch at the Tahoe Inn's Blue Room, as guests of "Pop" Bechdolt, the owner. When Janet arrived, she handed me a note dated October 14, 1947, which read, "Bill McGee, please call Lena Geiser." I figured it for another job lead and decided it could wait a day or so until I was back in Reno.

Scates kicked off our "season ending party" with a first round toast to our host, Pop Bechdolt. West followed with a toast of his own "to all of you hard workin' cowboys." And so it went. It's a safe bet any pretense of work later that afternoon flew out the window soon thereafter.

We partied as if there was no tomorrow. The few weeks we had spent together reminded me of the military. Great teamwork, comradeship, long hours with little sleep, and—this is important—new friendships based on a common bond—love for horses, adventure and the great outdoors.

Most of us hit the sack early that night hoping to sleep off pending hangovers. Some of us had a long day ahead of us tomorrow.

Trailin' to Reno

Sure enough, Tracey roused us around six the next morning. While we were having our first cup of coffee, Pete said, "Okay, men, here's the plan. Bud and Red head for home today. Bill will assist Chaska and his men, Neill, Thayer and McGinn, trailing Chaska's string of twenty-some horses to Reno, fifty-plus miles, mostly on blacktop. Any questions?"

As we were having breakfast around the picnic table, Scates handed out our paychecks and thanked us for the umpteenth time, counting last night, then said goodbye. He and Janet were packing for the move to their winter home in Auburn.

Pete Tracey followed in his pickup as we rode through town to the pasture. He then manned the gate while we cut out West's string and headed them northeast on Highway 28. Pete will be heading south in a few days to his "winter grazing grounds" at the Arizona Biltmore in Phoenix.

Chaska rode a half-mile ahead in his pickup, with the lights on to warn oncoming traffic to slow down. John McGinn rode point while Neill and I controlled the herd from the sides and rear.

It was a beautiful fall day, but with subtle reminders that winter was not far off. As we rounded Carnelian Bay on the North Shore and rode toward the home of Chaska West's Brockway stables, several horses tried to break for home, then seemed confused when we stopped them. Other than that, they followed McGinn's point lead without much trouble.

Our biggest challenge was speeding drivers and horn honkers who seemed to enjoy spooking the horses as they went by. We entered Nevada at Stateline Point, then skirted Crystal Bay until we came to the fork in the road where the Mount Rose highway drops down to join Highway 28.

As the saying goes, "It's just another day in paradise." We have been passing private residences perched high above steep drops and choice summer homes on the beach all along the North Shore. It reminded me of a couple of Mark Twain's passages in *Roughing It*:

> Three months of camp life at Lake Tahoe would restore an Egyptian mummy to his pristine vigor and give him an appetite like an alligator.... The air up there in the clouds is very pure and fine, bracing and delicious. And why shouldn't it be? It is the same the angels breathe.

Now it's time to tackle the Mount Rose Highway, the shortest, but steepest, route to Reno from the Lake. The grade is relatively mild for about two miles, then loops back toward the Lake for a last spectacular view, before starting back up the mountain in earnest.

By the time we reach the 8,900-foot summit, we have gained 2,700 feet in altitude in just seven miles. Mount Rose is off to our left at 10,778 feet elevation and Slide Mountain to our right at 9,688 feet. Horses feel the altitude and thin air just like we do, so we gave them a breather while we enjoyed our cigarettes.

The descent is even steeper. Consequently, the bends in the road are much sharper with auto speed limits as low as twenty-five mph on most curves. Needless to say, these conditions try the patience of more than one driver since there are no wide shoulders and very few passing lanes. Of course, not everyone is in a big hurry. The curious sight of a herd of horses and four dusty, unshaven cowboys coming toward them is, I imagine, as strange as anything they've seen all day. The kids love being close to so many horses. All in all, it is a memorable experience for them, as well as us.

By the time we reach the junction with U.S. 395, we have dropped down to around 4,500 feet,

The summertime crowds have gone and a dusting of snow cover the peaks. Time to contemplate the past days of summer and the approach of winter. (Photo Larry Prosor)

with a little less than ten miles to go. The sun slips down behind Mount Rose as we approach the gate to West's winter pasture, about three miles southeast of Reno.

It has been a full days' ride through some of the most scenic country in the West. After we unsaddle our mounts and turn them loose, we pile our gear into the back of Chaska's pickup and head for town.

I offered to buy a round of drinks at the Round Up Bar, but they all seemed eager to get home.

McGinn spoke for all of them when he said, "Thanks just the same, Bill, but I think we did enough damage to ourselves last night to last awhile." They dropped me off at the Nevada Hotel on East Second Street about eight p.m. along with my saddle and footlocker.

After a shave and a long, hot shower, I was as good as new, so I decked myself out in my dress boots, favorite shirt, and a clean pair of Levis and headed for the Round Up to see what Lena Geiser's message was all about.

Part II—The Famous Flying ME Ranch and the Changing Cast of Characters

V&T steaming south, past the Flying ME
(Courtesy R. C. Greenleaf)

Bill McGee with Zorro (left) and Alley Oop at the Flying M E, 1947. (Authors' Collection)

CHAPTER 5

Landing the FLYING M E Wrangler Job

Lena Geiser put down her cigarette and came out from behind the bar at the Round Up, Reno's popular hangout on West Second Street for ranch hands and cowboys. Lena greeted me with a big smile and a hug. "Welcome back, stranger. Did you get my message?"

"Just yesterday," I replied. "What's up, Lena?"

"Let's sit down," she said, motioning to a corner table. "I don't want the whole bar listening." I ordered us a couple of drinks, then she continued.

"I had a call from the Flying M E about a week ago, from a gal by the name of Allie Okie. They're going to be in the market for a dude wrangler real soon. I told her a little about you, Bill, and she said to call her as soon as you can. Emmy Wood would like to talk with you, the sooner the better."

"Holy mackerel!" I blurted out. "The famous Flying M E! I've got a real shot at the wrangler job! I can't thank you enough for calling me, Lena." I gave her a big hug.

"Hold on now, cowboy," Lena said. "You can thank me if you get the job. It's too late to call tonight," she counseled, "but I'd give them a call first thing tomorrow."

"You can count on that," I replied as Lena went back to tending bar. The Round Up was really jumping.

About that time, my cowboy friends, Utah Bob and Frank Burrows, walked in, and we played catch-up for an hour or so. Then I headed for my hotel and a good night's sleep. I wanted to be at my best for the next day.

The following morning I phoned the Flying M E about nine, and a maid answered. "Mrs. Okie is having breakfast. May I tell her who's calling?"

"Tell her it's Bill McGee, please. Lena Geiser's friend."

Mrs. Okie picked up the phone, and we must have talked for twenty minutes. Then she paused, "What's your day like, Bill? Can we meet later at the Riverside Corner Bar? I'm pretty sure Emmy has to be in court this afternoon. Hold on while I ask the cook. She'll know Emmy's schedule. Will four p.m. at the Corner Bar work for you?"

"You bet. I'll see you there."

Hiring On

At four p.m. on the dot, I entered the Corner Bar in the Riverside Hotel and spotted two women at a corner table. One was wearing frontier pants and a Western shirt; the other a tailored suit and hat.

The taller of the two, a lanky, attractive type in her late twenties, walked up to me. "You must be Bill McGee?"

"That's right, Ma'am," I replied.

"I'm Allie Okie. Very glad to meet you."

The other woman then rose to greet me. She was a handsome woman, maybe about fifty, and stood about five feet tall, with a youthful figure and very erect posture. She radiated charm and poise even before speaking.

Allie Okie made the introduction. "Bill McGee, please meet Mrs. Emmy Wood."

"Hello, dear," Emmy Wood said in a deep, whiskey voice. "It's nice to meet you. Lena thinks the world of you."

"It's a real pleasure to meet you, Mrs. Wood. I've heard so much about you and the Flying M E," I said, just a bit nervous.

"Oh, please call me Emmy. Everyone does. Did you enjoy your job with Bobby Scates at the Lake?"

"You bet I did. The camaraderie in the backcountry was really special. Bob Scates and Chaska West are a couple of pros from the old school."

"Now I don't know how much Lena has told you," Emmy said, "but we need a wrangler to start by the first of November. Tell us something about yourself, dear. About all we know is that you were born and raised on a ranch in Montana."

I gave them my verbal resumé, which seemed to make a favorable impression.

"Sounds like you could fill our needs very nicely," Emmy said. "Now let us tell you what we expect from our wrangler."

Between the two of them they described the duties of a typical dude ranch position, with one exception: unlike many dude ranches, Emmy discouraged fraternization between guest and wrangler. I could see potential problems with that down the road but decided to let sleeping dogs lie.

"What are we talking about money-wise?" I asked.

"Three hundred a month plus room and board and the use of the ranch pickup," Emmy replied. "You'll also earn some good tips, Bill, especially from the frequent riders. How does that sound?"

"More than fair. When do I start?"

With that, Emmy and Allie looked at each other, then nodded.

"November 1, if you can arrange it, Bill."

"Great," I said. We shook hands and then toasted each other with our drinks. Later as I was heading for the door, Allie called out, "Call me in about a week, Bill, so we can arrange to have you picked up."

"Will do," I replied.

I left the Riverside in a festive mood. I couldn't wait to tell Lena and Laurie the good news. You've no doubt heard the expression "in the right place at the right time." Lucky me, I thought, as I rounded the corner to Second Street and headed for the Round Up. But I reminded myself it wasn't just luck that got me the job. I had planned my approach, with Lena's help, then worked the plan.

I had eleven days off until starting at the Flying M E. They seemed to whiz by. Days and evenings I mostly hung out at the Round Up with my cowboy friends, Utah Bob and Frank Burrows. We spent a lot of time with our hero figure and cowboy friend, Frank Polk, watching him carve lifelike figures out of a piece of wood with his pocket knife and listening to his stories about his romances with the ladies. Frank was old enough to be our father and we all looked up to him, some of us hoping to have his kind of luck with the ladies. (See "The Cowboy and the Lady" in this chapter.)

My late nights were reserved for Laurie, who had filed for divorce shortly before I left for Tahoe. I called Star Taxi as soon as I got back to the hotel and Laurie answered the phone.

"Welcome home, stranger. The phones are ringing off the hook. Are you at the Nevada Hotel? Can I call you back?"

"Sure enough," I said.

A few minutes later, Laurie called back, and we made a date to meet at the Roaring Camp at midnight for a feast of Ramona's Mexican food, the best in Reno. Laurie was still working the four-to-midnight swing shift.

Celebration

We had a couple of tequila shooters with our combination plates and caught up with each other's fall happenings. Then we headed for my hotel. We had no sooner entered my room when Laurie, in a series of quick movements, kicked off her shoes, unfastened the buttons on her dress, and wiggled in pure joy as her dress cascaded to her feet. She then pulled her slip over her head and tossed it on a chair. She was wearing nothing else.

Naked and smiling, her firm, beautiful body with its pert breasts and her jet black hair took my breath away. She walked, with pride, across the room and kissed me fully on the lips. My hands reached out and touched her forward-thrusting nipples and, inadvertently it seemed, my fingers curled and tightened. Sensual waves shot through me.

"That's very nice," Laurie purred. "Let's go to bed."

We had been together several times before I left for Tahoe. On each occasion I had experienced sexual ecstasy like never before. Laurie knew incredible things to do to a man which both surprised and delighted me. Her skill aroused wave and wave of sensual pleasure until I had to cry out for her to stop.

Afterward she was gentle, caressing, loving, and patient until, to my male surprise, I was aroused once more.

"Bill, darling," she whispered. "You're hurrying too much. Lie still awhile. Hold back." She stroked my naked shoulders and then my spine. Her fingernails were sharp, but light. She was in full charge.

It was now my turn to moan—a mixture of sensual pleasure, pain and postponed fulfillment—as I obeyed Laurie's commands.

"It'll be worth waiting, I promise you," she whispered again.

I wondered how someone so young could have learned so much. She was so experienced, uninhibited, and gloriously emancipated.

"Not yet, cowboy! I'll tell you when!"

Her hands, skilled and knowing, went on exploring my body. It was best to do everything exactly as she said, I thought.

"Oh, that's good, Billy Boy. Isn't that lovely?"

"Yes, yes," I said, holding my breath.

"Soon, cowboy, very soon."

Laurie's black hair was spread over the pillows. Her kisses devoured me. Her fragrance was ambrosial. Her beautiful body was beneath me. This, I said to myself, has to be the best ever.

"Now, Billy, now! Now!"

After each lovemaking we dozed, awakened, then made love again, although not with entire success. We were both becoming physically drained and finally fell into a deep, exhausted sleep as the sun was rising.

When I awoke, Laurie was kissing me softly. She was dressed and leaving for work. We had slept until nearly four p.m. the next day.

"See you tonight, Bill." With that. she walked out the door and I fell back to sleep.

I would see Laurie several more times before joining the Flying M E. Not long after that when her divorce was final, she returned to her hometown somewhere in the Midwest—a free woman.

(Photo Valerie Vondermuhll, Courtesy George A. Vondermuhll Jr.)

Flying M E dude horses (Authors' Collection)

First Day

On November 1, 1947, Allie Okie pulled up in front of the Nevada Hotel. She was driving the ranch station wagon, a '47 forest green Buick "Woody" with the Flying M E brand on the front door panels. After an exchange of greetings, she opened the tailgate so I could load in my gear and we were off.

"Hope you don't mind if I ask you a few questions, Bill. I'm always curious about people's backgrounds."

"Don't mind at all, Mrs. Okie. Fire away."

"Call me Allie. It's short for Alys. However, the formalities will be just right for the guests. Now where in Montana did you say you're from?"

"Livingston, the southern part of the state, about forty miles north of Yellowstone Park. But it's a little more complicated than that. I was born in Livingston, but my dad's ranch was in Shields River Valley some twenty miles north of Livingston. I love Montana but it sure gets cold in the winter."

"You're going to like the weather around here, Bill. What I really love is it's seasonal without the extreme weather changes we had back East."

"What part of the East are you from, Mrs. Okie, I mean Allie?" I asked.

"I was born and raised in New York and moved to Virginia when I got married. I came out to the ranch last year for a divorce. When it was final, I agreed to stay on to help Emmy for just a few weeks.

"Emmy was going through a very traumatic time when I arrived. She won't volunteer this information, but since it's common knowledge around the Valley and in Reno, I'll explain so you'll know. Emmy and her husband, Dore—his real name was Theodore—were Easterners who came out West and fell in love with Nevada. Dore got involved with a young divorcée who was staying at the ranch. She was supposed to get lots of money when her divorce was final and, as these things go, Dore decided to divorce Emmy and take off with his new, wealthy girlfriend. The one good thing Dore did, he signed over the ranch—which was called the Tumbling DW then—debt free to Emmy, as part of the divorce settlement. Well, here I am a year later! Emmy really needs help when the ranch is full."

"That's some story, Allie. I'm glad you confided in me. Should help keep me from putting my foot in my mouth."

"Emmy's fine now. Last year she changed the name of the ranch to the Flying M E—for Emmy. She added more rooms and a swimming pool. Business is good.

"Emmy's very special, as you'll see. She's one of a kind. Some people come here very upset, and Emmy's a good listener at a time when they really need it."

Allie must be special, too, I thought. She was wearing Levis and cowboy boots, but had a way about her that suggested a very refined Eastern background.

"Not to change the subject, Bill, but we're in Washoe Valley now. That's Little Washoe Lake off to the left. Big Washoe is just to the south. We're going through Washoe City; it's a ghost town now, but it was Washoe's first county seat in the 1800s. Just ahead on the right is the historic Bowers Mansion."

Allie slowed down, then pulled over on the shoulder. "There it is, Bill," she said as she pointed toward the big Flying M E sign on the other side of the highway. "Do you like history?"

"Yes, you bet I do. It was my favorite subject in school."

"Then you're really going to love Nevada. You know, the original ranch building was the old Franktown Hotel, built about 1861. It was also a station stop for the Virginia & Truckee Railroad during the Comstock boom days. The V & T still stops here every day to take on water on its Reno-to-Carson City run. Emmy has lots of books on the history of the state. She shares your interest, so don't be afraid to ask her to loan you some."

We drove up the lane and turned toward the rambling two-story ranch house painted white with black trim. What a beautiful setting, I thought. Several large cottonwoods provided a close-up backdrop to the buildings, while to the west, the blue-green Sierras touched a cloudless sky. Off to the east, one could see Washoe Lake and the treeless burnt sienna Virginia Range hiding

Virginia City and the remains of the Comstock.

Several good-looking saddle horses were grazing in the pasture to the right, and straight ahead the old red V & T water tower was standing beside the railroad tracks just east of the ranch house.

Allie pulled in and parked alongside several other cars in front of the ranch house. "Not exactly the 'Old West' many guest ranches try to look like, is it Bill? It looks more like a gentleman farmer's country place in Virginia or New England. Remember, Emmy caters to a little older, well-to-do clientele who prefer the comforts of home to the 'roughing it' concept of some guest ranches.

Allie Okie (left) and cook Edith Riley in the kitchen
(Photo Valerie Vondermuhll, Courtesy George A. Vondermuhll Jr.)

"Let's put your saddle in the tack room, then I'll introduce you to Jimmy Murray. Jimmy is a former jockey, and he was the first dude wrangler here when Dore and Emmy operated the ranch as the Tumbling DW. He had a stroke some time ago which left him paralyzed on one side, so Emmy is putting him up 'for as long as he needs a roof over his head and three meals a day.' That's Emmy for you."

I pulled my saddle out of the back of the Buick and followed Allie to the stable's tack room. After stowing my saddle, she knocked on a door in the corner where the multi-car garage joins the stables and called out, "Jimmy, are you decent?"

"You're damn right I am! As decent as I'll ever get. Come on in, Allie."

We entered, and Allie said, "Jimmy, this is Bill McGee, our new wrangler."

"Howdy, partner. Emmy's already told me about you. Is it true you're on the run from some Montana sheriff?"

I guess I looked surprised, because he broke into a grin. "Just kiddin', cowboy. Good to meet you."

"Same here, Jimmy," I said as we shook hands.

In spite of Allie's briefing, I wasn't prepared to meet this pint-sized old-timer with a big voice and a firm handshake who couldn't have weighed a hundred pounds soakin' wet. As we were leaving, he added, "Drop in anytime, Bill. I can tell you a thing or two about this here operation."

We walked towards the ranch house, and Allie said, "I want you to meet our cook, Edith Riley. She's been with Emmy from the Tumbling DW days, too. Sometimes she's a residence witness for our guests, since she sees them everyday."

We entered a side door and walked down a hall to the kitchen. Edith Riley was having a cup of coffee when we entered, and Allie introduced us. I noticed that Edith had a long cigarette holder balanced on the counter with a lit cigarette dangling precariously from the end, a long line of ashes ready to fall at any moment on the floor. This would be the first of many times I would see Edith in the kitchen, sometimes leaning over a table kneading dough, with her long cigarette holder held loosely between her lips, and ashes dangling precariously from the end. We all wondered about the ashes, but never dared to say anything.

"I'm really looking forward to your cooking, Mrs. Riley. I've heard nothing but raves." She smiled with obvious pleasure at the compliment. "Thanks, Bill, and call me Edie."

Effie Kearney, the upstairs maid, walked in to get her mid-morning coffee. Edie did the introductions this time. Effie had also been with Emmy since the Tumbling DW days.

"Hmm," I noted, "Riley, Kearney, and McGee. Sounds like a winning combination to me."

As we headed for the dining room, we passed through a small room with a food service area on the left and a booth on the right with a window facing south. "This is where you'll eat," Allie said, "except for special occasions." Aha, I thought, a sign of Emmy's anti-fraternization rule.

The dining room table was already set for lunch. The room was paneled in knotty pine and had a window with a view of the lawn and swimming pool. "We can seat ten comfortably. During busy periods we usually have two seatings at dinner," Allie explained.

As we moved on into the living room, I expected to see some guests lolling about, but this time of morning the living room was empty. I supposed the guests slept late or had their breakfasts in their rooms. The living room window featured a great view of Slide Mountain. There was a stone fireplace and comfortable overstuffed sofas and chairs. Navajo rugs covered the floor. A well-stocked bar was set up in one corner, and it looked like a few glasses were left over from the night before.

Allie went on, "We can accommodate up to sixteen guests providing some are willing to double up. We only have nine at the moment. Three are late sleepers and usually skip breakfast, and two left early to tour Lake Tahoe in their rental car. I don't know about the other four. Emmy, as you may already know, is a night owl, and she's seldom seen before noon.

"Well, so much for the tour, Bill. Emmy wants you to take the first day to acquaint yourself with the ranch. Don't be afraid to ask questions. Now

Flying M E Dining room
(Courtesy Gail Greenleaf Hencken)

Living room
(Author's Collection)

let's get you over to the bunkhouse so you can unpack before lunch." As Allie drove the two hundred yards or so to my new quarters, she asked "What do you think so far, Bill?"

"Great, Allie. I love everything about the place."

I pulled my footlocker out of the Woody and carried it into the bunkhouse. As Allie drove off, she called out, "See you later. Hope you enjoy your 'private suite' at the M E!'"

My "private suite" was a good-sized cabin furnished with a bed, bedside table and lamp, and a small bureau. It was everything this single cowboy needed. The only hitch was the "head," which was in the ranch house some two hundred yards away— a definite handicap during the winter months.

It took me five minutes to unpack. Then I headed for the tack room with my bridle and saddle blanket. It was a bright, sunny day, but cool and windy. You could tell winter wasn't far off.

Jimmy Murray was sitting outside his door in the sun, but sheltered from the wind. It was as if he was posing for a photographer, with a cane in hand and his hat at a jaunty angle. It would become a very familiar picture.

It was still more than an hour until noon chow, so I started to chat with Jimmy. "How long ago did you start working for Emmy?" He cleared his throat two or three times, then went on to tell me the story.

Jimmy Murray, retired wrangler
(Photo Valerie Vondermuhll, Courtesy George A. Vondermuhll Jr.)

Wrangler's bunkhouse (Courtesy Gail Greenleaf Hencken)

"Well, lemme see. I first met Emmy and Dore in the thirties, when I was wranglin' at the old Monte Cristo Ranch overlookin' Pyramid Lake. It was a small outfit with about two hundred head of mother cows, until Bud and Phyllis Blundell built a row of small cabins and started takin' in dudes. But it was a real workin' ranch, too.

"Then, as I recall, Dore's brother, George, talked Dore and Emmy into comin' out West for a look-see. To hear Emmy tell it, it was love at first sight when they saw this valley from the

Emily Pentz Wood, proprietor of the Flying M E Ranch, with Dinklespiel
(Photo Valerie Vondermuhll, Courtesy George A. Vondermuhll Jr.)

old V & T. There was nothin' here at the ranch then but that old red water tower and the Franktown Hotel. Anyhoo, as I understand it, they leased this place on a trial basis, then bought it outright in '41. They did some major fixin' up and changed the name to the Tumblin' DW. That's where I come in. They asked me to come on over and take charge of the livestock and the dudes.

"Things were lookin' good when this good-looker, half Dore's age, checked in to get a divorce.

She sure turned Dore's head. Well, you can't blame him entirely. Here he is, surrounded by all these good-lookin' women. Anyway, the rumor was the good-looker was going to get a lot of money from her "ex" in the divorce settlement. Pretty soon, Dore and Emmy are splittin' blankets.

"But Emmy's a fighter. After the divorce, she did some more remodelin' and changed the name to the Flying M E. Things have been hummin' along pretty good ever since, 'cept for me, and

The Cowboy and the Lady

Here is the classic story about Frank Polk, "Reno's whittling cowboy." Frank hung out at the Round Up Bar and was a hero to the younger cowboys. This is one of the more popular stories about Frank—and it's absolutely true:

The story of Joan Kaufman Biddle Wintersteen Polk Ladd, her romancin' and two marriages with Reno's whittlin' cowboy, Frank Polk, is worth repeating here not because it's exceptional, but because it's so terribly typical of such Reno romances.

Joan is the daughter of the Kaufmans of New York and Palm Beach. Her father was one of Manhattan's most influential bankers and Joan and her family could walk up to Mrs. Vanderbilt any time, any day.

Joan had lived her life in the Ivy League set until she went west to divorce a brace of extremely social husbands. The first was George Drexel Biddle of Philadelphia and the second was Joseph M. Wintersteen.

It was on her second trip to Reno that Joan met Frank Polk, a prominent member of local cowboy

Frank Polk, "Reno's whittlin' cowboy," and Joan Kaufman Biddle Wintersteen Polk Ladd.
(Special Collections Department, University of Nevada, Reno Library)

and artistic sets. A whittlin' virtuoso, Polk bowled Reno over with his art, including a remarkably accurate and artistic whittled reproduction of a ranch complete with fences, barns, building, house, and requisite animals.

To make a long story short, Joan married the whittlin' cowboy on January 31, 1941. But the spring thaw included Joan. She divorced him on April 11, 1941.

Reno has long since given up trying to fathom the way of a cowboy with a divorcée, or vice versa. So it simply shrugged its collective shoulders when she remarried him the following day, April 12.

that's another story—one I choose to forget."

"What's your take on the horses, Jimmy?"

He smiled. "Now you're talkin'. Well, lemme see. First there's Zorro, a fine Standard Bred ropin' horse. You'll want to make him your personal mount. Then there's Alley Oop, a good lookin', but spirited, Arabian gelding. He's for your more experienced riders. He'll sometimes crow hop on a chilly morning if he can get his head down. The rest are nice and gentle dude ponies. Little Joe and Half Pint are the most popular with beginners, 'cause they are so close to the ground."

"Thanks. Those are good tips. What's with that Jersey cow out back?"

"Well, pardner, you lucked out, 'cause she's dryer than a boneyard. Gave her last milk in July. Emmy just agreed to trade her to our neighbor, Johnnie Jackson, in return for fresh dairy products. He should come get her any day now."

"You better believe I lucked out, Jimmy."

After Joan divorced her cowboy on April 11, her attorney put her on the eastbound plane for home and mother. But when Joan went to take her seat—surprise, surprise! The whittler was there!

Apparently Frank was as handy with gab as with a pocket knife and a piece of wood. For by the time the plane came down at Elko, Nevada for more fuel, Frank had persuaded his ex-wife to return to him. They were remarried in Elko.

But the second try was no more successful than the first. Joan finally divorced Frank once and for all on July 17, 1941.

At the time of the second divorce, Polk was with friends at the Round Up Bar and made a classic statement for all time regarding The Cowboy and the Lady.

His lament, in part, pointed out:

"Ladies ain't for cowboys because a good cowboy is just a glorified chump. When I get straightened out, I'm going to forget all about Eastern women.

"People seem to think cowboys marry these here Eastern women to get money out of them, but I married Joan Wintersteen because I loved her. I don't know if she ever loved me, but if she did, well, then she should have stayed put in the buggy.

"My cowboy friends in Arizona preached to me for years that the big thing was to come to Reno and marry an Eastern divorcée. But take it from me, that sermon is the nuts. A few weeks or months and then the whole thing is busted.

"But don't get me wrong. Any cowboy is just as good as any Easterner. The only thing a cowboy lacks is education. Those Eastern girls go to finishin' school and learn how to get into trouble.

"Now Western girls really know what's what. They won't marry cowboys because cowboys won't stay put in the saddle, but these Eastern girls think we're romantic. They must be loco, because there's nothing romantic about a cowboy, a jughead horse and a couple of steers.

"Like the rest of Eastern women who marry cowboys, Joan put me on a pedestal and then kicked the pedestal out from under me. Look at me—I've just landed!"

— Excerpted from the ten-part series, "Out of This World in Reno" by Inez Robb for *The American Weekly*, Chapter 8, June 25, 1944.

Then I told him about my fiasco at the Donner Trail Ranch in August. He broke up laughing, coughed a couple times, and said, "I met Fugitt once or twice so that don't surprise me none. Now I know he's a no account S.O.B.!" Then he glanced at the old-fashioned alarm clock beside his bed. "Time to eat, Bill." Slowly he pulled himself up, grunting as he leaned on his cane. After steadying himself he said, "Edie's cookin's 'bout the only good thing left for this here good-for-nothin' jockey."

Jimmy and I ate the first of many lunches to-

What is a Dude?

dude [Origin unknown] 1. A non-westerner or city-dweller who tours or stays in the west of the U.S., esp. one who spends his holidays on a ranch; a tenderfoot; Also a man who is overfastidious in dress and manner. **dude ranch**, *a ranch which provides entertainment for paying guests and tourists;* **dudess**, *a female dude.*

—OXFORD ENGLISH DICTIONARY, 1933

The terms *dude* and *dude ranch* developed a number of confusing meanings in the industry. To some people, dude implied tenderfoot or greenhorn and, while many dudes did fit the description, the word meant something much different when used by Westerners. A dude was simply someone from another area who came out West and paid for his or her food, lodging, riding, and/or guiding services.

With dude defined, one would think the meaning of the term *dude ranch* would be obvious, but not so. Some people have differentiated between *dude ranch* and *guest ranch* with the latter considered a bit more elaborate than the former. Generally *dude ranch* has been more common in the Northern Rockies and *guest ranch* in the Southwest; but both phrases are still in use throughout the Western states.

Generally, the word *ranch* has meant a place that raised a large amount of livestock. Most early dude ranches did raise cattle and/or horses, yet some of the very earliest ranches had no livestock other than the horses that the ranch workers and dudes rode. Certain characteristics developed and were considered the most important features of a dude ranch: (1) It was generally the year-round home of the owner where the visitor was considered a guest; (2) it was located in western North America, usually in the United States but occasionally in Canada; (3) it offered food, lodging, and horseback riding, most often at one price (i.e., the American Plan); (4) its location and activities were remote from crowded areas; (5) its main activities were horseback riding, fishing, hiking, hunting, sightseeing, and ranch work, although few of these activities were regimented and none mandatory; simple relaxation was always an option for the dude; (6) reservations were required, and transient trade was refused or formed little of the ranch's business; (7) atmosphere was the key ingredient; it was informal in manners and dress, people were on a first-name basis, hospitality was genuine, and guests did things together as part of a ranch family.

—Excerpted from Lawrence Borne's *Dude Ranching, A Complete History*

The preceding meanings of the words *dude ranch* and *guest ranch* are used throughout this book, along with the words *divorce ranch*, a uniquely Nevada term used by the national media during the "quickie divorce" era of the 1930s to the 1960s.

gether in the small booth between Edie's kitchen and the dining room. Jimmy was never at a loss for words. Thanks to his radio and the newspaper, he was well informed and opinionated on most any subject.

"I meant to tell you earlier, Bill, Emmy leases additional pasture land from Bill Pedroli, another neighbor. The gate to this pasture is about a mile south next to the highway. The Pedrolis are one of Franktown's earliest pioneer families and one of the nicest, too. When business slows, as it usually does in the winter, we always put some of the

What About Those Cowboy-Dude Relationships?

The Cowboy And The Lady Romances. Although it sounds like the makings of a Hollywood movie, marriages between Nevada cowboys and Eastern ladies truly happened. Inez Robb summed it up best in her colorful series in 1944 for *The American Weekly*, "Out of This World—in Reno":

RENO, Nevada. Out here in the great open spaces where men are men and the wimmen aim to keep 'em that way, the colorful story of the Cowboy and the Lady is very familiar. There are three possible endings to the inevitable romances between the lady tenderfeet and the cowhands.

No. 1 is the rare and happy ending, about 1 out of every 100.

No. 2 is the transitory marriage lasting from 24 hours to a year before the party of the first part gets fed up with the party in the Stetson hat, the tight-fittin' britches and the wingtip boots.

No. 3 results in marriage until such time as the innocent ol' Cowboy has mulcted the Lady of every penny in her possession, including the cattle or dude ranch she inevitably buys her lanky lover along the banks of the Truckee River or in the beautiful Washoe Valley.

True Tales. A cowboy by the name of Jack Watt wrangled dudes at the Tumbling DW in the early 1940s. Jack was a tall, handsome kid and a real handyman with either a horse, a guitar, or a lady dude. He went to Hollywood where he became known as Brad King, a sidekick in William Boyd's "Hopalong Cassidy" series. But before he left the Tumbling DW, he made some home recordings of his playing and singing for Dore and Emmy Wood. One of his classics—and there is little doubt that it contains more truth than poetry—follows:

I work on a dude ranch near Reno,
Givin' thrills to these divorce-seeking
    dames,
Every morning it's a splittin' headache,
Every night it's one or more flames.

One was a lady from Frisco,
One was a gal from Spo-kain,
One was the wife of a guy servin' life,
Another was a gay one from Maine.

A gay young divorcée, she won me,
Seekin' love in the West for a change,
Now I'm a gigolo in spurs
And the fault was all hers;
Gosh, I wish I was back on the range!

horses in that pasture to save on the feed bill."

As we were getting up from the table, Emmy appeared in the doorway, coffee cup and cigarette in hand. "Welcome, Bill. Glad to see you two have met. Is everything okay so far?"

"You bet. Jimmy's full of answers."

"Good. Let's get together with Allie this afternoon, say about three, in the office."

That afternoon we covered a lot of ground. It was a good meeting, and I left with a greater understanding of what it takes to run a successful dude ranch operation.

First we reviewed my primary wrangler duties. Some had been covered during my interview at the Riverside Hotel, such as taking the dudes on trail rides, horseback picnics, and pack trips. Other horse-related duties included the purchase of hay and grain, stable and fence maintenance, and the shoeing of horses.

My secondary duties were more indefinite. From time to time, when and if I wasn't occupied with my primary duties, I might be asked to take the guests on daytime sightseeing tours by auto. Or drive and accompany the guests at night to visit the local watering holes. The latter was only if Emmy and Allie were not available to do so. There were some miscellaneous duties, too, like hauling the trash every week to the Carson City dump.

"How do you share the hostessing duties?" I asked.

Allie began, "Some chores are done once a week, like going to Reno for food shopping. Others, like appearing in court as a witness, depend on whose time it is to go. We try to combine the two trips whenever possible.

"I do most of the taxiing of guests into Reno to see their lawyers, doctors, hairdressers, or to do some shopping. I also drive the guests on most of the sightseeing trips to Tahoe, Yosemite, Pyramid Lake, Virginia City, and the like.

"On week nights, I chauffeur the 'Allie Cats'—

as we call them—to town after dinner so they can gamble or drink at their favorite watering holes.

"Sunday is Edie's day off, and Emmy likes to host our Sunday night dinners out and pick the restaurant. Well, that about covers it. We're both pretty flexible, so it works out, but it can be tiring."

"That's where you come in, dear," Emmy said. "In time, we want you to assume some of these duties, especially in the evenings. But first we need to get to know you better. I'm sure you understand." That said, Emmy stood up and our little meeting was over.

I thanked them both for a very informative meeting. As I was leaving, Allie informed me I would have two riders, Helen Swanson and Elizabeth Sinclaire, for a nine a.m. trail ride the next morning. They were both novice riders.

"May I make a couple of suggestions, Bill. Give them Half Pint and Little Joe and take them up to Little Valley, just about everyone's favorite trail."

"Will do, Allie. Jimmy's already clued me in on the dude horses."

After doing a few of my primary chores around the stable, I dropped in on Jimmy. When he heard I was going up to Little Valley for my first trail ride with "green" guests, he opened a drawer in his bedside table and rustled through some papers. "Ah, here 'tis. This little 'ole booklet is crammed with Little Valley history. Emmy gave it to me and now it's yours. Allie told me you liked history.

"The trail you'll ride tomorrow is loaded with history. Most of the guests like to hear tales of our local history. Read this little book, young Bill, and you can be our next expert on Little Valley, and I ain't kiddin'."

I thanked Jimmy and gave him a pat on the shoulder. "You're a gentleman and a scholar, Mr. Murray. I'll read it tonight. You can count on that.

CHAPTER 6

The Flying M E

A bit of the Ritz dropped down in Nevada

Franktown Hotel Beginnings

The Flying M E began life about 1861 as the Franktown Hotel. George Seitz built the hotel shortly after the discovery of the silver-rich Comstock Lode on Mt. Davidson in Virginia City. The hotel was located on the southwest corner of 4th and Main Streets (formerly Union) in Franktown, just twelve miles from Virginia City as the crow flies.

Cesare and Rosie Belli were the owners when the historic hotel was sold to two Eastern ladies, Drika Noce and Mary Waterman, in 1936.[1] They made minor repairs and improvements, inside and out, and operated it as the Franktown Hotel, until Theodore and Emily Pentz Wood appeared on the scene in the late 1930s.

Tumbling DW Days

George Wood had moved to Reno to live and work, and it was his glowing picture of northern Nevada that enticed his brother and sister-in-law, Theodore and Emily, to visit him. The couple were born and bred in New York, and their plan was to stay "just a few weeks.

When Dore and Emmy first arrived in Nevada, they stayed at the Monte Cristo Ranch, owned by Ike and Bud Blundell, high on a peak overlooking Pyramid Lake. The Monte Cristo was a genuine working cattle-dude ranch catering chiefly to "six-weekers" taking advantage of Nevada's newly enacted 1931 divorce law which lowered the residency requirement to six weeks.

Like most visitors to the area, Emmy and Dore rode to Carson City in the picturesque cars of the Virginia & Truckee Railroad and were enchanted with the beauty of Washoe Valley, with its lakes to the east and the High Sierra to the west.

When the Woods first saw Franktown, there was nothing at the train stop except the old red water tower and the Franktown Hotel—a two-story structure with a bar, a dining room, and a few rooms offering Spartan accommodations and services to travelers. For many years, the Franktown Hotel had served as a station stop for the V & T Railroad. Passengers would alight, have a drink and a meal or, if they were hardy enough, spend the night. It was certainly not deluxe.

By now, Dore and Emmy knew that Nevada was the place they wanted to live. They were young and filled with energy. They had an idea and a little capital. Why not buy the hotel, remodel it,

The Franktown Hotel was built about 1861. (Nevada Historical Society)

The Franktown Hotel had a long and distinguished history. Washoe Valley historian Myra Sauer Ratay, a granddaughter of one of the early Washoe Valley pioneers about whom she writes, was born in the Valley on the Twaddle Ranch, next door to Bowers Mansion. She grew up listening to her father tell exciting stories about people and early days in Washoe Valley, and gained an intimate knowledge of the settings for the events she describes:

> The Franktown Hotel was known variously as the Seitz Hotel, Ent's, and the Franktown Hotel. In 1860, George Seitz and Frederick A. Ent had entered the mad rush to lay claim to Washoe Valley's timber preserves and had General Marlette survey out several hundred acres west of the village. Seitz and Ent (pronounced "aunt"), with Henry Arbuckle and company, bought out water rights on Franktown Creek and built a little mill on the Creek about one-half mile west of the hotel and a hundred feet above Stockham's Mill.

When the mining slump hit the Comstock in the mid-1860s, the mill was closed and Seitz moved to Pleasant Valley in the Ruby Mountains of eastern Nevada. Ent took over the hotel. He lived at the hotel and, as County Treasurer for the newly established county of Washoe, every day carried the county funds on horseback in a rig, back and forth between the county seat at Washoe City and Franktown.

A complete history of the Franktown Hotel is unattainable as accurate records go back only to 1888 when Narcesse Dufault and his wife, Philomena, homesteaded the land.

The long, narrow frame structure, more than any other in Franktown, reflected changing conditions. When times were good the hotel flourished, but in hard times it languished. In 1891 the place was sold at public auction to satisfy the debts of the Dufaults. It then went through a succession of owners including Jerry Correco (1893), Stephen Mazotti (1893), and Nelson Belli (1905).[2]

—Excerpted and condensed from Myra Sauer Ratay's *Pioneers of the Ponderosa*

and open it as a modern guest ranch?

The Woods first leased the historic hotel from Drika Noce and Mary Waterman in 1938, on a trial basis, and called it the Franktown Guest Ranch. Then they purchased the hotel on October 30, 1941, after a complete title search and survey gave them insurable title to the property.[3]

The Woods immediately set about remodeling and enlarging the hotel, according to their concept of what their Eastern friends and acquaintances would find attractive and comfortable.

Dore and Emmy Wood at work (Authors' Collection)

The old hotel was completely gutted inside. A modern kitchen was built where only a lean-to had been before; a new wing with five comfortable bedrooms was added (in addition to the four in the original building); a large master bedroom-office was created where the Woods would live and work; and quarters for the cook and maids were provided.

A five-car garage and a seven-box stall stable with tools and tack room were constructed; paddocks and pastures were fenced and painted; and a dozen good saddle horses were acquired—along with Jimmy Murray, a former jockey and veteran wrangler of the Monte Cristo Ranch, who arrived to take charge of the livestock.

The Franktown Hotel was renamed the Tumbling DW (for Dore Wood) and the dude ranch soon became known as one of the best furnished and managed in Nevada.

In 1943, the Tumbling DW received national media exposure when First Lady Eleanor Roosevelt paid a visit for some rest and relaxation. Her syndicated "My Day" columns, datelined "TUMBLING DW RANCH, Franktown, Nevada," helped put the Flying M E and the Woods on the map.

Business was good. However, Dore, being surrounded by the many temptations thrust upon a man at a divorce ranch, became enamored of a young and soon-to-be-wealthy divorcée. In 1946, Emmy and Dore got divorced. Emmy took over the ranch and continued to operate it for fifteen years, building a business that was known and talked about by society both in the United States and abroad.

Washoe Valley History Highlights

Here, in the prosperous days of the Comstock, little Franktown had grown up around a couple of mills, one for lumber and the other, using Franktown Creek for power, for grinding Comstock ore. Washoe Valley is full of history. Here's a thumbnail sketch of its nineteenth-century history by third generation Nevadan, Myra Sauer Ratay:

Washoe Valley, like her neighboring valleys—Carson, Eagle, Pleasant and Truckee—spawned booming frontier centers for the lumbering and milling businesses with their ancillary freighting industry. Washoe Valley secured a spot in history by being a vital part of the Comstock's frantic rush to gouge out of their receptacles the ores that haunted men's souls.

During the hectic decades of the silver-rush era of the 1860s and '70s Washoe Valley sprang to life, and never again was the valley to be the idyllic haunt of the wild birds, animals and the Washoe Indian....

The preferred east-west trail of early wanderers and emigrants, after winding its way westward across the arid Great Basin, followed the Carson River to the beautiful but perilous Sierra Nevada range and then struggled over one high desolate pass after another into the foothills of California.

In 1850 H. S. Beattie's log structure served as a summertime trading post for weary travelers intent on crossing the rugged mountains to jump into the California gold scramble. Here, the gold-rushers and emigrants took time out to recoup energy and supplies after the hard, slow, dusty 600 mile struggle across the desert from Salt Lake City. Here, the east-bound traveler paused before setting out across the alkali and sagebrush wastes.

Travel increased to a steady parade as tens of thousands crossed the continent to California. Some pioneers and their families, overcoming their zest for gold, built homes about Mormon Station and in the nearby valleys. So it was that the first known wayfarers into Washoe Valley probably came from the south, and halted on the ridge between Eagle and Washoe Valleys to rest and to take stock of the paradise spread out before them.

The Mormons who journeyed over the ridge between the two valleys stopped here to give their animals a breather and Orson Hyde, their leader, saw that the road was kept in good condition. He had no sooner settled in Washoe Valley in 1856 than, as Judge of the Probate Court, he authorized the construction of a direct road through the Valley to connect the two main emigrant arteries over the Sierra—one along the Carson River and the other along the Truckee.

Several seasons came and passed, then in the summer of 1859 pastoral life in Washoe Valley was brought to an end by the discovery of riches on Sun Mountain (later renamed Mt. Davidson). With a joyous cry, "Ho! Washoe!" thousands from all walks of life, of all nationalities and backgrounds, from every nook and cranny of the globe clogged the roads over the Sierra Nevada for the next three years. They swarmed to the

Washoe City, circa 1865 (Courtesy Nevada Historical Society)

eastern ridges of the mountain range between Washoe Valley and the desert.

Some of the mob spilled over into Washoe Valley to take part in the fast developing lumber, milling and hauling trades that supported the rush for gold and silver. Following the hard winter and the Indian trouble of 1860, Washoe Valley became a busy lumbering and trading area. (Several new sawmills were established to provide firewood and lumber to the new and flourishing mining district.) The mills gave work to tree fellers, choppers, loggers, edgers, sawyers, timber weavers, lumber clerks, millwrights, and laborers of all kinds.

Quartz or stamp mills—mainly Lytle, Gallagher and Co.'s and John Dall's—were built to handle ore brought from the mines for processing. The stamp mills employed engineers, amalgamators, burners, assayers, metallurgists, and laborers.

To provide for the needs of the workers there were a score of Chinese cooks, several saloon and store keepers, a couple of shoemakers, a wagon builder, carpenter, blacksmiths, stonemasons, hostlers, coopers, and farmers. Two dozen or more teamsters wove their way to and from the mining area, hauling wood or ore. From California they brought into Franktown the heavy machinery required for the industries and the food and household supplies for the several hundred souls who had come to make a living in the former Mormon hamlet.[4]

—Excerpted from Myra Sauer Ratay's
Pioneers of the Ponderosa

Emmy's favorite view of Slide Mountain (Authors' Collection)

Flying M E Days

After Dore left, Emmy added more guest rooms, a swimming pool, and changed the name to the Flying M E (for Emmy). Nevada journalist Basil Woon described the "M E" as "a bit of the Ritz dropped down in Nevada."

Located twenty-one miles south of Reno in beautiful Washoe Valley, the Flying M E enjoyed views of the majestic pine-covered Sierras to the west, and Washoe Lake and the sagebrush-covered Virginia Range to the east.

Activities and Attractions

During the day, guests had a wide choice of activities. For the horse set, there were daily trail rides to Little Valley or around Washoe Lake, some as picnics. Pack trips into the Sierras were scheduled upon request. For the less adventurous, there was swimming and sunbathing. There were sightseeing trips to Lake Tahoe, Pyramid Lake, Virginia City, and Yosemite.

A Buick station wagon and a Chrysler Town and Country convertible (both "Woody's") provided the guests with stylish, comfortable transportation into Reno or Carson City for trips to the lawyer, hairdresser, or to shop or go to church.

At night, there was bar and casino hopping, usually in Carson City. Once a week, on "cook's day off," guests dined out at one of Emmy's favorite restaurants, such as the Christmas Tree on Mount Rose Highway or the Bonanza Inn in Virginia City.

The days were more or less organized around a ranch schedule:

8:00-9:00 a.m.	Breakfast served in the dining room
10:00 a.m.	Horseback rides
1:00 p.m.	Lunch served
Afternoon	Trips to town for appointments, shopping, or sightseeing
5:30 p.m.	Cocktails
7:00 p.m.	Dinner served in the dining room

Guests were given service comparable to that in the finest hotels, but with a Western touch.

From the large picture window in the living room, with its spectacular view of Slide Mountain, guests could enjoy their cocktails while watching the horses kicking up their heels, as they playfully loped around the paddock.

Dress at the ranch was casual. Most guests enjoyed Western wear—frontier pants, Western shirts, cowboy boots and cowboy hats—all newly-acquired at Parker's in Reno. The only time most of the ladies donned a dress was to appear in court or go to dinner at one of the swankier restaurants.

Rodeos were a popular attraction. The Reno Rodeo, held every Fourth of July, was the big show. Yerington was a smaller but good rodeo. As one Eastern guest put it, "Those rodeos—to some-

V & T takes on water at Franktown (Nevada Historical Society)

one who had never been out West—were the most thrilling thing because what you didn't get at the Madison Square Garden shows was to get down in the dust and up close. In Yerington you had this sort of rickety fence, and these bulls, cows, and horses would be coming right up to your face. It was scary, but that was what was so neat. And the cowboys!"

A daily attraction was the Virginia & Truckee Railroad which stopped twice a day to take on water at the red tower. The steam engines looked exactly like the ones used in Western movies. The railroad—called "a toy built with a man-size purpose in the heydays of the Comstock Lode"— operated from Reno to Carson City and Minden up to about 1950. The high costs of upkeep had already forced the abandonment of the line from Carson City to Virginia City. To ride the train was a "must" for every visitor.

Guest Relations

The Flying M E was considered to be the most exclusive of all the dude ranches that operated in Nevada. It catered to a somewhat older and wealthier clientele. References were always required, and walk-in business was generally not accepted. Socially prominent people, largely from the East Coast and Europe, were referred by their lawyers or their friends to Emmy Wood's luxurious dude ranch "Out West."

Members of America's "first families," such as Margaret Astor and Ethel du Pont Roosevelt Jr. came for divorces. Hollywood celebrities, like Clark Gable and Ava Gardner, visited for rest and relaxation. Titled Europeans, such as the Duchess of Argyle from Scotland, came for a Western experience. The names of Flying M E guests did not make the papers, as did the names of famous and notable guests staying at other dude ranches. Emmy's guests wanted their privacy, and the press and photographers were banned from the ranch.

Emmy's reputation was extensive. She came from an upper-class background similar to that of her guests, and was the epitome of grace and manners. She was a good listener and offered hope of better things to come to her frequently depressed and distraught clientele. In spite of the business she was in, Emmy believed in the good in people.

Flying M E, looking west to the Sierras

The Flying M E from all Sides

Flying M E, looking east toward the Virginia Range
(Photos Gus Bundy, Authors' Collection)

Above, *Looking south at the poolhouse*

Left, *Looking east from the paddock*

Below, *Looking north from the pool*

(Photos Authors' Collection)

The Changing Cast of Characters

More than one person, including this writer, had urged Emmy to write her memoirs, but her response was always the same and would go something like, "Dear, I wouldn't dare. There are only so many types of guests. No matter what I would write, someone would think I was writing about them. You can be sure I would offend someone on every page. I care too much for my guests to take that chance."

Acclaimed journalist Robert Wernick first visited Reno in the 1950s and stayed at the Pyramid Lake Ranch to get a divorce. He had a special talent for analyzing and defining the distinguishing characteristics of people—in this case, his fellow divorcés staying at the ranch:

A fire is roaring in the great fireplace... Some of the inmates who have been around a few weeks are drifting in: they look tanned and relaxed, and they are wearing expensive variations on ranchhand attire....

As more and more of the guests troop in,

the cast of characters grows. It is a cast that will change continually throughout the six weeks as graduation days come and go. But though different groups will give different overall impressions—some will be more sedate, or more *sportif*, or more gossipy, or more alcoholic than others—there are certain types that will keep reappearing:

- There is the poor, shell-shocked girl, silent in her corner, ready to jump if she thinks someone is going to touch her, still quivering from the nameless enormities of her two-week marriage.
- There is, on the other hand, the boastful gold digger. "Wasn't it sweet of Stanley?" she says, stretching out her dazzling arms. "He brought me these two bracelets to choose from, and I said they were both so gorgeous I couldn't make up my mind, and he said to keep them both." Stanley is her husband, who flew out to Reno last week trying to persuade her to come back. Tomorrow her boyfriend is arriving, with gifts of his own.
- There is the bouncing, simpering little thing whose mother has come along to keep an eye

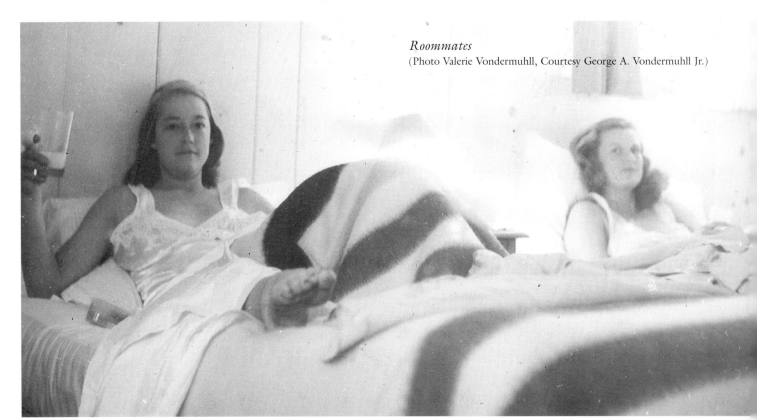

Roommates
(Photo Valerie Vondermuhll, Courtesy George A. Vondermuhll Jr.)

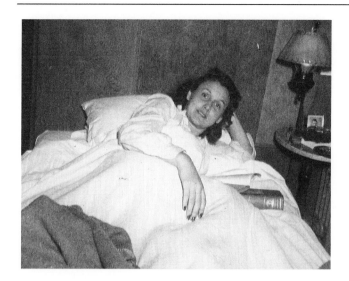

Private room
(Photo Valerie Vondermuhll, Courtesy George A. Vondermuhll Jr.)

on her. "Oh Mummy, you know what? I'd like to be a blackjack dealer, it's just fascinating."

"Nonsense, my dear," rumbles Mummy, "you know you always get into trouble when you aren't at home." And a stage whisper to the rest of the room: "It took her father and me six months to get her away from that dreadful man she married. We're not going to let it happen again."

• There is the secret drinker who lurches into the dining-room table as she is seated and knocks over a tureen of soup.

• There is the all-too-public drinker who will at unpredictable moments during the evening be amorous, or combative, or loquacious, or sodden.

• And there is the girl with hard eyes who specializes in instant analysis of her fellow-guests: "It's your inner lack of security that makes you give all that candy to your kids. You're just trying to buy their affection, that's all. It's a psycho-motor reaction."

The whole place has something of a dormitory air when after dinner the little groups form, split up, play cards, gossip. Everyone is on a first-name basis. Some of the girls are

heading for a night on the town. Others will settle for bridge or Scrabble or in a fit of loneliness will line up and practice [dancing]. Mostly they will talk—perhaps cattily about the overage girl in the undercut gown who makes violent plays for every man who crosses the threshold, perhaps concernedly about the poor girl who is being driven crazy by midnight long-distance calls from her husband. But especially they will talk about themselves, because whatever their differences in age and background, they do have one thing in common—they are all at the bad, broken end of a marriage.

It doesn't take long to pick up the common language, the patois of the divorce trade—cures and graduations, default decrees and visitation rights, *nunc pro tunc* and mental cruelty—and all the flitting problems of the American home: husbands who don't come home for dinner, conniving friends, meddlesome mothers, truant children…

Through the days that follow, an easy routine will form. There will be horseback rides in the morning. There will be tours of desert and mountain and trips into Reno to shop or see the shows or to gamble….

There are pitfalls on every side. There is, for example, the constant danger that the girls will go wild. Most people who come out here for a divorce are quiet, ordinary people who want to get it over with with a minimum of fuss. The trouble is that Nevada has a peculiar effect on ordinary people. There is the loose and lively Western atmosphere, the bars and casinos open 24 hours a day, the casual clothes and casual friendships. And it is 3,000 miles from home, no neighbors to snoop, no public opinion to fear….

The average divorcée will settle by choice or necessity for something other than primitive love in the wilderness. She will see the six weeks go by fast enough, punctuated by reproachful letters from home and by moments of self-doubt and panic. The panic grows especially on graduation day. Waiting in the cold halls of the Washoe County courthouse, all the doubts and anxieties come to a head. There is a feeling of "I can't go on. I can't go through with it. I won't be able to answer when he asks me what my name is...."

In the courtroom, though, things work out. The state of Nevada does its best to make the proceedings private and painless. The ranch's residence witness gives her testimony that she has seen the plaintiff every day for six weeks and then slips out. Alone with the judge and her lawyer, the plaintiff has nothing to do but answer a few kindly questions, and then she is free...It is quite possible that when our Sally or Betsy stands up and swears to the judge that she intends to be a permanent resident of Nevada—even with that return ticket to New York nesting in her pocketbook—she means every word of it.[5]

From my own observations as the head dude wrangler at the Flying M E, I would add a few guest types to Wernick's list:

- The wealthy and dignified matron.
- The male guest. Some made the trip to Reno because their wives weren't up to it, either emotionally or physically. Some had wives who were hospitalized or institutionalized with no hope of ever returning to normal society. Some men, being of independent means and not having to mind the business, came to Reno for a pleasant six week vacation.
- Hollywood celebrities and other well-known personalities.
- The Social Register, high society types.
- The successful career woman.

During the peak migratory divorce era, 1945-

1965, Nevada drew divorce seekers from abroad and every state in America. The six weeks' residency requirement, which became the law in 1931, was attractive to people whose home states had a one-year (New York) or even five-year (Massachusetts) requirement.

Most of the divorce seekers weren't the distraught and depressed types depicted by Hollywood. The hard part, the decision to get a divorce, had been made, and now it was a matter of filling out the six weeks with things to do.

Newspaper correspondents assigned to cover the Reno divorce scene and celebrity photographers were always on the lookout for stories about prominent, newsworthy people. Ranch owners, managers, hostesses, and wranglers all shared the responsibility of protecting the privacy of their guests, and no one was more adamant about this than Emmy Wood.

The top ranches seldom, if ever, advertised. They used their own mailing lists of former clients and could count on repeat business and referrals.

Accommodations and Rates

The ranch had accommodations for twelve-to-sixteen guests. The rates in 1948 ranged from $70 to $145 per week per person, depending on the type of room. Everything was included. Residence witness service was provided as part of the package. Extras included laundry, dry-cleaning, cigarettes, liquor, postage, and long-distance telephone calls.

Ranch Staff

Typical staff positions at a dude ranch consisted of a hostess (often the owner or manager), cook, food server, maid, and a wrangler. These positions were often supplemented by short-term help in the busy seasons, often divorcées working their way through their six weeks' residency.

The Divorce Seekers: Class of '47

The Flying M E catered to the more affluent divorce seekers. Socially prominent names like du Pont and Astor filled much of the ranch register. Eastern attorneys paved the way by arranging for a Reno lawyer and a luxurious dude ranch like the Flying M E. The Reno divorce seekers tried to forget their troubles by riding, sightseeing and gambling. Some enjoyed sunning on the pool-house deck or taking long walks on crisp autumn days; others skiied at Mount Rose. Evenings at the ranch were spent reading, playing bridge or backgammon, or simply talking—for whatever their differences in age and background, the divorce seekers had one common objective: to get "Reno-vated."

(Photos Valerie Vondermuhll, Courtesy George A. Vondermuhll Jr.)

The Divorce Seekers: Class of '47

The Divorce Seekers: Class of '47

  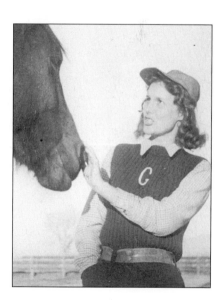

Effie Kearney, upstairs maid, with visiting cowboy friend (Photo Valerie Vondermuhll, Courtesy George A. Vondermuhll Jr.)

During my years at the Flying M E, a remarkable woman named Allie Okie was the hostess. Alys Matthiessen Okie, a well-born New Yorker, came to the ranch in late 1945 to get a divorce. The ranch was the Tumbling DW then, and it was about that time that Emmy and Dore were getting their own divorce.

The ranch was busy, so after Allie received her divorce decree she offered to stay on for "just a few weeks" to help Emmy out. The few weeks turned into four years, and Allie became a beloved and popular member of the Flying M E family.

After Allie left, the next ranch hostess was Nancy Johnson. Nancy was also a New Yorker, born in Scarsdale, and a Vassar graduate. Nancy came to the ranch to get a divorce and, just like Allie, she stayed on to help Emmy out "for just awhile." Nancy ended up marrying the neighboring rancher, Johnnie Jackson, and spent the rest of her life in the West.

Edith "Edie" Riley, the cook, baked fresh bread daily, and her recipes were known far and wide. She worked for Emmy from the Tumbling DW days of the early 1940s until the day Emmy retired in 1961. Edie developed a perfect menu of breakfasts, lunches and dinners that rotated every six weeks. At the end of each six weeks, the menu cycle would begin all over.

Edie smoked with a long cigarette holder, and the ashes would dangle precariously over the food she was preparing. This caused a lot of speculation about where the ashes fell. On "cook's day off" Edie donned a hat and headed straight for the bingo parlor. When Emmy retired, Edie retired to Reno, where she was the proud owner of an apartment house.

Lunch and dinners in the dining room were sit-down affairs, although informal dress was acceptable. Women could wear their frontier pants to dinner, and men were not required to wear jackets or ties. The meals were usually "Eastern" fare. Guests were expected to be there on time because, of course, "Cook" had to keep to her schedule.

Effie Kearney, the head maid, was a gem as she flitted about her upstairs bedroom duties. She taught each guest—most who had never done such things before—how to properly fold a blanket at the foot of the bed. She appeared wizened and old, with her wrinkles and white hair pulled tight into a topknot, yet energy and determination persisted despite her years. She was proud of her position and wore her white uniform proudly.

Other staff positions were a second housekeeper and a food server. These were usually filled by young women working their way through their six weeks' residency.

The Dude Wrangler

The top dude wranglers I came to know were personable and talented individuals who saw dude work as one type of cowboy work. Here's what Lawrence Borne, author of *Dude Ranching*, had to say on the subject:

Wranglers were actually more versatile than cowboys since they had to socialize with the guests and have a genuine liking for people. They could even be drifters in their work, just as cowboys had been, since they headed north in the summer to work on the mountain ranches and then turned to the Southwest to work where there were winter vacation sites. Knowledgeable ranch owners sought such men because they learned that the personal popularity of their wranglers was a valuable asset and sometimes the key factor in the success of a ranch.

Both dude wranglers and rodeo riders present the image of the cowboy to the American public. Rodeo cowboys travel widely, compete in violent and dangerous sports, and maintain a high degree of independence. While dude wranglers will probably not supplant these ropers and riders as the accepted successor to the "old-time cowboy," they have presented the cowboy image to tens of thousands of western visitors throughout the twentieth century. Their jobs are not as dramatic as riding a wild Brahma bull for eight seconds, but then, seldom were the cowboy's daily activities either. Dude wrangling is not a pathway to riches or fame, but neither was riding fence or trailing Longhorns.

Regardless of whatever image or mythical qualities easterners expected of wranglers, the dude rancher was faced with the reality of hiring men to handle horses and riders.[6]

Wranglers at Washoe County's top four guest ranches in the late '40s and early '50s were all cow-

The Flying M E Dude Ponies

*Bill McGee
and Zorro*
(Authors' Collection)

Bucky and her colt, Smoky (Photo Valerie Vondermuhll, Courtesy George A. Vondermuhll Jr.)

boys long before they became dude wranglers. Dude wranglers still had to know horses, since horses and everything connected with them were the key to dude ranching. A good wrangler would add to his cowboy skills by acquiring knowledge of the local history and the environment, so that he could answer questions of every conceivable sort and thus develop a working knowledge of history, plant life, animals, geology, wildlife management, and forest conservation.

Such a variety of duties did not appeal to many former wranglers, however. One old-timer summed up his feelings in this *Wrangler's Lament*:

> I'm a tough, hard-boiled old cowhand
> with a weatherbeaten hide,
>   But herdin' cows is nuthin' to teachin'
> dudes to ride.
>   I can stand their hi-toned langwidge an'
> their hifalutin' foods,
>   But you can bet your bottom dollar I'm
> fed up wranglin' dudes![7]

Jimmy Murray was a jockey on the county fair circuit before becoming a wrangler. He was working at the Monte Cristo Ranch in the 1930s when he met Emmy and Dore. They talked him into moving over to their Tumbling DW as their first wrangler. About 1945, Jimmy had a stroke and was never able to work again. Now he was old and craggy, with a full head of salt and pepper hair, and always needed a shave. But he still had a great sense of humor. The stroke left him paralyzed on one side but, with the help of his cane and a gimpy walk, he could make it from his room by the stables to the ranch house for his meals. Jimmy had a son living in Half Moon Bay, California, but Emmy insisted on providing for Jimmy's retirement on the ranch "for as long as he lives." That was Emmy.

There were other wranglers before and after my time at the ranch. "Maverick," Bill La Duke, and Glenn Llewellyn are three that come to mind. Duties and responsibilities varied from ranch to ranch. At the Flying M E, my primary duties consisted of all outdoor activities like taking the dudes on trail rides, horseback picnics and pack trips.

Secondary duties were much more indefinite. From time to time, when and if I wasn't otherwise occupied with my primary duties, I would be asked to take guests on daytime sightseeing tours by auto, or escort them at night to the local casinos and watering holes.

Riding was important to Emmy, and she expected me to promote it. "The guests need an incentive to get up and get going," she would say.

Dude horses are an important part of the dude ranch business, and good horses are the mainstay of the ranch. Dude horses have to be gentle-broken and reliable. All kinds of people ride them, and most of them are strange, either to horses in general or to western horses in particular. So the dude wrangler has to pick his stock carefully. Nothing is left to chance. One mistake can cost the ranch a lot of business. The horses must be plumb gentle and not too big or far off the ground, as it is easier for an inexperienced rider to mount and dismount from a low pony than a big horse.

To put together a string of gentle, well-broken dude horses which any kind of rider can handle is no easy matter. A lot of stock has to be looked over and carefully chosen before the string is right.

That wraps up the history of the Flying M E, from its origins as the Franktown Hotel in 1861, through its days as the Tumbling DW from 1941-1946, to my days at the legendary ranch from 1947-1950. In the following chapters, I'll recount many of my favorite memories of the changing cast of unforgettable characters I came to know during my time at the ranch.

CHAPTER 7

Eleanor Roosevelt Vacations at the Tumbling DW

Dateline: Franktown, Nevada

In July 1943, the early part of World War II, First Lady Eleanor Roosevelt was traveling the country to bolster America's morale. On her way to Seattle by way of Reno and San Francisco, she stopped at the Tumbling DW for some rest and relaxation and to visit her friend, Mrs. Gertrude Wenzel Pratt of New York, who was staying at the ranch for a divorce.

The First Lady had been writing a daily syndicated newspaper column, "My Day," since 1936, and it was carried by more than 140 newspapers across the country. During her stay at the ranch, the columns were datelined "Tumbling DW Ranch" and "Franktown, Nevada." Overnight both the ranch and its owners were thrust into the national and international spotlight, and the luxury dude ranch "out West" and Emmy and Dore Wood were now famous.

It was generally the policy of the Reno press to not print stories about well-known personalities staying at the dude ranches. After all, these people had chosen a dude ranch for its privacy. However, a visit by a First Lady was an exception and Mrs. Roosevelt graciously agreed to be interviewed by an excited Reno press corps. The *Nevada State Journal* carried the interview on July 9, 1943:

"Mrs. Roosevelt Keeps Busy During Her Stay at Ranch"

by Leola McDonald

Mrs. Roosevelt arrived Wednesday evening by plane and showing no signs of fatigue got up early yesterday and took a walk around the neighborhood, stopping to chat for about fifteen minutes at the William Pedroli ranch.... For her early morning hike, Mrs. Roosevelt was dressed in a short blue skirt, topped with a coral colored blouse, walking shoes and cotton stockings. Her hair was held back with a woven band of blue and white. Following her hike, she went back to the ranch and sat on the porch, busily writing her column "My Day" until Reno newspapermen arrived at ten thirty.

We were all ushered into the living room by Dore Wood, owner of the ranch. Mrs. Roosevelt came in. She had changed from hiking clothes and was now dressed in a very plain white tennis dress, made with detachable skirt and blouse in conventional shirtmaker style with open neck and short sleeves. She wore white cotton ribbed stockings and white buck low-heeled shoes, which looked decidedly comfortable, as they showed evidence of much wear. Her smiling face was completely devoid of any makeup and her nails were minus polish.

When Mrs. Roosevelt sat down on the window bench before a large window overlooking Mt. Rose and Slide Mountain, we all sat and waited for each other to start the interview.

Outside several cowboys were putting their horses through a few stunts and a woman guest at the ranch in cowboy attire walked through the room.

For a whole hour and one-half, most graciously, she talked on a variety of subjects —the President's health, her visit

Mrs. Roosevelt on the porch of the Tumbling DW talking with the press. (Courtesy *Nevada State Journal*)

with Madame Chiang-Kai-shek, her children.... Just like any other mother, she seemed worried when she said they had had no word from Franklin, Jr. (somewhere in the Atlantic) in over eight weeks.

The interview was ended not by Mrs. Roosevelt, who seemed to be enjoying her talk, but by a couple of reporters, who had been nervously taking cigarettes out of their pockets and then putting them back, not knowing just what the smoking etiquette was in the presence of the First Lady. She very graciously posed for pictures with Mr. Wood and his horse. Another snap was taken of Mrs. Roosevelt and one of the reporters, who was still trying to run down the rumor that [her daughter] Anna Roosevelt Dahl Boettiger was someplace in this community for a divorce. As we left we saw her chatting and laughing with some of the residents at

the dude ranch. I hope she wasn't laughing at us and I know she wasn't. She is too gracious and kindly for that.

While here she will have a visit with her daughter's friend, Mrs. Robert Zeimer Hawkins, the former Katherine Mackay.

On July 11, 1943, columnist Gladys Rowley reported on the early morning walk taken by the First Lady and Mrs. Pratt:

It was 7:45 a.m. Glancing through the kitchen window above the sink where she was washing breakfast dishes, Mrs. William Pedroli saw America's First Lady entering her gate.

Unable to believe her eyes, she then heard a knock at the door and a voice asking, "Can you spare a moment?" Whereupon one very surprised housewife—deep in the dishpan—found herself face to face with Eleanor Roosevelt.

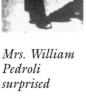

"But no matter how awed you might feel at the prospect of talking with the wife of the President," said Mrs. Pedroli, "you get over it right away in her presence. Mrs. Roosevelt is just as natural and as easy to talk to as you and I. Instead of being awed, you find you're being yourself, just as she is being herself."

Mrs. William Pedroli surprised

We asked Mrs. Pedroli what it was like to have the First Lady drop in for an early morning call. Mrs. Pedroli told us that Mrs. Pratt, who had previously stopped to chat during walks, had introduced her to Mrs. Roosevelt and they spent 15 or 20 minutes "wandering around the yard while Mrs. Roosevelt asked about the number of cows, the milk supply, and expressed amazement at the amount of water we have here."…

"But we want to hear more about how it feels to have Mrs. Roosevelt drop in on you," one of the reporters persisted.

"Well, it certainly makes you realize you're living in a democracy when you can have a breakfast-time visit from America's First Lady" was the answer.

Admitting that she herself is a Republican, Mrs. Pedroli said she had nonetheless admired the democratic Mrs. Roosevelt.[1]

"My Day"

First Lady Eleanor Roosevelt touched millions of Americans with her syndicated daily newspaper column titled simply "My Day." Written in an open, friendly manner, as if writing to a friend, the daily diary allowed the First Lady to describe White House life and her varied activities and to comment on events that would affect America. She wrote about children, married life, and what women could and should do. She often mentioned famous people, but she also had a keen sense of the average American. She drew readers close by being candid about her own life. She often included anecdotes and discussed books and plays.

During her vacation days at the Tumbling DW, Mrs. Roosevelt wrote about the local scenery and people. *Nevada State Journal*, July 15, 1943:

FRANKTOWN, Nevada—Some days ago as the newspapers have recorded, I came to spend a few days in this beautiful valley. I have a room that looks across a little lake to the mountains. There are farms around us settled long ago by some hardy pioneers. Gurgling streams run down even now from the mountains. Wild flowers bloom in the meadows, the pine trees and the cottonwoods give you shade.

I have walked in the early mornings with the sun coming up, and again in the evening under the moon and watched the stars come out, and renewed my understanding of our pioneers who gave us this vast land of ours. They had no fear of new adventure, there was no pattern to follow in their lives, they accepted men as they proved themselves in the daily business of meeting emergencies.

Have we lost this spirit, do we fear to face the fact that we have new frontiers to conquer? I was sick at heart when I came here, over race riots which put us on a par with Nazism which we fight, and make one tremble for what human beings may do when they no longer think but let themselves be dominated by their worst emotions.…

Saw Stewart School. We visited an Indian school near here yesterday. It was a great satisfaction to see the nice dormitories, simple living rooms and workshops. The girls—who learn to garden, care for the chickens and cows and horses—who live in the little two-room practice cottage and care for the baby—will take much back to their reservation to raise the standard of living.…

On the Comstock. We passed through extraordinary and ghostly Virginia City. What fortunes were made and lost there! There are still the remains of houses which give an inkling of the money spent. All materials came from far away and the difficulties of transportation must be hard for us even to imagine. The old opera house still stands with the list of famous people who appeared on its stage. Jenny Lind and the great Patti were among the number.

One of the things which warms one in this part of the country is the friendliness of the people. If your cattle get out, help is there as soon as your neighbors know you need it. I doubt if they have more time than the rest of us, but they are not afraid to be kind.[2]

—E. R.

In another column she commented wistfully on leisure time:

Someday I am going to live a life of leisure, but so far I never find that I do half the things I want to do in a day. I am here in the country and I have to acknowledge that if someone were to ask me what I was doing, I should have to say, practically nothing!...Of course, 1 have not mentioned that we swim and lie in the sun every day and that we do take a little exercise and see something of our neighbors, either on foot or on a bicycle. But I always wonder where the time goes and why it is so late at night when I finally go to bed![3]

When "My Day" first ran in 1936, the First Lady was not to write about politics. But the character of her column changed slowly. The simple, recorded daily diary gave way to strong opinions on a great variety of controversial subjects. By 1939, hardly a subject undergoing national attention failed to find its way into her column.

President Roosevelt had tried to discourage Eleanor from undertaking this project. Writing a five-hundred word column six days a week would be considered a full-time job for even the most experienced journalist. With a relentless deadline to meet, the column had to be written under many strange circumstances. The First Lady, with her typical energy and efficiency, managed to complete "My Day"—sometimes during meals; sometimes with a grandchild on her lap; sometimes in a speeding limousine, on a wartime destroyer, or in bed at the end of a packed sixteen-hour day. Often the problem arose of locating a telegraph office or phone to transmit the column to the UFS in New York by deadline time. But the column had to be delivered in rain, wind or sleet.

Mrs. Roosevelt produced five hundred words per column and often more, six days per week, with virtually no interruptions for nearly twenty-six years (1936-1962). Her one hiatus was a four-day break after President Roosevelt died on April 12, 1945.[4]

CHAPTER 8

Little Valley Trail Ride

Saddling Up

My first working day on the job, I broke open a bale of hay early in the morning, and watched as the horses scrambled for the best feeding positions. It was soon obvious that Little Joe, a buckskin mustang with a black mane and tail, was boss of the herd. Half Pint, a sorrel mustang with a light red mane and tail, was more passive yet refused to be pushed around. Mustangs were tough little horses.

Then it was breakfast time. I thoroughly enjoyed Edie's hearty and delicious meal of bacon, eggs and hash browns. Now I was ready to catch up Little Joe and Half Pint for the morning ride. I hitched them to the paddock fence, curried and saddled them. Based on Jimmy Murray's recommendation, I decided to claim Zorro, the handsome bay, trained as a roping horse, for my personal mount.

The two guest riders, all decked out in Western wear, appeared right on time. As they walked across the gravel driveway toward the stable, I greeted them.

"Good mornin', ladies. I'm Bill McGee, your new wrangler."

Zorro (Authors' Collection)

"Good morning, Bill. I'm Helen Swanson and it's nice to meet you."

"And I'm Elizabeth Sinclaire, still learning to ride."

Helen was a very attractive brunette and looked to be thirty-something. She cut a smart figure in her tan frontier pants and black Western shirt, all no doubt newly-purchased at Parker's in Reno for her six weeks' "costume."

It wasn't long before I observed a pattern with the guests. One of their first stops was at Parker's at 200 N. Center Street in Reno to get outfitted in Western wear. I knew the Parker brothers, Harry and Mush, since I shopped there myself. The next stop on the ritual tour was at Hoot Newman's

Parker's, 200 N. Center Street, Reno (Courtesy Harry Parker)

"Allie told us you're new here, from Montana," Mrs. Sinclaire said, breaking into my private thoughts. "Please take it easy on us today," she said smiling. Elizabeth Sinclaire looked to be about fifty, give or take a few years, and carried a little extra weight. She seemed less enthused about the ride than her friend; however, she was dressed for it and looked pretty sharp, too.

"Now don't be afraid, ladies. You can be assured you'll be riding the two most gentle horses on the ranch. Mrs. Sinclaire, you'll ride Half Pint, and Mrs. Swanson, you'll be on Little Joe," I said pointing to their horses. "First, let's get you aboard so I can adjust your stirrup length for the most comfortable ride."

The two small mustangs made it easy for the ladies to mount without my assistance. After adjusting their stirrups, checking the cinches, and handing them their reins, I swung aboard Zorro and we were off. I knew then that the only variations in this routine from this day forward would be the number of riders, their level of experience, and the horses assigned to them.

As we rode past the ranch house, Allie called out, "Have a great ride, ladies, and take care of Bill. Remember, it's his first day on the job!"

It was a perfect day for a ride. About sixty

Silver Shop at 120 W. Second Street to purchase a sterling silver concha belt. Newman's was next door to the Round Up Bar, so I was familiar with the fine silver bracelets, earrings, buckles, spurs and bits, and cigarette boxes displayed in the shop window. Hoot also made beautiful hand tooled leather belts and purses, all of it out of this cowboy's price range. Hoot's father showed his sense of humor when he named Hoot's brothers Holler and Yell.

Allie Okie bids riders goodbye
(Photo Valerie Vondermuhll,
Courtesy George A. Vondermuhll Jr.)

Those frontier pants really suit Helen, I thought, and wondered if she knew how good she looked in them. I also noticed she was wearing English riding boots. Maybe she had to get this first ride behind her before buying cowboy boots. Anyway, her boots would be okay for the gentle ride I was taking her on.

Looking east, Washoe Valley as seen from the Little Valley trail above Franktown Road. Johnnie Jackson's ranch is to the left of the Flying M E ranch. Washoe Lake and the Virginia Range can be seen in the distance, circa 1948.
(Photo Valerie Vondermuhll, Courtesy George A. Vondermuhll Jr.)

degrees with a light breeze and only a few cumulus clouds overhead. I pulled up Zorro as we approached the ranch exit to Highway 395, the north-south highway between Reno and Carson City, to offer a brief word of caution.

"We're going to turn right and go north along this side of the highway for about a hundred yards, then we'll cross over to Franktown Road when the coast is clear. Stay behind me and cross when I do. The horses are used to this so there's no reason to worry." Elizabeth looked a little worried but shook her head in agreement anyway.

Automobile traffic was very light so the crossing was without incident. We rode down Franktown Road for a short distance to the Little Valley trailhead.

"Hold up here for a minute, ladies, while I brief you on the trail ahead. But first take a look at one of the better views of the ranch down below. That's Johnnie Jackson's place to the left. According to my reading last night, our Little Valley destination is just two miles up the trail, but we'll be gaining about 1,500 feet in elevation, so we should take it easy on the horses."

"Oh, no," Elizabeth exclaimed, "I'm still trying to adjust to 5,000 feet."

"You'll be just fine," I assured her, "if we take it easy. But first, has anyone briefed you on the rich history of today's route?"

"No, Bill," Helen replied, "We're both interested."

"Great, that makes three of us. Well, let's see. The first thing I learned from my read last night was that this trail was once part of an early 1860s immigrant route that followed the creek up the canyon ahead through Little Valley, then crossed the summit at about 8,000 feet and zig-zagged down the western slope to Lake Tahoe."

"Very interesting," Helen said, "and to think that was less than a hundred years ago."

"I'm afraid I wouldn't have made a very good pioneer," Elizabeth volunteered. "I need my hot bath and a soft bed every night."

"Oh, come on, Elizabeth," Helen smiled. "You're far tougher than you think."

"Let's move on now. I'll share more history with you on our next stop," I said.

We wound our way up an easy foothill grade dotted with scrub pine for about a half-mile until we arrived alongside Franktown Creek at the mouth of the canyon.

"What kind of trees are these, Bill?" Elizabeth asked.

"I'm no expert on trees in this neck of the woods yet, Mrs. Sinclaire. Most of them are probably Ponderosa pines and firs. I've also seen some Jeffrey pines. It's hard to believe now, but according to what I read last night, every tree on this side of the valley an inch thick or more was downed by the logging industry just seventy-five years ago. More about that later."

A short time later we had to ford the creek, a small spring-fed stream this time of year, as the trail continued on the other side.

"Bill, we aren't going into the water, are we?" Elizabeth asked with a little terror in her voice.

"It's very shallow, Mrs. Sinclaire. These horses are used to it. Just follow me, and Mrs. Swanson will be right behind you."

I turned in my saddle to watch Half Pint with Elizabeth aboard wade through about six inches of crystal clear water. As he clamored up the bank on the other side, Elizabeth heaved a huge sign of relief, then broke into a big smile for the first time on the ride. "I did it!"

Helen showed none of the same fear as Little Joe crossed the creek.

At about the halfway point, the trail crossed a small clearing. "Looks like a good spot to give the horses a breather," I announced.

We dismounted and lit up cigarettes. Then Helen asked, "Bill, where in Montana do you come from?"

"Well, it's a bit complicated. I was born in southern Montana about forty miles north of Yellowstone Park and later on we moved to the northern part of the state near the Canadian border. If you don't mind my asking, where are you ladies from?"

"Pound Ridge, New York, but I've been living in New York City ever since I got married. And please, call me Helen."

"I'm originally from New Canaan, Connecticut, but now I live in Boston. Please call me Elizabeth."

"Sure, if you like, but my mother taught me to always address a lady with respect, and it is my first day here. Are you feeling the increased altitude? We've probably gained a thousand feet so far."

"I know I am," said Elizabeth.

"Me, too," Helen added, "but I'm sure we'll live."

"Okay, let's mount up and see if we can find Little Valley. It can't be more than a half mile up the trail."

A short time later, the trail branched off from Franktown Creek in a northwesterly direction. After a fairly steep climb, we reached the ridge overlooking Little Valley.

"What a beautiful sight!" Helen exclaimed.

"Isn't it, though," Elizabeth added.

"It's bigger than I expected. Looks like it's at least a mile long and more than a half-mile wide," I guessed. "And it's a high valley. A good 1,500 feet above Washoe Valley. Little Valley's floor is only two-to-three hundred feet below this ridge. Let's go get a closer look."

We followed the trail down to the floor of the valley and out to a large meadow.

"Would you like to lope your horses for a little ways?" I asked.

"Not today, please!" Elizabeth cried.

"I can wait, too," Helen said. I sensed she might have liked to but didn't want to make her friend feel uncomfortable. Maybe Helen and I would go on a ride together before her six weeks were up.

"That's okay, there'll be another day. Let's hitch our horses to those trees over there for a little break, then we'll circle the valley before heading home. Are you ready for another history lesson? Allie might give a quiz at dinner tonight.

"During the Comstock boom years of the 1860s and 1870s, several logging companies operated sawmills up here in Little Valley until they'd cut down every tree in the surrounding forest. One of them built a two-and-a-half mile V-flume slide to carry the lumber and cordwood down the canyon to Franktown. Then it was loaded on freight wagons or V & T railroad flat cars for the trip to Virginia City.

"Not long afterwards, this little valley was under fifteen to twenty feet of water as part of the struggle to supply water to Virginia City where water was almost as precious as gold. Several companies were concocting plans to supply this scarce natural resource to the mining industry, resulting in water fights in and out of court for years.

"Washoe Lake, the nearest body of water, was an obvious source of supply. One company, I believe it was the Virginia City and Gold Hill Water Company, acquired all of the water rights to Franktown Creek, including its headwaters, in a highly questionable legal transaction.

"The ranchers in Washoe Valley rose up in anger when they heard what had happened and filed suit to regain their water rights. But by this time, the water company's amazing engineering system was carrying water from upper Franktown Creek to Virginia City.

"To appease the ranchers, the water company gave them land for a dam over there," I said pointing to the head of Franktown Creek Canyon.

"But here's the kicker. In early 1881, heavy rains dumped a huge amount of water on the mountains surrounding Little Valley, filling the reservoir to a depth of forty feet—more than anyone had ever thought possible. Workmen tried to release the surplus water, but the floodgate refused to budge. The dam gave way without warning and water burst through and surged through the narrow gorge of the canyon as it roared down into Washoe Valley.

"A huge, twenty-foot wall of water, once free from the confining walls of the canyon we rode up this morning, raced toward Franktown two-and-a-half miles below the site of the dam. It knocked Washoe Valley houses and barns off their foundations, snapped the steel rails of the V & T tracks like kindling, and flooded Franktown as it rushed toward Washoe Lake."

"My goodness. Were there many casualties?" asked Helen.

"Fortunately no lives were lost because the collapse of the dam had been expected due to the heavy rains and a floodgate problem. Residents of the valley were warned to evacuate. The dam was never rebuilt and Franktown, thanks largely to the declining Comstock bonanza, reverted to its earlier pastoral existence.

"Okay, ladies, that's enough history for today. Let's mount up and give Little Valley the once over, then we'll head back down the canyon. We'll explore it more thoroughly on our next visit."

As we circled Little Valley, we could still see some high water marks on the rock outcroppings

Little Valley boulders (Photo Gus Bundy, Bundy Collection, Courtesy of Special Collections Department, University of Nevada, Reno Library)

and giant boulders. The return trip down the canyon was uneventful and we were back at the ranch in plenty of time for lunch.

As we dismounted, Elizabeth, much to my surprise, expressed her gratitude for "a most enjoyable and informative ride." Helen jumped in with, "I agree, Bill. Let's do it again and soon."

My first day on the job and, if all the guests were as nice as these ladies, this is my kind of work, at least for now, I thought.

A Soft Knock at the Bunkhouse Door

Later that night, I was in bed reading when I heard a soft knock at the bunkhouse door. I figured there must be an emergency of some kind so I quickly pulled on my Levis and opened the door. Much to my surprise it was Helen Swanson (not her real name) lighting up the night with her beautiful smile.

"Helen, what a nice surprise! Is something wrong?"

"Nothing we can't fix, cowboy."

I sensed what she wanted and took her in my arms. She pressed up to me, and I kissed her pretty lips and felt her fantastic body pressing against mine.

Emmy's rules about "non-fraternization" with the guests flashed before me briefly as they flew out the window. Whatever was going to happen was already happening.

Helen's smoldering sensuality had become a fierce flame, and soon we moved over to my bed. This young dude wrangler, only one day on the job, was learning that it was the quiet fillies who were full of surprises!

Cowboy Chic

In 1935, Harper's Bazaar advised stylish ladies on their "...uniform for a dude ranch or a ranch near Reno..." This included Levis worn low on the hips, a studded leather belt, high-heeled Western boots and a Stetson hat—all worn with "a great free air of bravado."

The Western costume described above was more becoming to some dudes than to others. There were the Levis and the dressier frontier pants frequently a size too small for the derrieres they graced. There were the heads under Stetsons which would be more at home in a chapeau or a Homburg, and there were the feet gingerly treading the sidewalk in high heeled cowboy boots which ached for Oxfords.

Western wear had a purpose: the hats, boots and pants were for working people who lived and worked on the range, whose clothes were adapted to riding long trails, roping mean steers and enduring blistering summer heat and the coldest of winters.

Hat styles were usually a reflection of the weather and working conditions in different parts of the country, and at one time told people what part of the country its owner was from. For example, cowboys in the northern plains and Rocky Mountain states were partial to the high crowned, wide brimmed, "ten gallon" hat. The extra high crown served as an extra insulating factor (dead air space on the man's head) in the severe cold of that region. The wide brim with a slight roll to it not only provided protection from sun and wind, but also prevented the heavy rain and snow from exerting their full impact on the cowboy's upper body. The slight roll to the brim enabled the wearer to "funnel" water from his hat brim away from his clothes by tilting his hat or his head.

The Nevada cowboy found a low, telescoped crown sufficient protection from the cold and a medium wide flat brim adequate protection from the sun. The cowboy from the southwest usually wore the low telescope crown with hat brim rolled up on both sides so he wasn't so likely to get it knocked off while chasing wild cows through the mesquite.

The cowboy boot, too, was designed with the needs of the cowboy in mind. The toe was pointed to allow easy entrance into the stirrups on a saddle. The sole was leather because leather tends to "slicken up" when most of the walking is on dirt or grass and a slick sole is not likely to hang up in a stirrup. The high heel is to keep the foot from slipping through the stirrup. The reason for the taper and small heel cap was to give "breaking power" on the ground.

To quote the famous cowboy artist and author, Will James, "Some people wonder at the clothes and riggin's of the cowboy, why the silver on spurs and bit, or anything a little fancy. It seems to them that some things are useless and only for show. But the range riding cowboy has nobody around him to show off to and everything he wears is altogether for use....There's nothing the cowboy wears that could be near as useless as an imported necktie or a stiff collar."

—S. V. M.

—Excerpted from: Hage, "History of Hats and Boots" from "Cowboy Chic," *Nevada Magazine*, July/August 1979; Reynolds and Rand, *The Cowboy Hat Book*; James, *Lone Cowboy: My Life Story*

Illustration from *Harper's Bazaar, 1935*, Courtesy Levi Strauss Co.

Rita Hayworth in Nevada to divorce Prince Aly Khan, circa early 1950s.
(AP Wirephoto, courtesy Special Collections Department, University of Nevada, Reno Library*)*

CHAPTER 9

Branding Chores

Some Chores Are More Fun Than Others

Johnnie and June Jackson were living on the old Dick Sides place when I joined the Flying M E in 1947. It was a small farm just east of the V & T tracks and north of the Pedroli farm.

One brisk November day, several neighboring cowhands got together to help Johnnie put his "J up J down quarter-circle" brand on some newly-acquired dairy cattle. Johnnie really wanted to be a cattle rancher, not a dairy farmer, so from day one their place was the "Jackson Ranch," not farm. As Johnnie once said, "Fate dealt me a different hand—at least for the time being."

Branding a full grown cow or steer is quite different from branding a calf. Catching a calf is done with one good ropin' horse and one cowboy who catches the calf and dismounts, then ties the calf's feet for branding.

Catching a full grown animal requires the talents of two mounted cowboys. One catches the head, the other lassoes the heels (hind legs), then they stretch the cow or steer out on the ground between them while someone else does the branding.

We branded around sixty head that day with ample supervision, I might add, from both neighboring ranchers and Flying M E guests.

• • •

Later that night, Helen Swanson knocked at my bunkhouse door again. I was half-expecting her this time.

"Helen, I was hoping you'd come tonight. Our smoke signals must be cooking."

"I couldn't wait to see you, cowboy."

I took her into my arms and she pushed me back on the bed. "Bill, we're being illegal! We're fraternizing!"

I quickly dropped my Levis and slid my illegal cock inside her. While happy to oblige, I was a little surprised and embarrassed by Helen's earthy language.

After our lovemaking, she kissed me and said gently, "Bill, my love, what's happened between us has been magical. It's something I never expected. Would you like me to stay after my divorce is final?"

"Sweetheart, you're a beautiful woman. You come from a different world. You wouldn't be happy staying with me and my plans for ranching. Things will look different when you return East. I'm sure you'll meet the right man in New York."

Later, when Helen slipped out into the night and walked back to the ranch house, I looked out, and a full moon was lighting her way.

Branding at Johnnie Jackson's ranch, circa 1948.
Bill McGee in black shirt. (Authors' Collection)

CHAPTER 10

Valerie Vondermuhll, Letters Home

Valerie Vondermuhll arrived at the Flying M E for a divorce on November 4, 1947, just three days after I started working at the ranch. Valerie hailed from a socially prominent Eastern family whose roots went back to Colonial times and whose names appeared with regularity in the Social Register.

In time I would recognize that Valerie was not typical of most of the upper-class guests at the ranch for, as young as she was, she was already a highly successful career woman, an editor for *Life* magazine, and a talented photographer.

In researching for this chapter, the authors sought out Charles Champlin, the retired arts editor and Critic-at-Large columnist of the *Los Angeles Times* for twenty-six years. Champlin was a young trainee news writer at *Life* magazine in 1948 when he first met Valerie. Champlin recalls: "Valerie ran foreign news editor Gene Farmer's staff of five or six researchers. She gave them their assignments and checked their work. She was a delightful gal to have around and really cheerful. Always on the move, always had a good word, and smart as hell."

Champlin also recalled Helen Deuell, another *Life* magazine staffer and Valerie's traveling companion in 1948, when the ladies spent a vacation week at the Flying M E: "Helen was head of the copy desk at *Life*. All copy at *Life* magazine funneled through her office. Valerie and Helen were both alike in that they were damn good administrators and extremely hardworking."

In later years, Valerie would handle syndication and reprint rights for all Time-Life magazines.

Letters Home

Valerie shared her impressions of Reno and dude ranch life with her parents, whom she affectionately addressed as "Pama," in a series of letters home:

> November 5, 1947
>
> Dear Pama,
>
> The train got me here at lunchtime yesterday...you will probably be relieved to know that the office caught up with me...only to discover that actually I couldn't help them very much.
>
> The ranch is set down in the valley about 5 miles north of Carson City...nothing very big or fancy but attractive and comfortable and apparently pleasant people. About 10 here

Valerie Vondermuhll on horseback.
(Courtesy George A. Vondermuhll Jr.)

at present…they come and go. So far I barely know one from the other…but have just sat around with my feet up…that was the only drawback to my train trip…sitting up for two nights and a day my feet got puffy…not uncomfortably so, but just rather unsightly.

We had quite a snowfall here yesterday, and they say that it has been snowing steadily up in the mountains…so as soon as I buy a pair of ski pants I will go up and try my luck. A couple of days should take care of the altitude acclimation…I haven't noticed it, but everyone says I would be silly to rush out and exercise violently right away…Riding I will do, too, but with less enthusiasm…just to shake the fat off. The senior member of our little group (about 40) is going in for steam baths. I'd rather do the work myself!

My room is a bit longer and wider than a hall bedroom…dresser, desk, bed, comfortable chair, bookcase. The bath is right across the hall…closet space ample. The book supply is fantastic…they must have a lot of people who do nothing but read. A pretty good selection, too, with a minimum of the trash novel and detective story. No magazines…which I consider a very good sign.

I seem to have figured right on my clothes…at least I don't need anything dressier than I have and will probably end up buying a couple of "western" shirts. The one I bought in Wyoming in '37 is still going strong, so I figure they'll be a good investment.

—Love, Val

• • •

November 12

Dear Pama,

I haven't been riding yet, sheer inertia… but went for a day to Virginia City with a local photographer and had a fine time taking pictures and chatting with various people. I have also been to Tahoe and Pyramid Lake…these little side trips are included in the tariff and apparently Mrs. Wood is sufficiently interested in the country so that she doesn't mind taking a carload here and there whenever the weather is just right….

This country is really wonderful and if you can get used to seeing roulette wheels and slot machines all over the place, it is really rather appealing country. The bar replaces the hot-dog stand and drug store, and if you go into any bar or store of almost any kind it is almost automatic to put 5, 10, 25 or 50 cents or a silver dollar into one of these machines. Of course, my luck is always lousy, but one of the gals here got $9 one time and two hours later $18 out of one of the machines. And we were told a story yesterday of some woman in town who went into a joint with $9 and had $1500 when she woke up the next morning. In another place, 75 jackpots of $150 each were paid out in the space of 2 hours! So you can see the temptations are tremendous.

We all sit around in slacks and jeans…in fact you can tell who is going to see the lawyer by the sudden appearance of a dress. From observation I would say that the longer you are here the more times you appear in a dress, or at least a skirt…Sort of retraining for Eastern civilization.

Your report about W. was the first we had heard about it, so created quite a bit of excitement. No one bothers to read the papers very much, and though we do listen to radio news broadcasts, often you can miss the interesting thing by just not being tuned in at the right time.

The afternoon errand-running is just being arranged, so I must go to see if my commissions are the kind that I can palm off on someone else.   —Love, Val

• • •

Dec 5

Dear Ma,

Heavens, thank goodness, you didn't send any food or "sweets" out here. Not only do we eat very well, but the between times stuff is just what I have been doing my best to avoid. The thought is appreciated however….

It has been snowing hard the last few days, so that the prospects of skiing are very good. Up 'til now it has been very scanty… they'd ski on it in the East, but the terrain is more rugged here so you really need more snow before it is safe. Dinner calls.—Love, Val

I finally got Valerie up on a horse near the end of her second week at the ranch. She joined Helen Swanson and Elizabeth Sinclaire for a ride to Little

Valerie Vondermuhll at Mount Rose Ski Bowl, 1947
(Courtesy George A. Vondermuhll Jr.)

Valley. Valerie was a good rider but seemed more interested in skiing Mount Rose as snowpack conditions improved.

By the time her six weeks were up, she was more than ready to get back into the harness as this note confirms:

• • •

Dec 12, 1947

Dear Family—

I would much rather you did not meet me as I'm not sure exactly which train I shall take and I plan to go straight to the office in any case.   —Love, Val

In 1948, about nine months after her first visit, Valerie returned to the Flying M E with her friend from *Life* magazine, Helen Deuell:

Dear Parents,

Well, we seem to have gotten bogged down on our trip as we are still here and now not leaving until Monday. We got here last Tuesday expecting to stay for 2 days, 3 at the outside....but after two postponements of 1 day each we suddenly decided that we really wanted to stay a whole extra week....

Two former LIFE people live in Virginia City and a number of friends from previous visits are around so we have had a wonderful time.

The ranch itself was full so we have stayed with another couple, the Pedrolis, but we ate at the main house. The advantages are great, especially when it comes to sleeping late. The couple are local people, real ranchers, and completely charming. Italian-Swiss—at least he is—so there were many questions about what Switzerland was really like.[1]

We had quite a bit of excitement last Saturday when a brush fire broke out and got out of hand. It was never closer than 3 miles away but a fierce wind was blowing and several other ranches were in danger. Fortunately the wind died down at about midnight.

Meanwhile Emmy and Allie (who run the place) had been getting coffee and sandwiches to the firefighters. The main highway into Carson City was closed as the fire was on both sides of it.

We came home from dinner at about that time and found a very funny situation here. Effie, the maid, had really panicked—waked

Valerie's Vacation

Valerie Vondermuhll's Vacation (Caricature by Joan Allison)

everybody, including the children, gotten them all packed, etc., etc. Actually we were never in that kind of danger but it looked pretty awful as even at 3-4 miles you could see the flames and the whole sky was red to the south. They finally got it out in the early morning. One thousand acres burned....

I was at the movies in Carson City with a date that night when the show was interrupted by a call for volunteer fire fighters. I walked my date across the street to the Old Corner Bar and left her to wait for me. She felt comfortable there as she recognized some guests from the ranch. By the time I made it to the line at the Lakeview saddle that divides Carson and Washoe valleys, the fire had jumped Highway 395. The fire was brought under control about three a.m. which allowed us to return to the ranch.

Val's letter continues:

The people around here are quite amazing. When the fire started, the first thought was to get coffee etc. and the next morning when one spot flared up again, and the men were out in the blazing sun, Allie rushed beer down to the line.

We passed a lost cocker spaniel on the road and then spent 1½ hours catching it and feeding it and now it is at the vets being wormed so they are trying to decide where the best home for it will be.

Emmy performed another humanitarian labor yesterday afternoon taking the new waitress's beau around to all the valley ranches trying to find him a job. She succeeded, too.

The ranch atmosphere is quite different from the last time I was here as there are four children around. Two have been here for months and two others just arrived. All most appealing and presently I have to supervise a skip rope lesson.[2]

The car has behaved perfectly and was much admired by truck drivers and locomotive engineers on the way out. The weather was bad at the start but cleared up in Nebraska and from there on we had the top down and got a lot of sun. Helen turns very interesting shades of brick!

The one drawback to the West at this time of year is that baseball news is hard to come by. Helen is nearly frantic!—See you soon, Val

Valerie Vondermuhll, Life *Magazine staffer, at Lake Tahoe, 1947. Val's photographs of the era enhance the collection of pictures in this photo memoir.*
(Courtesy George A. Vondermuhll Jr.)

The Research Trail

In researching this book, there were several challenges. One: how do you find people you last saw or spoke to over fifty years ago? Another: to collect photographs suitable for publication. Here is how the authors' research trail led to the discovery of Valerie Vondermuhll's letters home and her Flying M E photo album:

May 2001 – At the Nevada Historical Society in Reno, Eric Moody, the curator of manuscripts, showed us a booklet, "In Memoriam: Emily Pentz Wood," written in 1966 by Basil Woon. The credits page read, "The names of all photographers were not known. Among those whose pictures do appear are Mr. Gus Bundy of Carson City, Nevada and Miss Valerie Vondermuhll of New York, N.Y."

A phone call to either party and we would be rich in photos, so we thought.

January 2002 –To our great disappointment, Rootsweb.com revealed that both parties were deceased. Valerie Vondermuhll was deceased in April 1978. We decided to look for a Vondermuhll relative. The AOL White Pages listed two Alfred Vondermuhlls; one in Connecticut, the other in New York. We left messages at both phone numbers. A few months later, we left a second round of messages.

April 2002 – One evening our phone rang and it was George A. Vondermuhll Jr., Valerie's brother! We sent Mr. Vondermuhll a caricature by Joan Allison that we believed to be of Valerie, and he confirmed that it was indeed his sister. We inquired

about photos taken by Valerie at the Flying M E. Would someone in the family still have them?

May 2002 – Sandra emailed Mr. Vondermuhll to gently remind him to please look for photos.

June 6, 2002 – Mr. Vondermuhll found a packet of letters written by Valerie to her parents when she was at the ranch for a divorce in November-December 1947, and when she returned for a vacation in 1948. Mr. Vondermuhll sent us the letters with a cover note, "I'll keep trying for photos."

June 22, 2002 – We received an email: "Gold! This afternoon I finally dug into my basement archives and struck pay dirt—nay, the Comstock Lode—an album of Val's devoted entirely to the Flying M E Ranch and environs made during her first visit there while awaiting her divorce. I'll get it off to you on Monday. –GV"

To come upon a collection of letters and more than 200 valuable photos is rare and exciting. Furthermore, Valerie had documented the photos with the names of people and places!

The authors are extremely grateful to Mr. George A. Vondermuhll Jr. for sharing his sister Valerie's personal collection, which so greatly enhances the content of this book. It should be noted that following publication of this book, Mr. Vondermuhll will be donating Valerie's Flying M E photos to a historical repository in Nevada for archival preservation, research and enjoyment by future generations.

George A. Vondermuhll Jr. and his sister, Valerie Vondermuhll, in Litchfield, Connecticutt circa late 1930s.
(Courtesy George A. Vondermuhll Jr.)

Ann Walton and Emmy Wood opt for a quiet evening at the ranch. (Photo Valerie Vondermuhll, Courtesy George A. Vondermuhll Jr.*)*

Martini Anyone?

Sybil Clarke epitomized the wealthy New York Fifth Avenue matron. Listed in the Social Register and with memberships in all the swank clubs, Sybil knew it was back to New York for her as soon as her divorce was granted. No Western garb for this lady, not even for six weeks.

Sybil covered herself with diamonds and other jewels. She sparkled as she shook her martinis each evening. Frequent trips to a Reno hairdresser kept her fingernails bright red and her hair slightly blue. In spite of a regal and haughty bearing, one young and shy new arrival remembers, "Sybil was the first person to pay any attention to me. In spite of her grand bearing, she was motherly to me and some of my homesickness faded away."

Martini?

(Caricature by Joan Allison)

Looking west at the Sierra from the driveway of the Flying M E (Photo Valerie Vondermuhll, Courtesy George A. Vondermuhll Jr.*)*

CHAPTER 12

Ranch Life Not For Everyone

Or All Those Chattering Divorcées

Lucy Dodsworth Allison was an attractive matron from the New York suburb of Englewood, New Jersey. She came to Reno to get a divorce, her attorney having made all the arrangements for her to stay at the Flying M E.

Like Sybil Clarke, Lucy passed on wearing Western garb, preferring her conservative dresses and skirts at the ranch. She had no interest in riding but enjoyed taking long walks, sometimes alone, sometimes with other guests.

Lucy had a lovely voice for singing. Her soon-to-be ex, John "Jack" Allison, was a gifted songwriter and artist whose paintings were featured in many one-man shows in New York. The couple were a popular duo on New York's WOR radio and the café circuit.

John's father, William O. Allison, was a highly successful businessman and served as the first mayor of Englewood Cliffs. He was also a staunch

Lucy Dodsworth Allison & John Allison on the café circuit, circa late 1930s (Authors' Collection)

preservationist. Upon William's death in 1924, he left acres of land in the public trust as parkland (Allison Park) and several millions of dollars to the state of New Jersey "for the benefit of my fellow man."

In spite of her comfortable, affluent suburban lifestyle, Lucy had a taste for the Bohemian life and preferred the company of other artists to socializing with people of her own background.

Lucy lasted less than two weeks at the Flying M E, moving first to the Riverside Hotel, then to a boardinghouse for someplace "a little tawdry."

Someone who knew her well offered this insight:

> People from places like Englewood, New Jersey were a straight-laced, provincial lot—not particularly cosmopolitan or sophisticated. They lived in a kind of sack despite the close

proximity to the most sophisticated city in the world. Divorce was still something decent people did not do. There was shame and stigma all around you when you 'got back from Reno' like you had been away to some mysterious, evil place and you were forever damned. So despite her living in the affluent suburbs, Lucy Allison would have felt a little intimidated and uncomfortable around the more cosmopolitan, sophisticated ladies from Park Avenue. We in Englewood were the straight-laced parcel of the landed gentry.

• • •

Chester Gwinn was another short-timer at the Flying M E. If Emmy knew why it was Chester who came to Reno for a divorce rather than his wife, she didn't say.

Chester was a quiet, soft-spoken gentleman from the Washington, D.C. area. He couldn't stand being around "all those chattering divorcées." He tried to make the best of it, but the ladies drove him crazy. After two weeks, he confessed his misery to Emmy, apologizing profusely for any inconvenience he may be causing her, but that he just had to leave. Emmy accepted his early departure with her usual understanding manner and helped him find more suitable accommodations elsewhere.

Chester was grateful as he drove off in his rented Chevy to the Riverside Hotel, where he remained in semi-seclusion for the rest of his six weeks' sentence.

We never saw Chester again. Lucy, however, would pay us a surprise visit during the harsh winter of December 1948.

Chester Gwinn
(Caricature by Joan Allison)

Joan Allison 94

CHAPTER 13

Museum Director Romances Socialite

What a Tangled Web We Weave

It was not at all unusual for a woman to come to Reno, intent on divorcing one man to marry another, and to forget both in her enthusiasm for the new man she met while doing her time "out West."

When Margaret Astor arrived at the Flying M E for a divorce, her next husband was waiting for her back in England.

"Maggie," as she liked to be called, was a thirty-something, striking redhead, about five-foot six, with a fabulous figure. We were informed that she was a member of the English Astors and had resumed the use of her maiden name.

Maggie was not the outdoor type, and she never rode or hiked. She was a night owl who liked to bar hop and gamble in Carson City until dawn—if she could get someone to stay up with her—and she never got up before noon. She ran up enormous long distance telephone bills—considered extravagant at the time—talking to her future husband in England.

Maggie Astor ironing (Caricature by Joan Allison)

Maggie did have one unusual habit. She liked to iron her clothes in the ranch house living room—clad in pink pajamas or a shirt and panties. This cowboy walked in on her on more than one occasion, and it didn't bother her in the least.

• • •

Soon after Maggie's arrival, Emmy introduced her to Tony Green. Tony was the director of the Nevada State Museum in Carson City and was on Emmy's short list of acceptable single gentlemen who were frequently invited to the ranch for dinner. Maggie and Tony hit it off right away. They could be seen in the Old Corner Bar in Carson almost every night, and Tony's green pickup became a familiar sight at the ranch.

Emmy was frantic trying to keep track of Maggie. As a residence witness, Emmy had to testify in court that she had seen a prospective divorcé at least once in every twenty-four hours of their six weeks' stay. Witnessing was a no nonsense busi-

Left to right: *Maggie Astor, Tony Green and Joan Allison* (Authors' Collection)

ness in Nevada. Swearing falsely in regard to someone's residence was among the most serious of crimes, with the penalty of up to fourteen years in prison. Emmy was a stickler for this law and would not lie under oath for anyone.

Maggie was soon facing a big problem. She came to Nevada to divorce one man; she was already engaged to another man waiting eagerly for her back in England; and now she had fallen for local man, Tony Green. She would have to break it off with someone, but who? She was still weighing her options the day she went to court to receive her decree.

Maggie stayed on at the ranch for several

days after her divorce was final, then up and married Tony Green in a quiet Justice of the Peace ceremony—or so we were told. They left the ranch together for La Jolla, California, and that was the last we saw of them as a couple. We never saw or heard from Maggie Astor again. However, a few years later, Tony would reappear at the Flying M E.

• • •

One evening at the Old Corner Bar, I learned why Tony had left his position at the Nevada State Museum. Tony never talked about himself, so I was fascinated to learn more about his background. He was trained as a taxidermist and a preparator,

The Glenbrook locomotive at the Nevada State Museum, late 1940s. One of the most popular exhibits at the museum during the late 1940s—especially among the small fry who were permitted to climb into the cab—was "Old Glenbrook," an 1870 narrow gauge locomotive donated by the Bliss family. The locomotive was used to pull flat cars of lumber and cordwood from the sawmills at Glenbrook, Lake Tahoe, up to the Spooner Summit where the wood was speeded down to Carson City via the flume. (Courtesy Nevada State Museum, Carson City, NV)

J. Elton "Tony" Green, taxidermist, and Mbongo at San Diego's Natural History Museum, 1942
(Courtesy Jan and Barry Hundemer)

Tony Green, museum director, working in the mining exhibit at the Nevada State Museum in the late 1940s.
(Courtesy Nevada State Museum, Carson City, NV)

preserving animals and constructing their authentic natural habitats.

Before coming to Carson City, he worked at San Diego's Natural History Museum. One of his proudest achievements was in 1942, when he stuffed and mounted Mbongo, the celebrated Belgian Congo gorilla that was captured in 1930 and brought to the San Diego Zoo. When Mbongo succumbed to valley fever, he was taken to the Natural History Museum because of Tony's excellent reputation as a taxidermist. It reportedly took Tony two weeks just to pin all the wrinkles in the face just right.

In World War II, Marine Captain Green found the jungle areas surrounding his Marine outposts teeming with strange insect and plant life, which he collected and studied. He authored a booklet, "Food Is Where You Find It," a pocket survival guide to native foods in the South Pacific. The booklet was designed for emergency use to identify and prepare plants of food value, in order to live off nature in the jungle. Many pilots valued the booklet highly, and in some instances it became required reading for men in combat zones.

At the Nevada State Museum in Carson City, Tony wanted to build a children's petting zoo with native Nevada birds and animals. He had gotten a start with a few donated animals, such as a hawk, an eagle, a couple of raccoons, an opossum, and a fawn, and he was mostly taking care of the animals himself.

However, the museum's board of trustees had other priorities. Major Max C. Fleischmann, the museum's major contributor, had put up $50,000 to create a mining exhibit. He and Judge Clark J. Guild, the founder of the museum, wanted the mining exhibit finished in time for Nevada Day 1950.

So it came down to a difference of opinions and priorities, and the museum board won. It was said that Major Fleischmann, who always carried pearl-handled pistols, threatened Tony with a gun if he didn't concentrate on finishing the mining exhibit.

Judge Clark J. Guild and Major Max C. Fleischmann

Judge Clark J. Guild was born in Dayton, Nevada in 1887. He graduated from the University of Nevada, and was the auditor and recorder for Lyon County from 1908 to 1916. Guild was admitted to the Nevada bar in 1914. From 1924 to 1953 he served as District Court Judge for Nevada's Eighth (later redesignated First) District Court. Judge Guild founded the Nevada State Museum in 1939. The historic museum building originally housed the Carson City mint. Silver dollars stamped "CC" are valuable collectors' items.

Major Max C. Fleischmann was heir to a fortune derived from his family's founding of Fleischmann's Yeast and Standard Brands, upon whose board of directors he served. Long a resident of Santa Barbara, California, Major Fleischmann, in 1935, moved to Nevada to take advantage of the state's favorable tax climate. He constructed a substantial mansion at Glenbrook, on the east shore of Lake Tahoe. Until his death in 1951, Fleischmann was a benefactor of many charities and public projects in Nevada, including the State Museum.

Following Tony Green's departure, James W. Calhoun became the next director of the Nevada State Museum. He successfully finished the basement mine exhibit by Nevada Day 1950. As an authentic replica of a real Virginia City mine in the 1800s, it shows visitors how Nevada's wealth from the Comstock was developed.

—From James W. Calhoun's "Building the Mine Exhibit and Becoming Museum Director," Oral History Program, University of Nevada, 1987.

CHAPTER 14

Allie Okie, Flying M E Hostess

Who are the 'Allie Cats' Tonight?

Allie Okie came to Nevada in 1946 for a divorce and stayed at the Tumbling DW. She was divorcing Jack Okie, not to be confused with the actor, Jack Oakie. Business was thriving at the now-famous dude ranch, thanks to the national publicity it received when First Lady Eleanor Roosevelt vacationed there in 1943.

When Allie arrived at the ranch, Emmy and Dore Wood were having problems in their own marriage. Dore had taken up with a wealthy divorcée at the ranch, and the Woods were in the process of going through their own divorce.

The ranch was busy, so when Allie's divorce was final, she offered to stay on "just a few weeks" to help Emmy out

Allie Okie, Flying M E hostess extraordinaire (Photo Valerie Vondermuhll, Courtesy George A. Vondermuhll Jr.)

with the hostess duties. Those few weeks turned into four years, and Allie became a popular and beloved member of the Flying M E family.

Life on a dude ranch suited Allie. She was in her late twenties, close to six feet tall, and probably what we'd call a tomboy. She had short, wavy black hair and was attractive in a sporty, outdoors way. She was slim and trim and looked great in Western wear. I remember Allie in Levis, a man's Oxford button-down shirt, penny loafers and sox, and a hand tooled black leather belt adorned with silver and turquoise from Hoot Newman's Silver Shop.

Alys Matthiessen Okie was a native of Hudson, New York, some eighty miles north of New York City. She was the great granddaughter of Frederick William Matthiessen (1835-1918), a prominent industrialist and philanthropist from LaSalle, Illinois. F. W.'s main business was the Matthiessen-Hegeler Zinc Company in LaSalle. He also reorganized The Western Clock Manufacturing Company, later known by its trademark name "Westclox." After F. W.'s death in 1918, his 176-

Allie Okie at the Flying M E, 1947 (Photo Valerie Vondermuhll, Courtesy George A. Vondermuhll Jr.)

acre private park in central LaSalle County was donated to the State of Illinois. Matthiessen State Park later became a public park and grew to 1,938 acres.

I'm not sure of this, but I doubt that Allie took a dime for her four years of helping Emmy. She might even have put some of her own money into the ranch as a silent partner, but there's no factual evidence of this. There were times, especially during the winter months, when we only had three or four guests. Summertime was another matter, and we were usually full up with anywhere from twelve to sixteen guests.

Allie was very much a take-charge gal, and nothing seemed to faze her. We hit it off from the start and had a mutual respect and admiration for each other. Allie offered me the opportunity to go in with her on a Colorado cattle ranch. Nothing romantic. She offered to put up the money if I would run the ranch. Somewhere down the road I was to receive a piece of the action, but we never got beyond that point in our negotiations for reasons which will become obvious later on.

As I recall, Allie made one attempt at reconciliation with her "ex" in 1948. She flew back east and was gone for about three weeks. I remember

The Treed Cat. Edith Riley, the cook, heard her cat crying for help. Chased up a tree by the dachshunds, the situation attracted an audience of ranch guests, who tried to bring the cat down by pole and hose. Allie Okie came to the rescue and climbed up the tree to fetch the cat. There was no telling what a dude ranch hostess might be called upon to do in a day's work. (Photos by Valerie Vondermuhll, Courtesy of George A. Vondermuhll Jr.)

Emmy received a telegram, after she arrived in New York, that read something like, "All's fine. –Jack and Allie." But two weeks later there was great excitement when Emmy announced, "Allie's coming back!"

Allie was quick to sense the moods of the guests, especially if they were feeling the blues. Joan Allison Borg recalls her first weeks at the Flying M E in 1948:

When I arrived at the ranch, I heard brief but reverent words in reference to someone called Allie. I had somehow missed meeting her when I arrived. Then on Sunday we met. Allie had decided to do Sunday dinner for all the guests. I was feeling mopey and homesick, too shy to break the ice with the other guests, and had declined to go out with them that day. I was sitting on the sofa in the living

room by myself thumbing through a magazine. Suddenly, this tall, lanky gal came striding in from the kitchen.

"You must be Joan. I'm Allie. I'm making beef Stroganoff for dinner tonight. How do you feel about raw meat?"

"Raw meat? Oh, doesn't bother me at all."

"Then how about giving me a hand in the kitchen with Sunday dinner?"

Her manner was easy and comfortable. As I followed her, I wondered what she would ask me to do. I had no experience cooking and no idea what beef Stroganoff was. But with each slice of the knife, I felt my homesickness falling away. Allie was quick to sense the moods of the guests. She was creative in finding ways to remedy their blues.

Allie gave me importance and the beginnings of my place at the ranch. At this very moment, I can recall how she looked that afternoon. She had short dark hair cut in a wavy bob and was wearing Western riding pants, a man's white shirt, cowboy boots, and a belt trimmed with silver and turquoise. Oh, she also had on a big, white chef's hat!

Allie Okie on cook's night off
(Photo Valerie Vondermuhll, Courtesy George A. Vondermuhll Jr.)

The Allie Cats

Almost every night at dinner, someone would ask, "Who are the Allie Cats tonight?"—meaning who wanted to go out drinking and gambling after dinner with Allie. Questions followed such as "where to?" and "who's driving?" and soon the evening's group of Allie Cats was formed.

Allie Okie Inside and Out

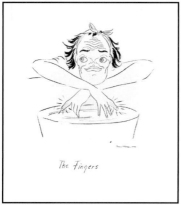

The Fingers

(Photos Valerie Vondermuhll, Courtesy George A. Vondermuhll Jr.;
Caricature by Joan Allison)

Clockwise from top left: *Beer break at Lake Tahoe with Bill McGee; evening at the ranch sewing; with the Buick "Woody" wagon (note the "M E" brand on the side panel); loading horse trailer; sign painting; and softball casualty.*

The Old Corner Bar in Carson City, just ten miles away, was by far the favorite destination for drinks and gambling. Allie, Emmy or I would drive the Buick station wagon and-or the Chrysler convertible. When we had a full house, one or more of the guests with rental cars would drive, too.

The guests loved the Old Corner Bar, where they could mix with the locals—from firemen, cowboys and policemen to lawyers, politicians, and museum directors. The local men knew there was always a chance that they might meet a nice

lady from the Flying M E—maybe even marry her. So there would usually be guys hittin' on the gals. For the most part, the gals enjoyed the attention.

Emmy's driver-escort rule was: Bring the guests home in one piece. Emmy was always worried about drunks offering to drive a guest home only to run off the road or something. She didn't try to play dorm mother, but she did worry and feel responsible for her guests' safe return to the ranch.

Above, *Carson Street looking north in the 1940s*
Opposite, *Carson Street with Broderick's Bar,
the Old Corner and Carson Theatre*
(Courtesy Nevada State Museum, Carson City, NV)

*Old Corner Bar, Mike Demas
at the wheel, late 1940s*
(Courtesy Nikki M. Demas-Butz)

Allie bids Emmy goodnight before heading out to the Old Corner Bar with her "Allie Cats."
(Photo Valerie Vondermuhll, Courtesy George A. Vondermuhll Jr.)

CHAPTER 15

Virginia & Truckee Railroad

The Crookedest Short Line in the World

During the 1940s, the Virginia and Truckee Railroad noisily whistled its way daily through Washoe Valley, steaming south in the morning and north in the evening. When the V & T locomotives—just like the ones you see in the old Western movies—whistled, then huffed and puffed to a stop beside the red water tower in Franktown to take on water, it was the highlight of the day for many Flying M E guests. The sights and sounds of the old engines generated applause for

V & T takes on water at the Flying M E
(Courtesy Nevada Historical Society)

the engineer and his fireman. The trains were even more spectacular on a winter night when the brilliant headlight of the powerful engine pierced the darkness and the locomotive belched steam like a dragon.

It was said that the old-timers could set their watches by the V & T. She was more than just a mining railroad born out of necessity. Over the years she became an institution, an integral part of a growing Nevada. Her whistle was as familiar as the sound of the wind through the sagebrush as she clickity-clacked and chugged her way through the valleys, canyons, and hills of a fledging state.

Built between 1869 and 1872, the V & T supplied the people and the mines of Virginia City with supplies and materials and transported ore to the mills in the valley below.

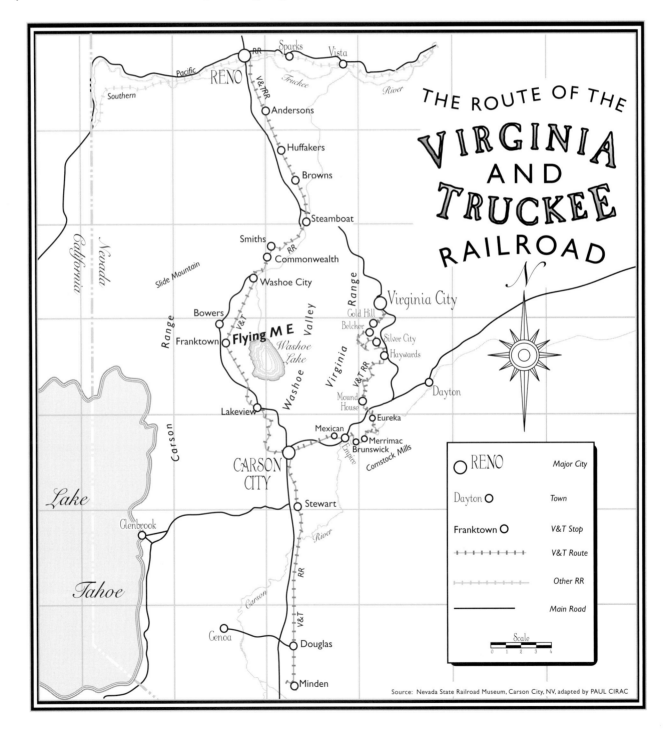

THE ROUTE OF THE
VIRGINIA AND TRUCKEE RAILROAD

RENO	Major City
Dayton	Town
Franktown	V&T Stop
	V&T Route
	Other RR
	Main Road

Source: Nevada State Railroad Museum, Carson City, NV, adapted by PAUL CIRAC

V & T History

Of all the settlements in Washoe Valley, Franktown was the one most closely associated with the fabulous Virginia and Truckee Railroad.

By November 17, 1871, the V & T had rails laid from Reno as far as Steamboat Springs, a resort settlement five miles north of Washoe City. The land owners of Washoe Valley, however, were prudent with their rights-of-way, and were disillusioned with the "Bank of California Crowd" which had gone back on its original plan to permit the counties to purchase stock in the company and instead asked for gifts of bonds. Neither were the Valleyites enamored with the mine companies which milked the Valley's natural resources, so it took almost another year for the V & T to span Washoe Valley and connect with the rails near Carson City.

Washoe City, circa 1863
(Dr. Effie Mona Mack Collection, Courtesy of Nevada Historical Society and Mrs. Dan Boyd who lived in Washoe City in 1863)

Of course, the delay may not have been entirely the fault of the Washoe farmers because one of the most difficult sections of the road was that piece near Lakeview where a tunnel had to be cut through solid rock.

Finally the last wheelbarrow of dirt was dumped, the last tie put in place and the final joining of the rails for the $3,000,000 railroad was scheduled to take place on August 24, 1872. At four o'clock in the afternoon of the great day, a train of cars filled with people pulled out of the Carson station for a spot one mile north. There the Reno end of the road faced the Carson City terminus.

Surrounded by the train crew and a crowd of about five hundred, H. M. Yerington and I. E. James drove in the last spike. Yerington, with his usual haughty non-chalance and his magnificent grey-white whiskers and droopy mustache trimmed to perfection, stepped up to accept the sledgehammer. Through long years of practice his eyes had developed a decided squint and on this happening the squint was most impressive as he aimed at the spike. "The driving was done with a will (except for an occasional miss-lick by Yerington) in a workmanlike way."

The crowd gave three cheers as the spike was pounded into place and then the tracks were cleared of the train from Carson City so that the pioneer locomotive from Reno, the *Storey*, which had performed yeoman's duty during the construction of the road, would have the honor of drawing the first train over the road.

Regular train traffic between Reno and Carson City did not begin until September 15 because the road needed ballasting in several places, but by January 6, 1873, the Carson City *Daily Appeal* was able to announce that twelve V & T engines were daily "snorting and cavorting on the tracks between Reno and Virginia City," a distance of 52 miles.

Little Franktown, which had lost out to Washoe City in the choice for a county seat and which never was in the running with her sister city as a freight center, finally came into her own with the coming of the railroad through the Valley. The city of Reno with her Central Pacific railroad snatched the headquarters of the county government from Washoe and when the V & T service annihilated mule and ox-drawn freighting, Washoe City disintegrated and Franktown with the iron horse took over as the shipping and passenger hub of the Valley.

The old Mormon hamlet also became a refueling depot for the dissonant wood burning engines, with brass brightly polished, whose hunger for cordwood equalled that of their owners for wealth and power, and whose tenders had to be kept stocked with wood and their tanks filled with water. All but five engines of the V & T fleet were named. Most of them—the *Storey, Nevada, Carson, Washoe, I. E. James, Ophir,* and the beautiful *Inyo,* to name a few, pulled up to the water tower and thirstily accepted the water from its long spout.

From the very first, the V & T was a busy little railroad. No sooner had the first freight, the printing press and other materials for the new *Daily Appeal* newspaper office in Carson City passed over the rails from Reno to Carson City, than there were freight trains on the tracks at all hours of the day and night. In one day alone, twenty-nine carloads of wood, twenty-one of lumber, nine of ties, seven of steel rails, two of pig-iron, one each of machinery, coal, fruit and potatoes went through Washoe Valley. Luxuries and supplies of all descriptions from art objects, rare fruits and liquors to heavy, clumsy mine machinery and delicate instruments from all parts of the globe were whisked by the Franktown station to the Comstock (which in 1873 was staggered when the Consolidated Virginia mine

Bowers Mansion, circa 1870s. Note the barren foothills behind the mansion due to clear-cutting for the Virginia City mines. (Courtesy of Nevada Historical Society)

V & T steaming across the Crown Point trestle (Courtesy Neal Cobb Collection)

struck the silver heart of the lode).

Throughout the remainder of the decade, Virginia City boomed with a population of about twenty thousand plus a thousand or more transients. Past the Franktown station journeyed the known and unknown from near and distant lands, riding in ten luxuriously appointed coaches with red velour seats fastened to the floor with gilded iron rungs. The new long, yellow coaches manufactured in 1874 by the Detroit Car Works had walls of ash and black walnut, and gleaming oil lamps hung from ceilings of painted oil cloth. Sleeping cars were also ornate, if not overly comfortable.

Perhaps some of the notables who rolled through Washoe Valley took cognizance of her beauty, despite the timber-shorn hills. Many residents of the Valley took note of the distinguished guests and some were in the audiences of Piper's Opera House in Virginia City to thrill to the performances of Maude Adams, Adah Menken, Edwin Booth, Helena Modjeska, Adelina Patti

and many, many others. Baron Rothschild and Presidents Ulysses S. Grant and Rutherford B. Hayes visited the Comstock, receiving ovations along the way.

Washoe Valley residents were more excited about the great excursion trains than they were about the special Palace cars or Pullmans that went through the Valley. Every weekend during June, July, and August of the 1870s long trains from both Reno and Virginia City transported noisy crowds to Franktown to regale themselves under the trees at Dall's Grove, or to Bowers Mansion which was the favorite retreat because of Eilley Bowers' lovely warm swimming pools.

When there were no special events, the V & T ran "Sunday Trips." The *Nevada State Journal* on June 27, 1878, wrote, "The excursion train with its cheap rates of fare, enabling everybody on the Comstock to go wherever they desired on Sunday, will become more and more popular, and will greatly add to the popularity of the Virginia and Truckee Railroad Company."

One historian reflected the prevalent attitude of the

times toward the V & T when he wrote, "For years the road made immense profits and gave as little as possible to the people." James G. Fair, one of the Bonanza Kings and a rival of the Bank of California enterprise, was in a constant hassle with Superintendent Yerington over freight rates for ore hauled from The Big Four's mines to the mills. He threatened to build his own road and thus won some concessions. Even before the railroad was completed, the Company began to pay dividends and the account books of the V & T show repeated entries of extra expenses to William Sharon, Henry Yerington, and to some of the other trusted employees.

Stories about the V & T were legion. The train's velocity and prowess were not alone in furnishing material for jibes; the schedules were frequently attacked, sometimes with, and more often without, justification. Although timetables were posted, weather, accidents and other acts of God turned them into a farce. Even then, during all the eighty years of its bumptious life, there was not one big catastrophe on the line. To be sure, there were accidents and newspapers frequently carried stories of injuries, Indians or Chinese being killed, drunks rolling under the wheels, and all were tragic for those involved.

One such calamity involved five Washoe Indians. It was during January 1890, that a particularly nasty snowstorm raked Washoe Valley heaping the snow into eight to ten foot drifts. The storm was so extensive that even the huge Southern Pacific trains were abandoned in the mountains. Before the wind and sleet had really gotten underway, the V & T engineer on an evening sprint to Reno through Washoe Valley tried to outrun the weather by throwing the throttle wide open and speeding over the rails. This particular maneuver had often worked in the past, but just when all was thought to be safe the snowplow in front of the engine barreled into a spot where the ties had warped. The pilot, engine and mail-express cars hurtled into Theodore Winters' field, spewing steam in all directions.

Five Indians who were riding free in the tender, as was their custom, went sprawling into the snow just as the boiler pipes exploded. Nearby ranchers harnessed their horses to sleighs and rushed to the wreck. Fortunately the passenger cars had remained on the tracks but the Indians were badly scalded. Andrew Sauer and his son George took them to Washoe City, and arranged for someone to care for them in an empty house that was made into an emergency hospital. Before medical help could reach the Valley, the Washoe Indians died.

V & T with snowplow, Carson City, January 1890
(Courtesy Nevada Historical Society)

V & T heading for Minden
(Hugh Tolford, Mallory Hope Ferrell; Neal Cobb Collection, Courtesy of Nevada Historical Society)

The weather in Washoe Valley had induced the idealists to long for a railroad, and was as disrespectful to the trains as it had been toward the stage coaches. In the winter of 1890, one V & T train was stalled for three weeks in the Washoe cut—the little canyon between Washoe and Pleasant Valleys—and had to be dug out by a gang of shovelers. The five engines and snowplow sent to the rescue from Carson City became snowbound near Franktown, and the plow sent from Reno had to be shunted to a siding at Steamboat Springs.

Cloudbursts in Washoe Valley stopped the trains several times. For five days prior to November 19, 1875, the rains deluged the Valley and carried away a bridge between Mill Station and Franktown. All the trains were delayed while a force of men constructed a new bridge.

In 1902, the V & T engines were converted to oil-burners so the little engines with their large top-heavy smoke stacks no longer needed to take on cord wood. However, they still stopped at

Franktown to refill their water tanks.

In 1904, the V & T tracks were extended a few miles from Carson City south to the Indian Reservation at Stewart. In 1906 the railroad finally completed the track from Carson City to Minden to bring into reality an idea first proposed by the Washoe newspaper, *The Eastern Slope,* which had suggested in 1867 that a Carson Valley branch be built to serve the agricultural trade of that region.

During the 1920s and 1930s the combined passenger and freights stopped at Franktown station, and excursion trains again brought hundreds to picnic at Bowers Mansion which had been revived as a summer resort.

In 1932 Ogden Mills, who had inherited his grandfather's holdings, purchased the remaining stock of the railroad from the Sharon estate. Mills kept the trains running, but his death in 1937 foreshadowed the end of the V & T. There was no longer anyone left to provide for the railroad, which all its life had accepted charity of one kind of another, never once contributing to the well-being of anyone but its own family, and it was unprepared to function as an independent business.

In the early 1940s the red station house beside the tracks at Franktown was shut down, the post office having previously been transferred elsewhere.

In 1941 the Carson-Virginia branch of the V & T— that crooked, trestled, steep, magnificent stretch of the road—was abandoned. Virginia City had melted away; the Fourth Ward School, the court house, the water works, the *Enterprise* offices, the opera house, the elegant saloons, and the beautiful big homes of the Bonanza Kings remained, but only as shadows of the past. Not until tourism came into its own after World War II, did the mining town come alive again—and then only as a shadow of its former greatness.

Washoe City remained a ghost town until the 1940s when a few newcomers bought up small plots of land. Slowly a new community has grown up where once there was all the industry, excitement, and glory of a pioneer settlement.

In 1940 a petition to vacate the road came up for a hearing before the Interstate Commerce Commission and the Nevada Public Service Commission. To no one's surprise, the arguments for closing the route were as exaggerated (in an opposite direction) as those used to start the road in the beginning. The types of slanted, false statistics, and pleas put forth to activate the V & T were used again to encourage its demise. No consideration was given to the benefits of those living along the railroad, or to depreciation of real estate values in Carson Valley. There never was a thought turned toward the historical value of such a railroad that had played such an important role in the settlement and development of this part of the State.[1]

—Excerpted and condensed from
Myra Sauer Ratay's
Pioneers of the Ponderosa

Lions Club members on the V & T Reno to Carson City run, 1945.

V & T train crew members on the Reno to Carson City run, 1945.
(Neal Cobb Collection, Courtesy of Nevada Historical Society)

No. 26 southbound out of Reno, November 12, 1948 (Courtesy Nevada State Railroad Museum, Carson City, NV)

A Farewell Excursion, Memorial Day Weekend, 1949

Invitations were sent to rail fans across the nation stating that the railroad society "regrets to announce the passing of the Virginia and Truckee Railway, age 80 years. Services will be held Sunday, May 29, on board the train en route Reno to Minden and return." The invitations were a reproduction of an old-time funeral announcement with a black border and formal script. The farewell excursion only cost $5 and included a big buffet luncheon at Carson City in the V & T Railroad car repair shops.[2]

Among the more than 300 passengers lucky to get tickets for the farewell excursion were railroad historians Lucius Beebe and Charles Clegg, and prominent Reno attorney, Clel Georgetta. Beebe and Clegg from *Virginia & Truckee, A Story of Virginia City and Comstock Times:*

A Sentimental Journey to Washoe

When the California-Nevada Railroad Historical Society chartered a "Comstock Express" over the Southern Pacific and brought 450 fans of all ages and degrees of railway sophistication for a last excursion over the V & T over Memorial Day weekend in 1949, every piece of V & T equipment except locomotive No. 5 was pressed into service for the occasion. Powered by Nos. 26 and 27, the special between Reno and Carson included four flat cars with rails and benches built for the occasion, the sole remaining box car, a long unused tunnel car, a flanger, combine, mail car and caboose. Memories of similar excursions long ago to the Bowers Mansion at Franktown, to the pools at Steamboat or to the shady pavilions of Treadway Park in Carson City were recalled as the bizarre train and its jampacked occupants rolled noisily across Washoe Meadows and up the grade to Lakeview overlooking Washoe Lake and the stately lawns of Lord Wellesley. The trippers lunched in the V & T shops at Carson where the chivalry of the Comstock had once danced at the great Fourth of July Ball of 1873, exposed untold quantities of film, went on to Minden and Virginia "for to see and to be seen."[3]

Reno attorney Clel Georgetta wrote in his diary:

Memorial Day, Sunday, 29 May 1949 – We made a bit of history today. Some 350 people from out of state and probably about 50 Nevada residents, and I was one of them. About 8:15 a.m., old engine 27, followed by 26, pulled away from the Reno station with a train of 12 cars. There wasn't even standing room left on any car. I selected an open flat car so I would be free to take pictures. I did take many pictures, but a cold wind chilled my ambition for anything but a chance to get warm. As the V & T goes from Reno it crosses the Truckee meadows and then passes through about 2 miles of narrow canyon with red rocks before it enters Washoe Valley.

Our first stop was at the old Washoe City stop. Then we slowly bumped along the ancient rails across the beautiful meadows of Washoe Valley and on up the grade to the old Summit Station [Lakeview]. Another stop, then on around the hill to the old caved-in abandoned tunnel now bypassed by a sharp bend of track around the curve of the hill. Another stop and hundreds of pictures taken with every kind of camera known to man from the simplest Brownie Box Camera to my Zeiss Contax III and the Graflex Speed Graphics 4x5 used by the photojournalists.

At Carson City, the crowd heard some speeches read from a small platform in front of the station. Oh, yes, we had lunch in the old stone Round House where I ran into our renowned Nevada historian, Effie Mona Mack, who introduced me to Lucius Beebe and Charles Clegg, the authors of *Virginia and Truckee* and *Mixed Train Daily*. Beebe does the writing and Clegg takes the pictures to illustrate the books.

After lunch the crowd divided, about half going on to Minden and then back to Reno on the train. The other half went to Virginia City in 6 big buses. I went to V.C. to keep warm. At Virginia City, I went to Boot Hill, the famous old graveyard, and then far down toward 6 mile canyon. When I got back to Piper's Opera House, all the buses were gone so I began looking for a ride. Walking down the street, some lamps in the window of an antique shop caught my eye. I looked inside and there was Edie Palmer, a woman I met when I first came to Reno. She would give me a ride to Reno. On the way down, I mentioned dinner. Very well, we went into the Sun Flower—crowded—so on up Mount Rose to the Christmas Tree we went.[4]

Lucius Beebe and Chuck Clegg devoted much of their highly creative lives to keeping the memory of the grandeur and excitement of railroading's golden age alive. In their own passionate prose:

Up to the very end the V & T maintained its flavor of the long gone 1870's in its operations, properties and pervading atmosphere. Much of the iron between Carson and Reno was the original Sheffield rolled steel laid down when the road was new. Its stub switches with their red and white painted target stands were never changed in its lifetime of eighty years.

The canary yellow and deep Gloucester green of its coaches were the same in 1949 as that which had gladdened the Nevada heart on the first rolling stock long ago in the eighties, although this had originally been painted green in its entirety.

The V & T was something that had survived out of the riding years of the coaches with six horses, the years of the great venturings and interminable landfarings. When it was new the distances of the old West were great distances and the railroad a greater miracle than anything in the American record until that time. There is nothing in the terms of the twentieth century to lay hold upon the heart and fire the imagining comparable to the first coming of the graded rails.

And if anyone should doubt the heroic proportions of the V & T's importance in the history of Nevada he has but to look upon the Great Seal of the commonwealth, where a V & T locomotive crossing the Crown Point Trestle above the hoists of the Yellow Jacket Mine is the heraldic emblem of the state.

The V & T was a wonderful and uncommonly beautiful railroad, the most beautiful, many people believe, in the terrain it traverses of any short line anywhere. The ramparts of the High Sierra have changed only with the seasons since the first year of the V & T's going. Its late afternoon departure from the depot platform at Carson with the ringing of the ancient warning bell swung from the eaves was one of the homely dramas of American existence.

From the high grade at Lakeview the traveler could see the whole of Eagle Valley, the cottonwoods in autumn yellow with the setting sun, the rolling hills beyond, soft in twilight as monstrous mounds of chocolate ice cream. Washoe Lake a thin sliver of turquoise; the mansion of Sandy Bowers hidden in its corona

of Lombardy poplars on the other side of the track. The shadows of Washoe Canyon are deep on the northbound run and by the time the little train has cleared Steamboat and entered the fringes of Reno the lights are on in cottage windows and the smoke of a hundred kitchen fires ascends, vertically, into the Truckee twilight. Parents hold their children on fencetops to see the train's nightly passing.

It is a microcosm of a way of life, vanished perhaps, but infinitely more valid than anything that has yet been devised to succeed it.

What promised to be the last winter of the V & T's existence was one of the most fearsome in the history of Nevada. Temperatures on the ranges dropped to forty below zero and sheep and cattle perished by uncounted thousands or were saved by the most heroic efforts of owners and public agencies. So great was the snowfall in the High Sierra and on the Great Plains that for days at a time no through trains passed over the mainline of the Southern Pacific. The high passes of the Rockies were impervious even to the most powerful Mallets and giant rotaries and at one time no transcontinental passenger train passed through Reno for five days. But the V & T missed no single run and, with a wedge plow ahead and Nos. 5 and 26 in tandem, schedules were made daily, bucking the drifts in Washoe Canyon and achieving their terminals even when there was no mail to deliver.

The Virginia & Truckee has banked the fires of its engines for the long night, as have so many little railroads before it. It will come not again, for the dead return not. But, like the sparkling Concords that went before it down the dusty highroads of yesterday, its memory will live forever in the minds of men, trailing an unforgotten banner of woodsmoke across the Nevada sagebrush where once the railroad ran.[5]

V & T Reborn

On May 31, 1965, Robert Gray was on a visit to Virginia City and noted the right-of-way for the V & T remained undeveloped. Gray was a businessman and railroad buff from California, and saw the potential in the rebirth of this historic monument. Thus began a quest to revive the most famous of all American short lines.

On May 31, 1972, Gray received approval from the Storey County Commissioners to operate the rail line and reincorporated the V & T Railroad. Old right-of-ways were purchased, steam trains were renovated, and the V & T entered a new life with vigor and enthusiasm as an excursion train for history and for railroad fans visiting Virginia City and the once mighty Comstock Lode.

As of this writing, the V & T makes a 2-1/2 mile round trip between the "F" Street Station in Virginia City down to the Gold Hill Depot in Gold Hill. The leisurely 35 minute trip allows passengers to get off at Gold Hill and reboard a later train. The conductor gives a narration of the many historic sights along the way. The train, still following its original 133-year-old right of way goes right through some of the most famous of the bonanza Comstock mines.

The Northern Nevada Railway Foundation (NNRF) is in the ongoing process of raising funds to rebuild the historic railroad. Plans call for extending the railroad seventeen miles from the end of the existing track in Gold Hill to Carson City. The intent is to rebuild the railroad on as much of the original right-of-way as possible, through spectacular scenery in American Flat and the Carson River Canyon.

The project is expected to inject an additional $40.9 million into the local economy and create more than 800 jobs. According to Janice Ayres, president of the Railway Foundation: "Rebuilding the Virginia & Truckee will not only create a positive and monumental economic impact on Northern Nevada,

it will be an invaluable artifact for all of American railroading. Its rails shaped generations long after it ceased operations and its operative portion enriches and brings back the old West to thousands each year. Let us drive the spikes that will resound for another. All aboard!" (*Nevada Appeal*, October 17, 2002. *For more information on the Northern Nevada Railway Foundation's program, visit their website at www.steamtrain.org.*)

As the V & T disbanded in the 1950s, parts of the famous line were sold for the movies or for scrap or donated to the state. Out of 27 surviving engines, 8 are currently on exhibit in museums and 1 is still used in the movies.

The Nevada State Railroad Museum in Carson City displays No. 18, *Dayton*; No. 22, *Inyo* (probably the most famous and also known as the Brass Betsy); and workhorse No. 25.

The historic mining town of Virginia City has Engine No. 27 on display.

The California State Railroad Museum in Sacramento displays No. 12, *Genoa*; No. 13, *Empire*; and No. 21, *J. W. Bowker*.

The Railroad Museum of Pennsylvania displays No. 20, *Tahoe*.

No. 11, *Reno*, made its first movie in 1937, and is still doing so today at the Old Tucson Studios in Tucson, Arizona.

The V & T Railroad is not just a piece of Nevada nostalgia; it is a treasure of national importance. Linked inseparably with the fortunes of Virginia City and the Comstock mines, it was the V & T that carried the silver and gold that helped to transform the American West.

Risen like the Phoenix Bird, born again from the ashes of the past, the V & T steams on, into a bright future, once again the "Crookedest Short Line in the World."[6]

CHAPTER 16

Lucius Beebe and Charles Clegg

Enterprising Journalists

Lucius Beebe began his literary career at the New York *Herald Tribune* in 1929, and went on to write articles for such periodicals as *Town & Country*, *Gourmet, Esquire*, and the *San Francisco Chronicle*, to name a few. Beebe and Charles Clegg, his partner and co-author of half of his thirty-four books, brought their private railroad car, the *Gold Coast*, to Nevada in 1948. They purchased a home in Virginia City and took over publishing and editing the *Territorial Enterprise*, where Samuel Clemens had his roots.

Nevada historian Andria Daley-Taylor has graciously granted the authors permission to excerpt and condense portions of her very informative and entertaining article from *Nevada Magazine*, "Boardwalk Bons Vivants":

"There is more glamour and nostalgic escape literature to be written about the west and Nevada, and Clegg (left) and I intend to do it. Properly mined, the literature field of the historic west could make Clegg and I rich—well almost, that is—as the people and times we have written about." (Lucius Beebe to the Reno Reporter, *October 6, 1949) St. Bernard, T-Bone Towser with the duo in Virginia City.*
(Photo courtesy Ann Clegg Holloway)

One summer's day in 1948, a gilded Pullman named the *Gold Coast* came to rest under the shady cottonwoods that lined the railroad siding in Carson City. Folks in Carson hadn't seen such overstuffed opulence parked on the Virginia & Truckee tracks since the nabobs had poured into the capital city for the Corbett-Fitzsimmons fight in 1897.

Lucius Beebe and Charles Clegg, noted authors and men about town, had arrived in Nevada, ready to conquer new frontiers. When the two splendidly attired gentlemen stepped down the *Gold Coast's* red-carpeted steps into the blazing noonday sun, a new literary era in Nevada began.

Lucius Beebe and Charles Clegg, two of America's foremost railroad historians, had come to Nevada to write about the Comstock's fabled Virginia & Truckee Railroad for their series of railroad books. They would create a sensation with their revival of the *Territorial Enterprise*.

At the time Beebe and Clegg arrived in Nevada, Beebe was the more famous of the pair. He was well known for his magazine articles, books, and syndicated New York *Herald Tribune* column, "This New York." The column documented the city's "Café Society," a term which Beebe coined and copyrighted.

Scion of a staid Boston banking family, Beebe frequently topped the nation's best-dressed list. He graced the cover of *Life* under the headline, "Beebe Sets the Style." "I'm as vain as a whore," he once confessed.

Beebe had paid his first visit to Reno and *Virginia City* in 1940 while covering the premiere of the film Virginia City. He panned the film but applauded Warner Brothers' three-day press party.

That same year he met his future collaborator, editor, photographer, and lifelong companion, Charles M. Clegg, when the two were house guests of Washington hostess Evalyn Walsh McLean, owner of the Hope diamond. "Chuck" Clegg was 24, fourteen years Beebe's junior, and known for his sense of fun, wit, and style. Clegg enlisted in the Navy at the onset of World War II, but they stayed in touch.

After the war, the two men teamed up to begin what would be their life's work: a definitive study of America's short line railroads. However, Beebe may have simply wanted a change of scenery. Clegg later said that Beebe left New York "because the Café Society was evaporating back into the mist from which it had sprung." He added that his friend's motto had always been to leave the party while it was still good, before melancholy drunks began singing off key.

Although Beebe and Clegg considered Carson City a little dull, they found the state of Nevada much to their liking—no taxes, limitless gambling, and champagne for $7 a bottle—and so they settled in Virginia City.

"Keedo," Clegg remembered Beebe saying as they walked the town's rickety old boardwalk, "do you realize that there is a saloon for every 20 men, women, and children in this town? Do you realize the absolute ultimate in Progress when you encounter it? Well, I do. Why, the alcoholic proof is so high, the moral tone so low, that we can be absolutely inconspicuous. Let's see if there is a house for sale."

Beebe purchased the tumbling remnants of a home on A Street. The house had been in the Piper family, owners of Piper's Opera House, and Beebe was proud of the theatrical association. Taking ownership required extracting an itinerant cowboy (later expanded by Beebe to two cowboys and their horses) from the parlor.

Clegg, the perfectionist, set about restoring the mansion "in Victorian vulgarity." He added elaborate gardens, a pool (Virginia City's first), and a six-car garage to house Beebe's Rolls-Royces and Clegg's Jaguar. Clegg also installed a fireproof walk-in banker's vault to house the writers' manuscripts and papers.

The two *boulevardiers*—always immaculately groomed and dapper, and often sporting Stetsons or top hats, as the occasion called for—met kindred spirits on their strolls around Virginia City. There were the remittance kids, children of the rich who were paid to stay away. A Delaware du Pont was tending bar at the Sky Deck Saloon. An Eastern socialite was running a hotel. A chef from Maxim's was cooking at the Bonanza Inn. Numerous members of Café

Dapper authors Lucius Beebe (left) and Charles Clegg arrived in Carson City in 1948 on their private railroad car, the Gold Coast. Beebe may have simply wanted a change of scenery from New York "because the Café Society was evaporating back into the mist from which it had sprung." (Courtesy Ann Clegg Holloway)

Society were on hand, waiting out their six-week residencies at divorce ranches near Reno. And there were locals like "Honest Len" Haffey, who spun the roulette wheel at the Delta Saloon.

Soon pals and colleagues from back East were migrating to Virginia City, and townsfolk took it in good stride when hobnobbing with the likes of a Cole Porter and other celebrities.

Beebe continued sending his stories to the *Herald Tribune*

Charles "Chuck" Clegg and Lucius Beebe—"Enterprising" journalists (Courtesy Ann Clegg Holloway)

and magazines like *American Heritage*, *Gourmet*, and *Esquire*. Remarkably, Beebe and Clegg produced three books in 1949, including the best sellers *Virginia & Truckee* and *The U.S. West: The Saga of Wells Fargo*, a handsomely illustrated story of the company which made Western transportation history. The latter remained on the *New York Times* best-seller list for a year.[1]

Beebe and Clegg at the Flying M E

About a week after their acclaimed arrival, Beebe and Clegg dropped in at the Flying M E one afternoon to say hello to Emmy, whom Beebe had met during his earlier junket to Virginia City. Emmy insisted they stay for dinner—the first of many over the next few years.

When I first met Beebe and Clegg, I had no idea who they were. This Montana country boy had never heard of them. Their and my love of trains did give us one thing in common though. When they first learned I had ridden the freights throughout the West in my wanderlust years (1940-41), prior to joining the U.S. Navy at age seventeen, they became very interested. Our conversation went something like this:

Beebe: "What was your impression of the average hobo you met?"

McGee: "Well, for the most part, the old-timers I met in the hobo jungles were unemployed men—with a sense of wanderlust, too. They seemed to be honest guys who worked when they could. Of course, there was always a chance one would just as soon slit your throat as look at you." He seemed rather surprised with my answer.

Clegg: "So you weren't really afraid of them?"

McGee: "Not really. We were more concerned with avoiding the 'salami slicers.' That's hobo speak for train wheels." [2]

As I recall, Beebe and Clegg traveled to warmer climes in their private railroad car during the harsh winter of 1948-49. They left in style after a gala bon voyage party at the Old Corner Bar hosted by Emmy and the bar's owner, Ella Broderick.

Chuck Clegg turned out to be a very nice guy, and we talked trains several times after that. But Lucius Beebe was quite another matter. He was arrogant and haughty towards almost everyone—and not surprisingly that included us cowboys. (We wondered if he ever heard our nickname for him, "Luscious Lucius.") I'm not sure how Emmy really felt about him, or how he felt about Emmy, but Lucius was friendly toward Emmy and loved the attention of the patrician population "serving time" at the Flying M E.

Some guests seemed bored with all the talk of trains and private parlor cars when Beebe and Clegg were visiting at the ranch. But everyone seemed in awe of the splendor of the *Gold Coast* when Emmy and her guests were invited for cocktails aboard the private car. Beebe and Clegg entertained frequently and extravagantly and were noted for the unusual. They staged one dinner party in the *Gold Coast* where guests were served pheasant and partridge eggs—hard-boiled in New York's Club 21 and flown to Nevada—to the accompaniment of suitable vintage wines.

The *Gold Coast* consisted of six rooms, with two bedrooms, three baths, a dining salon, servants' quarters, and a communication system. The drawing room was replete with crystal chandeliers, ornate drapery, brocaded couches, and a marble fireplace. Beebe claimed to be searching for someone like himself who lived in an ornate private railroad car so he could compare notes on how to provision, entertain, travel, and "keep a cook."

Here's a Lucius Beebe anecdote I've never forgotten. Joan Allison, the talented artist who created the ranch guest caricatures in this book, drew one of Beebe straddling a toy locomotive and wearing a cowboy hat and boots. Joan recalls:

> It was a miserable idea from the start that someone, meaning well, had dreamed up. A party had been planned with Beebe as the guest of honor. 'Wouldn't it be great if Joan could do caricatures of the guests while the party is going on?' Well, I knew better, but as always, I was trying to please.

Actually, Beebe's caricature turned out quite good, looking just like him. But he hated it and tore it up in front of everyone. At the time, I was the youngest guest at the ranch, just twenty, and was terribly embarrassed in front of all the guests. But he seemed to like being surrounded by glitter and chitchat. And I think he was jealous of the cowboys.

The pair contributed their time and talent to many civic affairs, such as writing the pageant outline for the Admission Day celebration on October 31, 1949. Their presence in Virginia City attracted national media attention, and soon the old mining town was becoming a tourist attraction. In 1949, the Virginia City Restoration Program was launched to restore and preserve the gradually disintegrating town. Its leader was Mrs. Helen Thomas whose grandfather was a financial leader in the days of the Big Bonanza. The idea was to restore the existing buildings and restrict all new buildings to the styles of the 1870s.

TERRITORIAL ENTERPRISE Reborn

The first edition of the *Territorial Enterprise* was printed in Genoa, Utah Territory, in 1858. The paper moved to Carson City in 1859 and then found a permanent home in Virginia City in 1860. During the 1860s, the golden era of the Comstock, the newspaper included among its reporters William Wright and Samuel Clemens, otherwise known by their respective pen names Dan De Quille and Mark Twain. Twain and De Quille would become synonymous with the lively *Enterprise,* which was being quoted in San Francisco and New York as the authentic voice of the frontier. The *Enterprise* had been published for eighty-eight years and had been dormant since

Territorial Enterprise offices
(Gus Bundy Photo, Bundy Collection, Courtesy of Special
Collections Department, University of Nevada, Reno Library)

1946, until Beebe and Clegg arrived on the scene.
Andria Daley-Taylor:

> In 1952 Beebe and Clegg took on their
> greatest literary challenge when they decided to
> buy the *Virginia City News*. They paid $5,500
> for the *News* and, for a $20 gold piece, ac-
> quired the rights to the venerable *Territorial
> Enterprise*. Clegg immediately spent $15,000
> on Victorian typefaces to recreate the look of
> the newspaper.

> On May 2, 1952, their first edition of the
> *Territorial Enterprise* appeared. Beebe and
> Clegg's joint statement explained: "We propose
> without contrived archaism to recreate some-
> thing of the identity and personality this news-
> paper achieved in the great days of the
> Comstock and to this end are reverting to its
> original style and title as the *Territorial

Enterprise." Every national publication was sent
a press package announcing the revitalization of
the famous Nevada newspaper.

The paper attracted an impressive list of
contributors such as Nevada's own Walter Van
Tilburg Clark, Pulitzer Prize-winning historian
Bernard DeVoto, folklorist Duncan Emrich,
and the "two Katies"—Katherine Hillyer and
Katherine Best, both contributors to national
magazines—wrote a column called "Comstock
Vignettes." The "Suburban News" section told
about happenings in the suburbs—Reno and
Las Vegas—and was written by a man in the
know: a traveling liquor salesman. The wisdom
of Miguel Augerreberre was quoted quite
extensively. Augerreberre was Virginia City's
lone sanitation person and lived in a cave.
However, Beebe regarded him as a natural
gentleman.

It was Beebe's and Clegg's desire to have
the newspaper reflect a rich western heritage
and to create a scholarly quarterly with impor-

*Former New York socialite Penna Tew Hinton Hart, a
Flying M E graduate, with "Garbage Mike" Augerre-
berre, left, and "21" dealer Mike Demas at the Brass
Rail Saloon, 1957.* (Courtesy Nikki M. Demas-Butz)

Fountain pens poised, the two authors at a book signing in Virginia City. (Courtesy Ann Clegg Holloway)

tant historical writing and important book reviews on regional subjects by authorities in their fields.

But satire was equally as important. San Francisco columnist Herb Caen noted that most newspapers had signs posted to remind their writers to think, "but at the *Enterprise* there were signs advising staff to smirk, sneer, conspire, plot, deceive, gloat, connive, leer, and defame."

By 1953, the number of paid subscribers had climbed to 2,875. The *Enterprise* had a national following and was often quoted in the national press. By 1954, there were more than

6,000 paid subscribers, making the paper the largest weekly circulated in the West. Soon the old mining town became one of the top tourist attractions in Nevada and the nation.

Beebe strong-armed his pals in San Francisco, the East, and England, and the *Enterprise* ran ads for Rolls-Royce, Antoine's in New Orleans, the Ritz, and Jack Daniels.

The Delta Saloon was the meeting place for the daily five o'clock editorial conferences. The bar would sparkle with martinis and whiskies, positions would be taken, and on signal the staffers would hoist. Staffers were tested for both their verbal proficiency and

Duo places bets with "Honest Len" Haffey at Delta Saloon. The Delta was the meeting place for daily five o'clock editorial conferences. (Courtesy Ann Clegg Holloway)

their ability to hold liquor.

But Beebe was finding the tourism boom—which ironically his presence had helped to promote—intolerable. In 1957 Clegg purchased a villa in Hillsborough, near San Francisco, and it became the pair's winter home. In 1960 Beebe and Clegg sold the Enterprise to Roy Shelter, who owned the historic part of the *Enterprise* Building. The names of Beebe and Clegg were to remain in the staff box.

Beebe died in 1966 at age 63. In 1978 Clegg sold their Virginia City home and spent most of his time at his secluded Hillsborough estate. He returned to the Comstock occasionally for visits, a lonesome figure. He died in 1979, also at age 63.

The happiest and most productive days of Beebe's and Clegg's lives had been those spent in Virginia City, where they wrote sixteen books (Beebe penned another three, solo) and succeeded in reviving one of the West's great newspapers.[3]

When Lucius Beebe died in 1966, San Francisco columnist Herb Caen ran an unpublished manuscript which Beebe had written in 1960. The manuscript was a sort of autobiographical assessment of Beebe's dreams and aspirations. In Beebe's words:

> I admire most of all the Renaissance Man, and, if it can be said without pretentiousness, like to think of myself as one, at least in small measure...perhaps a poor man's Cellini or a road company Cosmo d'Medici....In the Territorial Enterprise, we run a paper of outrage that only incidentally is the largest weekly west of the Missouri....If anything is worth doing, it's worth doing in style. And on your own terms....I'd like the obits to say: "Everything he did was made to measure. He never got an idea off the rack."[4]

The *Gold Coast* railroad car is now a popular attraction at the California State Railroad Museum in Sacramento. As of this writing, a new *Territorial Enterprise* was progressing toward start-up in a new format as a monthly magazine published both online and in print. In the tradition of the original *TE*, the new *Enterprise* plans to offer the reader a mix of satire, sarcasm, history, nostalgia, and current affairs. (*For updated information visit www.territorialenterprise.com*)

Left to right beginning with second man from left: Walter Van Tilburg Clark, folklorist Marian Emrich, historian Roger Butterfield, folklorist Duncan Emrich, and poet Irene Bruce at an authors book signing party in Virginia City in 1949. Virginia City had the highest percentage of professional authors of any town in America. (Gus Bundy Photo, Bundy Collection, Courtesy of Special Collections Department, University of Nevada, Reno Library)

Writers of the Comstock:
Virginia City's Literary Legacy of the 1940s

During the 1940s, a celebrated roster of writers came to Virginia City to live and write. The illustrious group included Lucius Beebe and Charles Clegg; Dr. Duncan Emrich, chief of the folklore section of the Library of Congress and author of *It's An Old Wild West Custom,* a collection of Western legends and folklore; Walter Van Tilburg Clark, author of the best sellers *The Track of the Cat* and *The Ox-Bow Incident* (published in 1940 and 1949 respectively); former *Life* magazine editor and nationally-known magazine writer Roger Butterfield, also author of the best seller *The American Past* (1947); poet Irene Bruce, whose latest book of poetry was *Crags and Sand;* folklorist Marian Emrich, whose *A Child's Book of Folklore* was a collection of folklore stories especially adapted for children; Pulitzer Prize-win-

ning Harvard historian Bernard DeVoto; and the "two Katies," Katherine Hillyer and Katherine Best, whose joint byline appeared in *Reader's Digest, Coronet, McCalls* and other nationally known magazines.

Most of these "name" authors were bona fide residents of Virginia City, giving the town—with a population of 800—the highest percentage of professional authors of any town in America. Roger Butterfield, a Virginia City resident since 1945 when he came to Nevada to get a divorce, owned the mountain top house which was once the home of Judge Clayton Belknap, a prominent Nevada jurist of early times. Beebe and Clegg purchased the residence built by John Piper, proprietor of Piper's Opera House. Clark lived in the red brick mansion which was the office and manager's home of the Con Chollar Mining Company.[5]

Cal-Neva Lodge entrance, circa 1930s (Courtesy Cal-Neva Resort)

CHAPTER 17

Cal-Neva Lodge

A Starry Night to Remember

One summer night over drinks at the Old Corner Bar, Allie announced that Frank Sinatra was opening at the Cal-Neva Lodge at Tahoe. She polled the "Allie Cats," and the vote was unanimous—everyone wanted to go see "Ol' Blue Eyes."

Emmy made the reservations, and Allie worked out the transportation. I would take four guests in the Buick wagon, Allie would take three in the Chrysler convertible, and a guest would take four in their rental car. Since the Cal-Neva's dress code was evolving from black-tie to dressy casual, it was agreed that the women could wear slacks or a dress, but jeans were out.

I had one problem with Allie's plan. Ava Gardner was a guest at the ranch then, and Allie had outflanked me by arranging for Miss Gardner to ride with her before I could offer our celebrity guest the front passenger seat in the wagon—next to me.

Ava Gardner had to be the most beautiful woman I had ever met—even more beautiful than in her movies. I knew a little something about her. Who didn't? She had been divorced twice, first from actor Mickey Rooney and then from bandleader Artie Shaw. She was from North Carolina and spoke with a soft and sexy drawl. She was stay-

ing at the ranch for some rest and relaxation, according to Emmy—not for a divorce—and wanted absolute privacy from the press and photographers. So far, she had not been riding with me, but I was hoping to change that. The "kitchen spies" informed me she was spending afternoons by the pool with a book.

I was reminded of a humorous story I heard during the war about Artie Shaw. He was entertaining the troops in the South Pacific and after finishing a gig one evening, he climbed a hill to go to the head, and a bunch of sailors followed him. They followed him right into the head. Shaw asked what they were doing, and one of the sailors answered, "We want to see the prick that screwed Ava Gardner!"

The next afternoon we left the ranch right on schedule at four p.m. Two of my passengers, Patti Allen and Anne Marie Baker, were regular riders. I knew little about the other two, Janet Van Cleef and Cynthia Callahan.

Allie wanted to stop in Carson City, so she took U.S. 50 over Spooner Summit to the lake. My route took us north about twelve miles through Pleasant Valley toward Reno, then west up the steep, winding Mount Rose Highway to the 8,900 foot summit between Mount Rose and Slide

Mountain—an elevation gain of about 4,400 feet in eleven miles. After a brief pause at the summit to take in the spectacular view of Reno and the Truckee Meadows, we headed down to Crystal Bay on the north shore of Tahoe.

While descending to lake level, we made another vista stop overlooking the Tahoe Basin. The questions started to come fast and furiously.

Patti: "What a magnificent panorama! How big is the lake, Bill?"

Bill: "About twenty-two miles long and twelve miles wide."

Anne Marie: "It's so blue! How deep is it?"

Bill: "Around 900 feet on average but 1,600 feet in the deepest areas. The blue you see is a reflection of the sky."

Janet: "Is there an outlet for all that water?"

Bill: "Yes, over in Tahoe City," I replied, pointing west. "That's the start of the Truckee River, which runs through Reno, then north all the way to Pyramid Lake."

When we were back in the wagon and headed down to the Cal-Neva, Cindy asked, "How did the lake get its name?"

"It's interesting that you should ask, Cindy, because I was reading about that just the other day. It's a long and controversial story, but I'll try to keep it short. The simplest and most logical explanation is that Spanish explorers discovered the lake in the early 1800s, and gave it the Spanish name 'Tajo'—pronounced 'Ta-ho.' It means 'a deep chasm filled with water.'

"But the lake had several names before it finally became Tahoe. In the 1840s, Captain John Frémont named it Lake Bonpland after the French botanist-explorer Jacques Bonpland. A decade later California's surveyor general named it Lake Bigler after the state's third governor, John Bigler. It took seventy-five years for the California legislature to officially recognize the name 'Lake Tahoe.'"

During the rest of our drive along the picturesque north shore of Lake Tahoe, I described the Cal-Neva Lodge.

"The Cal-Neva Lodge is built on the Nevada-California border at Crystal Bay. The Lodge is well-known for its top flight entertainment and for attracting wealthy people—just like you—who are seeking a Nevada divorce. Celebrity types like the Lodge and Tahoe because they have a better chance of avoiding the press. They usually stay in the cottages surrounding the Lodge.

"The old-timers of Tahoe speak with real sentiment about the days when they dressed for dinner and a show at the Cal-Neva. One old-timer told me he remembers his mother and father in the '30s going to the Cal-Neva, and his father was always in black-tie.

"A word of advice. Lots of folk have lost small fortunes here, especially during the days of the hoods during Prohibition. An old-timer in the area told me that a carpenter friend of his did some work at the Cal-Neva in the '30s. The work called for removing and demolishing some roulette tables. The carpenter said he never saw so many wires running through table legs in his life. The roulette games were totally wired!"

As we approached the Lodge, my passengers "oohed and aahed" at the dramatic structure built of logs and immense granite rocks. I dropped the ladies at the entrance and, after finding the parking lot full, left the car with the parking attendant. The guests continued "oohing and aahing" as they entered the rustic Lodge. On one side of the room was a massive stone fireplace flanked by boulders. On the other side were wall-to-wall windows with a spectacular view of "the most beautiful lake in the world."

We spotted Allie and her group, Ava Gardner, Tom Waring and Carol Robbins, at one of the "21" tables in the casino area. There must have been at least a dozen spectators standing behind the players hoping to see Ava up close. She looked

Cal-Neva Lodge, circa 1936.
(Images of Lake Tahoe, Courtesy of Special Collections Department, University of Nevada, Reno Library)

Cal-Neva Lodge gaming room, circa 1938
(Images of Lake Tahoe, Courtesy of Special Collections Department, University of Nevada, Reno Library)

*Historic Indian
Room in the 1930s,
Cal-Neva Lodge*
(Courtesy Cal-Neva Resort)

especially ravishing wearing a simple man's white shirt, unbuttoned just enough to expose a modest view of cleavage.

Cindy announced she was buying, so I agreed to a bourbon and water. As the driver, I limited myself to two drinks when I had "the duty." That was Emmy's rule. My second drink would be during dinner and the show.

Around half-past seven, Allie, Ava, Tom, and Carol tore themselves away from the "21" table and joined us, as we made our way into the Indian Room for dinner and Sinatra. As we waited to be seated, Allie said, "It's a good thing Emmy has VIP pull. She made our reservations yesterday, and it looks like a sellout crowd to me." We were seated at a great table not far from the stage, next to a man-made waterfall that splashed down over some rocks into a trout-filled pool.

Allie pointed out the giant map of Tahoe painted on the dance floor. It was bisected down the middle by the California-Nevada Stateline. "Couples can dance in both states. The game is to shout 'Jiggers, the judge!' and watch the divorcées scramble back to the Nevada side!"

I added my two cents worth to Allie's story. "According to one source, the game originated long ago when there used to be an elderly judge in Reno who, liking his liquor, frequently visited the Lodge just to watch the fun. Sometimes on arriving he would call, 'Jiggers, the judge!'"

We had the usual lively conversations over dinner but I was struck by one thing. Ava never once tried to dominate the conversation in spite of her celebrity status. In fact, she was very reserved, almost shy.

Dinner was excellent and the show terrific. It was my first time to see Sinatra live and he didn't disappoint. I had always thought of him as a teenager's idol, but from that night on I was a big fan.

Ava and Frank Connect

After the show, Sinatra headed straight for our table to say hello to Ava. It was obvious they had met before. A reporter suggested that Sinatra was in Reno taking advantage of the Mapes Hotel's special rates for six-week residence. "Heaven's sake, no! I'm still happily married, and we are never going to be divorced," Frank was quoted as saying in the *Reno Reporter* (August 4, 1949), referring to his wife, Nancy. "I'm in Reno because it's a lot of fun." (It would be another two years before Frank and Ava would begin their tempestuous romance. Sinatra would divorce his first wife Nancy and marry Ava Gardner in 1957.)

Ava introduced Frank to each of us and then excused herself to dance with him. He brought her back to the table and excused himself and left the club. Ava, with her quiet composure, fielded a number of questions about Frank, some serious,

some witty. No one could throw her a curve.

It was getting late, but several guests wanted to try their luck in the casino, so the rest of us waited for them in the Circle Bar. Many six-week visitors love to gamble, anytime, anywhere. As one guest put it, "Gambling was a time-killing, life-saving distraction for me during a very trying time in my life." Of course, there were plenty of others for whom cards, dice and chips, and the sound of the whirling roulette wheel held no fascination. We left the Cal-Neva about one a.m. and caravanned to the ranch via Spooner Summit.

A couple of days later I noticed Ava's convertible was gone. One morning, she thanked Emmy and Allie for a relaxing stay and off she drove—probably back to Hollywood. I would see Ava again when I took her and Clark Gable duck hunting near Walley's Hot Springs. Meantime, we all agreed—our night out at the Cal-Neva Lodge had been a starry night to remember.

Frank Sinatra with Ava Gardner
(Courtesy Cal-Neva Resort)

Cal-Neva, poolside, 1950 (Courtesy Cal-Neva Resort)

History of the Cal-Neva

The original lodge at Crystal Bay, Lake Tahoe, was built in 1926 by Robert Sherman, a wealthy San Franciscan. He named it Cal-Neva Lodge and used it to entertain his friends and real estate clients. The rustic Lodge was patterned after the log cabin in the hit Broadway play, *Lightnin'*. The play was written on the site of the famous resort. The storyline was about a couple who owned and operated a hotel which straddled the California-Nevada state line. The location was exploited to drum up business, mostly among divorcées who could check into the hotel to establish Nevada residency without leaving California. The play opened on Broadway in 1918, and was a smash hit and was, for

several decades, one of Broadway's longest-running plays. The 1930 film version of *Lightnin'* starred Will Rogers, Louise Dresser and Joel McCrea. References to the play and the film were used to great advantage in Cal-Neva's publicity.

In 1928, the Lodge was acquired by Norman Biltz, later dubbed "The Duke of Nevada" by *Fortune* magazine. No one really knows how Biltz and Sherman became involved, except that Sherman deeded the property to Biltz for real estate commissions owed him.

In 1931, Biltz worked with several other Nevadans on a plan to populate the state with about seventy-five millionaires who had managed to survive the crash of '29. The incentive was that Governor Fred Balzar would promise they would escape the state income taxes, gift taxes and inheritance taxes they faced in California and other states. At least eighty millionaires, including Max Fleischmann (heir to a yeast fortune), E. L. Cord (creator of a famous automobile), the family of newspaper publisher E. W. Scripps, and Cornelius Vanderbilt III made the move to Nevada. Biltz and the others were not doing this entirely as a public service. Along the way Biltz himself became a multi-millionaire.[1]

During the Prohibition years, the Cal-Neva Lodge bar was an uproarious rendezvous, one of the most stylish speakeasies in the West. The Lodge quickly became the playground for celebrities and socialites who wanted to escape from the public eye. The Lodge earned the nickname "Lady of the Lake," weathering a succession of owners, remodelings and heavy snowfalls.

Big-name entertainment in the '30s included Sophie Tucker, Tallulah Bankhead, Spike Jones, and Xavier Cugat.

Other gaming clubs, some palatial, some small, sprang up in the 1930s on the Nevada side of the North Shore. One was the Crystal Bay Lodge, also built by Biltz. However, the Cal-Neva Lodge remained the largest gambling house at Lake Tahoe.

Graham and McKay. In the 1920s, serious gamblers Bill Graham and James "Cinch" McKay came to Reno and were soon involved in a number of illegal businesses. Included among these were the Willows, the Cal-Neva Lodge at Lake Tahoe, the Bank Club, the Miner's Club, and the "Stockade," the latter an area of prostitution located just a few blocks from downtown Reno.

During the McKay-Graham ownership, the Cal-Neva Lodge was one of several hideaways for gangsters like "Baby Face" Nelson and "Pretty Boy" Floyd, who took sanctuary in the surrounding cottages.

In 1931, when gaming became legal, Graham and McKay simply opened their Nevada businesses to the public. They had already been in operation illegally for years, so it was easy for them to get into action. Their Bank Club on Center Street in Reno was the premier gambling casino in the early 1930s and was considered the largest casino in the world for many years.

McKay was especially interested in sports and horse racing, and was active in promoting professional boxing matches in Reno. McKay and Graham were also involved with Jack Dempsey, former heavyweight boxing champion, in promoting horse races at the old Reno Race Track, now the Washoe County Fairgrounds, on North Wells Avenue.

In 1934, McKay and Graham were arrested for mail fraud. The subsequent disappearance of a key witness for the prosecution, Roy Frisch, and the three-week trial generated nationwide headlines. The trial resulted in a hung jury. Another trial, held in 1935, also resulted in a hung jury. It wasn't until a third trial, held in January and February 1938, that McKay and Graham were convicted, sentenced to nine years in a federal prison and fined $11,000. After numerous delays and appeals, Graham and McKay entered Leavenworth Prison in November 1939. They remained there until their release in October 1945. They had served just under six years. In 1950, Nevada senator Pat McCarran interceded with President Harry Truman, and Graham and McKay were both given full pardons.

Shortly after their return to Reno, they were once again active in the Bank Club. In 1950, they bought back from Jack Sullivan the one-third percentage of the Bank Club that they had sold him before they went to prison. In 1952, James McKay's and Bill Graham's partnership in the Bank Club was dissolved. [2]

The Sinatra Years, 1960-63. During Frank Sinatra's ownership, he and his associates built the now famous Celebrity Showroom. They also installed a helicopter pad on the roof to make access easier for their colleagues and guests appearing at the Cal-Neva during summer months.

Hollywood followers were enamored with Sinatra and the "Rat Pack," an unforgettable fraternity that linked itself with the White House through Peter Lawford, brother-in-law of then President-elect John F. Kennedy. Dean Martin and Sammy Davis Jr., among others, "sang for their supper" in the Celebrity

Gambling at the Willows, circa 1930s. (Courtesy Neal Cobb Collection)

Chuk-a-Luck   Reno, Nevada

with the Nevada Gaming Control Board, he voluntarily gave up all his interests in Nevada casinos, which also included interests in the Sands and Desert Inn in Las Vegas. He was still allowed to perform in Nevada, but it was not until 1981 that he managed to obtain a new gaming license.

Cal-Neva Resort Today. The "Lady of the Lake" had suffered from neglect for nearly twenty years before she was purchased in December 1985 and given another chance by present owner, Charles P. Bluth, a prominent real estate developer from Southern California.

The Cal-Neva Resort is now a full-service, year-round destination resort featuring 200 lake-view rooms, cabins, and chalets, and a complete casino.

Frank Sinatra and Bert "Wingy" Grover entertained Marilyn Monroe at the Cal-Neva Lodge.
(Photo Don Dondero, Courtesy Cal-Neva Resort)

The Rat Pack at Cal-Neva Resort
(Courtesy Cal-Neva Resort)

Showroom and the Indian Room, while politicians and Hollywood stars played at the tables and in the private cottages overlooking Lake Tahoe. Marilyn Monroe was a frequent guest of the Lodge, and scandal generally surrounded her because of the "alleged" secret rendezvous with John F. Kennedy.

When the presence of one particular guest, Sam Giancana of Chicago, was noticed by authorities, it finally cost Sinatra his gaming license. In a losing battle

Ella Broderick, the first woman roulette operator in Nevada (Photo Noreen I. K. Humphreys)

CHAPTER 18

Gamblers – Before and After

Sis Brings a Spare

"Sis" Black was the epitome of a classy New York socialite. She attended fancy private schools, made a splashy début in society, and moved about with an air of confidence and finger-pointing authority. Now in her thirties, Sis was attractive, slim and blond, wearing her hair in a casual over-one-eye style like Veronica Lake.

Sis was getting a Reno divorce and, to keep her company during her six weeks, she brought "a spare," the Reno divorce term for the man or woman with whom the plaintiff is living and whom the plaintiff intends to marry when the decree is granted.

Sis' spare was Reese Harris, or "Reese Boy" as Sis called him. Reese had proper parentage, too, but little money. He was learning to gamble —with Sis' money.

According to one guest, "This crowd used nicknames a lot. The names were like passwords. If you were given one, you were 'in;' without one, you were 'out.'"

There was much banter among the guests about Sis' relationship with Reese Boy. Would she marry him when she got her divorce? Couldn't she do better—especially with her money? Does her husband know about Reese?

Of all the guests I met at the Flying M E, Sis

was the closest to a snob. As another guest put it, "She was a hard one to run into on your first day. She could look you right in the eye without saying hello."

Sis and Reese were night owls and late risers. They had a set routine. After lunch they would spend the afternoons at the pool sunbathing and reading. After dinner they would go into Carson City for gambling. When it was time to leave, without fail, Reese would beg everyone, "Wait just a little longer so I can get even." Rarely would it be, "You don't want me to quit now when I'm on a hot streak, do you?"

• • •

One night Emmy and Allie took everyone who wanted to go, up to Virginia City for dinner at the famous Bonanza Inn. Sis and Reese opted not to go, so I was elected to take them into Carson. One of my regular riders, Patti Allen (not her real name), decided at the last minute to go into Carson, too.

As we entered the Old Corner Bar, Mike Demas greeted us from behind the crap table. Patti, Sis and I watched Reese roll the dice a few times. Then Patti and I moved to the bar.

As a regular rider, I knew quite a bit about

Before.....

After !

Gambling, Before...After! Sis Black with her spare, "Reese Boy" Harris at the Old Corner.
(Caricature by Joan Allison)

Patti. She was a beautiful woman, pushing forty, with classic aristocratic features, a straight nose and high cheekbones. Her light brown hair, thick and shining, fell to her shoulders. She wore tan frontier pants and a black western shirt with a silver concha belt. She was perfectly groomed in every way.

Patti was a professional woman, an attorney with a major firm in New York City, and was divorcing her lawyer husband of eighteen years on grounds of infidelity.

I felt Patti's eyes on me when we went to see Sinatra at the Cal-Neva. As we sipped our drinks at the Old Corner, I felt her leg brush against mine ever so gently. I pressed back as I looked into her eyes and knew at once she was sending me a subtle signal. We were mutually attracted to each other and the attraction was now simmering.

"Would you like to take a walk, Patti? Sis and Reese will be here for hours."

"Sure, Bill. Maybe we could take in the movie across the street."

After confirming our gamblers weren't going anywhere for a few hours, Patti and I left the bar and crossed the street to the theatre. We ruled out the movie that was playing. We continued walking up Carson Street for two or three blocks, then stopped in front of a small motel.

"What do you think, Patti?" I asked. "Are you tired?"

"Not really," she answered as she reached for my hand. "Never too tired for what you and I have in mind—and it's not another drink."

As we checked in, Patti leaned over and brushed her tongue across my ear. "I'm not sure I can wait," she whispered. Then she teased me with her hand.

At the door to the room, I leaned over and kissed her gently. "Would you like to come in?"

"Just as badly as you want me to," she whispered playfully.

I opened the door, gently pushed her inside and closed the door. The room was dark. Patti leaned against the wall as I pressed against her. I felt her breathing quicken and her body pulsate with eagerness. As I kissed the back of her neck, I slipped my hand around her waist and into her pants.

"Bill," Patti whispered, "I want you." Then she smothered me with her moist lips.

As we struggled out of our clothes, our kissing grew more desperate. "Christ, you're beautiful," I muttered.

With that, she pushed me onto the bed and crouched on top of me. "I want you now, cowboy. Don't you dare make me wait another second."

Afterwards, I was surprised when she began to sob quietly.

"What's wrong, cowgirl?" I asked, as I took her back into my arms.

"Oh, nothing's wrong, my dear," she whispered. "I guess it's just been so long since I felt like this. I'm weeping for joy, I guess. Does that make sense, Bill?"

"I was afraid you weren't satisfied."

"Nothing could be further from the truth," she assured me as she climbed back aboard for an encore performance.

By the time we got back to the Old Corner Bar it was after midnight, but no one seemed to have missed us. Reese and Sis had moved over to a "21" table and were in no rush to leave, so Patti and I had a drink.

Because we had such a great time together, I decided I'd better explain how I had violated Emmy's "no fraternization" rule and that we might not be able to get together again, at least not out in the open. She was disappointed but reluctantly agreed it made sense.

"But don't worry, Patti, you're always welcome for a late night rendezvous at this cowboy's bunkhouse," I said, knowing I was heading straight for trouble if I wasn't careful.

Joan Allison Borg, Flying M E guest, and Bill McGee saddled up for a ride. "You'll be perfectly safe, dear, on horseback with Bill McGee," assured Emmy Wood. (Authors' Collection)

The Summer of '48

You'll be Perfectly Safe on Horseback with Bill McGee

During the summer of '48, the Flying M E was booked solid. The cast of characters was a little different than usual, because there were a variety of age groups. There was the typical age group of thirty-, forty- and fifty-somethings doing their time for a divorce. There were three women my age (early twenties) awaiting divorces. (One of them would become my first wife.) Then there were the college kids.

The Ghost of the M E.

When Allie and I met Carol Greenley at the Reno train depot, it took both the "Woody" and the convertible to transport all her luggage to the ranch. She had steamer trunks, hat boxes, makeup cases, and what looked like a portable bar. Mrs. Greenley was from England and had come "out West" for a dude ranch vacation. She was treating her college-age son and a classmate to

The Ghost of the Flying M E
(Caricature by Joan Allison)

join her during their summer vacation. They were driving cross-country from Princeton in the son's new Frazer Manhattan.

Emmy, Allie and I were looking forward to showing our British guests the sights. Emmy and Allie would take her sightseeing and gambling, and I, of course, would take her riding.

As it turned out, Mrs. Greenley had other ways of spending her time. What we thought was a portable bar was a silver tea service—with China cups and saucers, silver spoons and a variety of teas. She drank tea continuously, all day and all night. During the day, she held court in her room and invited the other guests to stop in for a cup of tea and a chat. During the night, she wandered around the ranch house with her tea cup in hand. This habit earned her the nickname, "The Ghost of the M E."

Mrs. Greenley rarely dressed to go out and spent her days in dressing gowns and peignoir sets. She never unpacked her trunks, leaving them open to display rows of gowns, cosmetic jars and make up. While most guests opted to wear little make up and get a tan, Mrs. Greenley packed hers on heavily.

Little Audrey, the young and perky maid who was working her way through her six weeks, loved her special assignment of preparing Mrs. Greenley's tea trays. Audrey took her assignment very seriously and was seen studying magazines like Town & Country to see how a proper tea tray should look. This special effort pleased Mrs. Greenley very much, and she thanked Audrey with gifts of English beauty creams and French lotions.

The College Boys. Mrs. Greenley's son, Colin, was a nice-looking, charismatic, young man with the good manners one expects from an English-bred gentleman. His love of the moment was his new car. Why a Frazer Manhattan was anyone's guess. He was always working on it or talking on the phone to the Kaiser-Frazer dealer in Reno. At Emmy's request, I finally had to ask him to please take it

into Carson City to work on it. "It makes the driveway look like an auto repair shop lot," she opined.

Bud Henry, Colin's Princeton classmate, was a jovial jock-type with a blond crew-cut and a stout muscular frame. He was into sports —and shorts—at all times except for dinner.

My Age Group. Now for the ladies in my age group. Dee Allen was from Newport, Rhode Island and flew in from Providence. Flying cross-country was still new and considered adventurous, not to mention expensive. Dee was tall, a little tomboyish, and dressed like what we would call today "Preppy" —complete with the strand of Tiffany pearls. She didn't act like the debutantes or rich girls from Newport that had been to the ranch before. I thought Dee was very nice.

Ruth Gordon arrived by train from Cleveland, Ohio with her mother in tow. They were inseparable the entire six weeks. "Very Midwestern," was the catty guests' verdict for Ruth. Colin, Bud and I tried to get Ruth away from her mother to participate in ranch activities, but we had no luck.

Then there was Joan Allison Borg, who also arrived by train from Englewood, New Jersey.

The Social Asset

Colin Greenley's 'Geyser' Frazer   (Caricatures by Joan Allison)

Joan's mother, Lucy Dodsworth Allison, had been at the ranch—albeit for only two weeks—to get a divorce from Joan's father. So when Joan needed a divorce, Lucy called Emmy to make the arrangements. Emmy made a special point of welcoming Joan and met her at the train as if she was one of the family. It was a court witness day for Emmy, so she was dressed in a suit, hat and gloves. This was Joan's first trip "out West," and it surprised her to see someone "dressed up."

Being "family" had its advantages and disadvantages, as Joan recalls:

> Upon my arrival, I was assigned to the downstairs corner room. It was more luxurious than the others with its own entrance, private bath and brick fireplace. The knotty pine walls were washed pale yellow. It was a warm and charming place. It was usually reserved for "special" guests who were willing to pay "special" rates. I was not in that category.
>
> As new faces kept appearing at the ranch, one day, in her refined and kindly manner, Emmy took me aside and asked if I would mind moving to the other end of the ranch house as there was a shortage of rooms? Or would I mind taking one of the twin beds in her room while Allie was away? So I moved to Emmy's cozy, combination bedroom/office. I was able to observe some of the behind-the-scenes workings of the ranch.
>
> That happened two or three times. Of course, if a guest was willing to pay extra for a private room, it could usually be arranged and guaranteed.

Trail Rides. The energy level and constant demand for activities by the younger group was a welcome change for me. We had daily morning trail rides and/or horseback picnics, afternoon sightseeing trips, plus evening jack rabbit shoots. A

Sierra pack trip was tentatively planned.

Colin and Bud were a cut above novice riders, but Dee and Joan were rank beginners. Joan still remembers her first ride:

> As I recall, Emmy encouraged me to try riding. I was terrified of horses, always had been, and still am. But Emmy sensed I was terribly unhappy and homesick. She insisted I would be "perfectly safe on horseback with Bill McGee as a guide." So to please Emmy, I said okay.
>
> The trail Bill took me on had a brook that had to be crossed. The horses would make a small jump. I was frozen with fear. But I did it! We went this way more than a few times and, even though I'd been warned, one time a

Joan Allison Borg and Bill McGee. (Authors' Collection)

"Where d'ya say that screen was, Bud?"

The boys of summer '48: Bud Henry and Colin Greenley, earning their "pilot's license."
(Caricature by Joan Allison)

branch knocked me off Little Joe's back. I pretended I was getting to like riding. I even went into town with Emmy and some of the guests to buy Western wear at Parker's. Instead of the baggy jeans from New Jersey I'd been wearing, I came back with slim-fitting riding pants and a pair of two-toned, brown cowboy boots. Finally, I was "in." I even began forgetting to count the days.

Pilot's License. Before and after each trail ride, the saddle horses would be tethered to the paddock fence while they were being groomed and saddled or unsaddled. Of course, this routine resulted in the almost daily dropping of "road apples" in the white gravel driveway area. Naturally, if Colin and Bud were around, I wanted them to help with the clean-up, and in no time at all they earned their "pilot's license"—learning to "pile it here, pile it there."

Jack Rabbit and Coyote Shoot. In the 1940s,

the eastern side of Big Washoe Lake was the home of hundreds of coyotes and thousands of jack rabbits, the latter having long ears and long hind legs. They were not the kind of rabbits you eat, like cottontails.

In the summer months, when the days were long, we would drive around the lake in the evening in the pickup. On the far side of the lake, there was an old gravel road, but not a house in sight. One of us drove the truck, while the others in the back took turns shooting the .22 rifle. It was a sport that was both innocent and fun.

Mostly we shot jack rabbits, but once in awhile someone got a shot off at a coyote. This kind of hunting, I'm told, is now illegal. Back then, the cattlemen encouraged it because they never had enough grass for their livestock.

Joan Allison Borg's 21st Birthday. Colin and Bud surprised Joan with a birthday gift in mid-August. Joan:

Those fellows gave me a silver and jade

bracelet for my twenty-first birthday. It matched my green dress. The dress was bare-shouldered with thin straps and a little jacket that matched.

Colin sort of courted me. He had a terrible crush, but I was a year older than he. I didn't know that younger guys ever went for "older women."

As I recall, Colin and Bud also sang me a song on my birthday. It went something like, "She was only a Borg in a gilded cage." My first husband was Eddie Borg. The real song, of course, was "You were only a bird in a gilded cage."

I was only a year older than Joan and maybe two years older than Colin and Bud, but at the time, they thought I was much older. Four years fighting a war can do that to you.

French Nude. Danielle Masiere (not her real name) created quite a stir among both guests and staff the day she first disrobed and went skinny dipping in the pool. Danielle was quite beautiful with a sexy, French accent. Emmy, who was closed-mouthed about the guests' ages, hinted that she may be in her mid-thirties. But she looked ten years younger. Her dark hair was short and chic and she dressed very stylishly.

Tom Waring, our only male guest at the time, gave me a full report. "Every morning, without fail, Danielle strolls to the pool about eleven o'clock in her robe with only a towel underneath. She faces south, away from the ranch house, to disrobe, then dives into the pool. After several laps, she gets out of the pool and casually climbs the steps to the top of the pool house. Judiciously, she drapes her towel over the railing in consideration of us other guests and then she lies down to sunbathe—nude, of course!"

I overheard two women discussing Danielle's delightful routine:

"She uses a depilatory while taking a sunbath."

"I know. I saw her white creamy mustache as she lay there with her eyes closed. She must have a lot of hair on her upper lip."

Colin and Bud swapped more than one morning ride for a swim. Word of our French nude must have spread like wildfire, because we had more neighbors than usual visit the ranch during her six week stay.

Bunkhouse Rendezvous. During a trail ride, Patti Allen got me aside to request a private audience around nine that evening. I confirmed it on the spot.

When she arrived that night, we made passionate, violent love; so violent, in fact, that she pounded her fists on my shoulders as she climaxed.

"Jesus, Patti, that hurts," I protested.

"Sorry, darling, I didn't mean to hurt you, but it felt so good it hurt me, too."

Patti was very beautiful and very desirable. It was hard to believe she was almost forty. The sight of her, the scent of her and the sound of her excited me. She transmitted sexuality like a beacon.

The more we talked, the more I understood that to her, sex was about power.

"I need and want to dominate," she said. "Does that shock you? Most men seem to enjoy it."

I didn't say anything.

"With you, Bill, I don't feel the need to dominate. It's different. I don't know why. Oh, just love me, cowboy," she said as we began another round.

Later when we were resting, Patti gave me a tender kiss and said, "Bill, I've said it before and I'll say it again. You're a delicious lover."

"That goes double for you, my little city slicker."

And so went the Summer of '48.

Clark Gable liked hunting, fishing, horses, gambling, fast cars, drinking, and women—not necessarily in that order. (© Eve Arnold/Magnum Photos)

CHAPTER 20

Clark Gable

Clark Gable at the Flying M E

I got to know Clark Gable from his frequent visits to the Flying M E in the late '40s. He'd stop by just to say hello to Emmy and have a drink, or perhaps stay for a few days of rest and relaxation. He liked Emmy and felt comfortable at the ranch. He knew that Emmy and the ranch staff would guard his privacy and never leak his visits to reporters.

The "King" was a big star then and admired by both men and women. Women loved him for the obvious reasons. Men liked him because, in spite of his celebrity status, he remained a man's man. He liked hunting, fishing, horses, gambling, fast cars, drinking, and women—not necessarily in that order. I remember him as always arriving at the ranch in some sporty automobile, which he took pleasure in washing each morning in the driveway.

Emmy and the ranch staff adored Clark for his down-to-earth friendliness, good manners and lack of airs. During cocktail hour, he enjoyed "waiting"

Emmy Wood and Clark Gable at the Flying M E (Authors' Collection)

on the guests, shaking their martinis or manhattans at the bar.

Clark Gable met Ava Gardner in 1947, when they worked together for the first time making *The Hucksters* at MGM. Like Clark, Ava enjoyed coming to the ranch for some relaxation and privacy. One time, the three of us drove to Genoa in Clark's Caddie convertible—with Ava seated between us. As you know from the chapter on the Cal-Neva Lodge, I had a big crush on Ava Gardner. When the three of us arrived in Genoa, we tied up the Caddie in front of the Genoa Bar, the oldest bar in Nevada. Inside, we tethered ourselves to three bar stools and ordered drinks and sandwiches. Clark and Ava created quite a stir, and the three of us were photographed at the bar. I think some of the bar patrons were wondering who I was.

Clark and I went riding together several times, and though he didn't talk about it, he still bore the sadness from the tragic death of his beloved wife, Carole Lombard, in 1942. (Carole Lombard and her mother were flying home from Indiana where the star was helping to launch a national campaign to sell war bonds. Their plane crashed just minutes after taking off in Las Vegas. There were no survivors.) In December 1949, he would marry a Lady Sylvia Ashley, but their marriage lasted less than eighteen months. Their divorce provided Gable with legal reasons to come to Nevada, where he established residency at Glenbrook.

During my years at the Flying M E, Clark made several movies for MGM including *Homecoming* (1948), *Command Decision* (1948), *Any Number*

The Making of THE MISFITS

A lot has been written about the filming of *The Misfits*—the drama and tragedy surrounding its stars Marilyn Monroe, Clark Gable and Montgomery Clift. Although the film was made after my time at the ranch, there are a few background points of particular interest I'd like to share.

The origin of the story itself is interesting. The noted writer and journalist A. J. Liebling came to Nevada in 1949 to get a divorce and stayed at Pyramid Lake Ranch. While there, he became so interested in the various issues surrounding the Paiute Indians and their reservation lands that he returned in 1953 with his second wife, Lucille, to do further research for a series of articles he was writing about these issues. Joe and Lucille were invited to go on a roundup of wild horses on the Smoke Creek Desert, north of Pyramid Lake. The wild horses—or mustangs—were being rounded up and captured for slaughter for dog food. Liebling wrote about how the cowboys herded the mustangs by airplane, then captured them with a rope tied to a tire and let the horses run until they became exhausted. His two-part series, "The Mustang Buzzers," appeared in *The New Yorker* on April 3 and 10, 1954. Part two ends with a dramatic description of the capture of a wild stallion who nearly escapes and of Lucille's unsuccessful plea to save his life.

In his autobiography, *Timebends: A Life,* Arthur Miller describes the origins of *The Misfits*. The theme first appeared as a short story published in *Esquire* in October 1957. It was written after Miller spent time in Nevada in 1956, while waiting for a divorce so he could marry Marilyn Monroe. Like Liebling, he also stayed at Pyramid Lake Ranch. The Nevada desert provided him with the figures who were to be the heroes of his story: cowboys rather adrift in the modern world, free-spirited men who lived an outdoor life, making a living by catching wild horses they would then sell to be made into dog

Arthur Miller (Courtesy of Special Collections Department, University of Nevada, Reno Library)

food. He was interested in the way they lived on the margins of society. One day, two of the cowboys invited him to join their hunt for wild horses. Miller studied these men closely as they used their lariats to rope a horse from the back of a truck. The other end of the lariat would be tied to a large tire so it was only a matter of time until the horse became exhausted from dragging the tire, allowing the cowboys to capture him.

In the short story, three male characters dominate: Guido, the pilot; Gay Langland, the hunter of wild horses; and Perce Howland, a young rodeo rider. Roslyn, the female character, hardly appears.

In 1960, when the short story became the basis for the screenplay, *The Misfits,* Miller greatly expanded the part of Roslyn for his new wife, Marilyn Monroe, so she could show her gift for serious drama.

Can Play (1949), *Key to the City* (1950), and *To Please a Lady* (1950).

The last time I saw Clark Gable was in September 1960. I was in Nevada on a business trip and stopped by the ranch to say hello to Emmy. I knocked on the door and who should answer but "the King" himself. He was on a break from shooting *The Misfits* and had come to the ranch for some privacy.

The film was released in 1961, and among Monroe's many dramatic scenes is the final, heartrending scene where Roslyn dramatically protests the capture of the wild mustangs.

In 1963, Lucille Liebling reportedly told some friends, "Arthur Miller's screenplay for the film was really 'my story.'"

• • •

When Gable first saw the script for *The Misfits*, he told Miller, "It's supposed to be a Western, but it's not a Western." The playwright found a definition that settled the question: "It's a sort of Eastern Western." To Miller, while the story was set in the West, it was a story about the indifference he had been feeling not only in Nevada, but in the world at that time.

• • •

The Misfits was shot in various locations around northern Nevada: Reno (Harrah's Club, the Courthouse), Quail Canyon Ranch (for Guido's ranch), Dayton (for the rodeo scene), and Pyramid Lake (for the capture of the mustangs).

The Quail Canyon Ranch, in north Washoe County on the old Pyramid Lake highway, was owned by a Mrs. Adine Haviland Stix who rented the ranch to the film company. This location was the very ranch where in 1956 Miller had met a young woman who had come from the East to get a divorce, as well as the two cowboys who inspired the story of *The Misfits*.

One day, there was no shooting, and Gable was absent from the set. So Mrs. Stix cooked dinner for Marilyn and others of the cast and production crew that were around. She added lots of garlic, which Marilyn liked and Clark didn't. Just as they were finishing dinner, in walked Gable. He took one sniff and walked out again. According to Mrs. Stix, Clark hardly spoke to her after that. Later on, she learned that it was not her garlic-flavored dinner that had bothered him. He had just returned from a visit with his doctor and knew he had just suffered a mild heart attack.

• • •

The Misfits turned out to be Gable's and Monroe's last film. Clark Gable died of a heart attack on November 16, 1960, at age 59, just twelve days after shooting the final sequences in Los Angeles. He never saw the final version of the film. Marilyn Monroe separated from Arthur Miller. She died in mysterious circumstances that have still not been fully explained, on August 5, 1962, at age 36. Montgomery Clift would make three more movies, including the acclaimed *Judgment at Nuremberg*, and suffer a fatal heart attack on July 23, 1966, at age 45.

In Miller's words, "*The Misfits* has been Clark Gable's elegy. He and Gay Langland are now one and the same person; I no longer know where one ends and the other begins."

About the film, Miller said, "It's both sad and happy. What's very sad, is that I had written it to make Marilyn feel good. And for her, it resulted in complete collapse. But at the same time, I am glad it was done, because her dream was to be a serious actress."[1]

• • •

There are still plenty of hard-working cowboys in the West who do the work because they love it, not because they're getting rich. The only difference: They may ride the range in a Jeep for some jobs, terrain permitting, and they might wear a baseball cap in windy or sweaty conditions to save wear and tear on their cowboy hats. But for cowboy work like moving cattle, roundups and branding, only a good horse will do.

Gus Bundy first made his mark in photography in 1951. While driving a truck in the Nevada desert for a Life magazine photographer, Bundy was able to snap some 300 photos of wild horses being rounded up by hunters using trucks and airplanes. The Life magazine photographer was prevented from completing his assignment by the hunters, but Bundy's photos became the focus of a national effort to protect these wild herds. The photos are regarded as a principal reason that legislation was eventually secured in 1959.

(Wild horses series from the Bundy Collection, Courtesy of Special Collections Department, University of Nevada, Reno Library; Bundy photo: Courtesy Tina Bundy Nappe)

Scouting the trail (Authors' Collection)

CHAPTER 21

Sierra Pack Trip

Bill, What's on the Other Side of that Ridge?

One July morning, on a loop ride up in the Sierras, we stopped on the ridge overlooking Little Valley and the high Sierra sweeps in the distance. Colin Greenley asked, "What's on the other side of that ridge across the valley?"

"Well, due west of us, about three miles as the crow flies, is Lake Tahoe. Just beyond that tallest mountain to the south of us is Marlette Lake, the primary source of Virginia City's water supply," I answered.

"Can't we keep going, Bill, so we can see for ourselves?" asked the beautiful Patti Allen.

"Sorry, folks, that's more than we can tackle in one day. We need at least three days to go in there and have time to ride around some. That means two nights in a trail camp. If you're still interested when we get back to the ranch, we'll make some plans to do it."

I stressed the importance of planning and preparation for a successful pack trip. "It calls for a step-by-step plan that needs to be organized and executed much like a small military operation. The more planning, the more likely it will be a smooth and enjoyable experience for all concerned."

Planning and Preparation for a Successful Pack Trip. That night after dinner, I spread out my trail and topo maps on the dining room table, and plans were made for a three day pack trip.

Step #1. This first and most necessary step is to determine who is going, which fixes the number of saddle horses that have to be assigned to the trip and the number of pack horses needed. Joan Allison Borg and Dee Allen gave it some thought, then decided they weren't ready to "rough it." So plans were made for four guests and myself. We would leave in five days.

Pack-trippers and saddle stock:
Anne Marie Baker - Topsy
Colin Greenley - Little Joe
Patti Allen - Alley Oop
Bud Henry - Jeff

It was agreed we would not accept any last minute additions to the group, as it would throw a monkey wrench into our plans.

The composition of the party governs the type and amount of camp gear and equipment and the grub that must be assembled and ready to load on the pack horses.

Step #2. Pack horses must be selected. As a general rule, one good horse can carry the camp equipment and supplies for two people. I picked Half Pint and Bucky to carry the loads.

The packsaddles must be carefully fitted to each horse, with the buckles of the harness for each packsaddle adjusted to each horse.

Step #3. Finalize the "Grub" list. After figuring the number of meals we'll need for the time we'll be out, a shopping list can be created. For our trip, I estimated 10 breakfasts, 15 lunches and 10 dinners. Patti and Bud volunteered to meet with Edie to plan our meals and create a shopping list for Allie or Emmy to purchase when they next go to market. My suggested rations list (see Sidebar) is a little too Spartan for this group of dudes.

Step #4. Assemble all bedding, cooking and miscellaneous camping gear items, using my proven "Wilderness Camping Checklist" (see Sidebar). Everything should be checked off as it is assembled and stacked in the garage stall nearest the tack room.

Step #5. All non-perishables on the Grub list can be assembled in the garage prior to Tuesday, our departure day.

Step #6. Pack poke bags. Each "tripper" is responsible for packing his or her personal items in a poke bag, with a name tag, and bringing it to the assembly point before breakfast on Tuesday morning.

Bill McGee's Wilderness Camping Checklist

Bedding & Tents

Sleeping bag – Foam pad and air mattress – Ground cloth – Tube tent – Tent, fly stakes

Cooking Gear

Backpacking stove, fuel – Matches (waterproof) – Pots, pans (nesting set) – Pot lifter – Grill – Ax – Saw (folding) – Knife, fork, spoon – Plastic water bottles

Grub

Spirits – Breakfast #___ - Lunch #___ - Dinner #___ – Trail snacks* – Salt & Pepper* – Oil (small bottle) – Coffee, tea – Sugar, Pream* – Mustard, ketchup* – plastic bags
*Small individual servings in plastic bags

Miscellaneous

Trail & topo maps – Bag of oats (small) – Camping permit – Compass – Spare horseshoes – Swiss knife – Short-handled shovel – Flashlight (batteries & bulbs) – Toilet paper – Insect repellent Biodegradable soap – Kleenex (small packs) – Band-Aids – Aspirin – Ace bandage – Water tablets – Long food line – Fishing gear, license – Solar shower bag

Clothing/Personal Items

Sunglasses (elastic strap) – Suntan lotion – Chap stick – Toothbrush, toothpaste – Towel – Comb – Camera, film – Jacket – Sweater – Jeans – Shirts – Socks – Underwear – Bandana – Poncho – Hat

Rations List

Suggested minimum rations list for one camper for one day: ¾ lb. of meat: bacon, ham, or equivalent – 1 lb. potatoes – ⅕ lb. dried beans, peas, or ⅛ lb. rice – 1¼ lb. flour or the equivalent in bread – ⅛ lb. coffee – ⅕ lb. sugar.

It is possible to use this as a one-day ration, substituting other foodstuffs for the basic items indicated. This ration list is on the Spartan side for people willing to "rough it."

Step #7. Perishable grub. Bud and Patti have agreed to bring these last minute items to the assembly point.

Step #8. Pack the panniers (the box-like containers draped over the packsaddles) with the food, small cooking utensils and personal poke bags (space permitting). Now we are ready to bring everything together and load it on the pack horses.

Departure Day. I packed the panniers, then went in for some chow. After breakfast, I went over Edie's menu plans for our trip, then tucked them in my pocket. Allie caught up the saddle horses and, with Patti's help, was saddling them as I headed for the tack room.

Patti was the most experienced rider, and Bud, thanks to his Boy Scout training, seemed to be the most knowledgeable camper. So I designated Bud "assistant packer."

"Okay, Half Pint," I said, "age before beauty." I tightened his two packsaddle cinches, then adjusted the breast collar and breeching harness. By this time, we had an audience.

Anne Marie: "What is the purpose of that stuff?" pointing to the harness.

"Well, the breast collar, as this is called," pointing to the collar, "keeps the packsaddle and pack from sliding back when we are going uphill. The breeching harness back here keeps the load from sliding forward when we are on a downgrade.

"Bud, we're ready to put the panniers in place, so will you please get on the other side of Half Pint, so that as I lift the pannier up you can grab the leather loops and fit them down over the crosstrees?"

"Sure, Bill," he said. "Hoist away." With Bud's help, we had both panniers in place in no time.

Next, we put two of the poke bags in the space

Bill McGee loading gear on Half Pint for the backcountry trip. (Authors' Collection)

Headin' out (Drackert Collection, Courtesy of Special Collections Department, University of Nevada, Reno Library)

between the crosstrees and above the panniers.

"That little spot is the most protected place in the pack," I explained to the group.

"Now, Bud, let's place three of the bedrolls on the packsaddle, so that one rides fore and aft on each pannier and one lies in between them. Then we'll cover them with a tarp and secure everything with a lash rope and a diamond hitch. It should hold for hours of hard trail travel, if I tie it right. You should all sleep like babies tonight, because we provide the latest thing in bedrolls: down-filled sleeping bags, air mattresses and foam rubber ground pads, neatly rolled up together. Not long ago, a bedroll was a couple of blankets wrapped up in a tarp."

"That's good to know, but why is the diamond hitch so good, Bill?" Colin asked.

"Good question, Colin. It's because every section of the lash rope pulls against all others. To be perfectly honest, I'm never sure when I 'throw' a diamond hitch that it will do the job. Usually it does, but sometimes it turns out lopsided. Pete Tracey, an old packer I worked with at Tahoe last year, showed me how. But please don't ask me to draw you a diagram!"

After two false starts, I finally secured Half Pint's load with a proper diamond hitch. Then Patti led Half Pint out of the way as Bud moved Bucky, a good-looking buckskin mare with a black mane and tail, into position, and we repeated the packing process. Only this time we put the cooking gear in the space between the saddle trees and lashed the duffel bag of miscellaneous supplies and the remaining two bedrolls above the panniers.

By this time, most of the guests and the ranch staff were out to see us off. After one last check of the saddle horses—cinches tight, halter ropes tied to the near (left) side of the horn, and rolled ponchos tied behind the saddles—we headed for the Little Valley trail head.

The first two-and-a-half miles of the trip followed the now familiar Franktown Creek up to Little Valley. I led with Bucky in tow, followed by Anne Marie, Colin and Patti. Bud and Half Pint brought up the rear. When we stopped to give the horses a breather, Colin asked, "When can we canter?"

"Not until tomorrow," I replied, "when we take a loop ride out from camp. Loaded pack horses can't canter and seldom even trot. Today's trail is much too steep. We've already gained about 1,800 feet. Our objective today is to get this outfit through to our campsite safe and sound, hopefully by mid-afternoon. That reminds me," I added, "a wise packer once wrote, 'It isn't how far you travel on the trail that counts. It's the pleasure per mile and what you find at the end of the trail that counts.'"

I wound up my little talk with this history reminder. "The traditions and routines of pack train travel go way back to the frontier explorers, trappers and mountain men, who had no other method of traversing the wilderness."

We continued along Franktown Creek in a southerly direction through Little Valley for about three miles, then made a lunch stop. "Why don't you tie your horses up to those trees over there, using the halter lead ropes tied to your saddle strings, while I unpack the sandwiches in my saddle bag," I suggested.

"Feels good to stretch the legs," Bud offered, as he led Jeff to the clump of trees.

"You said it," Anne Marie added, as she followed Bud with Topsy.

Edie's sandwiches, a choice of ham and cheese or chicken salad on rye, were a big hit as usual.

"What a perfect day for a ride, Bill," Patti said.

"Sure is, Patti. Seventy-five degrees, I'd guess, with a light breeze and just a few clouds. Doesn't get much better than that. Anyone interested in a local history lesson today?"

"Oh, yes!" was the answer, so I retold my favorite Little Valley story of the logging boom during the Comstock era, followed by the collapse of the dam in 1881, which flooded Franktown.

I brought out my topo maps and showed the group where we were at the moment, then pointed out Twin Lakes, our campsite for two nights. It's less than a mile as the crow flies but more than two miles on the trail, a steep upgrade from about 6,800 feet here to 8,000 feet at Twin Lakes.

After checking cinches and the packsaddle harness, we mounted our trusty steeds and continued south alongside Franktown Creek for a quarter mile, then southwest for a steep half mile climb up one switchback after another.

We were about to head northwest on the last leg of the trail to the campsite, so we gave the horses a blow (a breather); then I suggested we walk a ways leading the horses to stretch our legs.

Setting Up Camp

We rode into our campsite about four p.m., and everyone was eager to help pitch camp. It was a good campsite with plenty of level ground for our sleeping bags, back a ways from the lakes, where the pines were growing in scattered, open stands. There was a mat of pine needles carpeting the ground. We had plenty of water for both riders and horses, grass for the stock and dry wood for our cooking fire.

After dismounting, the saddle horses and the pack horses were kept separate. Patti agreed to keep an eye on the saddle horses. She would see to it that the halter ropes were loosened from the saddle strings and in her hands before the saddles were pulled off and stashed on an old log. The blankets were thrown over the saddles so they could dry out. The bridles were then hung over the saddle pommels.

Meanwhile, Bud and I led Half Pint and Bucky over to the sleeping area and threw off the bedrolls and ditty bags. We then moved to the "supply section" where the food would be stowed and the cooking would take place. The loaded panniers were stowed on two nearby tree stumps.

The packsaddles were then pulled and stowed near the other saddles.

I transferred all the provisions to an old Army

surplus duffel bag. The bacon, cheese and other strong smelling foods had been previously packed in air tight containers by Edie. While I was doing this, Bud and Colin climbed two Jeffrey pines about a hundred feet from camp and strung a heavy-duty line between them about ten feet off the ground. Meanwhile, I attached a separate line to the duffel bag to be tossed over the tree line in order to hoist the provisions well above a black bear's reach.

"Sounds like a real nuisance, doesn't it? Well, it is, but it's a must for all backcountry campers. Follow this rule and you'll never wake up to an empty larder," I said.

Next chore. Patti and I picked up two pair of hobbles, the horse bell and a half-bucket of oats and strolled out to the little meadow where the horses were grazing. We put hobbles on Zorro, my personal mount, and Bucky, the lead mare ("old lady") of the string. We also put the bell on her. All seven horses got a bite of oats out of the bucket—makes them easier to catch the next morning.

On the way back to camp, Patti smiled at me. "Does Emmy's non-fraternization rule apply up here?"

"I'm afraid so, Patti. I don't want to chance it with these kids around. I hope you understand. But Thursday night looks good."

"I understand, sweet William. Thursday night it is."

I had one more chore before I could relax a bit. "Bud, grab the shovel in the camp gear duffel bag and follow me. We have to create a camp 'john.' It's simple, but I want you to know how. First we dig a human waste trench about two feet long behind these trees and a good hundred feet from camp, our water supply, and the trail. Then each day we simply cover up and add to the trench as needed."

"That's easy enough, Bill. Can do."

"Thanks a lot, Bud," I said as we walked back to camp. "You and Patti have made my day a lot easier."

The sun was low in the sky, and the evening shadows were lengthening. Colin and Anne Marie had studied Edie's meal plans and had already laid out the supplies for tonight's supper: New York steaks, mixed green salad, and—one of my favorites—Edie's chocolate cake.

"But first things first!" I announced. "The bar is now open! We have Bourbon and Scotch with mountain spring water as a chaser. Any takers?" I asked as the group gathered round.

Later, I broiled the steaks on a little 9"x18" grill supported by boulders on each end while Patti and Anne Marie prepared the salad.

Our cooking fire was small, so we all got close to it as the night air cooled. Later on, we added bone-dry aspen and pine knots, my preferred fuel for a campfire.

It had been a long day. Night comes and sleep refreshes.

Day 2. As a new dawn broke, I crawled out of my sleeping bag, got dressed and headed for the lake to wash up and brush my teeth. Then I went with the bucket of oats to catch the horses, remove the hobbles, fix the lead ropes to the halters, and, finally, bring them in ready for saddling.

Meanwhile, Patti and Bud made breakfast. We planned to take a daylong ride after breakfast down toward Lake Tahoe and Marlette Lake and back. I cautioned everyone to remember "looping out from a backcountry camp covers trails less traveled, so don't go off on your own." Then I added, "Getting lost or having an accident in the backcountry can be very serious, so be sure you don't depart from our plan of the day, as you could end up ruining everyone's enjoyment.

"Before we saddle up, I promised some of you a Q & A session this morning. So fire away."

Anne Marie: "Are there 'rules for the trail' like

there's 'rules for the road' for cars?"

Bill: "That's a good question. Saddle travel actually has something similar, only it's called a code. Certain actions should be performed or avoided, depending on the circumstances. For example, you may be tempted to gallop your horses this morning when we start out on our ride. But if there's ever a time a spirited horse like Alley Oop might start crow-hopping—a mild form of bucking—it's when he's fresh and, pardon my French, full of piss and vinegar. That, in turn, can trigger a bad reaction by the other horses.

Dudes in the high country (Courtesy Joel H. Bernstein Collection)

"Another example. Please don't allow your horses to graze along the trail, meaning don't let them swoop their heads down to snag a mouthful of grass. It's a bad habit and can slow up and irk the entire group. Next question."

Colin: "How big is the average horse here, and would you also explain gaits? I'm confused."

Bill: "Dude horses generally weigh between 900 and 1,100 pounds and stand between 14 and 15 hands high. They're not show horses by any means, but a few are trained to pace or single-foot. Some, like Little Joe, come by it naturally, but don't ask me why. So, with some exceptions, they usually walk, trot, canter, or gallop and have no other fancy gaits. But you can count on them to show heart and stamina, be sure-footed and have plenty of horse sense.

"You should enjoy your horse at all gaits. There are times to trot your horse and places to gallop, assuming, of course, you are not in a pack train like yesterday. Sound trail savvy comes from experience. In 'slow country' with steep or rocky trails, you walk. Enjoy a jog trot across a meadow or sage flat, for a change of pace. Or, if I suggest a gallop over safe, fairly level ground, spread out in open formation and gallop, but avoid following too close behind other riders. At any gait, keep a good distance between horses where the trail narrows."

Bud: "Just what do you mean by 'horse sense,' Bill?"

Bill: "That's not easy to answer. The average dude horse is both a good and intelligent animal, if you meet him half way by sitting in the saddle reasonably well, speaking normally, never shouting, reining him firmly, never jerking, and avoiding sudden, spooky moves.

"It's also important to give him his head, meaning, let him have his own way at times—like when he makes it plain he doesn't want to jump over a log or cross a swift stream or pick his way through a boggy spot. When in doubt, it's usually best to give the horse his head, as he's probably been over the trail before and knows how to handle himself and protect his rider. One more question, then we better saddle up."

Anne Marie: "Is it okay to drop our reins when we dismount, like the cowboys do in the movies?"

Bill: "Most horses will stand 'rein-tied' as it's called with unknotted reins dropped to the ground. But for longer times, it's best to use their lead rope and halter and tether them to a tree."

After checking the condition of the horses' feet and shoes and finding them okay, we saddled up

Looking down on Crystal Bay from Marlette Peak (Photo Larry Prosor)

for the day's ride. Patti and Anne Marie gave me the sandwiches they had made earlier to stow in my saddlebags. I said, "Since summer showers are not unusual in the mountains, please be sure to tie your ponchos behind your saddles."

We left camp about eight-thirty, under partly cloudy conditions, and headed down slope for about a half-mile in a northerly direction. Then we made a 180-degree turn and climbed a few hundred feet, until we came to the box flume aqueduct running north from Marlette Lake to Tunnel Creek Station.

We kept our eye on the flume as we traversed the steep mountainside, heading south. About a mile after turning south, we climbed a ridge and rode out on a small mesa about a half-mile west of Herlan Peak.

"You're now looking at Lake Tahoe to the west and Marlette Lake to the south," I announced.

"Oh, what a magnificent view!" Patti exclaimed. "Can we stop for a few minutes?"

"Sure, let's all dismount and take five."

"How big is Tahoe again, Bill?" Anne Marie asked.

"About 22 miles long and 12 miles wide. Off to the north, you can see Crystal Bay and the Cal-Neva Lodge at Stateline. Everything you see west of the Cal-Neva is in California. You can also see Marlette Lake south of us, our destination for today. Notice how it lies in a natural depression some 1,800 feet above Tahoe. We'd ride down to Tahoe, as we're only a mile away as the crow flies, but it's almost a perpendicular drop with no established trail.

"I believe I mentioned yesterday, the snow water of the Carson-Sierra Nevada Range is the source of Virginia City's water supply. It's a long and complex story dating back to the 1870s

Comstock era, but I'll try to summarize it.

"Virginia City imported its first water from Franktown (Hobart) Creek. Remember, we rode alongside of it yesterday? Engineers built a diversion dam above Little Valley, then developed an incredible combination of box flume and pipe installation to carry the water to the mines, by way of Lakeview on the Washoe-Eagle Valley saddle.

"About that same time, lumbermen Bliss and Yerington built a dirt-filled dam across the head of Marlette Creek forming Marlette Lake to add to their water supply. The reservoir water was conveyed six miles south by way of a V-flume to Summit Camp just east of Summit Station, where it was fed down twelve miles of trestled V-flume to the lumber terminal south of Carson City.

"About three years later, the Virginia City water people made a deal with Bliss and Yerington to draw water from Marlette Lake and move it north along the Carson Range in a covered box flume 1,800 feet above Lake Tahoe. The flume—we've been riding beside it this morning—runs four and one-half miles around the mountain rim to the west portal of a 4,000-foot tunnel blasted through solid granite under the Sierra Summit. The tunnel is due north of us.

"On the east side of the tunnel, another box flume carries the water another three miles from the tunnel down to a junction with the Franktown/Hobart Creek system.

"This complex system of flumes and piping between the high Sierra and Virginia City extends

Marlette Lake (Images of Lake Tahoe, Courtesy of Special Collections Department, University of Nevada, Reno Library)

over 32 miles to meet the insatiable demand of Virginia City, and is still considered a miraculous engineering achievement by the Silver State.

"If you want the full story, let me know and I'll loan you my favorite book on the subject."

We continued riding south, with magnificent views in all directions. We also enjoyed several deer sightings along the way.

By the time we reached Marlette Creek and the lake's dam, it was lunch time. From the dam, we had a panoramic view to the north of Incline Mountain and the Mount Rose range off in the distance. After a quick look at the lake, we went back down to the creek and dismounted for lunch under a clump of scrub pine.

It had turned warm, probably more than eighty degrees with a cloudless sky.

A half-hour later we were back in the saddle. First, we skirted the southern shore of Marlette Lake and went through North Canyon, then headed north.

As the crow flies, we were only about four miles from our trail camp, but we were blazing trail now at an elevation of approximately 8,200 feet, so the going was slow.

We went around the eastern slope of Marlette Peak, elevation 8,780 feet; "About halfway to camp" I called out.

"I don't think I can make it," moaned Colin.

"Don't worry, you will, but let's give the horses another rest here, then we'll walk some to give your backside a break."

We pulled into camp around five p.m. with a bunch of saddle sore but satisfied campers. Everyone pitched in, and in nothing flat our horses joined Half Pint and Bucky in the meadow.

Fifteen minutes later, we were all in the lake—skinny-dipping—with various degrees of modesty. The water was a bit chilly, but no doubt therapeutic for greenhorn aches and pains.

Later, as we were preparing chow, we had some

"hellacious weather"—as packer friend Chaska West used to call it. One thunderhead after another rolled through, delivering brilliant lightning strikes followed by rolling claps of thunder. Everyone broke out their ponchos, but we had very little precipitation. Tents were out for this trip, as we had all opted to sleep under the stars.

Supper would be easy tonight. Two giant cans of Dinty Moore beef stew, one large can of Del Monte mixed vegetables tossed with a tasty salad dressing, and plenty of coffee with the last of Edie's cake.

It had turned into a warm evening. The moon climbed out of the pines and lit up the camp with its warm glow. "It doesn't get much better than this, does it?" I said to four tired but happy campers. All enthusiastically agreed in one way or another.

By nine o'clock, the storytelling, laughter and campfire camaraderie had ended, as everyone hit the sack.

Day 3. By sunup Thursday, there wasn't a cloud in the sky. All you could see was the bright blue Sierra sky. Good weather, I thought, for our return ride to the ranch. Everyone in camp was ready and waiting for a scrambled eggs and bacon breakfast. By the time we were done, Patti and Bud were catching up the horses and Colin and Anne Marie were washing the dishes.

I packed the panniers, then loaded the pack horses, with Bud's help again, and we were ready to move out by eight a.m. "One more tip before we get started. On steep, downhill grades, give your horse his head so he can see where he's going. Sit back in your saddle against the cantle, straighten your legs, and press forward in the stirrups. It'll make for a more comfortable ride. It's trails like this that call for the Western saddle. The English flat saddle just won't cut it in the mountains."

I took the point (or lead), as we started our

descent down the steep slope with its many switchbacks. Bud took the drag. By the time we had worked our way down Little Valley, the trail widened, so I encouraged my four "experienced dudes" to canter ahead for a change, while I hung back with the pack horses. Patti and Bud jumped at the chance. Anne Marie and Colin never got their horses out of a trot, but seemed pleased with the progress.

We pulled into the Flying M E early Thursday afternoon. Our welcoming committee was small but vocal, especially the dachshunds and Jimmy Murray.

All four riders thanked me profusely for a "new and exciting experience."

Patti hung back, as I knew she would, but then surprised me. "Do you mind terribly if we get together tomorrow night instead of tonight, Bill?" she whispered. "I'm positively exhausted."

"No problem, my little cowgirl. See you tomorrow."

Groves of quaking aspens such as these at Marlette Lake leave little doubt of winter's coming. Aspen-filled canyons reveal some history of past sheepherders and explorers who left their marks on the white bark. (Photo Larry Prosor)

Glenbrook rodeo—Hatherly and Will M. Bliss on deck of stable tack room, where ropers lined up to pay entry fees.
(Julian P. Graham photo, Courtesy William W. Bliss)

CHAPTER 22

Glenbrook Inn

Glenbrook's Popular Rodeo

A couple days after the Sierra pack trip, Jimmy Murray and I were "shootin' the bull" by the tack room. "You goin' up to the rodeo at Glenbrook come Sunday and, ifin' you are, can I tag along?" he asked.

"Damn, Jimmy, I plumb forgot. The answer is 'yes' and 'yes.' I'm going and you're joining me. I'll spread the word at dinner tonight and see who else wants to go. I'm pretty sure we'll have some takers."

All four of my Sierra pack-trippers—Patti Allen, Anne Marie Baker, Colin Greenley, and Bud

Glenbrook Meadow with the Glenbrook Inn buildings beyond. (Julian P. Graham photo, Courtesy William W. Bliss)

Henry—were rarin' to go, plus Dee Allen, Joan Allison Borg, Danielle Masiere, Tom Waring, Sis Black, and her "spare," Reese Harris. Allie and I would drive. We tried to talk Emmy into coming, because we knew she loved Glenbrook, but she felt obligated to stay at the ranch with Carol Greenley and a few others.

Come Sunday morning, we were ready to shove off by half past nine and took my favorite southern loop to Tahoe via Jack's Valley (a Pony Express stop in 1860), Genoa (Nevada's first permanent settlement, established as a Mormon trading post in 1851), then up over the steep, winding Kingsbury Grade to the South Shore, and finally north on U.S. 50 to Glenbrook.

Of course, we had to make a stop at the Genoa Bar, "Nevada's oldest thirst parlor." I never tired of showing guests Nevada's sights and telling them a little bit about its history. It was still morning, but the bar was busy.

Around noon, we pulled into Glenbrook. The rodeo grounds were in a large meadow next to an apple orchard at the base of the surrounding mountains and Shakespeare Rock. It was spectacular.

"Before we get separated, allow me to give you a little background on the Glenbrook rodeo," I said.

"Will Bliss—he's top boss of the Inn and a self-proclaimed, frustrated weekend roper—and a group of his friends and neighbors built this arena and the cattle chutes and pens in the 1930s, for roping practice and for entertaining the Inn's guests. Many of the guests had never seen calf roping and team roping, so roping practice became a popular attraction. Cowboy friends of Will's from nearby ranches in Carson, Smith and Mason valleys began to show up on weekends, and the Glenbrook rodeos were born. As the story goes, the cows and calves grazing in the surrounding meadows could no longer count on endless summer days of peaceful grazing.

"Although they were simple family and neighbor get-togethers, the rodeos always remained competitive. Entry fees were collected from each contestant by Will, his wife Hatherly and other members of the Bliss family. The fee money was divided into prizes and returned to the cowboys for first, second and third place winners. There was no admission charge for spectators.

"Today's events will include calf and team roping, cowgirl barrel racing, and a wild cow milking contest. Cowboys will prod the cattle from the catch pens into the chutes. Will and his friends will be the timers and provide the commentary. Flagging in the arena, part of the timing process, is usually done by a volunteer. Allie, would you like to add something?"

"Just this. Be sure to take some time to walk around. This is a beautiful and very historical place. There's a pier down by the lake, an interesting cemetery where many important people are buried, and the historical Glenbrook Inn. Let's plan to meet back at our cars when the rodeo is over or at five p.m., whichever comes first."

Some eighty to a hundred competitors were taking part in today's events, and the apple orchard was jammed with horse trailers.

The rodeo got off to a flying start at one-thirty. The cowboys and guests taking part in the events made their "Grand Entry" to the accompaniment of a scratchy recording of "The-Star Spangled Banner." The bleachers were overflowing with spectators, some perched atop the fences surrounding the roping arena. For a small show, there was plenty of entertainment and excitement.

In the calf roping competition, local cowboy Chris Cordes caught his calf, threw him and tied him in eighteen seconds flat, winning top prize money.

First prize in the cowgirl barrel race went to a Glenbrook high schooler who lived nearby.

Glenbrook rodeo, cowboys moving the rodeo stock (Courtesy Patricia Cramer)

Chris Cordes calf-roping at Glenbrook rodeo
(Courtesy William W. Bliss)

Bottom, *Glenbrook rodeo*
(Courtesy Patricia Cramer)

History of Glenbrook Inn

Glenbrook began its history in the mid-1860s, when Captain A. W. Pray built the Lake's first sawmill on the south side of Glenbrook Bay.

In 1873, the Carson & Tahoe Lumber & Fluming Company (C&TL&FC), headed by Duane L. Bliss, began acquiring large tracts of land in and around the Glenbrook area. Under Bliss's direction, a narrow gauge railroad was built to carry cordwood and lumber from the Company's new Glenbrook mills to the top of Spooner Summit for transportation by flume to Carson City. Here the wood was loaded onto Virginia & Truckee Railroad flatcars and carried to Virginia City for use in the Comstock mines. By 1881, Glenbrook had become Nevada's leading logging town.

In 1896, Duane L. Bliss launched a new era with the christening of his new passenger ship, the S. S. *Tahoe*. Within a short time, this once little known logging lake became the foremost mountain resort in the western United States.

Three generations, left to right: Will M., William W., and William S. Bliss, 1936.
(Courtesy William W. Bliss)

In 1907, the Glenbrook Inn opened its doors to accommodate the new tourist trade. The Inn itself was composed of two former hotels, Lakeshore House and Jellerson House, together with new construction and parts of an old general store. The interior of the large Bliss house, no longer used by the family, was modified to provide still more space. A number of cottages were also constructed. Most of the Inn's guests arrived via steamer from Tahoe City, after a short journey by train from the Southern Pacific Railway station in Truckee to the Tahoe Tavern.

In the early 1920s, all of the cottages had hot and cold running water, and a number had private baths.

Automobile "sheds" were also added.

The Glenbrook Inn, by now, was well-established and benefiting from regular clientele. For many families, a summer vacation at Glenbrook was a tradition, with the children claiming they "grew up" at Glenbrook. The attractions were simple and wholesome, and most often guests stayed for several weeks at a time, or for a full month in July or August.

During the '20s and '30s, the roads through the mountains were paved, marking the decline of the steamship era. The use of the automobile enabled people from every level of society to enjoy the magnificent "Lake in the Sky" and smaller, middle-class lodges began to develop. However, the affluent continued to retreat to Glenbrook or to their private family compounds elsewhere around the Lake.

The Inn, in spite of its popularity, was a seasonal operation. The big boom in winter sports would not begin at the Lake until the 1960 Winter Olympics in Squaw Valley. In the meantime, the Bliss family still owned thousands of acres on Tahoe's Nevada side, including approximately six miles of lakefront. The phrase "land poor" was applicable in a very real way and would continue in the Depression years ahead.

There were excellent Bliss lakefront properties in the Glenbrook area, which third-generation Will M. Bliss believed could be sold without altering the tranquility and unique atmosphere of Glenbrook. The Inn would remain surrounded by several hundred acres of meadow and thousands of acres of forest land. Twenty-five hundred feet of beachfront would be retained for the use of Inn guests. Several well-known, wealthy men, including Max C. Fleischmann and "Captain" George

Whittell, purchased large tracts of Bliss property during the difficult Depression years of the mid-1930s. By 1938, these purchases included all Bliss family holdings with the exception of 3,300 acres encompassing the Glenbrook Inn and a small parcel in Secret Harbor.

Activities. Outdoor recreation at Glenbrook included fishing, horseback riding, golf, tennis, and boating. A popular attraction was the rodeos held on three or four Sundays during the summer. Many of the guests had never seen calf and team roping and "practice sessions" became a popular attraction. As the rodeos grew in popularity with the guests, their interest in horseback riding increased. In 1942, Glenbrook wrangler Johnny Vance hired Wyoming-born Jack Morgan to assist in the stables. Jack Morgan would become a legend at Glenbrook—the quintessential cowboy blessed with native wisdom, warmth, intelligence, and sense of humor. He kept the guests and locals laughing with his witty and often spicy "Morganisms."

Will M. Bliss enjoyed being camp cook for Glenbrook's popular breakfast rides. (Courtesy William W. Bliss)

After the sudden passing of Will M. Bliss in 1960, the rodeo tradition was continued by his son and daughter, William W. "Bill" Bliss and Hatherly "Sis" Bliss, believing their father would have wished it. A treasured belt buckle in Will Bliss' name was awarded in team roping. The ages of the two members of the victorious team had to total more than one hundred years and, with rare exception, the winners of the "Will Bliss Buckle" were old friends of Will's when he ran the show.

Guests. The Glenbrook Inn was first and foremost a family-oriented resort. However, it attracted its share of well known personalities. In the 1950s, Clark Gable and Rita Hayworth stayed there during the same season, while establishing their residencies for Nevada divorces. (Gable was divorcing Lady Sylvia Ashley and Hayworth was divorcing Prince Aly Khan.)

Fourth-generation William W. "Bill" Bliss, manager of the Inn from 1960 to 1975, offered this perspective on celebrity guests: "A lot of people remember Clark Gable and Rita Hayworth stayed here. However, Glenbrook was first-and-foremost a family-oriented resort. There was the tradition of generations coming here year after year, in a very, low-key way. Often those who had spent their childhood summers here were hired as busboys and waitresses when they became of age, allowing them to wait upon their mothers and fathers. I started as a golf caddy and graduated to garbage man! My sister, Hatherly, was a waitress for several summers. It's true the guest register included some well-known names, but they chose Glenbrook to get away from the limelight."

In a series of interviews with William W. "Bill" Bliss in 2002, the authors learned that on average only about 2 percent of the Inn's guests might be staying there for a divorce in the 1945-1965 era. Bill usually served as the Inn's residence witness when a guest went before the judge.

Regarding the Inn's exclusivity and whether or not the restaurant was open to the public: "Well, it was and it wasn't. To be very frank, we took a look at you and then decided if we were full or not! It wasn't advertised. You couldn't count on coming in off the road.

Will M. Bliss and Clark Gable busing dishes at Glenbrook Inn dining room, after college student busboys had headed home after the summer. (Courtesy William W. Bliss)

Rita Hayworth comparing scores with Glenbrook golf pro Floyd Hudson. (Courtesy William W. Bliss)

Reservations were a good idea, and coat and tie were required right up to the end."

Bill Bliss remembers an average occupancy as being between 95-110 guests; 128 when the Inn was really full. The average rate per person in 1948 was $28 per day, or about $200 per week, American plan. Bliss recalls, "We had 65 to 70 employees. There were 14 in the kitchen, plus the usual maids and bartenders. Some were six-weekers whom I'd witness for. We used to raise our own vegetables and operate our own dairy. We had an irrigator and used to cut hay here. And don't forget the wrangler and his 20 to 25 head of dude horses!"

The Final Years. Gradually the old-time summer resorts on Lake Tahoe were closing; Tahoe Tavern in 1964, and Brockway Hot Springs in 1967. The reasons varied. Real estate developers converged on the Lake in the 1960s and, with no practical building or planning restrictions, condominiums were built and sold by the hundreds. Motels, heretofore a rarity, sprang up along with restaurants and dinner houses. The American plan was losing its appeal.

Perhaps the single most important factor in the loss of the old resorts was the increase in property values caused by development. Most resorts were not winterized and depended on a short summer season to make ends meet. This was becoming impossible.

Glenbrook was a beloved and reassuring holdout in a rapidly changing environment. Many employees remained loyal to the Bliss family and to Glenbrook for many years, and this loyalty lent a feeling of consistency which guests could count on from year to year. To many, it became a tradition—the last rite of a departing guest—to fill out a reservation for the following year, which usually was a request for the same accommodations and comparable dates.

To the end, the Bliss family insisted on fresh table and bed linen daily, waitresses with starched aprons and bus boys in immaculate white jackets—sometimes changed several times a day. Gentlemen were required to wear coats and ties at dinner.

However, the problems which had forced other old-time resorts to close their doors eventually began to seriously affect the Glenbrook Inn. An agonizing decision was made by the Bliss family in late 1975, and in January 1976, the following notice was mailed to hundreds of guests:

The Inn will not be open in 1976. The golf course, however, will be open.

The Nevada Industrial Commission requires us to totally rewire the Inn.

The Lake Tahoe Fire Protection District requires the same, in addition to major construction of additional exits and a totally new fire protection system.

The Nevada State Department of Health code requires many costly additions to our kitchen.

The Environmental Protection Agency requires all facilities to be connected to the Tahoe Douglas Sewer District.

Financially, it is impossible to comply with the above.

The decision to discontinue operation of the Glenbrook Inn has been an extremely painful one.

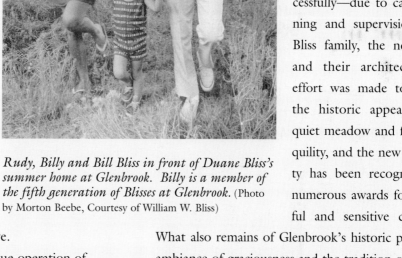

Rudy, Billy and Bill Bliss in front of Duane Bliss's summer home at Glenbrook. Billy is a member of the fifth generation of Blisses at Glenbrook. (Photo by Morton Beebe, Courtesy of William W. Bliss)

An avalanche of letters from former guests arrived, expressing dismay and disappointment, but at the same time offering thanks and understanding. Perhaps the most succinct read: "This is a very sad day for all of us who loved Glenbrook, as well as for you. It is another example of the days of vanishing simple, wholesome pleasures. I am glad to have enjoyed it and seen it at its best."

Today, only the faint shadow of the Bonanza days rests on Glenbrook's shoreline—a few historic buildings, rapidly disappearing mill foundations and the ghostly piles of the pier, from whence the steamer *Tahoe* disembarked passengers and guests in grand style. The grand old Inn, Ray Sendejas' clubhouse bar and the rustic cottages are cherished memories of yesteryear for hundreds of families and guests. However, unlike a lot of dowager properties of its kind, Glenbrook made a transition from a historic resort to a modern day residential community—successfully—due to careful planning and supervision by the Bliss family, the new owners and their architects. Every effort was made to maintain the historic appearance and quiet meadow and forest tranquility, and the new community has been recognized with numerous awards for its tasteful and sensitive conversion. What also remains of Glenbrook's historic past are the ambiance of graciousness and the tradition of family, as many former Inn guests still return each summer, however now staying in their privately owned residences.

— This history has been derived from *Tahoe-Heritage, The Bliss Family of Glenbrook, Nevada* by Sessions S. Wheeler with William W. Bliss; and personal interviews with William W. Bliss in 2002.

The wild cow milking contest was a big crowd pleaser as usual. The milkers—or should I say would-be milkers—ate lots of dust trying to squeeze even a few squirts of milk out of a wild mother cow, as their roper partners urged them on.

Everyone enjoyed the close-up action of the show; that is, with the exception of Danielle and Dee, who preferred spending their time sunning on the beach.

Jimmy Murray's running commentary amused everyone around us. Jimmy, being out of the mainstream since his stroke, was especially happy to meet the two Glenbrook cowboys he'd heard so much about, Johnny Vance and Jack Morgan. I first met Vance and Morgan at the Reno Rodeo in '47, and later at Lena Geiser's Round Up Bar. So when they came by to say hello, I made sure to introduce them to Jimmy. Johnny was a well-known Rodeo Cowboy Association professional roper, and both Johnny and Jack were popular figures at Glenbrook.

The rodeo was over a little before five and, after one round for the road at Ray's Sendejas' clubhouse bar—mainly so Sis and Reese could check out the golf course—we returned to the ranch by way of Spooner Summit and Carson City. Everyone really enjoyed the day.

Dinner at the Inn

Enthusiastic talk about our rodeo outing inspired Emmy to ask one evening, "Who would like to dine at the Glenbrook Inn this Sunday?"

She reminded her guests—who by now were getting used to going everywhere in their Western wear—about the Inn's dress code at dinner. Emmy called Will Bliss and a dinner reservation was made for ten, including two drivers.

With her usual thoughtfulness, Emmy said to me privately, "Bill, dear, I'd like you to join us, and you'll be fine in your Sunday-goin'-to-meetin' Western shirt, bolo tie, Levis and boots." I decided I'd also take my western-cut Pendleton jacket.

It was a warm August afternoon and quite a treat to see the ladies all dolled up in their fine dresses and jewelry. What a swell-looking group, I thought, proud to be their escort.

Emmy drove the Buick wagon with Carol Greenley, Sis and Reese Boy (who decided to forego gambling for one evening), Anne Marie Baker, and Tom Waring. I followed in the Chrysler convertible with Patti Allen, Joan Allison Borg and Dee Allen.

It was a beautiful summer afternoon for a drive, about eighty degrees with a few fleecy cumulus clouds and a light breeze, so we put the top down. Our plan was to arrive at the Inn by five so we could spend some leisure time by the lake before cocktails.

On the way over Spooner Summit, Patti asked, "About how far were we from Glenbrook on our pack trip, Bill?"

"Our Twin Lakes campsite was about ten miles to the north, would be my guess. Why do you ask?"

"Great! I just won ten dollars from Bud! He bet we were about twenty miles away when we were here the other day."

"You get to buy the drinks, Patti," Dee called from the back seat.

We arrived at Glenbrook a little before five and strolled down to the beach in front of the Inn. Everyone was in awe of the Inn's idyllic setting, looking out at the pristine blue lake.

As we walked out to the end of the pier, Emmy, always the perfect hostess, gave a brief verbal tour of the lake and its history. When we were out with an entourage together, I always deferred to Emmy as the senior "tour guide," knowing she would call on me if she wanted to.

"Well, dears," Emmy said looking at her watch, "our dinner reservation is for seven, so we can either continue strolling or go in the bar for cocktails."

Except for Joan and Dee, who wanted to walk along the beach, the group wanted their cocktails. So in we went, and the bartender took care of us in no time. Cocktail hour flew by, as we enjoyed our generous drinks and took in the beautiful lake view.

We were seated for dinner at a great view table. We had no sooner ordered a second round when Will Bliss appeared. He and Emmy were old friends, and their mutual fondness and respect for each other was obvious. Mr. Bliss thanked us all for coming, then excused himself, but not before saying, "This round's on me!"

Carol Greenley, our British guest, saw some friends from England and, after getting Emmy's nod of approval, took great delight in inviting them "out to the ranch" in her "veddy British" accent.

Our superb dinner at the Glenbrook Inn ended as we sipped our coffee and watched a spectacular sunset over Lake Tahoe.

Jack Morgan, Quintessential Cowboy

Jack Morgan was a legend at Glenbrook—the quintessential cowboy blessed with native wisdom, warmth, intelligence, and sense of humor. Fourth generation Nevadan Bill Bliss and celebrated author and artist Barnaby Conrad (*Matador*) share their fond memories of one of the West's most colorful dude wranglers.

Barnaby Conrad: Jack was the first person to put me on a horse when I was only four or five years old. It was up at the Lazy K Bar ranch near Big Timber, Montana. I remember he always wore a black hat.

Time goes by and thirty or forty years later I see him sitting by the corral at the Glenbrook Inn at Tahoe, but he's wearing a white hat. "Jack," I said," What happened to your black hat?"

Later that night, I find this old black hat on my pillow. It was Jack's and he'd put it there for me to have. That hat hangs on my office wall now.

Jack was an unforgettable character. He liked to say, "I really only had two jobs. Sixteen years with the Lazy K Bar, and thirty years at Glenbrook.

Barnaby Conrad, celebrated author and artist, wearing Jack Morgan's black hat, circa 2003. (Authors' Collection)

Bill Bliss: Jack was born in either Wyoming or Montana. He was a fourth grade dropout. He worked at the Lazy K Bar near Big Timber, Montana. Then he worked for the Deep Well Guest Ranch in Palm Springs, California, during the winter months. He joined us at Glenbrook about 1938.

Jack was a natural born storyteller. He had a way with words. The guests loved him. It didn't seem to matter what the subject was, he was never at a loss for words. I kept a journal with my favorite "Morgan-isms." Here's a few for posterity's sake:

Jack Morgan-isms

First impression of Glenbrook:
"Beats makin' a day camp out of a wet saddle blanket."

On travel:
"Come Monday, we're just going to piddle on the fire, wind the clock, and go."

"This has been a grand day— I've just ate it up."

The Grand Tetons: *"Plum wicked. Look at that peak over there—ruggeder than a whore's tits. And up that pocket, makes you think of the Great Beyond. And over there, a fairyland of color."*

Bryce Canyon: *"My good God, look what the ravages of time have did—sentinels, castles, cathedrals, bridges —extraordinary rock work—and the ole' Boy should be mighty proud of his color work, too."*

On dining:
"That meat was tender as a maiden's prayers."

Breakfast hashbrowns: *"Aggravated just beautiful."*

On dudes and dude ranchers:
"He's quite a cowboy now—come a long ways since last year sucking his thumb on a lead rope."

The horsemanship of a couple's children:

"Their mother and father think they're wonderful kids, but they wouldn't know how to empty a boot full of piss."

A dude between his seventh and eighth marriages: *"God damn, he must have a helluva hanger on him—or at least lovely bed manners."*

The Lazy K Bar ranch: *"Helped Paul Van Cleve double mortgage cattle by driving them from one side to the other to an intercessible ridge."*

On women:
"Did you notice the landing gear on that waitress—and the knockers—lovely eyes, too. No ringbone, no distemper."

"Now that one's too chunky—be alright in a cow camp if it was rainin' enough."

On philosophizing:
"It's fun just to sit here and conjuncture on the days ahead."

"The world don't owe me nothin'—I'm at rest with myself."

On Barnaby Conrad:
"He's the one that did that massive portrait of Don Coyote that hangs in Gardelli Square!"

Drawing of Jack Morgan by Barnaby Conrad

Just plain bad:
Looking for a friend's house: *"That's odd. It used to loom up like a diamond on a goat's butt."*
"It was raining like a cow piddlin' on a flat rock."

"Felt lower than a snake's ass in a wagon rut."

Favorite Watering Holes

And Sights Along the Way

Emmy Wood, tour guide, gathering her "flock" of Flying M E guests at Pyramid Lake on a chilly November 1947 day.
(Photo Valerie Vondermuhll, Courtesy George A. Vondermuhll Jr.)

Emmy was passionate about Nevada history, and many of her favorite restaurants and watering holes dated back to the Big Bonanza days of the Comstock. Once a week, she hosted the guests on "cook's day off" and was very discriminating when choosing the restaurant. Whether heading for Carson City, Genoa, Virginia City, Reno, Pyramid Lake, Lake Tahoe, or the Mount Rose Highway, she always enjoyed pointing out the sights and giving a little related history along the way.

Carson City
30 miles south of Reno
via U.S. Highway 395

Old Corner Bar &
Broderick's Bar and Casino

The Old Corner Bar, 517 N. Carson Street, was by far the favorite destination of the Flying M E guests for drinks and gambling. It was only ten miles away, with very little traffic, and the guests liked mixing with the locals, from ranch hands and firemen to lawyers and state legislators. Almost every evening during dinner, Allie Okie would ask, "Who are the Allie Cats tonight? Who would like to go to the Old Corner with Allie?"

The Flying M E entourage always enjoyed a warm welcome at the Old Corner—*With Your Old Friends*—as their ad slogan read. The local men knew there was always a chance they might meet a wealthy divorcée from the Flying M E. So there were always guys hittin' on the gals, and the gals seemed to enjoy the attention.

(Photo Valerie Vondermuhll, Courtesy George A. Vondermuhll Jr.)

The bar was quiet compared to the typical casino bar. Tim Martinez, the soft spoken manager of gaming, supervised the only two games in the bar, craps and "21." Mike Demas mostly dealt "21."

Next door was Broderick's Bar and Casino, 507 N. Carson Street, typical of the big and busy gaming establishments, with their noisy slot machines. Both establishments were under the same ownership, but the Old Corner was special, with its own entrance.

Ella Broderick, at the wheel, owner of the Old Corner and Broderick's Bar and Casino. In the world of business, very much a man's world in those days, Ella was ahead of her time and racked up a number

of firsts. "Who's Who in Nevada" for 1949-1950 listed Ella Broderick as "the first woman roulette operator in Nevada, and the only woman in Nevada to own and operate a gambling house to date. Also president of the Carson City Chamber of Commerce."

Many years later, Ella reflected, "It wasn't that I planned to pioneer. I knew when I was left a widow that I had to do it. I heard more than one businessman and other Carson folk predict I would be broke in three months, but I fooled them." (*Carson Review*, October 26, 1973)

Ella contributed greatly to the development of Carson City. She was a serious fund raiser for the Carson-Tahoe Hospital. She began a campaign drive in 1944, when she met philanthropist Max C. Fleischmann, who offered to match every dollar she could raise with a dollar of his own. In May 1949, the fully-equipped hospital opened, and Fleischmann had matched half of the $80,000 needed.

Ella Broderick, left (Photo Noreen I. K. Humphreys)

Left to right: Craps and "21" dealer Mike Demas, local habitué Kelly O'Keefe and publisher Grahame Hardy in the Old Corner, circa late 1940s.

(Photo John Nulty, Courtesy Nikki M. Demas-Butz)

In my first few months at the Flying M E, I developed a foolish habit. When I got my pay-check, I bought any personal items that I needed and then gambled the rest away. After all, my room and board were taken care of, so why not. One night at the Old Corner when business was slow, I was playing "21" with Mike, partly out of bore-dom and partly to keep him company. Mike said to me, "Bill, I know you understand the odds. The house always has the odds in its favor. You can't keep coming in here as often as you do and expect to win in the long run. So why don't you bank your hard-earned bucks? Ella doesn't need your money." He was speaking of Ella Broderick, the owner of the Old Corner and Broderick's Bar and Casino. (Today's Carson Nugget occupies the site of Broderick's and the Old Corner Bar)

Other favorite places in Carson were the Hunter's Lodge (400 S. Carson Street), famous for great steaks and generous pours at the bar; Melody Lane (309 S. Carson Street), a quiet place to sip cocktails and listen to Art Cooper play the Hammond organ; and the Fireside Inn in the Greeno Hotel (108 E. Proctor Street), a lively place to mingle with other locals.

Genoa
About 12 miles south of Carson City

Considered by most historians to be the first settlement in Nevada, Genoa was established in 1851 by Mormon pioneers looking to expand their influence over an unclaimed frontier. Originally called Mormon Station, this small cor-ner of the lush Carson Valley became a prominent stop along the emigrant trail to California.

The Genoa Bar, *Nevada's Oldest Thirst Parlor.* Nevada's oldest community is also home to its oldest saloon. In a little brochure, the Genoa Bar "speaks for itself":

"The building was built in 1853 and I was first open for business as Livingstones Exchange, then renamed "Fettic's Exchange" in 1884 and operated by Frank Fettic. I was well known as a "gentleman's saloon" back then and I was "kept in first-class style in every particular way." Mr. Fettic served fine wines, liquors, and cigars. According to one of his advertisements, "I would be pleased to have all my old friends call, and they would be treated in the most cordial manner."

"The top of my bar is original from the front to mid-way where you'll see a line across it. The medallions on the ceiling above the lights are original as is the one red oil lamp which is lit every New Year's Eve. The electric lamps are also original to the bar and were oil

Genoa Bar, 2003 (Authors' Collection)

but converted to electricity at the turn of the century. And, no, those are not blood stains you see on the ceiling—it's tomato juice. While there have been many rough and tumbles here, no one was ever killed.

"The Diamond Dust Mirror on the back of the bar came from Glasgow, Scotland, in the late 1840s. It was shipped around the "horn" to San Francisco, and then brought here by covered wagon. Originally, there were two mirrors, but one was sold to a movie company in the 1930s during the Great Depression. If you shine a flashlight into the mirror, you can see the diamond dust.

"There are many stories about the cellar—drunks are thrown down there to "sleep it off" and dancing girls come out at night.

"Many famous people have visited me over the years: Mark Twain when he first reported for the *Territorial Enterprise* which opened in Genoa before moving to Virginia City; Presidents Ulysses S. Grant and Theodore "Teddy" Roosevelt enjoyed "cool ones" here; and Carole Lombard and Clark Gable came here to play poker with the local cattle barons.

"A number of movies have been filmed here including *The Shootist* with John Wayne, *Charley Varrick* with Walter Matthau, *Honky Tonk Man* with Clint Eastwood, and *Misery* with James Caan, Kathy Bates, Rob Reiner, and Richard Farnsworth.

"Musicians seem to gravitate here. I've welcomed Willy Nelson, Charlie Daniels, Merle Haggard, Waylon Jennings, Johnny Cash, Slim Pickens, John Denver, and the Captain and Tennile to name just a few.

"There have been a lot of "high old times" within these walls over the years and that tradition continues to this day. I'm delighted that you stopped by to share your time with me in this little corner of history."

—*Genoa Bar brochure*

Virginia City
22 miles from Reno
via U.S. Highway 395 and
State Route 431 (formerly SR 17)

Virginia City was the leading city of the Big Bonanza days, when the Comstock Lode supported a population of about 30,000 and yielded $180 million in the one year of 1873. Many historic old buildings were still standing in the old

The Bonanza Inn, Virginia City
(Photo Gus Bundy, Bundy Collection, Courtesy of Special Collections Department, University of Nevada, Reno Library)

mining town, including Piper's Opera House and several famed old-time saloons. The presence of Lucius Beebe and Chuck Clegg in Virginia City in the 1940s attracted national media attention, and soon the old mining town was becoming a tourist attraction. In 1949, the Virginia City Restoration Program was launched to restore and preserve the gradually disintegrating town to its ornate Victorian architectural styles of the 1870s.

Bonanza Inn
The Bonanza Inn, corner of Howard and Taylor streets, was located in one of the oldest and most beautiful mansions on the Comstock, an elegant, white-pillared structure built in 1863 by prominent Comstock banker George Anson King. The location above town provided fabulous views of Six Mile

Penna Tew Hinton and Doug Moore tending bar in the cozy and dimly-lit confines of what was possibly the smallest bar in the world—only 32-inches long. On the right are the Bonanza Inn proprietors, Jinny and Halvor Smedsrud. June 1949. (Photo Adam Ooms, Courtesy Dirck L. Hinton)

Canyon, Sugar Loaf and the valley and deserts below.

The Bonanza Inn entrance, with its heavy black walnut doors, a vestibule of shiny Circassian walnut and Belgian glass, and the brass fittings of doorknobs and hinges, all harkened back to the glory days of the rich Comstock era. Inside, the restaurant's rich carpeting ran up the grand staircase. Candles were reflected in the pier glass, fires burned in the Italian marble fireplaces, and massive pieces of ornate furniture looked as if they were in their same place as during the days of

Doug's Bar, The Bonanza Inn, Virginia City
(Photo Gus Bundy, Bundy Collection, Courtesy of Special Collections Department, University of Nevada, Reno Library)

George Anson King's ownership. The Inn boasted a fireplace in every room. The high ceilings and heavy-paneled doors and walls gave each room a luxurious appearance. On the walls were paintings of local subjects by such prominent artists as Sheldon Pennoyer and Louis Siegriest.

The Bonanza Inn proprietors, Jinny and Halvor Smedsrud and their associate, Doug Moore, met in Europe during World War II. Jinny was a socialite from Boston and met Halvor while she was serving with the American Red Cross in Europe. In the spring of 1947, the Smedsruds and Moore signed a lease on the elegant Adams mansion and began renovation for a restaurant and inn.

When the Bonanza Inn opened later that year, it was an overnight success. Locals and visitors alike were clamoring for reservations to dine at the elegantly appointed mansion. Messrs. Lucius Beebe and Chuck Clegg contributed to the Inn's success by generating national publicity.

The talents of the three proprietors complemented one another perfectly: Jinny's culinary talents acquired in Europe; Halvor's continental background as a maitre d'hotel; and Doug's background in "stimulants." The menu featured continental cuisine complemented by Doug's selection of fine wines. A dinner might begin with Snails à la Bourguignonne, followed by Boeuf à la Mode, and ending with Peche Flambé and Café Diable.

Typical of the Smedsruds' flair, they hosted a farewell party for their loyal patrons before closing for the winter. The guests were entertained in the usual hospitable fashion and enjoyed hot glug and a delicious smorgasbord before the open fires of the Inn. Beginning in 1949, the Inn remained open year-round.

The guest list for 1948 and 1949 read like a "Who's Who" and included the famous, the near famous, celebrities, socialites, artists, and politicians: Hollywood's Desi Arnez and Lucille Ball; Irving Berlin and his wife, Ellin Mackay (Ellin was the granddaughter of Comstock Bonanza King John W. Mackay); writer Roger Butterfield and Mrs. Butterfield; Hollywood director Frank Capra; Hollywood restauranteur David Chasen; actress Irene Dunne; entertainer Dwight Fiske; socialite Mrs. Charles Gulden, who was staying at the Flying M E for a divorce; Lord John Hasketh and Lady Patricia of London, England (Lord John Hasketh's ancestor was William Sharon of the Bank of California in Bonanza days); writer Nunnally Johnson; actress Hedy Lamarr; Mr. Scott Newhall of the *San Francisco Chronicle* and Mrs. Newhall; The Marquesa Pellegrini from Italy; Governor and Mrs. Vail Pittman; editor of *The New Yorker* magazine, Harold Ross; Lord and Lady Wellesley of Washoe Valley; and artist Sheldon Pennoyer, to name a few. The local social set, such as Lucius Beebe and Chuck Clegg, and the proprietors of exclusive divorce ranches such as Emmy Wood of the Flying M E, kept the Inn busy with private dinner parties.

In 1952, the Smedsruds relocated the Bonanza Inn from one historical site to another. They leased a portion of Walley's Hot Springs, a mile south of Genoa in Carson Valley, and continued business as the Bonanza Inn. Their loyal clientele followed them from Virginia City to Carson Valley, where the Smedsruds continued to offer the same continental cuisine and the popular smorgasbord.

I enjoyed dining at the Bonanza Inn on many occasions, my first being in November 1947, when Jinny and Halvor hosted about forty guests in honor of Emmy Wood's birthday.

Piper's Opera House, B and Union streets, was built by John Piper in 1885 and is the third structure—the two previous having been destroyed by fire in 1875 and 1883. In its heyday, audiences in evening dress and diamonds arrived in stylish carriages drawn by horses whose harnesses were trimmed with Comstock silver. The ranking names of theater history were regularly billed: Maude Adams, Adelina Patti, Edwin Booth, Helena Modjeska, and Adah Isaacs Menken. David Belasco began his career as stage manager at Piper's. Today, the Opera House is being restored through donations and grants, and once again the stage is alive with theater and music. (Photo Valerie Vondermuhll, Courtesy George A. Vondermuhll Jr.)

Piper's Opera House, interior, 1946.
(Courtesy Neal Cobb Collection)

The Brass Rail

The Brass Rail, C Street, *Every Night is New Year's.* The site of the Brass Rail dated back to the Comstock times. It was razed by the great fire of 1875; rebuilt in 1876 as the Mollinelli House, where the best in French foods were served; and later became the famous Capitol Bar. In 1941, Pat Hart came to town and installed a brass rail at the bar and named it accordingly. Nevadans modestly insisted that the Brass

(Courtesy Dirck L. Hinton)

Left to right: *Pat Hart, Lucius Beebe and Chuck Clegg, 1951.*
(Courtesy Dirck L. Hinton)

Rail was the "doggonest, swellest ginmill and roulette den in the West." Under the ownership of the amiable Pat Hart, the bar boasted the tallest bar in the world and the oldest roulette wheel in Nevada. According to a sign on the back wall, the roulette wheel was made in Denver in 1860, shipped via Wells Fargo Express to the original Capitol Club in Virginia City, later used in Carson City, and then returned to Virginia City.

Left, Gail Hinton, daughter of Penna Tew Hinton, shown with "21" dealer Mike Demas at the Brass Rail in the 1950s. Comstock kids were frequently seen inside the local saloons.

(Courtesy Kit Hinton)

Versal McBride, proprietor
(Photo Gus Bundy, Bundy Collection, Courtesy of Special
Collections Department, University of Nevada, Reno Library)

The Bucket of Blood Saloon

The Bucket of Blood Saloon, C Street, *Virginia City's Most Historic Saloon and Museum.* The Bucket of Blood earned its name during the roaring days of the Bonanza boom. As the story goes, one Don Vasquez, a bandit and general badman, ended an argument in the back room of the saloon by cutting out the enemy's heart and throwing it on the table. Don Vasquez was later caught near Sonora, California, and given "a necktie" party.

Under Versal McBride's ownership in the 1930s, the Bucket of Blood Saloon became one of the finest sights in Virginia City. McBride's hobby was collecting historical things, mostly from Virginia City and Nevada. The saloon became a museum full of interesting and valuable pieces such as the portraits of Sandy and Eilley Bowers, painted in Europe while they hobnobbed with royalty at the height of their wealth.

There was the painting of Hank Monk and his stage, and the two sawed-off shotguns that Monk used to carry with him. There was the picture of Julia Bulette and her red lamp. There was the knife used by Don Vasquez, with a blade eight inches long and about two inches wide, on display in the saloon museum.

Bucket of Blood, 1946 (Neal Cobb Collection, Courtesy of Nevada Historical Society)

Looking at a Virginia City landmark, St. Mary's of the Mountains (Photo Valerie Vondermuhll, Courtesy George A. Vondermuhll Jr.)

The Fourth Ward School, circa 1900s. Built in 1875, it was the most modern school of its time, with artificial lighting and water fountains on each floor.
(Courtesy of Special Collections Department, University of Nevada, Reno Library)

Serious poker
(Photo Gus Bundy, Bundy Collection, Courtesy of Special Collections Department, University of Nevada, Reno Library)

Virginia City from the California Pan Mine
(Courtesy of Special Collections Department, University of Nevada, Reno Library)

Virginia City street scene, 1947.
(Photo Valerie Vondermuhll, Courtesy George A. Vondermuhll Jr.)

Harolds Club Float, Virginia City Parade, 1946
(Neal Cobb Collection, Courtesy of Nevada Historical Society)

*The Delta Saloon, C Street. The suicide table was the
subject of one of Virginia City's bloodiest legends and
was on display at the Delta. 1947.*
(Photo Valerie Vondermuhll, Courtesy George A. Vondermuhll Jr.)

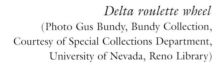

Delta roulette wheel
(Photo Gus Bundy, Bundy Collection,
Courtesy of Special Collections Department,
University of Nevada, Reno Library)

Crystal Bar, See the Historic Sparkling Chandeliers. The historic crystal chandeliers dated back to the Comstock years when they were installed in 1875 and originally burned kerosene.
(Courtesy of Special Collections Department, University of Nevada, Reno Library)

Heading for Reno down the Geiger Grade: Left, Looking toward Steamboat and Mt. Rose. Right, Looking northwest towards Reno and the Truckee Meadows, circa 1947.
(Photo Valerie Vondermuhll, Courtesy George A. Vondermuhll Jr.)

Aerial view of downtown Reno, circa 1946. The Mapes Hotel has not yet been built. Can you find the Riverside Hotel and the Washoe County Courthouse? (Courtesy of Nevada Historical Society)

Reno

The first Reno arch was erected on Virginia Street at Commercial Row in 1926, to celebrate the Transcontinental Highway Exposition in Reno. The original arch spelled out "RENO" and the title of the exposition in blinking electric bulbs. Later a contest was held to find a slogan for the arch. In 1929, a G. A. Burns of Sacramento won $100 for his or her entry, "The Biggest Little City in the World." Over the years, the arch went through several redesigns and then was replaced in the 1970s with a new one. In 1994, film-makers restored the original arch for the movie *Ty Cobb.*

The Reno arch, in rain. (Courtesy Neal Cobb Collection)

Mapes Hotel in the 1960s. Note the "Bridge of Sighs" in the foreground. (Courtesy Nevada Historical Society)

Mapes Hotel

Mapes Hotel, corner of First and Virginia streets. The grandiose Mapes Hotel opened on December 17, 1947, becoming the first high-rise hotel completed in the world after World War II and Nevada's tallest building (until 1956). The art-deco beauty, with its twelve-stories and 300 rooms, poised on the Truckee River overlooking downtown Reno, changed Reno's skyline.

The widely-anticipated opening of the luxurious Skyroom afforded those lucky enough to find a table, a spot at the bar or on the crowded dance floor, unexcelled views through the large windows, overlooking the twinkling lights of Reno and the surrounding foothills and mountains beyond. There was dancing to the music of Joe Reichman, the "Pagliacci of the Piano," and his orchestra.

The city of Reno turned out en masse for the grand opening. From Hollywood there were Bruce Cabot, the big ex-pug-turned-star Maxie Rosenbloom, and the much-publicized Johnny Weismuller, with his long hair, dark glasses, and unmistakable physique. Weismuller was staying at the Donner Trail Ranch while getting a divorce, and was frequently seen gambling and dining at the hotel, prompting one reporter to dub him, "Tarzan of the Mapes."

The Mapes Hotel and Skyroom immediately became the showplace of Reno and a venue for the most famous entertainers in show business. The Riverside and Golden Hotels soon followed with their own big-name entertainment.

Washoe County Courthouse, Hotel Riverside and Mapes Hotel, 1947-49.
(Neal Cobb Collection, Courtesy of Nevada Historical Society)

In 1980, with competition from many new hotel-casinos, the Mapes was forced to file for bankruptcy.

In the 1990s, attempts were made by the City of Reno and Oliver McMillan, a San Diego developer, to convert the Mapes into time-share units. This agreement was terminated, and on September 13, 1999, the Reno City Council voted to demolish the Mapes Hotel, rejecting three proposals to save the historic landmark. On January 30, 2000, the Mapes Hotel was imploded. As of February 2003, the Reno City Council has agreed on a plan to turn the prime riverfront site into a public plaza with fountains, trees, a riverwalk, and ice-skating rink.

The Riverside ad from The Nevada Magazine, *July 1947*

The Riverside

The Riverside, 17 South Virginia Street. In 1925, prominent Reno businessman, George Wingfield, purchased the vacant property at the corner of South Virginia Street and Riverside Drive. With an excellent downtown location, Wingfield's Riverside Hotel was destined to have a significant place in Reno history. It was conveniently located to serve the divorce trade: only four blocks from the "Divorcée Specials" (any train bringing clients to Reno), next door to the "Separator" (Reno's busy courthouse), and a few steps from the famous "Bridge of Sighs," where divorcées were said to cast their wedding rings into the Truckee River and then head to the "Widow's Corner"—the Riverside's Corner Bar—to celebrate.

Bill Harrah (in hat) in front of the Riverside during the Reno rodeo, 1946. (Courtesy Neal Cobb Collection)

The Corner Bar, which came into existence following the repeal of Prohibition (1933), became *the* meeting place of locals and visitors.

In 1949, the hotel was remodeled and featured a new wing and the first swimming pool in a Reno hotel.

Wingfield leased the gaming area to Mert Wertheimer, who made the Riverside famous for featuring big-name entertainers. Over the next several years, just about every big-name entertainer in America played the Riverside showroom. In fact, the Riverside, Mapes and Golden hotels, by competing with each other to present the top acts in show business during the forties and fifties, propelled Reno to "entertainment capital of the world" status.

EUGENE'S . . . *for*
BETTER FOOD
AT POPULAR PRICES

DANCING AND ENTERTAINMENT
TELEPHONE 8986

South Virginia Road   Reno, Nevada

Eugene's ad from The Nevada Magazine, *July 1947*

In 1997, the City of Reno took possession of the Riverside and demolished the newer sections, leaving the older portion built in 1927 untouched. In 1998, the Reno City Council gave the final approval to Oliver McMillan, a San Diego developer, to renovate the Riverside and convert the property into artists' lofts, restaurants, and shops.

Eugene's

Eugene's, 2955 South Virginia Road (later Street), was one of Reno's finest restaurants for many years. In December 1995, the building that had housed Eugene's for so many years, and was later operated as the Hacienda Del Sol, was sold to the Peppermill Casino. The building was razed, and the land where the building stood became part of the Peppermill parking lot.

Roaring Camp

The Roaring Camp, 128 Lake Street, opened on June 1, 1946, and housed what was probably the largest collection of Western memorabilia in the western United States. It featured over two thousand guns, including Tom Mix's personal gun collection, a "prairie schooner," a host of old-time carriages, hundreds of artifacts of all kinds related to western life, and dozens of mechanical pianos, player pianos, and organs. The restaurant was operated by local favorite Ramona and featured the best Mexican food in town. On more than a few occasions, the author enjoyed

Christmas greeting from the Stagg Tribe of Roaring Camp, circa 1946.
(Courtesy of Nevada Historical Society)

ending his day with a bowl of Ramona's hot chili and a bottle of Mexican beer at Stagg's Roaring Camp.

During its short life of less than three years, the Roaring Camp was plagued with problems in the gaming end of the business. Raymond Stagg was the prin-cipal owner of the establishment, but he frequently leased the gaming to other people, and he had trouble with some of them.

On February 19, 1949, local newspapers announced that Ray Stagg had sold the Roaring Camp to

Douglas Alley in the 1940s
(Photograph by The Camera,
Nevada Historical Society)

Pyramid Lake (Photo courtesy of Nevada Historical Society)

Raymond I. "Pappy" Smith of Harolds Club for $300,000. Stagg went to work for Smith as a public relations person and traveled all over the United States promoting Harolds Club. He traveled in a truck built to resemble a covered wagon, and always dressed in a fringed buckskin outfit. His hair was gray and worn long, giving him the appearance of a mountain man. This marketing ploy, tied in with the theme "Harolds Club or Bust," resulted in tens of thousands of people coming to Reno and Harolds Club.

The Roaring Camp was reopened on April 2, 1949, and remained open until late in the year. Then all of Stagg's memorabilia was transported to Harolds Club, and the collection was placed in a section of the club appropriately named the Roaring Camp Room. For years, all or portions of the one-of-a-kind collection were displayed in Harolds Club and were considered a famous piece of Reno history.

Following the sale of Harolds Club, Stagg's collection was sold to Butterfield and Butterfield. In 1994, Butterfield's sold it at auction, and the famous collection was no more.

Pyramid Lake
33 miles northeast of Reno,
via State Route 445 (formerly SR 33)

Pyramid is one of the strange lakes of the world. It is a cool lake in the midst of a parched desert. From its waters have been taken some of the world's largest trout. Around the lake there is little vegetation and hardly any habitation.

Pyramid Lake is what is left of a prehistoric ocean which covered most of Nevada and much of Idaho and Utah. Pyramid is in an Indian Reservation, and the Indians own the lake.

Pyramid Lake Ranch, Trading Post interior.
(Drackert Collection, Courtesy of Special Collections Department,
University of Nevada, Reno Library)

Captain John C. Frémont and his expedition were probably the first non-Indians to see Pyramid Lake. Frémont described his first dramatic encounter with the lake on January 14, 1844: "Beyond a defile between mountains and filling up the lower space was a sheet of green water some twenty miles broad. It broke upon our eyes like the ocean. We camped opposite a very remarkable rock on the lake which attracted our attention. It rose, according to our estimate about 600 feet above the water and presented a pretty exact outline of the Pyramid of Cheops. This suggested a name and I called it 'Pyramid Lake.'"

Mount Rose Highway and Lake Tahoe

The Christmas Tree

29900 Mount Rose Highway. The cozy and chalet-like restaurant and bar was lit up like a Christmas tree year-round and was a welcoming sight for travelers making the mountainous journey over the Mount Rose Highway between Reno and Lake Tahoe. Johnny and Alice Ross opened the Tree as a bar in the winter of 1946, and added the restaurant in 1947. (Alice was the widow of the famous cowboy artist Will James.) Overnight the place became popular with locals and

Washoe Valley as seen through a telephoto lens from the Christmas Tree deck on Mount Rose Highway.
(Authors' Collection)

(Authors' Collection)

Flying M E divorce seeker forgets her troubles on the slopes of Mt. Rose. (Photo Valerie Vondermuhll, Courtesy George A. Vondermuhll Jr.)

visitors and developed a reputation for the *best mahogany broiled steaks anywhere*. And the view was magnificent. The Christmas Tree is still going strong today.

The Mesa, overlooking Reno, was located a few miles up the Mount Rose Highway. The Mesa featured fine dining and dancing. The Mesa was sold, and the name was changed to the Lancer Restaurant in 1959. In 1971, the Lancer was completely destroyed by fire and never rebuilt.

Two more favorite watering holes at Lake Tahoe were the Glenbrook Inn and the Cal-Neva Lodge, both profiled in other chapters.[1]

CHAPTER 24

Hollywood Creative Types "Get Reno-vated"

Why Would You Ever Want to Leave Here, Bill?

In the fall of '48, Norman Tokar pulled into the ranch in a fire-engine-red Ford convertible. Norman was an actor-writer-director from Hollywood, and turned out to be a very entertaining guest—a real character with a wry grin and a great sense of humor.

Norman had a stocky build, boyish looks, curly red hair, and a twinkle in his eye. Despite his stature of maybe 5'2" to 5'4"—with lifts—the ladies found him quite the charmer. He and Half Pint, the gentlest pony on the ranch, were well-suited for each other, because Norman had never ridden before, and Half Pint couldn't care less.

A few days after Norman's arrival, film and TV series writer Terry Robinson and her best friend, Jean Taylor, arrived on the S.P. Overland Limited, after a three day ride from New York. It was not unusual for a divorcé to come out West with a friend or a relative to keep them company for six weeks. Emmy met the ladies at the station, then made the usual stops before heading for the ranch—the Riverside for drinks and to pick up any guests that rode into town with her, and Parker's for Western wear.

I had just returned from a trail ride with Norman and Joan Borg when Emmy drove up with Terry and Jean.

"Oh, Bill, what good timing," Emmy called out. "These young ladies are dying to meet you and schedule their first ride."

After Emmy made the introductions, I added the ladies to my "ride list;" then Norman and I carried their bags up to their room.

Terry and her friend Jean were opposites. Terry was brusque and loud compared to our typical ranch guests. She had a heavy Brooklyn accent and chain-smoked with a cigarette holder clenched tightly between her teeth. These traits tended to cancel out any chances of feminine attributes, as far as I was concerned. However, she did get right in the swing of things and loved wearing frontier pants, colorful Western shirts and cowboy boots. Her best friend Jean, who had come to keep her company, was quiet, poised, and very attractive. Jean didn't take to Western wear right away, but gave in wholeheartedly after a couple weeks.

On our first of many trail rides together, I learned that Norman and Terry were writers in the entertainment business. I was fascinated by their line of work, and I'm sure I asked too many questions. It would take several trail rides to get their full stories out of them.

Norman, particularly, was modest about his career successes. As a child actor, he was active on

Norman Tokar

stage and in radio in the '30s and '40s. He understudied Ezra Stone in the radio role of Henry Aldrich, and took over the part in June 1942, only to have to vacate the series a month later when he was called to active duty in the Army's Signal Corp. After the war, Norman turned his talents to directing and signed on with Walt Disney's talent pool.

I continued to follow Norman's career after he left the ranch. In the 1950s, he directed the TV series "Leave It To Beaver" and "Naked City," and was at the helm of several Disney TV projects. In 1962, he was given a feature film opportunity with *Big Red,* and this assignment established him as an "outdoors" director—a handy talent for a Disney employee. Norman displayed his talent for slapstick and family farce, and continued to direct right up to his death in 1979.

I talked to Norman a lot about the entertainment business. During one of our trail ride conversations, he looked at me and said, "Bill, why would you ever want to leave what you're doing? Most men would give their right arm to have your job." He meant it sincerely.

When I asked Terry Robinson how she broke into the business, she answered candidly, "It helps to know someone. In my case, I married him!" Her soon-to-be ex-husband was the vice-president and program director for CBS, New York.

"He was my mentor—and a tough taskmaster," Terry added.

"You're divorcing Hubbell Robinson, I gather?" Norman interjected.

"That's right, after long years of conflict," Terry replied. (A month after their divorce, Hubbell Robinson would marry Margaret Whiting.)

Terry wrote for the movies, and was also pioneering the new medium of television as a series TV writer. Her professional pen name was "Therese Lewis." One of her writing credits was on the screenplay for *What a Woman!,* with Rosalind

Left to right, Actor Hugh Beaumont, who played Ward Cleaver, the "Beav's" father, on the hit TV series, Leave It To Beaver, *and director Norman Tokar at an awards ceremony.*
(Photos Courtesy Deborah Tokar Schneider)

Terry Robinson, aka "Therese Lewis," successful writer for film and the new medium of TV (Caricature by Joan Allison)

Russell, which was released when I was overseas during the war.

I also followed Terry's career after she left the ranch. She became a prolific writer for the TV series "Robert Montgomery Presents" and "Goodyear Television Playhouse," which aired in 1950 and 1951 respectively. That's probably what she was working on in fall of '48 at the ranch.

According to a guest who prefers to remain anonymous, "There were hints among the gals that Terry was, uh, you know. In those days, no one ever said the "L" word and gay meant bright and happy."

Dinner at the Flying M E. Guests included left to right: Jean Taylor; fourth from left, screenwriter Terry Robinson; Emmy Wood; and Allie Okie in right foreground. (Authors' Collection)

Caught in a Washoe Zephyr

The fall of '48 was busy with riders. Terry and Jean rode everyday, weather permitting, sometimes for the entire day. Norman, Joan and the others kept me busy with frequent but shorter rides.

I've never forgotten one picnic ride with Terry and Jean, when we circled the valley. The morning started out with a clear blue sky and hazy, fleecy clouds. We skirted the south end of Big Washoe and dismounted at my favorite picnic spot, with a great view of Slide Mountain and the Sierra Nevadas.

Before we finished lunch, Washoe Valley's famous Zephyr started to blow. No season of the year is immune to the Washoe Zephyrs, when they sweep down through the valley, especially in the afternoons in the spring and fall. Valley farmers and ranchers tilled the soil and hauled their hay according to the dictates of the winds.

Sometimes the Zephyrs' winds lasted for hours, so I asked Terry and Jean if they wanted to continue the circle ride or double back to the ranch.

"You tell us, Bill. What should we do?" Terry asked.

"Let's continue up to Washoe City, then home, if you're game. The Zephyrs can be irritating and hard on the nerves at times, but I see no reason to cut and run. Let's put our ponchos on before we mount up, because they make good windbreakers. And here's a safety tip worth remembering: it's always best to put your poncho or slicker on while dismounted. The least little bit of fluttering motion can spook a horse, so it's best he sees

Jean Taylor and Bill McGee enjoying a beer break on a trail ride in Washoe Valley, 1948. (Authors' Collection)

what's happening to avoid trouble."

We loped off and on up the east side of the lake to Little Washoe Lake, as swirling clouds of dust filled the air, almost choking us. The Zephyr now blew in terrific gusts from all quarters of the compass.

When I spotted the little Washoe Bar through the gusts, I said, "Well, ladies, should we wet our whistles before heading home?"

"Absolutely," Terry said, with Jean seconding the motion.

We tied our horses to the hitching post in front of the old bar—"just like in the movies," remarked Terry—and went in for a tall, cool one. Thirty minutes later, we were on our way.

"The last four miles are always the longest, ladies, but we'll be home soon," I said.

We pulled into the ranch about four-thirty just as the Zephyr started to calm down.

"That was some ride, Bill," Jean said. "I didn't want to say anything, but I was scared the whole way home."

"Me, too," Terry added. "Guess I'm not as tough as I thought I was."

Private Lesson

A few days later, I took Terry, Jean and Norman up to Little Valley on a morning ride. In the afternoon, they were all going sightseeing to Pyramid Lake, and I was taking Joan Allison Borg out for a private lesson that Emmy had promised her a week ago. During the busy season, it was difficult to schedule "privates" in advance.

Joan Allison on the fence awaiting her first private riding lesson. (Authors' Collection)

I had my eye on Joan ever since she arrived in mid-July. She differed from the typical guest in that she was younger than me—a year younger to be exact. Most of the guests were ten or twenty years older than I. And Joan was beautiful. She stood about 5'2", with shoulder length, wavy, honey-blonde hair, and a great figure to boot. She had a soft and pleasant voice—a bit shy sounding, and almost seductive in tone.

I had spoken to her on several occasions, but it was always with other guests around; so today's private lesson would be my first chance to be alone with her. Joan showed up as I was saddling Zorro and Little Joe.

"You look great in your new outfit. Parker Brothers?" I asked.

"Of course. I couldn't keep wearing my baggy jeans with this group."

She had on a white shirt with pearl snap buttons, tan frontier pants, and two-tone tan and brown cowboy boots.

"Should improve your riding skills a couple notches," I added.

"Oh, sure," she said, and we both laughed.

We took the trail toward Little Valley for about thirty minutes, then crossed the Franktown Creek—much to Joan's chagrin, although without a problem—and then branched out to the north to a sunny little glen and dismounted.

I had promised Joan we would make this a short ride, with plenty of time to discuss riding do's and don'ts.

"First, let me unroll this ground cloth and

blanket so you won't get that new outfit dirty," I said, as I untied the roll behind my saddle and spread it out on the ground, in a level spot between two Jeffrey pines with just the right amount of sun and shade. We sat down together on the blanket.

"Cigarette?" I asked.

"Yes, please."

I lit two Lucky Strikes and handed one to Joan.

"My, you think of everything, don't you?"

"I try. It's part of my job. Let me know if you get thirsty. There's two bottles of Coke in my saddlebags."

It was a bright, warm day, about eighty degrees, with just a little Washoe Zephyr to keep us from getting too warm.

We talked for two hours about most everything under the sun, including her mother, Lucy Dodsworth Allison, who had been to the ranch to divorce Joan's father a few month's earlier (although she didn't stay the full six weeks). We talked about Emmy and Allie; Colin Greenley and Bud Henry and their crushes on Joan; why Joan's marriage to Eddie Borg was ending so soon and why she couldn't get an annulment in New Jersey; why Emmy had invited her to stay on at the ranch as an assistant ranch hostess; and finally, why Emmy had given Joan and me permission to date.

"This is nice, Bill," Joan said. "Just sitting here, talking."

"Then let's continue. But talking isn't the only…"

"I know. But there's the question of where we're going, if we're going, and why."

"Couldn't we just spin a wheel?" I asked.

"If we did, there'd be no gamble. Just a certainty. But our chemistry does seem favorable. So in the course of things, there'd be a natural progression, right?"

"I'm not only with you, I'm ahead."

"In bed, I suppose. I've a disappointment for you there."

I leaned back and blew a smoke ring, then a second and third, speculating on what she meant by "disappointment."

"I've always wanted to do that," Joan said referring to the smoke rings.

"What kind of disappointment?" I asked.

"A notion—call it silly, if you must—that if what could happen…happens, it ought to mean something for both of us."

"And could it for you?"

"It could, I think. I'm not sure yet."

She seemed even less sure of her own reaction to what might come next. I stubbed out my cigarette, then took Joan's and did the same.

"We need to get to know each other," I said, as I looked into her beautiful blue eyes, "and words aren't always the best way."

I reached out and took her in my arms. She moved closer, at first pliantly, then with more excitement. Her lips formed eager, incoherent sounds…my breath quickened…then there was a pause as we pulled apart, no longer touching.

"Sometimes," I said, "we remember things at the damnedest times," as I gently put my arms around her. "You were right. Let's give it time."

Then I kissed her gently, as she opened her blue eyes.

"Are you sure?"

"Of course. Besides, this ground is too damned hard!"

We both laughed, with relief, happy our first time alone wouldn't be ending on a bad note. We pulled into the ranch about five o'clock, and nobody seemed to have missed us. Before parting, we made a date to go see a movie in Carson City the following week.

CHAPTER 25

Autumn Leaves as Greenleafs Arrive

Oh, Gloomy

Labor Day weekend 1948 marked the end of the busiest season of the year. The "boys of summer," as Colin Greenley and Bud Henry were dubbed, left in Colin's "Geyser" Frazer to return to Princeton. Carol Greenley and Dee Allen flew east via San Francisco on United Mainliners, and the Gordon mother and daughter left by train for Cleveland. Patti Allen and Anne Marie Baker would be going to court soon, and then they'd leave.

That's the nature of the hospitality business—feast or famine. However, we were fully booked again by mid-September.

The new arrivals included Mrs. Ann Greenleaf and her two young children, Ricky and Gail—much to the chagrin of several guests. Everyone knew the Flying M E didn't take young children. Children made Emmy very nervous. Divorcées who brought their children with them usually stayed at the Washoe Pines or Pyramid Lake ranches, because they had stand-alone cabins. So why the exception for Ann Greenleaf and her two young ones, a lot of us wondered.

Ann McCormick Greenleaf with the fabulous smile, in the 1940s (Courtesy Gail Greenleaf Hencken)

Speculation ended when Emmy let it be known that Annie was an old and very dear friend of Allie's from finishing school days.

Ann McCormick Greenleaf, or "Annie" as she preferred to be called, was from Greenwich, Connecticut, a fashionable New York City suburb. She came from an Albany, New York family and had properly "come out" as a debutante. The 1948 Social Register listed her as Junior League and married to Lt. (Dr.) Richard Greenleaf.

Annie was a petite 5'2", with blond hair, eyes of blue and a great smile. Her teeth weren't perfect, but that didn't keep her from smiling.

Little Ricky, six, and Gail, four, were very well behaved, so in nothing flat both children had endeared themselves to guests and staff alike.

Annie, with Allie's assistance, enrolled Ricky in the little Franktown country school. I introduced the kids to Half Pint and Little Joe and let them ride around the paddock. They took to riding like a duck does to water. Speaking of water, I also taught them to swim, in my spare time.

As you can imagine, the kids spent lots of time with me around the stables. Instead of calling me Bill, they called me "Balls," not realizing other connotations of the word. They had another little expression, "Oh, gloomy." They used it many ways like, "Oh, gloomy, I don't want to go to school" or "Oh, gloomy, do we have to go to bed?" It was very expressive the way they said it. Little Gail came down with appendicitis and had to have an emergency appendectomy in Carson City. I was learning what it must be like to be a father.

Franktown School, 1947
(Photo Valerie Vondermuhll, Courtesy George A. Vondermuhll Jr.)

Annie Greenleaf was gregarious "from the git go" and her laughter was infectious. She loved to party, and became a steady member of the "Allie Cats." She was a regular night owl. I think she only rode twice, just to please her kids.

They say time flies when you're having fun, and it was definitely a fun time for this cowboy. I was dating Joan Allison Borg—with Emmy's approval—and there was a nice group of compatible guests at the ranch.

Too soon it was time for the Greenleafs to leave. Allie drove Annie into Reno and witnessed for her in court. That night, there was a graduation party for Annie at the Old Corner Bar. The next day, the Greenleaf family was on the train to New York.

About two weeks later, Allie flew east to visit her family in Virginia and, I believe, Annie in Greenwich. It was during this period that Emmy asked Joan to help her out with some of the chores Allie did, like taxiing guests to appointments and checking over the phone bill. In return, Joan received something off her room and board and a minimal monthly stipend.

I missed Ricky and Gail. The ranch just wasn't the same without them. Then, mid-December,

Ricky and Gail Greenleaf with "Balls" McGee
(Authors' Collection)

Gail Greenleaf sporting cowgirl boots, 1948

Ricky Greenleaf graining horses. Buckskin on right is Little Joe

(Authors' Collection)

word spread like wildfire, "The Greenleafs are coming back—only this time for a year!"

Two months later, when I was back on the job after a "cowboyin' mishap" (more about this later), Annie and the kids were ensconced at the ranch, just as if they had never left, and Ricky was back in school. Next thing I knew, Annie and both kids came down with the chicken pox. Ricky and Gail were not too troubled by the illness, but Annie became very ill. Emmy was away, so Allie moved Annie into one of the twin beds in Emmy's room to quarantine her from the other guests.

I kept in touch with Annie after I left the ranch. In the early 1950s, she invited me to a cocktail party in either Port Chester or Greenwich, Connecticut. She was giving a party for Kathleen Winsor, the author of *Forever Amber*. When the novel was published in 1944, it flew off the shelves, selling 100,000 copies the first week. It was considered very racy in its day. I remember Miss Winsor demurring, "I wrote only two sexy passages, and my publishers took both of them out." Annie remarried about twelve years after leaving the ranch. The last time we spoke—and this is almost unbelievable—she told me her married name had gone from a Greenleaf to a Carrott! We had a big laugh over that.

• • •

More than forty years later, I caught up with "little Ricky" and Gail Greenleaf via the Internet. There were thirty-eight Richard, Rick, or R. Greenleafs listed on Ancestry.com, and each was sent a postcard with the message, "Writing a book on the famous Flying M E in Franktown, Nevada. Looking for Ricky and Gail Greenleaf, children of Ann Greenleaf, who stayed at the ranch in the late 1940s. If this is you, please call collect!" Three days later, Rick Greenleaf called. The "kids" are still a joy to talk to after all these years. Gail is married, with two children and two grandchildren. Rick has been married three times and has two children. They both live in the East.

Gail shared her favorite memories:

Rick and I were suffering under the illusion we were there on vacation. We stayed more than a year the second time. Mom didn't want to pull Rick out of school.

The Flying M E guests were "party animals," according to Mom, and Mom knew how to have a good time.

I didn't know that Allie was part of the ranch management. I thought she was just a good friend of Mom's. I remember going down to Virginia later on, to visit Allie on her father's huge farm.

Half Pint was my horse. He was huge. I'm still sure he was the biggest, wasn't he, Bill?

Allie Okie and Annie Greenleaf, "party people" (Courtesy R. C. Greenleaf)

CHAPTER 26

Midnight Plumbing Problem

Joan Allison's caricature summarizes the problem. Now for the solution. The Flying M E had modern plumbing, but it was hooked up to a septic tank, not a city sewer system. Emmy and the maids used to caution all the guests upon arrival: please do not flush personal items. When this did happen, it drove Emmy crazy. As she put it, "Just one thoughtless guest inconveniences all the rest!"

If we were lucky, the plumber's helper would do the trick. But chances were the output pipe to the septic tank was clogged up, which in turn triggered the following scenario:

(Caricatures by Joan Allison)

• It's around midnight just after a major snowstorm in December. Someone pounds on the bunkhouse door waking this wrangler out of a deep sleep.

• I dress and wade through eighteen inches of snow to get to the ranch house.

• After giving the plumber's helper a go, I call an emergency septic tank service in Carson City. A live answering service lady promises to send someone out first thing in the morning.

• Next morning, after a hot cup of coffee, I locate and dig up the lawn sod over the septic tank, first having cleared the area of snow.

• The pumper truck arrives about eight, empties the tank and clears the pipe with a fifty-foot snake.

By ten a.m., we're back in business. A guest comments, "I've been sitting by the window having coffee and watching you. It looked cold!"

Bill McGee with the ranch's Chrysler Town & Country, 1948. (Authors' Collection)

CHAPTER 27

Three's a Crowd

Or a Play in Four Acts

Act I.

It was a crisp autumn day in early November 1948, and guests were as scarce as hen's teeth. The "Hollywood creative types" had left, as had the Greenleaf family. In fact, the ranch was so quiet that Emmy and Allie decided to fly to Europe for a well-deserved vacation. Joan Allison and I would be in charge, and Edie and Joan would act as residence witnesses for the few guests we have.

Joan's divorce was final, and she had resumed her maiden name, Allison. She had arrived at the ranch in mid-July and had been phasing in as Emmy's assistant since early September, helping both Emmy and Allie, and earning their trust and confidence.

Furthermore, Joan and I had been dating on

Flying M E management team: left to right, Emmy Wood, Bill McGee and Allie Okie. (Authors' Collection)

and off for a couple of months. Nothing serious, but who knows. She was one sweet lady.

On November 3, Joan and I drove Emmy and Allie to the Reno airport and watched their United flight take off. I was pleased with my increased responsibilities at the ranch. My long-range plans were right on schedule.

Joan's and my first assignment as interim ranch managers was to meet a "Divorcée Special" —the local jargon for any train bringing divorce clients to Reno—and pick up a Mrs. Nathalie Morgan from New York. Her train was late, which gave Joan and me some time to observe the passing parade over a cup of hot coffee and a cigarette. Another Joan, Joan Drackert from the Pyramid Lake Guest Ranch, was there to meet a six-weeker and we exchanged the

The majority of Flying M E guests arrived in Reno on a "Divorcée Special," the term used for any train bringing clients to Reno. More adventurous guests opted to arrive by air. (Courtesy Neal Cobb Collection)

latest on who was in town, and who was "bad news." "Bad news," in our business, meant a guest who was a bad drunk or a loudmouth. They usually would be asked to leave, after arrangements were made for them to stay someplace else.

Finally, the train pulled in, and we watched closely as the passengers descended the Pullman car.

"There she is," Joan whispered. "I can tell by how she's dressed."

Joan was right. There was our Mrs. Nathalie Morgan, the very picture of "society," in a full-length mink coat, collar turned up against the cold, kid gloves and a felt hat. A porter followed behind with her luggage.

I'd guess Mrs. Morgan to be in her fifties, although she looked much younger. She was very attractive, and greeted us in a confident and poised manner.

"You must be Bill McGee and Joan Allison," she said, extending her gloved hand. "Emmy told

me you'd be meeting me. I told her I'd miss her, but she was to have a wonderful time in Paris and not to worry about me."

We made our way through the crowded station, and I loaded her luggage in the Buick wagon. A lot of luggage for six weeks, I thought to myself, especially the four hat boxes. Most guests bought a Stetson at Parker's, and that was what they wore their entire stay.

"Mrs. Morgan, would you like to get something to eat before driving out to the ranch? We could go to the Riverside Hotel. Or maybe you have some other stops you'd like to make, like your lawyer's office?"

"I hope this doesn't shock you, but I'd love a martini."

"Oh, I don't know, ma'am. The sun's over the yardarm in New York, isn't it?" I said.

"I like your thinking, Bill. I hope you and Joan will join me."

We parked near the Riverside and entered the

Corner Bar. Heads turned to admire our elegant and stylish guest. She was used to this kind of attention, I could tell, as she walked with confidence straight to the best table with a river view.

Two martinis later, Mrs. Morgan was insisting we call her Nathalie. After the third, she was telling us why she was getting a divorce. Her reasons were not so different from those of the other guests. Emmy was always saying "there were just six stories," meaning each guest fit into one of six categories. I noticed that after three martinis Nathalie seemed to change not a bit. I was sure of one thing: word would soon get around town about this lady and the local male prospects—or should I say suspects—would be paying their court to Mrs. Nathalie Morgan, wealthy divorcée.

Despite the differences in their age and personality, Nathalie and Joan became good pals. Nathalie taught Joan how to play Canasta and Oklahoma, and they played every night that we didn't go into town. Joan became a champion card player, much to her amazement.

On a darker note, Joan recalls, "At first, I thought Nathalie was drinking lots of water. Naïve me. One morning I saw her pouring gin into her water glass. Turns out she drank gin all day but never seemed to get drunk."

Like others before her, Nathalie came to Reno intent on divorcing one man to marry another. Her fiancé was waiting for her in San Francisco. Their plan was for him to come to the ranch in early December, so they could be married as soon as she descended the courthouse steps, divorce decree in hand. But Nathalie seemed nervous about something, and one day she simply blurted out, "God, I don't want him here!"

Meanwhile, Joan and I were going about our various duties running the ranch. Joan met two more guests at the train station, Dotsie Wilson and Louise Rathbone, shopped for Edie in Reno, and took care of the bills and other chores. Dotsie was a belle from North Carolina and Louise was a Main Liner from Philadelphia.

As for me, I was down to one regular rider, Sidney Lawrence, a lawyer from Washington D. C. He was quiet and not much fun to be with, not like a Colin Greenley or a Norman Tokar. My guess was his divorce had him very depressed. When he wasn't riding, he kept to himself and stayed in his room. Joan and I took the guests who wanted to go sightseeing to Pyramid Lake, Virginia City and Lake Tahoe.

Since Emmy had given Joan and me her "dating okay," we had a few evenings out at the movies in Carson and a dinner at the Mapes Skyroom, to see Frank Sinatra. One night at the Old Corner, Joan surprised me when she said, "Mother sent me a diaphragm with a nice note saying, 'If you're going to continue seeing that cowboy, you'll need this.' Do I have a modern mother, or what?"

"Can't wait to prove her right!" We both laughed.

Best I can recall, we went straight back to the ranch that night and made passionate love in Emmy's room (Joan's for the month of November). We proved her mother to be right on more than one occasion, from that night on.

On December 2, Emmy returned from Europe in particularly good spirits and looking refreshed. Allie had stopped off in Virginia to visit her father. To celebrate Emmy's return, Edie made one of her favorite dinners, Boeuf `a la Bourguignonne, and Nathalie contributed the French wines.

Winter arrived with a vengeance on December 3, depositing several inches of snow on the ground. Donner Summit reported twenty-four inches with the snow still falling. According to a weather bureau report, "The snow season is here to stay. A long-range forecast from California predicts this year will have the heaviest snowfall in the mountains in forty years." (*Nevada State Journal*, December 4, 1948). That's exactly what happened.

A few days later, Allie returned from Virginia. She announced that Annie Greenleaf and her two kids would definitely be arriving around the first of February for an extended stay.

On December 15, the United States weather bureau in Reno forecast another big snowfall was on its way within twenty-four hours. The storm was moving south from the northern ranges of Oregon and Washington. Snowpack on Donner Summit was now sixty inches. During the winter of 1948/49, many heavy snowstorms raked Washoe Valley, dumping mounds of snow that piled into six to eight foot drifts, thanks to gale force winds. The storms were so intense at times that the V & T was stalled for days in the Washoe cut, the little canyon between Washoe and Pleasant Valley, and had to be dug out by gangs of shovelers. During one big snow, the drifts were so huge that even the big Southern Pacific trains were abandoned in the Sierras for days.

Act II. The Gathering Storm

The second act opens on a dark and chilly day following the latest storm. Nathalie's fiancé from San Francisco, Mr. George H. L. Peet, pulled into the ranch in his black Chrysler sedan. I was feeding the horses in the stables when George walked in.

"Hello, I'm George Peet, a guest of Nathalie Morgan's. I'll be spending a few days here," he said, stamping his feet to loosen the snow on his overshoes.

"Howdy, Mr. Peet, and welcome. I'm Bill McGee. I'll take you to the ranch house and introduce you to Emmy Wood. Let me give you a hand with your luggage. How was your drive? Did you have to chain up over the Summit?"

"No, but the snow plows were busy. I understand there's more snow to come."

Mr. Peet looked to be a distinguished gentleman in his fifties with a full head of silver grey hair, and a neatly groomed, pencil thin mustache. Despite the weather, he was dressed in a conservative blue blazer and grey flannel slacks. Nathalie was not at the ranch to meet him.

According to Joan, Mr. Peet was a non-stop talker and it wasn't long before Emmy and Joan had heard his life story. He was a Naval Academy graduate, a Lieutenant Commander in the Naval Reserve, and had skippered a navy cargo ship during World War II. He was divorced from a Knight of New York—the Knights being a very old and wealthy family—and she had divorced him. George was now living in an apartment on Russian Hill in San Francisco.

Joan also told me, on the q.t., that according to Nathalie, George possessed many attractive qualities: a good social background, perfect manners, he dressed beautifully, and made a good escort. However, he didn't have any money. He didn't even have a career. Nathalie wasn't too happy about that.

Act III.

On December 18, we were all surprised with the unannounced arrival of Lucy Dodsworth Allison, Joan's mother and the woman with the good sense to mail her daughter a diaphragm. Lucy had been to the ranch earlier in the year to divorce Joan's father, but she checked out after two weeks, to move into town to be closer to "the action." Her unannounced visit during this harsh winter came as a big surprise, especially to Joan. Lucy said she came to lend "moral support to her newly-divorced daughter," but I think maybe she came to size up Bill McGee.

Joan thinks her mother made the trip for a different reason. "I'd written mother a letter telling her my depression had fallen away and I was feeling much better, sort of in charge of myself, as they say. I told her this was a good time for me to start over and I wanted to return East and study to become a doctor. Money was no problem as far as college was concerned. Next thing, Mother's at the ranch! I think she came flying out to the ranch as soon as she read my letter because she was afraid I'd return East and cramp her lifestyle! "

Act IV.

Our cast of malcontented characters was housebound for several days. Conversation was polite but strained. You could cut the tension with a knife. The only escape was to go for a walk, and that meant in very cold temperatures and through —or over—snow drifts.

Nathalie Morgan was one very unhappy looking fiancée. Not only was she suspicious of George Peet's motives for wanting to marry her, she had tired of him, too. Seems Nathalie tired of men quickly and wanted out of her engagement to George.

George H. L. Peet, the perfect fiancé, was oblivious to Nathalie's change of heart. He simply mistook her distant behavior as pre-divorce as well as pre-marital jitters.

Lucy Dodsworth Allison was still keeping her real reason for coming to the ranch to herself.

Finally one evening, Nathalie announced to George that their engagement was off.

The next morning, George was seen out walking in the snow with Lucy. This would be the first of several long walks they would take together, just the two of them although sometimes Dotsie

Wilson went along. The snow continued to fall.

On December 19, the snow plows were finally able to clear the driveway into the ranch.

On December 20, Emmy and Joan took Nathalie into Reno for her court appearance, followed by celebratory martinis at the "Widow's Corner" in the Riverside. They bid Nathalie farewell at the train depot, and she boarded a Pullman for the return trip to New York.

On December 21, after promising to purchase a new set of chains in Carson, George decided to return to San Francisco.

On December 22, Allie and Joan took Lucy and Dotsie into Reno. Dotsie made her court appearance with Joan as her witness, and then Dotsie and Lucy, good friends by now, boarded the train to San Francisco. Dotsie had talked Lucy into looking at apartments there.

Back at the ranch, our dinner conversations speculated about our malcontented guests. Had wealthy socialite Nathalie Morgan arrived in Reno with her mind already made up to break it off with George H. L. Peet? Why did Lucy Dodsworth Allison show up unannounced at the ranch, and in the middle of one of the worst snowstorms? What would become of gentleman George H. L. Peet, who looked so forlorn as he drove off in the snow? Well, we discussed things up one side and down the other and laughingly decided we didn't have a clue. As long as guests departed with good memories of the ranch, we were happy.

The weather cleared, the sky was a brilliant blue, the sun was blinding, and the temperature was averaging about twenty degrees. Slide Mountain never looked more beautiful and Christmas was right around the corner. Life was good at the Flying M E.

Half Pint, Zorro and Bill McGee bring down a Christmas tree for the Flying M E, December, 1948. (Authors' Collection)

CHAPTER 28

Christmas at the Flying M E

Have You Ever Done the Reno Rhumba?

On December 22, after the last member of "Three's a Crowd" had checked out, I figured it was high time we created a little holiday atmosphere. So I saddled Zorro, put the packsaddle on Half Pint, and rode up the Little Valley trail about a half-mile, until I spotted the perfectly shaped Christmas tree I'd had my eye on for some time, a seven-foot sugar pine.

When I returned to the ranch, I built a stand for the tree, with plenty of supervision from my jockey friend, Jimmy Murray. The ladies of the ranch agreed on the ideal spot in the living room.

This would be my second Christmas at the Flying M E. It was much like a traditional American family get-together. Emmy and the staff were the family, and any ranch guests— usually less than six this time of year—were treated as visiting family. Decorating the tree was a very festive occasion, with everyone pitching in. Allie

Joan Allison and friend, Christmas 1948
(Authors' Collection)

played a record of Christmas carols, and Emmy and Joan played under the tree with the dachshunds. The tree was beautifully decorated by cocktail hour. To top it off, we had plenty of snow.

After several toasts of "Cheers" and a few sips of our drinks, Joan planted a quick kiss on me and asked if we could go somewhere quiet to talk. So, later on we excused ourselves and drove into Carson to the Old Corner Bar.

A Cowboy Christmas Surprise

"There's no easy way to tell you this. I'm pregnant." Just as Joan didn't know how to tell me, I didn't know how to react to this news.

"Are you sure? You've been using your diaphragm, right?"

"The answer to both questions is yes. I've always used my diaphragm, and the doctor called this afternoon. I didn't want to tell you until I was sure, but I had a pregnancy test yesterday, after putting Mother and Mrs. Wilson on the train."

"Holy mackerel. What are we going to do?"

"I'm not sure. I don't think either one of us has marriage in mind."

"You want to be a doctor, and I'm sure not ready to become a city dweller."

"The doctor estimates I'm three weeks along, so we have some time. How would you feel if I could arrange to terminate the pregnancy?"

"I have one problem with that, and it's a big one. From everything I've heard and read, your life could be on the line, unless we find a bona fide doctor to perform the abortion. Let's sleep on it and talk about it tomorrow."

"I'm afraid Emmy's going to be very upset about this," Joan said sadly.

"Yes, she will be, so let's not tell her until we've finalized a plan, okay?"

As we drove home that night, we were both silently weighing our options. With Emmy and Allie back, I was back sleeping in the bunkhouse, and Joan had the yellow room with a fireplace in the ranch house. Neither of us slept much that night.

The next day, after talking about it again, we told Emmy and Allie about our problem and the plan we'd worked out. I would take time off to search for a medical doctor in San Francisco who would perform an abortion under clean, safe conditions.

I left the ranch after lunch that day and was in San Francisco six hours later, in spite of the road conditions and chain controls.

At twenty-two, I was no country bumpkin. Having spent four years in the Navy (three of them in World War II), I knew San Francisco pretty well. Since abortion was illegal, I knew it would be pointless to start calling doctors in the book. So I did the next best thing—I talked to cab drivers and bell hops all over the city. I received several refer-

rals, but none of them were for a doctor. After chasing down these leads, I concluded that my mission was futile. I wouldn't let the people I met operate on my worst enemy.

Even though I'd had no success in San Francisco, I decided to try the same approach in Sacramento on my way home, just in case a smaller town might yield different results. But no luck.

I arrived back at the ranch on Christmas Eve morning with the disappointing news and a new plan. Joan should have our baby. When she starts to show, she should leave the ranch to "visit" her mother in San Francisco. Joan and her mother could make arrangements to put the baby up for adoption. This way, the baby would be born in a hospital with proper medical care for both baby and mother. In the event we had a change of heart, we could marry and keep the baby. That night, Joanie and I agreed to the plan.

"I don't think we have another choice," she said. "This way, we can both stick with our career plans."

Emmy breathed a sigh of relief when we told her our plan.

"Thank the good Lord. I was hoping you two would decide on that course."

• • •

Edie prepared a fantastic Christmas dinner. Roast turkey with all the trimmings, plus pumpkin and mince meat pies. The only guest we had was Sidney Lawrence, the D. C. lawyer. The holidays seemed to depress him even more. His divorce action was being challenged, and he had to stay on in Nevada longer than six weeks.

On December 27, Emmy held her annual open house for valley neighbors, Carson and Virginia City friends and—by invitation only—Reno lawyers and judges. It was a great mix of people.

With the open house in full swing, Allie

Emmy with Dinklespiel and Shätzie, under the Christmas tree, 1948
(Authors' Collection)

returned from Reno with a new guest in tow, Mrs. Theodora McMillan, a handsome, middle-aged matron from Boston. This was her second stay at the ranch, her first being back in '43 when Eleanor Roosevelt paid a visit.

"I guess that makes me a two-time loser," she said to Emmy.

"Oh, dear, your situation is not that unusual, believe me," said Emmy, in an effort to console.

With a stiff upper lip, Mrs. McMillan picked herself up, joined the party and mixed right in with the guests at the open house. She had confidence and poise and put people at ease. She encountered Sidney Lawrence on one of his necessary departures from his room to have a meal, and she seemed to know just how to cheer him out of his melancholy mood.

Have You Ever Done the Reno Rhumba?

The weather continued to make the headlines. The *Nevada State Journal* reported on December 28, 1948:

Reno Gets Biggest Snowfall Since '37

Not for 11 years had Reno seen so much snow all at one time.

It began early Sunday morning. People getting up after a late morning snooze looked out to see it coming down, not in the big wind-blown flakes common to Washoe County, but in small, thick-falling ones coming steadily and in dead silence from a leaden sky that reached from horizon to horizon.

From the very start it looked like a big one,

Manhattan anyone? (Photo Valerie Vondermuhll, Courtesy George A. Vondermuhll Jr.)

and it was. From six to eight inches of snow fell in low-lying areas around Reno and Carson City, and by yesterday had turned streets and highways into a welter of slush, ice and water.

As much as 24 inches of snow was deposited on high mountain elevations. Donner Summit reported a snow pack of 65 inches and said 22 inches of new snow fell Sunday.

United Airlines reported the snowstorm forced Reno-bound planes to fly over the city without landing on Sunday.

Below freezing temperatures continued throughout western Nevada, with a low of five degrees recorded in Reno yesterday morning.

Yesterday was the coldest December 27 on record as far as Reno is concerned, the local weather bureau reported last night.

The thermometer got down to five above, which is one lower than the next best record of six, set on December 27, 1916. Although there are still some days to go, this whole month has a chance to set a new record for cold Decembers.

As if record snowfall and freezing temps were not enough, earthquakes hit the area. From the *Nevada State Journal*, December 30, 1948:

Earthquakes Still Shaking Reno Area
Epidemic of Earthquakes Becoming Known
as the "Reno Rhumba"

Intermittent tremors continued to shake the Reno area last night many hours after a sharp earthquake rattled western Nevada and northern California, causing widespread but minor damage.

Reno residents were apprehensive and restive, fearful that the continuing temblors were an advance warning of another and even sharper jolt yet to come.

Prof. Vincent Gianella, University of Nevada seismologist, placed the center of the first violent shock as about 12 or 13 miles west of Reno, in the Verdi area.

The severe shakeup, which came at 4:53 a.m., rocked thousands of square miles in the two-state area, making a low rumbling noise.

The force of the jolt woke up most Reno residents, as well as those in Carson City, Truckee, Virginia City, Minden, and Portola and Quincy in nearby California.

Verdi Suffers Most Damage From Quake

Substantiating the earthquake theory was the discovery of another narrow crack in the ground immediately west of the Donner Trail Ranch, near Verdi.

A half-dozen divorce seeking residents of the Donner Trail Ranch, including silent screen heroine, Dorothy Mackaill, fled from their rooms in fear yesterday morning when the jolt shook the ranch house itself sharply.

Gianella described the force of the shock as "extremely severe. Had it occurred in Reno itself," he said, "I'm afraid we would have had a disaster on our hands."

As it was, only the small town of Verdi and open rangeland stood in the immediate center of the quake.

Almost every building in the community suffered minor damage but residents estimated $15,000 to $20,000 would cover it all.

The earth shaking continued throughout the afternoon in Reno, with several of the jolts noticeable in the downtown section of the city.

Gianella said he had never heard of such activity in the Reno area in the more than 30 years seismographs have been in operation here.

"This is unusual for Reno," he said. "We don't know what to think of it."

• • •

Between Christmas and the New Year, Emmy launched her annual New Year's card project. Joan and Allie addressed hundreds of envelopes, and Emmy wrote a personal note on each card.

Emmy took her time with this project. One year, she was still writing notes well into March. Friends, former guests, neighbors, and business associates looked forward to receiving Emmy's annual New Year's card, no matter what time of year it arrived.

Holiday Cards, 1948

CHAPTER 29

Cowboyin' Mishap

New Year's 1949

Northern Nevada's epidemic of earthquakes were becoming known throughout the nation as the "Reno Rhumba" and continued to produce occasional quivers. Professor Vincent Gianella, University of Nevada seismologist, was quoted in the *Nevada State Journal* on January 1: "Somewhere around a hundred separate tremors have been recorded in Reno the last five days."

Lady Luck shook me up on January 2. The day had begun just fine. It was one of those bright, clear days in Nevada—very cold, but no wind, and still lots of snow on the ground. In fact, the locals said we had more snow on the ground for longer periods of time this winter than they've seen in seventeen years. Some drifts were six to eight feet high

The Flying M E, January 1949 (Authors' Collection)

before Christmas, in some places.

Skiers were taking advantage of the excellent snow conditions by flocking to their favorite slopes. Snowplow crews were working overtime to keep the Mount Rose area open.

Ray Raymond, a retired San Francisco banker now a gentleman rancher, lived up the road from the "M E" about a half-mile. Mr. Raymond was a widower, and Emmy invited him to dinner with some regularity.

Several of Raymond's prized purebred Black Angus cattle had wandered off through some downed fence, apparently caused by the huge snowdrifts. His hired hand was away for the holidays, so Mr. Raymond asked Emmy if I could give him a hand.

An hour later, Zorro and I were making our way through the deep snow toward Big Washoe. There looked to be several dozen head of cattle

Reno when it's snowing, circa 1940s (Courtesy Neal Cobb Collection)

near the lake. It soon became obvious that more than one rancher would be looking for strays. In some cases, fence had been knocked down by the weight of the snow, or the huge, packed drifts had provided the cattle with a bridge over the fence.

Cutting out Mr. Raymond's Black Angus from the other cattle, all Herefords, should have been a breeze, but there was a hidden problem. Cattle had left deep hoof marks in the mud as the lake receded in the fall, and now the hoof marks were hidden by the recent snow storms.

Lights Out

As I was cutting out Raymond's cattle, Zorro— one of the most sure-footed horses I'd ever ridden—stepped in a deep rut below the snow,

and we somersaulted "ass over tea kettle." It's a wonder my neck wasn't broken. I was out cold for some time, and when I came to, Zorro was standing over me with his head lowered, looking me in the eye as if to say, "I'm sorry." (I've been having lower back problems off and on ever since as a result of this fall.)

Several things happened in quick order after the accident. My Reno doctor, Dr. Ernest W. "Ernie" Mack, a neurologist at 1155 Wells Avenue, put me in a body cast from my hips to my armpits. I was numb on the right side below the hip, and he was worried I might become paralyzed.

January had started out very cold, and January 3 bottomed out at minus 3 degrees, with a high of 26 degrees. Emmy insisted I move from the bunkhouse into an upstairs bedroom, so I could be looked after. "You'll be red-nosed and frozen-toed, even with your woolies on in that bunkhouse," she said.

Mr. Raymond insisted he would cover my medical expenses.

Reno R n' R

A few days later, when another big snowstorm was in the forecast, Dr. Mack ordered me to stay in town so he could check on my condition daily. Dr. Mack knew best. The *Nevada State Journal* reported: "The storm dumped one of the season's deepest snows on Reno. For local residents it was ankle deep and then some. By early evening the street was under several inches of snow and the flakes were still coming down. Cars were getting stuck in the drifts, and pedestrians were having to wade. The local forecast gloomily predicted cloudy skies, more snow, and temperatures colder than yesterday's high of 26 degrees and low of 6."

I arranged for a cowboy friend of mine, "Utah" Bob, to fill in for me at the ranch "for an indefinite period," as the doc put it.

When Edie Riley, the wonderful Flying M E cook, heard I was going to have to stay in Reno, she offered me the use of a vacant one bedroom furnished apartment in an apartment house she owned on West Fifth Street. Edie also offered it rent-free for the first month.

"Edie, you don't have to do that," I protested.

"Never look a gift horse in the mouth, Bill. I wouldn't have offered if I didn't mean it."

Her timing was perfect. Joan packed for me while Utah chained up the pickup, and we made it to Reno just before snow flurries changed to blizzard conditions. Later, I learned that Utah had to pull over several times due to zero visibility, but made it back to the ranch okay.

About a week went by. I saw the doc every day so he could check me out. The body cast was very

uncomfortable, and eating made me nauseated. I asked the doc for his best prognosis.

"You're making some progress, but my objective is still the same: to avoid surgery on your lower back if at all possible. If you don't have any setbacks, we should be able to replace the cast with a brace in a few days."

Then I asked the doc how long he thought it would be before I could resume my cowboy duties.

"It's too soon to tell. Probably six to eight weeks. But I want you to stay in town. Another big storm is said to be moving in. It's really some winter."

I relayed Dr. Mack's prognosis to Joan and

Bill McGee and "Utah" Bob, 1949 (Authors' Collection)

Emmy. The very next day, Allie drove Joan into town with some good news. Since it was still quiet at the ranch, Joan could keep me company for the rest of my Reno stay. Allie also reported that Utah was doing a good job.

The following week, the body cast came off—thank God for that—and I was fitted for a special lower back steel brace. I almost felt normal again.

Dr. Mack, a native Nevadan of pioneer Virginia City stock, had spent three-plus years in the South Pacific with "MacArthur's Army." He met his wife-to-be in Australia—Roberta Bowers Dawson, a WAC officer from Reno. It was a small world, we agreed, and decided that our paths had probably crossed in both New Guinea and Manila. Ernie was also an avid fisherman and a real man's man.[1]

In December, when Washoe Valley was covered with snow, several times we saw snow shoot up geyser-like immediately after the sound of an explosion. On January 16, 1949, the *Nevada State Journal* carried what we thought was the answer to these unexplained explosions:

Professor Vincent Gianella, eminent seismologist at University of Nevada Reno, believes the "explosions" heard last year may have been vertical earthquakes. Gianella says up-and-down shifts with the earth's surface probably would not be recorded on seismographs, but might very likely make a noise resembling a distant explosion.

He said such phenomena are fairly common throughout the world and are referred to by geologists as the "moodus rumbles."

The locals agreed the valley had more than its share of "moodus rumbles."

I finally got the green light from the doctor to see if Star Taxi could use an experienced driver. They had a relief driver position open, so I grabbed it. I needed the money. The only problem was you never knew what shift you would be driving from day to day.

It was great to have Joanie with me. We ate out most nights (she never learned how to cook) and saw a lot of movies. I introduced her to my old friend, Lena Geiser, at the Round Up Bar, and I took her to the Roaring Camp.

In spite of our being together, I could tell the whole Reno scene depressed her—Edie's apartment, the neighborhood, the pregnancy. It didn't help any when her mother and George H. L. Peet paid us a visit from San Francisco and confirmed the same.

I went to the pound and picked out a cute little puppy of questionable heritage and brought her home in the top of a bag of groceries. The puppy seemed to cheer Joanie up, at least for awhile.

In another attempt to cheer up Joanie, I made a dinner date for us with one of my favorite friends of the old Round Up crowd, Dick Sylvester. Dick promised me he would be "sober as a judge to meet your new lady friend." When Dick was sober, he was very interesting and had a great sense of humor; when he wasn't, he became very quiet and sullen. Dick was an alcoholic and a "remittance kid," a black sheep from an upper crust Boston family who had shipped him out West.

We met for dinner at the Riverside. In spite of his promise, I could tell that Dick had had a few by the slur of his words when I introduced him to Joanie. As "John Barleycorn" took over during dinner, Dick pushed his plate aside in the middle of our conversation and slowly lowered his head so that it rested on one of his hands and went to sleep—or so it seemed.

A few minutes later, our waiter came over and asked, "Is Mr. Sylvester all right?"

"He's had a little too much to drink. He's just resting," I said. "We'll take him home."

At this point, the maitre d' arrived and took Dick's pulse. "This man needs a doctor," he called out loudly. "Is there a doctor in the house?"

A doctor was sitting two booths away and came over and felt Dick's pulse. "Someone call an ambulance! This man is dying!"

Sad to say, Dick was DOA at Washoe General. He had choked to death on a piece of steak lodged in his throat. In retrospect, had he been sober, he no doubt would have signaled that he was choking, and someone might have been able to act in time to save him.

The Emergency Room nurse gave me several phone numbers of Sylvesters from the little address book in Dick's wallet, and I called from the hospital, even though it was about midnight in Boston. I got one of Dick's brothers on the first call. After he recovered from the shocking news, he thanked me and said, "One or two of us will catch the next flight to Reno. Would you please be good enough to arrange for the transfer of his body to a Reno mortuary for embalming? We'll be bringing him back to Boston for burial in the family plot."

As I write this some fifty years later, I am still haunted by that night and the "what ifs." I still wake up from a recurring dream fully convinced that I am choking to death.

John Friendly, Radio DJ

A few days later, Lady Luck returned. I had the day shift and had picked up a fare at the Reno airport. Turns out he was an executive with Western American Life Insurance Company. We were talking during the drive into town when he said, "Has anyone told you that you have a great voice? Ever done any radio announcing?"

"No, I haven't, but thanks for the compliment."

"Tell you what, why don't you call my office and I'll arrange an audition for you. Here's my card. I'm Mr. Tomlison. What's your name?"

"Bill McGee. Thanks a lot, Mr. Tomlison. I'll call you first thing tomorrow."

The rest of the way into town, he asked me questions about my background and seemed satisfied with the answers.

Joanie seemed please with the news. "I'd love to see you do something beside driving a cab."

My audition was at KOH Radio. A station man gave me some commercial copy to read. I was hired then and there and given the radio name "John Friendly."

I would actually be on the Western American Life Insurance Company's payroll, and they were headquartered at 153 N. Virginia Street. As "John Friendly," my job was to spin records, announce the births of new babies and salute the mothers on the air each morning. Later, "John Friendly" would deliver a free baby book to each mother, sometimes at the hospital, sometimes at their home. The sponsor's objective was to sell life insurance to the new parents. From what I heard, it was a successful approach.

It did strike Joanie and me as just a little ironic that the theme of my radio show was babies.

My hours as John Friendly didn't pay much more than cab driving, but the regular, daytime hours were a welcome change for Joanie and me. The job required I drive my own car, so since I'd been planning to buy one anyway, we shopped around and decided to invest in a new Plymouth coupe from Herrmann & Wilson on Island Avenue.

As hard as she tried, Joanie couldn't shake her feelings of depression. We went out quite a bit. One night we went to see the legendary country music singer Hank Williams perform in the Mapes Skyroom. He sang two of his biggest hits, "Hey, Good Lookin'" and "Your Cheatin' Heart." (He would die just four years later at age twenty-nine of a heart attack.) Joanie enjoyed his performance, much to my surprise. She told me her father, Jack

Allison, wrote and sang folk music and was a big admirer of Hank Williams' talent.

Back to the Ranch

About the middle of February, I received a call from Emmy. "Utah has made a fool of himself, and I'm going to have to let him go today. How are you doing? Has Dr. Mack given you a date when you can return to us?"

I apologized to Emmy about Utah Bob and called Dr. Mack. He was very obliging.

"I'd prefer you wait another two weeks, but go ahead. Just be sure you wear your brace and call me at once if you notice any significant changes."

Before calling Emmy back, Joan and I talked it over.

"Bill, I don't think I should return to the ranch right now. Emmy doesn't need a pregnant hostess around. I think it's time for me to stay with Mother until the baby arrives."

Sneaking to meet Cowboy
(Caricature by Joan Allison)

We had planned on this, of course, but not quite so soon.

"Let's get you settled at your mother's before I go back to the ranch."

Emmy was both pleased and relieved with our plan. She told us to take as many days as we needed, as things were still quiet at the ranch.

The insurance company wasn't quite as nice about my leaving, but they had known from the start that I was only temporary. I packed up what few belongings we had, and Joanie called her mother. Then we drove non-stop to San Francisco. Fortunately, U.S. 40 was open with no controls.

Lucy Allison had leased a three-bedroom apartment on Nob Hill with great views of the bay. I spent two nights and one day there and then returned to the ranch.

Before I could unpack, Jimmy Murray was filling me in on the "Utah Caper" as he called it.

"Your Utah cowboy friend took advantage of Emmy's kindness. You know that little room opposite the yellow fireplace room that looks out at the water tower? Well, Emmy puts him up there 'cause of the big snow. Then the other day he violates Emmy's house rules on fraternization, which made Emmy real mad.

"According to Emmy, she came in late from ridin' herd on some guests at the Old Corner. The livin' room was barely lit and she was emptying ashtrays and straightenin' up the bar. Lo and behold, here come one of the gals a tippy-toeing across the living room, candle in hand, barefoot, wearing only a little sheer blue nighty. Emmy watched her, and sure enough the gal was headin' straight to Utah Bob's room. 'Oh, no you don't, young lady!' Emmy said in a stern voice. 'We don't do that here.' Then she wheeled the gal around saying, 'Back to your room.'"

"Damn him," I said. "I warned Utah about that. He promised me if he fell in love, he'd wait 'til I got back and arrange his meetings away from the ranch. Wait 'til I see him. He's really let me down."

"Well," said Jimmy, "I suppose it's all Utah Bob's fault. But then, sittin' here and observin' the goings on every day as I do, let your elder tell you something, young Bill. You never can tell with some of them fillies. The gal just might of started the whole thing—and what was poor Utah to do!"

CHAPTER 30

Rustlers Nabbed

As Far As I Was Concerned, They Got What They Deserved

This story really happened shortly after I returned to the ranch after convalescing from my "cowboyin' mishap."

You remember two of my so-called cowboy friends, Utah Bob and Frank Burrows—Utah embarrassed me at the Flying M E, and Burrows was the "lady killer" cowboy from Arizona. Both were out of work, down on their luck and no doubt loaded to the gills, when they shot a steer beside the road one night near Steamboat Springs and butchered it on the spot. They tried to sell the two sides of beef to a Reno meat packer the next morning, but the packing house called the sheriff as soon as the "rustlers" walked out the door.

The charge was made by the rancher, who claimed that the pair had killed and butchered one of his steers, valued at $160. According to a sheriff's deputy, there was a large knife, a meat saw and the carcass in the cowboys' pickup. The pair were taken to the county jail and booked for grand larceny.

Under Nevada laws, the theft of animals such as cattle constitutes grand larceny, regardless of the cash value of the animal. Ordinarily, stolen property must amount to $250 before it is classified as grand larceny.

The cowboys paid for their drunken stupidity with two long years in the Nevada State Prison in Carson City. I visited them several times with cartons of cigarettes and Edie's cookies, but as far as I was concerned, they got what they deserved.

• • •

Big things were happening in Carson City. The new $80,000 Carson-Tahoe Hospital had its grand opening on January 26, 1949. Sure enough, our friend Ella Broderick, who was president of the Carson City Chamber of Commerce and instrumental in raising the money for the new hospital, was in charge of ticket sales for the opening day celebration.

• • •

About a week after the rustlin' caper, I got a frantic call from Lucy Allison in San Francisco.

"Bill, Joan's had a miscarriage. She's very upset. Can you get away?"

"Oh, no. Please tell her I'll leave within the hour."

Emmy as usual was very understanding. "Go, Bill dear, but drive carefully. The roads over the pass are treacherous."

U.S. 50 over Echo Summit wasn't all that bad,

Scene of the crime. Note hay crane in center. (Photo Valerie Vondermuhll, Courtesy George A. Vondermuhll Jr.)

and the little Plymouth coupe made it to San Francisco in a little under four hours.

Joan was sitting up in bed when I arrived. We kissed, and she held me for the longest time. Then she started to sob, and I joined in. Our feelings were a mix of sadness and relief. We had lost our baby, yet now we were free. That was what we wanted, wasn't it?

That night we talked a great deal about our future, Joan's medical school ambitions and my desire to own my own cattle and dude ranch someday. But we settled one thing. Joanie would come back to the ranch while we decided where our relationship would go from here.

Next day, I returned to the ranch. Joan and her mother would follow by train in four to six weeks.

CHAPTER 31

Washoe Valley Neighbors

Tour of Washoe Valley

Washoe Valley in the 1940s and 1950s was an interesting mix of third and fourth generation Nevada families and newcomers—who mostly came to northern Nevada for a divorce, fell in love with the open spaces and never left.

Author and journalist Basil Woon took the reader on a nostalgic tour of Washoe Valley ranches and farms in the following story written for the *Nevada State Journal* in 1956. The authors have chosen to excerpt Woon's work as he wrote it, even though some facts have subsequently been challenged.

Basil Woon at a book signing at the Old Corner Bar, Carson City, 1953. (Courtesy Nikki M. Demas-Butz)

Nonetheless, Woon had a sincere interest in Washoe Valley history and its people, and his writing style is highly entertaining:

Changes Taking Place on Long Settled Lands
Old Ranches Give Way to "Gentleman Farms"

by Basil Woon

One after another the old ranches and settlements have given way to the big "gentlemen's farms" or dude ranches. There are now three "dude" ranches in Franktown and Ophir. Gus Bundy, the well-known artist and photographer, has built one at Ophir. The other two are Mrs. Emily P. Wood's Flying M E, which was once the Franktown Hotel, and the equally celebrated Washoe Pines, which was once the home of cowboy artist Will James.

Bundy's highly original home was built by Gus himself, with the help of his wife and sundry guests. Most of the furniture was fashioned from old frame lumber and anything else Gus could find on his hunting trips.

Down from Bundy's place a mile is Bowers Mansion, a monument to the execrable taste of the Victorian age. Next to it is Dr. Samuel T. Clarke's [sic] Tumbling IQ Ranch. Dr. Clarke, a Massachusetts ophthalmologist, came to Reno for a divorce and has been in the Valley ever since.

The R. I. Raymond home, built of brick from the ruins of the old International Hotel in Virginia City and from the Sutro Tunnel, is one of the most distinguished ranch homes near Reno. Its owner is a former vice president of the Wells Fargo Bank in San Francisco. Mr. Raymond manages his own ranch which raises registered Herefords, but he has a prized right-hand man in the person of Bill Pedroli, who was born on the Pedroli ranch which was built by Ebenezer Twaddle in 1864, sold to Stephen Pedroli (Bill's father) in 1870, and is now the property of John Jackson. The present generation of Pedrolis now live on the Raymond ranch, where they have built for themselves a beautiful and commodious brick house.

A stone's throw from this house is the site of the old mill owned and run by Capt. William Dall. He sold it to Dick Sides and retired to spend the remaining years of a long life gazing from a window of the Palace Hotel [in San Francisco] at the bay, where his abandoned brig once lay rotting at anchor.

Along the county road which turns off opposite the Flying M E are a number of fine ranches. Besides Bill Sauer, whose family once owned a good slice of the Valley and whose stone cottage rises above the road just beyond the creek, there are several other old-timers. They include Henry Heidenreidt [sic] who sold his ranch opposite the Franktown school to Jack Whitehead and now owns Katie Lewis' old

ranch farther south, and Alvin H. Cliff, who owns one of the finest dairies in Nevada, the only dairy left in a Valley formerly full of them.

Then there is the Windy J owned jointly by James H. Lathrop of the marine motors family and his in-laws, Dr. and Mrs. George Leonard.

Adjoining the Washoe Pines dude ranch is Tony and Tonie Green's ranch. J. Elton Green, in a lucky moment, acquired the place from a Mrs. Campbell of Carson City and now, I believe, of Arizona. Mrs. Campbell was a prodigious and imaginative builder and the place more nearly resembled a village than one ranch as it is today. Her husband was a wood-worker and Mrs. Campbell's own interests lay in museum collections, so when Tony Green found the place it was part museum, part workshop and part home.

Mrs. Campbell was hard to please, so the story goes. Once disliking one of the buildings, she had a bulldozer push the whole structure into the mountain, where it remains, a heap of brick beneath the dirt. The Greens have had fun remodeling and adding (and often tearing down, for the collection of buildings were too many for their purposes) and the ranch is now a showplace of the Valley. Green himself is a skilled taxidermist, builder, and collector, so the place was exactly what he had been looking for.

Beyond, on the other side, is the San Antonio Rancho, built as a fortress by a wealthy Brooklyn oil man who was afraid of kidnappers. He sold it to a French family named Famel, who turned it into an herb farm. [The Famels, a time-honored name in perfume manufacture in France, also developed a perfume called Bonanza.] They in turn sold it to Jim McKay.

Still farther along is the B-Bar-E, another showplace that has had a checkered career. It was built by William Bassett of the Otis Elevator Co. and was originally operated as a dairy, using the famous brown Swiss Milchers. He sold to Louis Carlyle, who sold to Hill Smith, who sold to Edwin Thompson, one of the owners of the Hollywood Knickerbocker Hotel. Mr. Thompson, like most of the Valley ranchers (excepting Dr. Clarke) breeds prize pedigree Herefords. Dr. Clarke has a fine herd of Black Angus.

At the far end of the Valley is the commodious ranch home of the Frank List family. Mr. List is head of the extensive List Cattle Co. The house was built by a Lord William Wellesley, the fourth Earl of Cowley, who married a Reno girl and lived there until a few years ago under the name of Mr. Wellesley, which was his family name.

Washoe Pines dude ranch, popularly known as "The Pines," is successfully operated by Betty and Lyle Hardin. The original main ranch building was built as a studio for a couple of talented artists on parole from the Nevada State Penitentiary, Will James and Buck Nimi. In this studio James wrote some of his best stories and did several of his better-known illustrations, and Buck Nimi created the images of horses and cowboys that made him famous.

Two years ago Betty and Lyle Hardin,

Celebrated cowboy artist and author, Will James, at his Washoe Valley property in the 1920s. His log cabin home would later become the main ranch house for the Washoe Pines Ranch. (Courtesy Will James Art Co.)

newlyweds, were hired to run the Pines and a few weeks ago they were able to buy the ranch and it is now their property.

The Flying M E is a different sort of establishment and stresses the social life rather than that of the traditional "dude" ranch. I once described the "M E" as a bit of the Ritz dropped down in Nevada, and that perhaps adequately describes both its accommodations and the people you are apt to meet here.

Emmy and her husband, Dore, took over the old Franktown railroad hotel, built in 1862 as the hub of Franktown social life. When they finished making extensive changes, the Flying M E was perhaps the best furnished and most modern guest ranch in the state. Guests over the years have included celebrities and world famous people. But many of

Well-known author and international journalist, Basil Woon, described the Flying M E as "a bit of the Ritz dropped down in Nevada." (Photo Gus Bundy, Authors' Collection)

Left, looking north at Slide Mountain from the Washoe Valley floor; above, looking east from Franktown Road (note Flying M E in the distance); right, Big Washoe Lake as seen from Mt. Rose Highway. (All 1947)
(Photos Valerie Vondermuhll, Courtesy George A. Vondermuhll Jr.)

them came for divorce and it is Mrs. Wood's policy to surround all guests with a mantle of privacy. Thus her reputation has grown and her friends are legion.

Such is Franktown and Washoe Valley. It has become an aristocratic suburb to both Reno and Carson City, but hasn't forgotten its beginnings, and life there is centered about its ranches and cattle.   —Excerpted from
"Water Rights and Dude Ranches
Mean Much to Washoe Valley,"
by Basil Woon, *Nevada State Journal*, 1956

The Pedroli farm, looking southeast, as seen from the old County Road, circa 1947. (Photo Valerie Vondermuhll, Courtesy George A. Vondermuhll Jr.)

More About the Neighbors

Pedroli Farm

Stephen Pedroli sailed around the horn from Switzerland to California to join relatives in Virginia City. Before settling in Franktown, he worked as a miner on the Comstock, drove an ox team for the logging operations at Glenbrook and worked on a dairy ranch.

In 1874, he bought the John and Ebenezer Twaddle farm in Washoe Valley. Starting with a few imported Swiss dairy cows, Pedroli developed a large herd on his farm in the Valley. He made daily trips to deliver milk, cream, cheese, and butter to Virginia City, by way of the rocky Ophir grade. Later he shipped these on the V & T railroad. For almost forty years, every morning he sent fresh dairy products to Virginia City, Reno, Carson City and other nearby towns.

In February 1895, Stephen Pedroli married Camella (Camille) Mora, who was also from Switzerland. They met while she was visiting a relative in California. The Pedrolis raised their five children on their Washoe Valley farm, which had the picturesqueness of a scene in Switzerland.

Their son, William "Bill" Pedroli, took over management of the dairy farm in 1924, upon the

death of his father. In 1948, the farm was sold to the Harp Brothers Corporation.[1]

In 1943, the Pedroli farm made the papers when Mrs. William Pedroli received a surprise visit one morning from First Lady Eleanor Roosevelt, who was staying at the neighboring Tumbling DW ranch (later the Flying M E). Mrs. Roosevelt wrote about her visit to the Pedroli farm in her syndicated daily column, "My Day."

Jackson Ranch

Johnnie Jackson and I met in 1947 at the Round Up Bar during the Fourth of July Rodeo. He hung out with Utah Bob, Frank Burrows and me around the chutes that week. Johnnie and his wife June were living on the old Dick Sides place near the Flying M E at that time.

In 1948, June's father's business, the Harp Brothers Corporation, bought the Pedroli dairy farm and turned over its management to Johnnie and June.

Johnnie's dream was to be a rodeo producer and announcer, and you could say he got his start at the Flying M E. During '48 and '49, he and I practiced our calf roping skills a lot at the Flying

Johnnie Jackson's ranch (the old Dick Sides place), adjacent to the Flying M E, 1947. Jackson's ranch expanded to include the Pedroli ranch in 1948. (Photo Valerie Vondermuhll, Courtesy George A. Vondermuhll Jr.)

Ruins of Washoe City, circa 1940s. The center building was once Brow's saloon. (Photo Gus Bundy, Bundy Collection, Courtesy of Special Collections Department, University of Nevada, Reno Library)

M E's roping arena, using his calves and our chutes.

Sometime after I left the Flying M E, tragedy struck Johnnie and June. Johnnie's gun discharged while the couple were riding in their pickup truck and June was fatally wounded.[2]

While interviewing people for this book, I heard that Johnnie came to Nevada with his mother, who was getting a divorce. I have also heard, but been unable to confirm, that Johnnie had a twin brother, Nick, who was a silversmith and may have bought Hoot Newman's Silver Shop at some point.

After June's death, Johnnie married Nancy Johnson, whom he met at the neighboring Flying M E. Nancy was a graduate of Vassar and came to the Flying M E in the early 1950s to get a divorce. Just like Allie Okie before her, Nancy stayed on after her divorce as Emmy Wood's ranch hostess.

Johnnie and Nancy bought a ranch in California, and eventually he realized his dream of becoming a rodeo producer-announcer. The last time we had a drink together was at a rodeo in Salinas, California, where he was one of the announcers. We relived some Washoe Valley memories, and he was one happy cowboy.

As for the old Twaddle-Pedroli-Jackson place, most of the land today appears to have been subdivided into small home sites.

Washoe City

At the north end of Washoe Valley, one can still see remnants of the once bustling Washoe City, the first county seat for Washoe County.

Bundy Ranch

About a mile-and-a-half north of the Flying M E was the Bundy ranch. In 1941, Gus and Jeanne Bundy moved to Washoe Valley at the suggestion of a fellow photographer. The Bundy's were determined not to raise their children in New York and purchased a modest property along Ophir Creek at the mouth of Ophir Canyon. The property came with a one-room structure, and the Bundy's began raising chickens for eggs.

Gus Bundy (Courtesy of Tina Bundy Nappe)

Bundy ranch, main house, early 1950s
(Courtesy Tina Bundy Nappe)

Jeanne, Tina and Molly Bundy, Washoe Valley, 1947. (Photo Valerie Vondermuhll, Courtesy George A. Vondermuhll Jr.)

Bundy's Book

Thanks for making a happy time out of what would have been a boring sentence!

> *–Cecil W, 1948*

To Jeanne and Gus—With whom six weeks have seemed a short period of time, but broad in experience, deep in contentment, high in idealism and something long to remember.

> *–Karl W, 1948*

I didn't expect to find such a grand place to spend my days of exile.

> *–Nancy H, Essex Falls, 1950*

My stay here allowed me to make probably the most important choice of my life.

> *–Tod G, Boston, 1955*

In real appreciation for your warm and thoughtful hospitality—which enabled me to spend these weeks constructively and in contemplation.   *–Dr. R, New Haven, 1955*

As one of the "jaded vultures" who found a new lease on a lovely, lusty life after that B-therapy (Bundy-therapy), I shan't forget the learning and living.

> *–Jane M, Middleburg, 1956*

Thanks for an unexpectedly wonderful six weeks, complete with snow and freezing weather, 100-degree heat, wind, clear sunny weather, changing cloud effects, mist and snow on the mountains, local murder, forest fire, earthquake, water rights squabble, counseling service, children, puppies, dogs, ducks, hens and chicks, cat and kitten, gardening, venison, trout, raw fish, woodchuck stew, Virginia City, Pyramid Washoe beach, Mexican Dam, a desert storm, agate fields, Fort Churchill, brooks that are turned off and on, sagebrush and bitterbrush, photography, painting, art, philosophy at any and all hours, new friends, more stars than I ever saw before, the dump with the loveliest view of any dump in the world and reminders of my starry-eyed youth in NY when we all hoped to remake the world.   *–Helen S, New York City, 1954*

(Bundy's Book courtesy of Tina Bundy Nappe)

Following World War II and the decline of the egg business, the decision was made to become a divorce ranch. Gus started adding to the one-room house and transformed the chicken house into guest rooms, until three or four guests could be accommodated.

Being a talented artist, Gus also made the furniture for the ranch. As a result of some hiking in the Slide Mountain area, Gus discovered some abandoned old flumes from the Comstock era. He collected the wood and converted it into coffee tables, a bar, and, in some instances, walls. His artist's eye captured the beauty of the

Theodore and Maggie Winters (center, sitting) with their family, 1885
(Courtesy Nevada Historical Society)

wood grain, aged and water scarred, creating unusual effects. Creative uses were found for other items found on outings. A pair of huge bellows from the V & T Railroad became a double-deck living room table. Planks used for shoring-up mine shafts became bookshelves. Old rails became door handles. Rocks from an ore dump formed a large fireplace, and the fire grate was a section of V & T rail.

Lacking horses and a swimming pool, which the higher-end divorce ranches had, the Bundy's focused on other activities for their guests. Guests could join in art classes, gem cutting, picnics, and camping. Some of the guests brought their own work with them, like Al Deutsch, who wrote "Sorry State of Nevada" for *Collier's* as a result of his trip to Reno. Dr. Alfred Kinsey, famed for his Kinsey Reports, was planning his third trip to the ranch when he died.

Gus Bundy studied art at the well-known National Academy of Design and was an accomplished painter, printmaker, sculptor, and photographer. His photographs of Nevada capture the state's unique and beautiful heritage. Bundy first made his mark in photography in 1951. While driving a truck in the Nevada desert for a *Life* magazine photographer, Bundy was able to snap some 300 photos of wild horses being rounded up by hunters using trucks and airplanes. The *Life* magazine photographer was prevented from completing his assignment by the hunters, but Bundy's photos became the focus of a national effort to protect these wild herds. The photos are regarded as a principal reason that legislation was eventually secured in 1959. (Gus Bundy's stunning series of wild horse photos are featured in the chapter, "Clark Gable.")[3]

Winters Ranch

Scattered among the ranches and farms, the Valley had some opulent mansions built from fortunes made on the Comstock. One was the Winters mansion, about three miles from the Flying M E on Highway 395.

When the Winters brothers—John, Joseph and Theodore—sold their shares of the Ophir Mine on

Winters Ranch, circa 1950s (Courtesy Nevada Historical Society)

the Comstock Lode, it was in the 1850s, at the height of the strike, and they each received about a quarter of a million dollars.

In 1857, Theodore saw an opportunity to buy land cheaply from the Mormons, when Brigham Young called for all of his followers to return to Salt Lake City. Starting with a square mile of choice Washoe Valley land, which he bought for $50 and a team of oxen, he continued to expand his holdings until, ten years later, he owned 18,000 acres in Nevada and California.

In 1864, "Thee," as he was known to his family and friends, built a Victorian gothic mansion for his wife and seven children on his property known as Rancho del Sierra. The ranch first belonged to

William Jennings, a Mormon, reputed to be one of the wealthiest of the early settlers of the Valley. The ranch covered about four thousand acres.

The Winters mansion was elaborately furnished with ornately-carved walnut furniture, brass and crystal chandeliers, Oriental rugs, fine china and linens, and many other items of decorative beauty. The third floor had a ballroom-billiard room which also served as a schoolroom at one time.

Theodore built a race track and became the owner of a fine line of thoroughbred racing horses. Two derby winners were raised on the ranch, one the famous El Rio Rey, considered to be the fastest horse in the world. Hay raised on the Winters ranch was so prized that it was shipped to New

York and England.

In 1888, Theodore bought the neighboring Bowers Mansion and grounds. However, his wife, Maggie, refused to live there because of the previous owners' ostentatious lifestyle and reputation. During the five years that Winters owned the property, the mansion and the splendid grounds fell into disrepair.

In 1890, Theodore's fortunes turned. He ran for governor of Nevada on the Democratic ticket and was soundly beaten in the election. The campaign left him heavily in debt and he began selling his Nevada property. Financial problems continued to plague him.

After Theodore Winters' passing in August 1906, Rancho del Sierra was maintained for the next half century by his daughter, Nevada Winters Sauer, until her passing in 1953.

The gothic mansion fell into disrepair and went through a series of owners before it sat vacant for many years. Today the elegant structure is being renovated and, as the locals say, "it's nice to see lights on in the evening."

The Winters family continues to be a legend in Nevada. Fourth generation JohnD Winters [pronounced John-Dee] was the Grand Marshal in the 1995 Nevada Day parade.[4]

Bowers Mansion

Another mansion built from Comstock riches was the fabled Bowers mansion, about a mile from the Flying M E. Here are some highlights of the fascinating rags-to-riches-to-rags story of Eilley and Sandy Bowers excerpted from Myra Sauer Ratay's *Pioneers of the Ponderosa*:

In May 1856, Alisen "Eilley" Orrum Hunter Cowan and Alexander Cowan paid $100 for a log hut and 320 acres of one of the first land claims in Washoe Valley. The land lay along the western foothills of the Valley where there was a lovely hot spring gushing forth from a crack in a granite ledge. In 1860 the bonds of matrimony between Eilley and Alexander were dissolved and Eilley got title to the Washoe Valley property as alimony.

Eilley moved to Gold Hill where she operated a boarding house. She met a miner and mule skinner several years her junior, Lemuel Sanford Bowers, and the couple were married on August 9, 1859. From various accounts, Eilley may not have been legally divorced yet from Alexander Cowan, but such things were not unusual in those days.

Eilley and "Sandy" owned adjoining mining claims on the Hill and suddenly their adjoining twenty-one feet at Gold Hill began pouring out wealth. Overnight, Eilley was no longer a washerwoman and cook, but the first "Queen of the Comstock," and Sandy was no longer a mule skinner. Though never in the same league with the other Comstock barons like Flood, Fair, O'Brien and Mackay, the Bowers accumulated a total wealth of five to six million dollars.

The sudden glitter of silver and gold completely blinded them. Uneducated and unlearned in the ways of the world, they spent their new-found wealth lavishly, and often foolishly, on all the luxuries that money could buy.

In 1861, Sandy put his attorney in charge of building a mansion on Eilley's Washoe Valley property while the Bowers went off to Europe to sightsee and shop.

In the summer of 1863, the Bowers moved into their magnificent new home which cost $400,000 to build and was the most superb residence in the Valley. The interior was lavishly furnished with imported lace curtains and velvet drapes, thick carpets, crystal chandeliers and silver door knobs and hinges. The furniture was carved and heavy as was the fashion at the time and all the main rooms had Italian marble fireplaces. The piano in the main salon was said to have a keyboard of mother-of-pearl.

The library housed some 2,200 books for which Sandy had signed a $12,000 blanket order stipulating only that they be bound in the finest of leather and lettered in gold. Some of the volumes had blank pages inside as the library was for show, since neither Sandy nor Eilley could read.

For a few years, the couple lived elegantly and entertained extravagantly. Then about 1866, the first flush of the Comstock excitement began wearing off and Sandy began to feel the pinch of lowered production and poor investments. In April 1868, he became seriously ill and died in the early morning of April 21, 1868. His funeral was one of the most elaborate on the Comstock.

Eilley began selling off her treasures to bring in money. In June 1873, the piano, along with other furnishings and objets d'art, were raffled off. Grief

stricken by the sudden death of their adopted daughter, Persia, on July 14, 1874, and harassed by creditors, Eilley grew more and more irascible. Former friends and business associates deserted her.

In 1875, the Bowers Mansion was opened to the public for balls, meetings, picnics, and other events. Grand excursions on the V & T to the beautiful Bowers Mansion were elegant and

Bowers Mansion (Courtesy of Nevada Historical Society)

exciting outings. However, these events failed to help Eilley out of her financial difficulties and her home was auctioned off on May 3, 1876. Myron C. Lake, the founder of Reno, was the highest bidder. The buildings and some 180 acres of farmland that were valued at about $638,000 were sold for $10,000 to satisfy a $13,622.17 judgment. Eilley was given six months in which to redeem her property but she was unable to do so, and on November 27, 1876, she lost her beloved mansion forever.

For the next few years, Eilley found shelter with neighbors and friends and began telling fortunes. In 1887, she went to San Francisco where she lived in basement rooms on Larkin and O'Farrell Streets and eked out a living as the "Washoe Seeress."

In July 1901, she returned to Nevada, poor, deaf and friendless, and was placed in the Washoe County poorhouse. Late in August, the County Commissioners shipped her to the King's Daughters Home in Oakland. On August 20, 1901, a reporter for the Nevada State Journal wrote: "Thus Nevada shakes off the responsibility of the destitute Washoe Seeress. Western hospitality, me-thinks, has taken unto itself wings and fled. But fare you well Mrs. Bowers, and our blessings (if nothing else) be with you." On October 27, 1903, Alisen "Eilley" Orrum Hunter Cowan Bowers, former washerwoman and first "Queen of the Comstock," died alone and penniless.

Henry Riter, then owner of Eilley's old mansion and grounds, had her ashes brought back to Washoe Valley to rest in the little hillside graveyard beside Sandy and Persia.[5]

• • •

In 1948, a plan was announced to make the mansion into a museum. The Bowers Committee was formed and launched a drive to locate original furnishings and other items for the mansion. Mrs. Alice B. Addenbrooke of the committee kept the public informed in a series of articles she wrote for the *Nevada State Journal*, similar to the following one which appeared on December 5, 1948:

"Table, Table, Who Has The Table?"
Bowers Committee Would Like To Know

In the south parlor of Bowers Mansion there was an oval marble-topped table of walnut. This very table may be waiting in someone's home to find a permanent resting place just where Eilley Bowers put it when she arranged her furniture on their return from the European trip. It could be that the owner, in a very generous mood, may feel that his oval marble-topped table of walnut is more a part of the history of Bowers Mansion than of a private home.

A month later, the table was found. It was in the possession of a Nevada pioneer family who bought it from Eilley Bowers in her financially troubled days of 1875. The family donated the table back to the Bowers Mansion.

Through similar diligence, the Bowers Committee found other furnishings whose owners agreed to contribute them back to the Bowers Mansion. Among these was the spinet square piano which was raffled off in 1873, taken to a saloon in Carson City, and then passed through four owners before finding its way back to the main salon in the mansion.

Today the Bowers Mansion is owned and operated by the county, and the swimming pool, picnic grounds, and mansion are open to the public.

The lady, Penna Tew Hinton, and the gambler, Pat Hart at the Brass Rail Saloon, Virginia City, 1949.
(Courtesy Dirck L. Hinton)

CHAPTER 32

The Gambler and the Lady

*"The minute I saw this place, I knew
I would never go back to New York."*
—Penna Tew Hinton Hart

Penna Tew Hinton arrived at the Flying M E in early March 1949. Emmy clued me in that Mrs. Hinton was an expert "English" rider and was anxious to "ride Western," so I immediately booked her to join Elizabeth "Betsy" Scott, an intermediate rider, for a picnic ride around Washoe Lake.

Betsy was in her late thirties, with a full figure which her frontier pants heightened. A few telltale strands of gray could be seen in her short-cropped, flamboyant red hair. Her clear blue-green eyes had a quality of directness.

The next morning, I caught up Alley Oop, Jeff and Zorro for the ride. I decided to give Alley Oop to Mrs. Hinton, as he was a spirited Arabian gelding, more than enough horse, I figured, to satisfy a good rider. Jeff was a handsome black gelding with a nice easy gait, more horse than Betsy's earlier mount, but just about right for her now.

The two riders arrived at the stable while I was

*Penna Tew Hinton in a pensive moment,
September 1951* (Courtesy Dirck L. Hinton)

stowing our lunches in my saddlebags.

"Good morning, Bill. I'd like to introduce you to Penna Hinton," said Betsy.

"Glad to meet you, Mrs. Hinton. I hear you've won a bunch of ribbons with your jumper. Looking forward to hearing more about those meets."

"Nice to meet you, too, Bill. Please call me Penna. As for those ribbons, that was years ago when I was a teenager."

Penna was smartly dressed in jodhpurs and tall English riding boots. She was very attractive, tall, lean, and somewhere in her thirties.

"Betsy, I'm promoting you to Jeff this morning. I think you'll like him. Penna, I'm assigning Alley Oop to you. He's a full-blooded Arabian. He's been known to crow hop once or twice on a chilly morning if he can get his head down, but he doesn't really buck. I'm sure you'll like him."

After adjusting stirrups and tightening their cinches, I climbed aboard Zorro and we headed out. As we approached the ranch exit to Highway 395, I advised the ladies to follow me as we crossed the road and headed south for about two miles.

It became obvious Penna was comfortable on Alley Oop when he shied sideways as a big 18-wheeler roared by. She reached over and patted him on the neck as she said something to calm him down. Then she looked at me and smiled as if to say, "I'm fine, we're okay."

At about the two mile point, we crossed back over the highway and through a gate to the pasture where our extra dude horses grazed. As we made our way through the three-to four foot tall sage-brush, Penna was ready when Alley Oop shied again at the sudden sight of a jack rabbit heading for cover.

"Good goin', Penna. Your experience shows," I said.

We then headed east, skirting the southern shore of Big Washoe Lake for another three miles, to a small, tree-lined campground southeast of the lake.

After hitching the horses to some trees, I broke out Edie's delicious sandwiches and three bottles of beer. As we settled down on the ground cover I unrolled from behind my saddle, Betsy said, "It's time for another one of your fascinating pioneer stories, Bill."

"Great," Penna added. "I want to learn about Nevada, too."

"You never have to ask me twice, Penna. As Betsy knows, I'm a history buff from the word go. Well, since we're only a few miles from Nevada's main historical event—the discovery of the Comstock Lode—here's one of my favorite stories. But keep in mind, I'm still learning about Nevada's history, thanks to Emmy's library.

"The Comstock Lode on Mt. Davidson," I said pointing to the Virginia Range behind us, "was the richest known U.S. silver deposit. It was discovered in 1857 by two brothers, Ethan and Hosea Grosch. As educated Easterners with a working knowledge of geology, they were the first to find encouragement in the 'blue mud.' At the head of Gold Canyon, they found two silver veins and later four more veins crossing the canyon. A secret, preliminary assay estimated the ore value at $3,500 a ton. Keeping their discovery a secret, Ethan and Hosea staked out their claims and continued to outline the silver veins before going to California to raise capital to launch an all-out mining effort.

"Sadly, in the summer of 1857, their luck ran out. Hosea injured his foot with a pick and died of gangrene. Ethan set out for California in November with Richard Bucke, a Canadian traveling companion, to meet with bankers. For more than two weeks, they were lost in a winter storm. When the two men finally crawled into Last Chance, a little mining camp, Ethan died while fighting off attempts to amputate his frozen, gangrenous legs. No doctor was available and there was no anesthetic available, just a hunting knife and saw. Richard Bucke had one of his frozen feet amputated, then went home to Canada to recover. The silver lodes were still secret at this point. The Grosch brothers had been the Comstock's first quartz prospectors, the true discoverers of what would become the world-shaking Big Bonanza."[1]

"Oh, Bill, those poor brothers," said Betsy.

"I agree. I can't wait to visit Virginia City. It sounds so colorful," said Penna.

"We'll continue the Comstock story on our next ride. It's time to mount up now and head back to the ranch. We'll have covered about eleven miles round trip according to my topo maps."

It had been a nice day for a ride. About sixty-five degrees with a little nip in the air. Several thunderheads and an occasional flash of lightning over the Sierras warned us to hurry up to avoid a possible shower, but the return ride was uneventful and we were back at the ranch by two-thirty.

As we dismounted, Penna said, "Thank you very much for the ride, Bill, and my first Nevada history lesson. May I have Alley Oop again if we ride tomorrow?"

"You bet," I replied.

Betsy seemed in no hurry and offered to help me unsaddle the horses. Then Allie called out from the front porch, "Betsy, we're going into Carson and want you to join us."

"I'll talk to you later, Bill," she said as she headed for the ranch house. I could tell something was on her mind.

Miss Penna Tew, Debutante of the Season

Miss Penna Tew attended Miss Chapin's fashionable school and was one of New York's most popular debutantes of the 1930-1931 season. All the New York papers carried the news of her engagement. Cholly Knickerbocker wrote, "The very comely Penna Tew, as a member of the 1930-1931 debutante ranks, was one of the most sought-after 'buds' of the past season and many masculine cardiac organs were known to miss that well-known beat when, early in March, Mr. and Mrs. Tew made the formal announcement of her betrothal to Longstreet Hinton of Locust Valley, Long Island."[2]

The wedding was covered with splashy photos and glowing copy. The *Herald Tribune*, May 29, 1931: "Miss Penna Tew, daughter of Mr. and Mrs. William H. Tew, of 3 East Fifty-fourth Street, was married yesterday afternoon to Mr. Longstreet Hinton in the chantry of St. Thomas Church. A reception was given by the bride's grandmother in the Egyptian room of the Hotel St. Regis. Following their honeymoon in Bermuda, Mr. and Mrs. Hinton will live at 405 East Fifty-fourth Street. The bride is a graduate of Miss Chapin's

Socialite Penna Tew Hinton at a New York club (Courtesy Dirck L. Hinton)

school and made her debut last winter. Mr. Hinton is associated with the firm of J. P. Morgan & Co."

No effort had been spared to make the wedding one of the loveliest of the year. Inside New York's fashionable St. Thomas' Church, the pews were crowded with expensively attired guests. Outside, a battery of newspaper photographers waited to snap pictures. The groom was tall and handsome. Socially prominent, he was one of the bright young men in the Wall Street firm of J. P. Morgan and Company. The bride wore her mother's wedding gown and was described by her friends as having a talent for doing things "with a flair."

Now, in 1949, Penna, at age 36, found herself

in Reno getting a divorce after eighteen years of marriage.

Meanwhile, another socialite, Mrs. Ethel du Pont Roosevelt, checked into the Flying M E. Mrs. Roosevelt was there to divorce Franklin Delano Roosevelt Jr. The two ladies had met socially in New York and were both excellent riders. Soon they became "saddle pals," as well as bar-hopping pals in the evenings to the near-by watering holes and casinos.

From Salon to Saloon

Penna fell in love with Nevada and decided to stay on awhile after her divorce. The next thing I knew, she was tending bar and dealing "21" at Pat Hart's Brass Rail Saloon in Virginia City. She seemed to be loving every moment of it.

In the fall of '49, Penna and the Smedsruds entertained a group of their friends with a "hunt style breakfast" at the Bonanza Inn. The guests included Emmy Wood, Allie Okie, Annie Greenleaf, Doris Vander Poel, Bobbie Keeble, Elizabeth Walker, and Mrs. Kinsey Incognito (staying under a presumed name) all of the Flying M E; Nancy Truesdale and Tootie Foster of Washoe Pines; and Pat Hart of the Brass Rail. According to the *Reno Reporter*, "After a glowing start of Hot Swedish Glogg, Penna, Virginia and Halvor dished up New England fish chowder, onion soup au gratin, chicken livers, broiled kidneys, fish cakes, baked beans, sausages, scrambled eggs, pancakes, popovers, cornbread and coffee. Hunt-style breakfasts are an old Eastern custom, and will be continued each Sunday during the Autumn and Winter months at the Bonanza Inn, where Colony gourmets have been striking it rich the past two years." [3]

Saddle pals, Penna Tew Hinton (left) and Ethel du Pont Roosevelt, share a trail ride story over a snack in the Flying M E kitchen. (Courtesy Dirck L. Hinton)

It wasn't long before New York socialite Penna Tew Hinton and Nevada saloon keeper Pat Hart fell in love. The romance began when Penna and Ethel, along with other social figures staying at the Flying M E, journeyed frequently to Virginia City for nightlife, gambling and socializing with other members of Reno's divorce colony.

Penna and Pat were married on November 11, 1949 at the Bonanza Inn in Virginia City. The wedding was covered by all the papers and featured clever headlines like "Penna Goes From Salon to Saloon," "Gambler Wins—the Lady," "Penna Hinton Bride of Gambling King" and "Elegantly reared New York socialite, Mrs. Penna Tew Hinton, yesterday became Queen of the Comstock when she was married in Virginia City, Nev., to the King—plaid-shirted gambler Patrick J. Hart."

Here's the rest of the story courtesy of the *Virginia City News,* November 19, 1949:

HINTON-HART RITES PERFORMED

Historic Bonanza Inn was the locale of a simple wedding ceremony on Wednesday afternoon, November 11, when Penna Tew Hinton became the bride of Patrick J. Hart. Judge Clark J. Guild officiated at the ceremony.

The bride chose to wear an afternoon gown of gold lame, accented with antique gold jewelry. The bride's attendant was her cousin, Mrs. Nancy Bryce Truesdale of New York City, who wore a black and white afternoon gown and a corsage of American Beauty roses.

The bride is the daughter of Mrs. William Tew of New York City, and came to Virginia City several months ago. She was escorted by Simon Dadiani of San Francisco, brother-in-law of the bride's sister, Princess Georges Dadiani of Paris.

Patrick J. Hart, popular and prominent business man of Virginia City, and owner of the Brass Rail Saloon, is the son of Michael Hart of

Penna Tew Hinton and Brass Rail Saloon owner, Pat Hart, married on November 11, 1949 at the Bonanza Inn, Virginia City. Looking on, left to right, the groom's daughter, Joyce Hart, Emily Pentz Wood of the Flying M E, and Jinny Smedsrud of the Bonanza Inn.
(Courtesy Dirck L. Hinton)

Hazen, Nevada. Best man for the bridegroom was Larry Maloney, top bartender at the Brass Rail.

For the occasion the drawing room of the beautiful Bonanza Inn was decorated with white chrysanthemums, American beauty roses, and lighted tapers.

After the ceremony, cake, sandwiches and champagne were served and later in the evening the happy couple was honored at a dinner party at the Big Hat in Reno.

Guests included George Breed, Li Sanders, Emily Wood of the Flying M E, Lillian Kennedy, David Hayden, Mr. and Mrs. Fred

Every Night is New Year's at the Brass Rail

*Above: Penna Hinton Hart tending bar (left)
and dealing "21" (right).*

*Below left: Brothers Dirck (left) and Kit Hinton spent summers in Virginia City during their teenage years;
below right: Gail Hinton, shown with dealer Mike Demas, grew up in Virginia City.*

Clockwise from top left: Kit Hinton has a "heart-to-heart" with step-father, Pat Hart; (from left), Pat Hart entertains author Lucius Beebe and photographer Chuck Clegg of the Territorial Enterprise; *Bonanza Inn bartender Doug Moore celebrates his birthday at the Brass Rail with "Spud" and Lucius Beebe; Kit Hinton gets an English lesson from Bob Richards, Managing Editor of the* Territorial Enterprise.

(Courtesy Dirck L. Hinton and Kit Hinton)

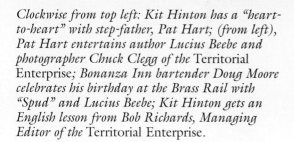

Young, the groom's daughter Joyce Hart, and the host and hostesses, Mr. and Mrs. Halvor Smedsrud.

As an aside, the bride's attendant and cousin, the attractive blond and blue-eyed New York socialite Mrs. Nancy Bryce Truesdale, went from wedding matron of honor on a Friday afternoon to divorcée on a Saturday morning, when she appeared in court the next day and won her freedom from Francis Scott Truesdale. That's the way things were in Reno's divorce colony.

As the wife of Pat Hart, Penna said she would take charge of the blackjack game at the Brass Rail while her husband operated the roulette wheel. In 1950, Penna told *The American Weekly,* "I've found that it's much less expensive to deal the cards than to play in front. I've had a long social life, but I want no more of it. The minute I saw this place, I knew I would never go back to New York to live. I think I'll be more contented and more happy than ever before in my life."[4]

William W. "Bill" Bliss shared his favorite Penna Hinton story:

One evening I was escorting a Glenbrook guest up to Virginia City. I'm dressed in grey flannels, Brooks Brothers button-down shirt, tie, navy blazer, and maybe white bucks—my usual uniform at the time. We go into the Brass Rail Saloon and Penna is tending bar. Now Penna's a socialite from the East and had been in this area for only a few months at this point. In fact, she had just gotten her divorce while staying at the Flying M E.

Well, Penna's all decked out in Western wear and is regaling her bar customers with the history and tales of the area. I casually mention that my great-grandfather was born in Gold Hill and supplied cordwood and lumber to Virginia City during the Comstock

boom in the 1800s. Then I casually mention that my grandfather built the Tahoe Tavern in Tahoe City in the early 1900s. A few drinks later, I let out that my father and I are running the Glenbrook Inn, started by my great-grandfather in 1907.

Penna was beginning to realize she was the newer kid on the block and all—and we all shared a good laugh! Penna and I became good friends from then on. She was one of those "to the manor born" Easterners. But she married Pat Hart and stayed in Nevada. Her thirst for Nevada history was never quenched. Such a priceless story—nobody would believe it today!

Penna and her first husband agreed that their daughter Gail would be raised in Virginia City and the teenage boys, Dirck and Kit, in the East. The boys spent the first of many summers in Virginia City in 1950. All three children have fond memories of their step-father Pat, and colorful stories of growing up on the Comstock.

Hart Night

On December 9, 1970, Pat Hart was killed in an auto accident on the icy Carson Highway at age 58. The regard in which his fellow Comstockers held him was displayed on August 30, 1971: the the businessmen of Virginia City bought out the Reno ball park for the last professional baseball game of the season and invited all fans to attend, without charge. The night was dedicated to Pat Hart, and a finer tribute couldn't have been arranged:

Pat and Penna Hart were among the most ardent supporters of the Reno Silver Sox baseball team. Their love for baseball didn't stop after the season ended as they would also attend spring training in Arizona. Many of the Major League players visited Pat and Penna frequently. What could be more fitting than to pay tribute to Pat by having Pat Hart Night with the Silver Sox team at the Moana Stadium in Reno.

This special night, August 30, is being sponsored by those who loved Pat and want to pay tribute to him. Also, money will be contributed to Pat's favorite charity.

Maggie Murphy, one of the Harts' oldest and dearest friends, will be playing the piano during the evening. A no-host cocktail party will be held at the Sharon House following the game.[5]

Helping Others

Not long after Pat's death, Penna became a full-time volunteer at the Carson-Tahoe Hospital in Carson City. She volunteered forty hours a week as an assistant to the hospital's ombudsman. Penna was honored many times, including recognition for 10,000 hours of volunteer service. From *MJR's Corner* by Margot Arthur:

Helping others is all I want. If I took a job and got paid for it in money, it wouldn't do the same for me as working as a volunteer does."

Boredom, the social disease of those who have everything money can buy, is unknown to Penna Hart. Her unceasing involvement in the world around her has kept her young and expanded her identity from the "me" to the "we."

"I've always been a volunteer. I didn't need to earn money, fortunately, but

everybody needs a purpose in life. If you don't get out and do something for others, you become not only bored but sooner or later you'll become a bore yourself. And what better place is there than a hospital?"[6]

Penna Tew Hinton Hart died on August 15, 1995 at age 82.

Mr. and Mrs. Patrick Hart, November 11, 1949, Virginia City
(Courtesy Dirck L. Hinton)

Duding it up at the Flying M E, 1947 (Photo Valerie Vondermuhll, Courtesy George A. Vondermuhll Jr.)

CHAPTER 33

Equestrienne Socialite Arrives Incognito

*"Ethel du Pont Roosevelt was a
true aristocrat."*
—Emily Pentz Wood

In late March 1949, Mrs. Franklin D. Roosevelt Jr., the former Ethel du Pont, arrived at the Reno airport under the assumed name of Mrs. Frederick D. Randolph Jr. High society names like du Pont, Astor, Vanderbilt, and Roosevelt always represented interest and excitement to the rest of the world. Add the additional dimension of divorce and you had a front page story.

Emmy was very familiar with the media's ability to sniff out stories at the airport and train station, so she encouraged her "name guests" to travel incognito. She would try and meet them personally when they arrived and whisk them away straight to the ranch.

Meanwhile, Allie was at the Reno train depot to meet Mrs. Roosevelt's close friend, Mrs. Laura Manning, due in from Lexington, Kentucky. Ethel and Laura had been friends since Mrs. Walker's School for Girls in

Mrs. F. D. R. Jr. in Reno for Divorce

(NEA Telephoto)
Mrs. F. D. Roosevelt Jr. (left), wife of the son of the late President, is in Reno to establish residence and sue for divorce. Mr. Roosevelt (right) in New York, declined comment on the step taken by the former Edith Du Pont. It is believed property and custodial settlements have been reached. This picture was taken before the rift. The Roosevelts have two children.

(Nevada Appeal, April 12, 1949)

Simsbury, Connecticut, and Laura was coming to keep her friend company for six weeks.

I met both of the new guests during cocktail hour the day of their arrival. Both were eager to ride and would become frequent riders. Emmy got me aside that night to tell me that both women were sports enthusiasts and excellent horsewomen. "In fact, Mrs. Roosevelt was a member of a Virginia hunt club," she said.

Ethel Roosevelt was pleasantly surprised to find that another friend of hers, Penna Tew Hinton, was staying at the ranch. Penna had ten days to go to qualify for her decree.

So I now had three excellent riders, all riding daily, schedules permitting.

During our get-acquainted ride the next day, the two new guests and I went up to Little Valley. Mrs. Roosevelt was on Alley Oop and Mrs. Manning on Jeff. It was a brisk May morning and

Alley Oop tried his best to crow hop, but Mrs. Roosevelt wouldn't give him his head.

In Little Valley, we put our horses through their paces, even jumped a few logs along the way. It was a treat for Zorro and me, as it wasn't often we could open up. (There was usually at least one novice rider in any group.)

We were on a first name basis by the time we reached Little Valley. Ethel was in her early thirties, 5'5", slender, with attractive, classic, aristocratic features, blue eyes and lustrous light brown hair. She wore conservative sports clothes and was used to a flat (English) saddle, but understood the value of a Western saddle in mountainous country.

Laura was about the same age, slim, 5'7", with honey-blond hair streaming behind a small, pretty, pert face with faint signs of freckles. Her family raised thoroughbred horses in the famous blue-grass region of Kentucky. Her soft southern accent was pleasing to the ears. Both women looked to be in excellent shape.

Ethel's heritage was somewhat familiar to me. The du Pont Company controlled the lion's share of the world's powder and synthetics business and, indirectly, a sizeable share of General Motors. And, of course, her father-in-law was president of the United States from 1932-1945 and Commander in Chief of the armed forces during World War II.

The du Pont and Roosevelt families were among the most powerful in America, but their political and economic philosophies were poles apart. Franklin Delano Roosevelt Jr., son of a President who thundered against the "economic royalists," was marrying Ethel du Pont, "a slim princess in gossamer white," whose great industrial family had contributed over three hundred thousand dollars to defeat the President the year before.[1]

At the time of their celebrated marriage in 1937, there was a definitely Montague-Capulet atmosphere about it all. Various important du

Ponts refused to attend the wedding. The President, apparently more delighted than the du Ponts with the match, was at the reception for the bride and groom. Undoubtedly he was surprised at what must have seemed to him to be a paucity of du Ponts in attendance. He probably never knew that many of them, not wanting to shake his hand, had put in an appearance by the back door to congratulate the bride, and then, ignoring protocol, slipped out a back door.[2]

Ethel, in spite of her family roots, was as down to earth as anyone I'd met at the ranch.

The day after our first ride, Emmy asked, "How did our new girls do?"

"Great, Emmy. They are both excellent riders. We're going to circle the Valley, today and Penna's going to join us."

The four of us circled Big and Little Washoe Lakes, a popular ride for intermediate to advanced riders because the trail is relatively flat and safe for letting the horses run at times.

Several days later we took a challenging loop trail ride. We entered Ophir Creek Canyon just west of the Bundy Ranch and followed Ophir Creek up to Lower Price Lake. After some lunch, we traversed Slide Mountain until we came to Winters Creek, then followed it back down to Washoe City to a point some three miles north of the ranch, and then on home.

Ethel, Laura and Penna loved their full day outing. I think the three of them could have ridden all day, most days, but I had to take the less-experienced guests out, too. So I worked out an alternate day schedule: beginners rode even days; advanced rode odd days; and intermediates could decide based on each day's trail ride plans. This schedule worked out well anytime we had guests with above average riding skills and experience.

One night, Ethel, Laura and I were sitting at the Old Corner Bar when the subject of when and how our mutual love of horses came about. I guess

Ethel du Pont Roosevelt, left, and Penna Tew Hinton relax after a picnic lunch at Lower Price Lake.
(Courtesy Dirck L. Hinton)

I triggered the discussion when I asked, "You two are the finest horsewomen I've had the pleasure of riding with. When did you start riding?"

Ethel answered, "My family always had horses, so I think it just happened naturally. As the oldest of four children, it was probably expected of me. I think I had my own horse by age six."

Then Laura responded, "I was raised on a farm in the bluegrass region of Kentucky. My father was a banker who loved and raised thoroughbreds as an avocation. Horses are part of my heritage. I'm sure I was riding by age six, too."

"Ethel, Emmy mentioned that you rode in a hunt club. Fox hunting, I presume?"

"Yes, Bill. It was ages ago in Virginia, shortly after I was married. My husband was in law school at the University of Virginia. A really bad fall put me in the hospital for several weeks. What about you? Did you always want to be a cowboy?"

"Yes, as long as I can remember. My dad put me on a horse before I could walk."

"I know you were born in Montana. What part?"

"Park County in south central Montana, just above Yellowstone Park. My dad was home-steading our place in Shields River Valley after the first World War and, to make ends meet, managed one of my uncle's nearby ranches. My uncle was my mother's older brother and we always called him our 'rich uncle' because he bought and sold ranches like some people trade in stocks and bonds.

"But to make a long story shorter, my parents separated when I was five and divorced two years later. Times were tough. It was during the

Branding spring calves, circa 1935. Left to right: Carl Holm, Bill McGee, Ralph Bergsagel. (Authors' Collection)

Depression. To make matters worse, Dad contributed nothing toward the support of his family. So we ended up living in the small town of Malta.

"To put food on the table, we operated as a family cooperative. Every penny my mother, two older sisters, kid brother, and I made went into a household kitty. In 1934, we moved into a larger rental house so we could take in boarders, mostly country kids who had to live in town to go to high school because of the Montana winters."

"Bill, that's a real piece of Americana. How did you acquire your cowboy skills?" Ethel asked.

"I was getting to that. In the spring of 1933, after school was over, I was 'farmed out,' as it was called, to the Holm Ranch twenty miles south of town to work for my room and board. I was eight years old. Carl Holm ran about 200 mother cows and a like number of calves. He also farmed with horses, even after many of his neighbors got tractors, preferring to think of himself as a cow man

who only farmed for diversification. Dryland farming, at that.

"We worked from dawn 'til dark almost every day. By the end of my first summer on the ranch, I knew what it was like to round up and brand cattle, fix fence, put up hay, and harvest wheat.

"Carl was a good teacher. Each year he taught me to do more until, by the end of my sixth summer on the ranch, the fall of 1938, I was capable of doing a man's job. I was a big, strong, thirteen-year old by then. I knew how to break a colt, shoe horses, and round up, brand and ship cattle.

"I could also handle most farm jobs such as plowing with four or six head of horses, or seeding and harvesting wheat, as well as various other chores like milking cows—which I hated—to haying, hauling water, and fixing fence. But cowboyin' was my first love.

"In 1940, my dad joined the Secret Intelligence branch of the OSS, meaning the Office of Strategic Services, and left for Alaska for the duration of World War II. Two years later, when I turned seventeen, I enlisted in the U. S. Navy."

"Oh, Bill, you've had such an interesting life. But you're so young," Laura said.

"Not really. Lots of guys my age grew up in a hurry, for two reasons, the Depression and the war. Say, it's getting late. Should we get going?"

"Let's," said Ethel, "but I want to hear more of your story, especially how you got to Nevada and started working for Emmy."

"I'll save it for our next ride," I said as we left the Old Corner to drive back to the ranch.

A few days later, we had a "graduation party" for Penna. She surprised everyone when she announced, "I'm not ready to return to New York and that life. I'm going to find a small place in Virginia City and explore Nevada some more. I love it out here."

Overnight Trail Ride to Virginia City

Ethel and Laura expressed keen interest in doing an overnight trip by horseback, so we decided to ride up to Virginia City. Rather than camp out, it was decided we would overnight in a hotel.

The April morning began as many others in Nevada—a clear blue sky with a few fluffy clouds and a mild sixty-four degrees. Ethel, Laura and I saddled our horses, then headed out. We went south about three miles, then east skirting the south shore of Washoe Lake, then north a mile or so to my favorite picnic area where we dismounted for a stretch and a cigarette.

Then we rode north following the western slope of the Virginia Range until we came to the Jumbo Grade heading up the mountain to Virginia City.

"We're due east of Bowers Mansion, roughly half way to Virginia City. Can you see the mansion?" I asked, pointing across Big Washoe. "We've

done the easy half. Now it's time to begin our climb."

I took out my topo map to show the ladies. "Based on the topo map, it looks like we'll gain some 2,000 feet in the next six miles. This Jumbo Grade, as it used to be called, was heavily traveled by horse, mule and oxen drawn freight wagons. That was before the V & T started running up to Virginia City. Okay, let's mount up."

In spite of the record winter snowstorms, the Virginia Range was still a rocky, barren brown, broken up by patches of gray sagebrush two feet tall and some three to six feet apart.

About two miles up the dusty grade, we spotted a small spring just off the trail where we stopped for lunch. Edie packed us sandwiches of summer sausage on her homemade bread. They were filling and delicious washed down with a thermos of hot, strong coffee. We watched a little sagebrush lizard and a digger ground squirrel a few feet off the trail study a five foot bull (gopher) snake.

"Aren't the little lizard and squirrel afraid of the snake? Why are they so close to it?" Ethel asked.

"They're staying just far enough away to be safe," I answered.

Meanwhile, a red-tailed hawk with at least a four foot wingspan circled overhead with a long, shrill "squee-oo" whistle as he watched the same stand-off below, waiting for us to move on so it could swoop down and strike with its large, sharp claws.

"That little lizard and squirrel better look out or the hawk will get them," said Laura. Then she added, "What about rattlesnakes? Are we going to see some on this ride, Bill?"

"The Western rattlesnake looks a lot like a bullsnake. They're the subject of much misinformation and folklore. Your chances of meeting one are not great except during the mating season which is this time of year. To avoid danger, when you're on foot, always look at the trail ahead and on the other side of a log or rock before stepping or jumping over it. Also, avoid putting your hands on a ledge or overhead rock when you can't see over the top of it.

"Rattlesnakes feed on rodents, baby rabbits, lizards, and some birds. The rattle on the tail can be vibrated to buzz somewhat like a cicada. It's usually rattling when the snake is approached, but not always. Anyway, they're something to watch out for when on the trail."

According to the topo map, due north within two miles of our lunch stop were the sites of the Jumbo, Empire, Pandora, Campbell, and Mahoney mines.

We had other sightings on the way up to Virginia City: a coyote, America's native "wild dog" with its high-pitched barking and wailing, mostly at night; several gregarious magpies with their long black tails, white bellies, and harsh "qua qua" calls; and numerous black-tailed jack rabbits, the long-eared hare named "jackass rabbit" by the pioneers.

About four miles ahead, as we resumed our easterly course, we could see Wakefield Peak, the highest point of this ride at 7,110 feet elevation. As we circled Wakefield at the 6,800 level we could look down and see the little town of Gold Hill about three miles east as the crow flies and some 1,000 feet lower in elevation.

After we stretched our legs and gave the horses a breather, we started our descent which took us past Suicide Rock where we connected with Ophir Grade, then in a northern direction through Cown Point Ravine and on into southern Virginia City where the grade meets C Street.

The final segment of our twenty-seven mile ride was the shortest but the most interesting. After crossing C Street (also SR 341) to E Street, we headed north until we came to Bud Taylor's Livery. As Bud put it, "There ain't no number on the place, but you'll find us 'cause it smells like a barn!" Bud's going to feed and water our horses tonight.

Ethel and Laura seemed to really enjoy that last mile through town, especially the school children who insisted on following us, but also the architecture of the old Comstock buildings.

After the horses were unsaddled, watered and fed, Bud Taylor hooked up his team of beautifully matched Chestnut mares to a superbly restored buckboard and gave us a lift to the Horseshoe Hotel on C Street, because "it ain't far, but the hills are mighty steep in this here town."

Emmy knew the Swiderski's, owners of the Horseshoe, and she had made our reservations. During the summer months, reservations were nearly impossible to get and could be difficult during the shoulder seasons, too. The historic Silver Dollar Hotel, owned by former New York socialite Florence Ballou Edwards, was our first choice, but it was already booked solid.

The Horseshoe Hotel opened in June 1946 in the Old Comstock building on C Street. The *Territorial Enterprise* reported on June 12, 1946:

> The lobby is decorated with wallpaper 50 years old, dug out of the basement of an old San Francisco store. The walls of other rooms have been covered with paper reproducing that of a much earlier day. An old parlor organ, plate rails with their decorative plates of the period, whatnots and ornaments of various types complete the decorative effect of 70 years ago.
>
> The bar corresponds as closely as possible to those in famous Virginia City hotels and clubs of earlier days. Above it, near the door, is a sign, "Check your guns here." Wednesday night a group of tourists got the thrill of their lives, and grew fairly pop-eyed, when the chief of police walked in as solemn as an old gray owl, checked his guns with the bartender,

looked the place over, and retrieved his guns and walked out.

The chandelier in the bar, incidentally, came from the Flood home in San Francisco, a home built on money made in Virginia City mines. The gold-leafed mirrors behind the bar are even older, running back for approximately 100 years.

Emmy reserved a large suite with a private bath for Ethel and Laura. My room, not much bigger than a closet, was down the hall and I shared a community bathroom.

"What do you say we have a drink in the bar before we head up?" I asked.

"A great idea but only if I buy," said Laura.

Ethel and I looked at each other. "Fine!"

We "checked our guns at the door" and "bellied up" to the bar.

"I can't go to the Bonanza Inn dressed like this. What shall we do for dinner tonight, Bill?" Ethel asked.

All we brought with us were the clothes we were wearing. No matter, I had a plan.

"How about if we rest up and meet in an hour. Then we'll go to the Brass Rail. They have bar food and really great hot dogs."

"Fine with us," said the ladies.

Bar-Hopping on the Boardwalk

Freshened up, we met in an hour and headed for the Brass Rail. Before the night was over, we had run into Penna and friends, and they joined us as we made the rounds of the Bucket of Blood, the Crystal Bar, the Delta, and Gordon Lane's Union Brewery. Returning to the Brass Rail for a nightcap, Ethel and Penna shared some laughs about "socializing" in a little Western mining town, dressed in Western garb instead of designer gowns —and loving it.

Turns out we never did have a sit-down dinner, but we enjoyed our hot dogs.

Next morning, we were the first customers to be served breakfast in the hotel dining room. At eight a.m. sharp, Bud Taylor picked us up in his buckboard for the short downhill ride to the stables.

We retraced our route over the Virginia Range and down to Washoe Valley. Then we turned north for a different route back to the ranch. We were all pretty quiet as we nursed the effects of last night's bar-hopping.

We broke for lunch under a couple of cottonwood trees and enjoyed more of Edie's delicious sandwiches with a thermos of iced tea. We also talked birds.

"I think I recognized sparrows on this ride, Bill. What were some of the others we've seen?"

"Well, you're right about the sparrows, Ethel. We've seen lots of Sage sparrows as well as some Vesper, Brewer and Bell sparrows. Other birds we've seen include ash-coated Flycatchers, Say Phoebes, and, speaking of sparrows, the Sparrow Hawk we saw yesterday. It's America's smallest falcon, not much bigger than a robin. Its principal foods are small rodents and grasshoppers and an occasional small bird."

"Bill, how do you know all that? Did you learn it in school?" asked Laura.

"I'm afraid not in school, Laura. Growing up in the country you learn those things. But I've always been extra interested in the flora and fauna, so wherever I go I look for a little book on the natural history of the area. Well, we better saddle up."

We made our way back to the ranch by way of the northern route around Little Washoe Lake, enjoyed a beer stop in Washoe City, then headed south for the Flying M E.

It was a great trip for everyone. I knew the ladies enjoyed it, and I enjoyed sharing the ride

Ethel du Pont Roosevelt and Bill McGee prepare to mount up after a lunch break. (Authors' Collection)

with such accomplished riders. It was a nice change of pace to visit Virginia City on horseback, too.

Every now and then, Penna would drop in at the ranch for a visit. She and Ethel were developing a nice friendship. But it wasn't long before Ethel's six weeks were up and she and Laura returned to their respective homes. And, as the reader already knows from the previous chapter, Penna became a Nevadan for life.

Postscript. During the six weeks that Ethel was at the ranch, we had developed a very special friendship. Her twelve year marriage to FDR Jr. was ending (he would remarry a month later), but she still had two young sons to raise, Franklin Delano III, age eleven, and Christopher du Pont, age eight. She also told me in confidence that she was being seriously courted by a new suitor. It had all happened very fast and she was feeling a bit distressed.

As for me, I was still free at twenty-three but in a questionable relationship with someone I really had nothing in common with. Ethel was ten years my senior, but as we grew closer there were times when I was the older one.

Years later, Joan told me she was aware of my special friendship with Ethel. "I knew she had a crush on you and, I knew you liked taking her riding because her riding ability was way above the average guests'. In my jealousy, I started a caricature of the two of you, with Ethel astride a horse packing you behind her across the horse's rump. I never finished it. She always wore a blue cashmere sweater when she rode. I remember she gave you one to match."

Ethel and I stayed in touch by mail for several months after her divorce. At her request, I purchased Western saddles for her boys and had them shipped to her.

On May 25, 1965, the *New York Times* carried the shocking news of her death:

> Detroit, May 25—Mrs. Ethel du Pont Warren, former wife of Franklin D. Roosevelt Jr., was found dead today in her suburban Grosse Pointe Farms home.
>
> The police said they found the body of the 49-year old du Pont heiress hanging by a braided bathrobe belt from a shower curtain rod in a locked second-floor bathroom. They listed her death as an apparent suicide.
>
> Miss Martha Weber, a maid, reportedly told the police that Mrs. Warren had complained of feeling ill after she was served breakfast in bed at about 9 A. M. The maid said she suggested to Mrs. Warren that she get some more rest.
>
> Mrs. Warren was married to Benjamin S. Warren Jr., a socially prominent Detroit lawyer, in December 1950, following her divorce in 1949 from Mr. Roosevelt. Family friends said the Warrens had separated, but recently were reconciled.

Emmy said, "Ethel du Pont Roosevelt was a true aristocrat. Many others are merely emulating her." What a waste of a beautiful human being. I am still haunted by her sad story thirty-eight years later.

CHAPTER 34

Yerington Rodeo

"Never a horse that can't be rode and
Never a cowboy that can't be throwed"
—Old Western Truism

Charlie Pittman, a fun-loving, textiles executive from the South, arrived in early April 1949, for "the cure." According to Charlie, his wife was a bit "delicate" and couldn't face coming West for the divorce, so Charlie pulled the duty. He was joined by a friend and fellow textile executive, Andy Topol, and the two of them entertained everyone at the ranch.

Charlie and Andy insisted I take them to Parker's in Reno and help them select authentic Western outfits. "None of that dude-looking stuff for us Carolina cowboys!"

At the other end of a catch.
(Authors' Collection)

I introduced them to Harry and Mush Parker and, in less than an hour, the brothers had them all "duded up" for about $65 each: Stetson 3X Beaver, $18; Western shirt, $12.50; Levi-Strauss jeans, $3.45; leather belt, $7.00; and cowboy boots, $24. The guys got a kick out of the advertising copy for their shape of Stetson, "the San Fran—with the lazy-curving broad brim, the smooth-tapered crown, that stamps you as a man who's at home on the range."[1]

Ropin' Demo

Calf roping demonstrations were always a popular activity at the ranch. What with the Yerington Spring Roundup coming up, Johnnie Jackson and I got in some practice at the ranch with the help of the guests.

According to Emmy, "Several friends helped us build the arena, catch pen and calf chute in the Tumbling DW days during World War II. Dore was a frustrated amateur roper. Bill Pedroli furnished the calves." Johnnie Jackson's calves now had the honors. The arena surrounded the Flying M E bunkhouse (but that would soon change).

Volunteers were key to the roping demonstrations. Someone had to chase the calf back to the catch pen after the roper caught or missed his calf. Another volunteer had to prod the next calf into the chute, then open the gate at the roper's signal. Very seldom did we have enough volunteers to time and flag these practice sessions, but it was still good roping practice.

Bill McGee on Zorro, rope and piggin' string ready, prepares to give chute operator the nod. (Authors' Collection)

Joan Allison had been my favorite—albeit reluctant—chute volunteer since she decided to stay on and help Emmy. On more than one occasion she had served as a one-woman "chute crew."

On this particular day, we were volunteer-rich for our roping demonstration. Charlie, Andy, Ethel, and Laura volunteered to man the catch pen and calf chute.

Zorro was one fine roping horse. He was well-trained and enjoyed the action. I roped and tied my first calf while Johnnie was getting ready, but I took too long to be competitive in a rodeo.

While I was waiting for Johnnie to catch his first calf, Laura asked me, "Have you ever entered a rodeo, Bill?"

"Sure, when I was in high school, and then a couple of times later in what was called the Montana County Fair Circuit. The high school events were pretty much the same as you'll see at the Yerington rodeo. The high school girls also competed in their own events which included barrel racing, team roping and, I think, goat tying."

Johnnie was a new Washoe Valley rancher. He was about twenty-five or thirty years old, slim (some would say skinny), maybe 135 pounds soaking wet. His one burning ambition was to be a rodeo producer and announcer, and a top hand with a rope.

We each roped, or tried to rope, six calves that afternoon.

Yerington Spring Roundup

Small-town shows like the annual Yerington rodeo were very popular with ranch guests because they provided the opportunity to see cowboys in action, up close and personal.

The Yerington Spring Roundup kicked off Nevada's rodeo season and was sponsored by the local VFW and American Legion posts. Entries in

Zorro, anticipating the coming action, is urged into position behind the barrier by Bill McGee. (Authors' Collection)

the five announced competition categories closed April 15. Contests that had been set with purses and entry fees were championship bronc riding, Brahma bull riding, calf roping, bareback bronc riding, and wild cow milking. In addition to the rodeo, there would be two days of entertainment that would include dances and a carnival.

We caravanned to Yerington, some seventy miles southeast of the ranch, in four cars. There were about fifteen of us, and we had plans to make a full day of it.

A record-smashing attendance sent the 1949 rodeo off to a flying start. The crowds overflowed the grandstand and bleachers to a point where even standing room only was hard to find. Many specta-

Yerington Rodeo Parade, 1949 (Courtesy Ethel Hall)

tors found perches along the roping and bucking chutes and atop rail fences.

All the familiar highlights of a rodeo—the Grand Entry parade, snorting broncs, daring riders, droll clowns, plus trick roping and riding exhibitions by the well-known Monte Montana troupe—were featured at the show on opening day.

Everyone seemed to enjoy the close-up action. The Brahma bull and bronc riding were the real crowd pleasers, especially when a snorting bull or bronc charged, with hoofs flying in a cloud of dust, toward the fence in front of the spectators.

The rodeo lasted about four hours, and the announcer was calling out the names of the day-money winners as we were walking to our cars. I didn't recognize any of the names, but most of the contestants were Nevadans. The size of the purses at the small shows like the Spring Roundup attracted very few top professional rodeo riders.

We were all in great spirits after the rodeo, as we headed north to Virginia City for the "Rodeo Special" dinner at the Bonanza Inn. As usual, I got hit with questions.

Annie Greenleaf: What are the origins of rodeo, Bill?

Bill: Rodeos date back to the 1870s, when it was pretty much a competition between cowhands who grew up working on ranches in the West. It's changed a lot over the years, and now the professional cowboys are exceptionally talented athletes — much like professional football or baseball players. But there are still many local circuit rodeos that provide competitive opportunities for amateur cowboys and cowgirls.

Charlie Pittman: What did the rodeo announcer mean when he said the rider was "disqualified for pulling leather," Bill?

Bill: That's when the rider grabs hold of the saddle horn to keep from being thrown, in saddle bronc riding.

We were all thirsty and couldn't wait to get to the Bonanza Inn. The Inn was already crowded when we arrived, and people were standing in line at Doug's little bar. When Halvor Smedsrud spotted Emmy and our entourage, he greeted us royally and showed us to a private room with a crackling fire. In no time, we had cocktails in hand and were watching the sun set over the High Sierras. Jinny Smedsrud's "Rodeo Special" was a winning ticket: Comstock salad, old-fashioned Western pot roast with mashed potatoes, and a chocolate soufflé, each course accompanied by wines selected by Doug Moore.

After dinner, Charlie Pittman muttered that he must have bought his Levis too small.

Then more questions.

Andy Topol: What's the difference between a cowboy and a wrangler, Bill?

He looked at Charlie Pittman and they smiled. I was sure they were setting me up for a joke but decided to play along.

Bill: A wrangler on a cattle ranch or cattle drive is the cowboy who is responsible for taking care of the horses. A wrangler on a dude ranch is respon-

Yerington Roundup, 1949

(Authors' Collection)

sible for taking care of both the horses and the dudes.

Charlie Pittman: Sounds like you have it made, Bill. You get paid for this?

Bill: Look at it this way, someone's got to do it!

We arrived back at the ranch around midnight. I could tell that Emmy was feeling relieved we were all back in one piece. You'd never know it by looking at her, but this kind of day was tough on her. She felt responsible for everyone's having a good time and coming home safely.

Before retiring, Allie reminded me that tomorrow morning movers were coming to move the bunkhouse. Emmy, Allie and I had discussed the pros and cons of moving the bunkhouse closer to the main house ever since the heavy snowstorms of December and January. The question was where would we move it *to*? We finally settled on a spot adjacent to the south side of the stone house with Edie's big walk-in refrigerator.

The decision to move the bunkhouse was a good one for two reasons. The wrangler would be more accessible to the ranch staff in case of an emergency, and he'd also be closer to the bathroom.

I was up early the next morning to move some horses, so I could open up the paddock fence before the movers arrived. Around nine, three men arrived and jacked up the bunkhouse, backed their moving rig under it, eased off the jacks, and within two hours the bunkhouse was set in place on a new cement block foundation. No more wading through 200 yards of snow in the winter to reach the john!

Ride 'em, Cowboy!

Charlie Pittman and his new Levis
(Caricature by Joan Allison)

CHAPTER 35

When Tony Met Tonie

The Two Tonys

Tonie

Mrs. Anthonie "Tonie" Kelly arrived in Reno on the Divorcée Special at three a.m. It had been a long and tiring three days since leaving New York, and she was looking forward to checking in at the Riverside Hotel, where her lawyer had made reservations for her six weeks' stay. As she settled back in the taxi, she thought how nice a hot bath and a long sleep in a real bed were going to feel.

Fifty years later, Tonie reminisced:

Was I surprised! When I arrived at the Riverside, the place was jumping! It was three-thirty in the morning and the place was packed. Everyone was singing, drinking, and gambling. I checked in and went up to my room which faced the main street. I stood there and didn't know what to do!

The bellman said, "You look tired. How about something to eat?" He left and returned with a chicken sandwich—and a Scotch! I certainly didn't want a Scotch in the middle of the night and asked for a glass of milk instead.

The next morning, Mrs. Kelly went to see her lawyer.

Mrs. Kelly: I can't stay at that hotel. It's...oh, I don't know what to do. I think I'll go back to New York.

Mr. Halley: Oh, no, you can't do that. Not if you want a divorce in six weeks. If the Riverside is too noisy, I think you should move to a nice dude ranch out of town, like the Flying M E.

Mrs. Kelly: Oh, I wouldn't go to a dude ranch, not for anything in the world. I would go back to New York and Mr. Kelly first.

Mr. Halley knew he had to do something, so he arranged a meeting at the Riverside with Anthonie Kelly and Emmy Wood, owner of the Flying M E. Tonie continues:

This tiny woman appeared at the Riverside. She was all done up in Western garb. Still, she looked like a proper little thing. "Would you like a drink, dear?" she asked.

I thought, gee, at eleven in the morning? I answered, "Go ahead and have one. I'll just sit here while we talk." We chatted and I think she figured out I wasn't too interested in staying at a ranch.

"Well, dear," she said, "it's up to you."

2

She was very nice about it.

Outside, she had a station wagon full of girls—I don't remember any men. She said they were going to someplace named Parker's to buy Western wear and a place called Newman's for belt buckles and turquoise jewelery, and would I like to come along. So I went along.

The girls were buying everything—pants, shirts, belts, boots, and hats. I was certainly no expert, but I remember thinking that this "costume" was more becoming to some than to others. Definitely not for me, I thought.

Then we drove out to the Flying M E, and I looked at the place. There were horses there, and that made me happy. So we drove back to Reno, and I called my lawyer. "I guess it would be better if I stayed at the Flying M E. Otherwise, I'll never make it here for six weeks," I told him.

My lawyer made all the arrangements for

From The Nevada Magazine, *1947*

Tonie Green, now a full-blown Westerner, enjoys a walk in the pines. (Courtesy Jan and Barry Hundemer)

me to move, while I packed my things. Then Emmy and I drove back to the ranch.

I still remember my first night there. Emmy drove a carload of us to Carson City to the Old Corner Bar. I remember saying, "I'm not going into that funny little place!" and I sat in the car while the rest of them went in to drink and gamble. Finally, I did go in and met Timmy Martinez, the manager, and Mike Demas, a dealer. Mike was a belly gunner in a bomber in World War II. He was a Greek from Brooklyn. We hit it off and I loved him.

Well, soon I was in Parker's and Newman's too, buying my own cowgirl garb, and the Old Corner Bar became my favorite habitat. This reluctant New Yorker stayed six weeks.

The above scenario was very typical of many divorcées' first reaction upon arriving in Reno. Tonie settled in, went sightseeing, and met some of the locals.

Tony

Tony Green was on Emmy's short list of acceptable single men whom she would invite to dinner periodically. To be on the list, a man had to have manners, behave like a gentleman and be a good conversationalist.

Tony Green appeared in an earlier chapter, when he was director of the Nevada State Museum in Carson City. Maggie Astor was staying at the ranch then, and Tony and Maggie became romantically involved.

Tony's background was in the Natural Sciences, and he had come to the Nevada State Museum from San Diego's Natural History Museum, where he worked as a preparator preserving animals and constructing their authentic natural habitats. He wanted to add a children's petting zoo of native Nevada birds and animals to the Carson City museum. However, Major Max C. Fleischmann, the major benefactor of the museum, and Judge Clark J. Guild, the museum founder, had a different priority which was to complete the museum's mine exhibit by Nevada Day 1950. So Tony left the museum and Carson City—with Maggie Astor in tow.

Joan Allison and I got to know Tony Green and Maggie Astor very well. We went out to dinner together on several occasions. When Tony and Maggie left the area, everyone understood they'd

The former Campbell ranch on Franktown Road became a showplace of Washoe Valley in the 1950s under the ownership of the "two Tony's," Tony and Tonie Green. (Courtesy Jan and Barry Hundemer)

Mr. and Mrs. J. Elton Green of Washoe Valley, are winter visitors at Hotel del Charro, La Jolla.
(*San Diego Union*, Courtesy Jan and Barry Hundemer)

gotten married. Emmy even gave them a farewell dinner at the ranch before they headed for La Jolla, California.

Tony Meets Tonie

A few years after leaving Carson and his position at the museum, Tony revisited the Flying M E. In Tonie's words:

During my six weeks at the ranch, Tony Green arrived one day and we met. I think he was up from Coronado with some friends. Nothing clicked one way or another. A few months after my divorce was final, I flew to San Francisco and met Tony at some function. This time we clicked.

On October 29, 1952, Tonie Kelly married Tony Green in Franktown, Nevada. The "two Tonys"—as they were called around the Valley—bought the Campbell ranch next door to the Washoe Pines dude ranch in Washoe Valley. The ranch had been built by Mrs. Campbell, a soup heiress, who had a reputation for building and tearing down, and her property was a mix of buildings — part home, part museum and part woodworking shop. This was a project made to order for Tony, an artist, builder and collector. The two Tonys had fun remodeling the property, and according to journalist Basil Woon their ranch became "a showplace of the valley." (*Nevada State Journal, 1956*)

After selling their Washoe Valley ranch, the Greens moved to La Jolla and eventually Nevada City, California for "the four seasons." They enjoyed a long and happy marriage of thirty-four years.

In our interview with Tonie Green in 2002, she was sure that Tony had not married Maggie Astor. Knowing Maggie as I did, it shouldn't have come as a surprise that her engagement or marriage to Tony might have fallen through. After all, she arrived at the ranch to divorce one man, was already engaged to marry another man, and fell for a new man in the meantime—all in six weeks.

But this chapter is about when Tony met Tonie—a happy couple whose paths crossed at the Flying M E.

CHAPTER 36

Eastern Gentleman Weds Western Lady

A snowy night, a serendipitous meeting

This is a love story with a reversal on the cowboy-and-the-lady theme, for it wasn't always Eastern *ladies* who came to Nevada for a divorce and stayed.

Janice Duncan Goodhue was born and raised in San Francisco. She was married to Gregor Duncan, the famous *Life* magazine and *Stars and Stripes* cartoonist, when World War II broke out. Wanting to help with the war effort, she first worked for the Office of War Information (OWI). Then, when Gregor was drafted, she volunteered for the American Red Cross. In 1943, the Red Cross assigned Janice overseas, first to Algiers in North Africa and then to Sardinia and Italy. During this time, she met another Red Cross volunteer, Jinny, who would later play a role in Janice's life. Tragically, Gregor was killed in 1944 at Anzio, which left Janice—along with thousands of other bereaved widows, widowers, and battle-fatigued veterans—at an unhappy crossroads in their lives.

Nathaniel and Janice Goodhue in Carson City, 1967, greeting the dog which was shipped to them by Nathaniel Jr. from Santiago, Chile.
(Courtesy Janice Goodhue)

The post-war years found Janice Duncan working in Carson City, Nevada, for the State Legislature. She learned through a friend whom she had met at OWI that her former Red Cross pal, Jinny, was at Walley's Hot Springs, just outside Genoa. Jinny was now married to Halvor Smedsrud, and the couple were enjoying success and popularity with their Bonanza Inn. The Inn first opened in Virginia City in 1947, and then relocated to Walley's in 1952.

The Bonanza Inn clientele followed the Smedsruds to Walley's Hot Springs, and this included Emmy Wood and her changing entourage of Flying M E guests. One evening, Jinny introduced Janice to the legendary dude ranch owner. As Emmy did so often with people she liked, she extended an invitation to Janice, that if it was ever snowing too hard to get home, she was welcome to spend the night at the Flying M E.

This is exactly what happened one night...

Nathaniel Mansfield Goodhue arrived at the Flying M E from Medfield, Massachusetts. Born into wealth and a descendant of an old Yankee shipping family, he was educated—as all proper New Englanders must be—by attending Milton Academy and Harvard.

Nathaniel, an avid sailor, had never been west of Wyoming, and now he was in the open spaces of Nevada for a divorce. One snowy evening, Janice Duncan arrived at the ranch to sit out some rough weather. Emmy introduced Janice to the ranch guests, which included Nathaniel. Tall and good-looking, Nathaniel had what many called "movie star looks," and it would have been natural to assume that after his divorce he was already spoken for. Whether spoken for or not, Nathaniel and Janice fell in love, and they married the same year in Needham, Massachusetts.

Janice and Nathaniel Goodhue at Holiday Farm, Medfield, Massachusetts, 1956 (Courtesy Janice Goodhue)

Happy times at Holiday Farm. Nathaniel and his new bride lived at Holiday Farm in Medfield, Massachusetts for the next eight years. Many of their Nevada friends came to visit them, including the writer and journalist Basil Woon, who spent six months as their houseguest. Janice Goodhue recalls Basil Woon's visit:

> Basil was a wonderful houseguest. We had lots of extra space, and he stayed in a separate wing with its own entrance. He loved to bake bread, and we had the real, honest-to-goodness sourdough, just like I remembered having in San Francisco.
>
> He was an early riser and very disciplined. No matter what he was writing, he worked at his typewriter every morning—whether he had anything to say or not!
>
> Basil was in his glory when Mr. Goodhue arranged a temporary membership for him at the Boston Athenaeum. It's one of the oldest libraries in the United States, and Basil would go there and spend days doing research. He loved it.

Nathaniel, like so many Easterners who came to Nevada for a divorce, had fallen in love with Nevada's open spaces, unmatchable vistas, climate, and people. The couple would visit every year, and in 1959 they purchased six acres on Winnie Lane in Carson City "when there was nothing there but sagebrush." Each year they'd come out and do some clearing, and one summer Janice planted over two hundred seedlings for a windbreak.

In 1964, when Nathaniel's daughter, Charlotte, married and his son, Nat Jr. was off to Chile for the Peace Corps, Nathaniel and Janice felt free to move. They returned to Carson and began construction of their home, which they moved into in February 1965. They became active members of the Carson-Reno-Tahoe community and shared

Nathaniel Goodhue helping out on a friend's ranch in Smith Valley, circa 1976. (Courtesy Janice Goodhue)

many close friendships with other locals, like Gus and Jeanne Bundy, Rudy and Bill Bliss, and the "two Tonys," Tonie and Tony Green.

Nathaniel served as a member of the Ormsby Library Board of Trustees and was a highly praised and respected volunteer fireman with Carson City's Warren Engine Company No. 1. *Sports Illustrated* interviewed Nathaniel for an article on retirement (November 12, 1973), which featured a two-page photo of "Nate" (as his fellow volunteer firemen called him) in his fire gear.

Nathaniel never forgot his Massachusetts roots and installed a Cape Cod weathervane on the roof of his Nevada home, which became a great source of discussion during cocktails-at-the-poolside.

Nathaniel and Janice lived happily in Carson City for twenty-one years until his death in 1986.

Janice, as petite and dynamic as ever, is living in Washoe County and stays very active pursuing her interests. Her memories of World War II have been recorded and published by the University of Nevada Oral History Program. And now her fond memories of a serendipitous meeting at the Flying M E have been captured in this book.

Nathaniel Goodhue in Sports Illustrated. (Courtesy Janice Goodhue)

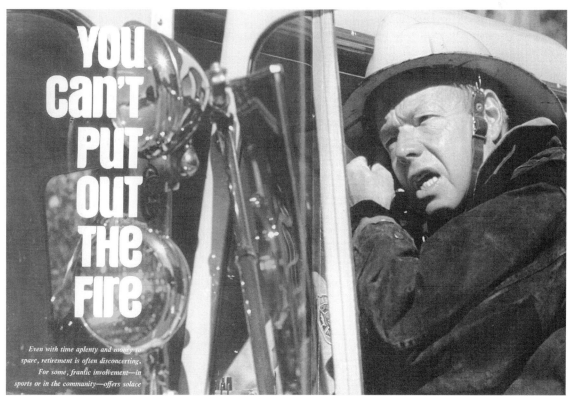

YOU can'T PUT OUT THE FIRE

Even with time aplenty and money to spare, retirement is often disconcerting. For some, frantic involvement—in sports or in the community—offers solace

Emmy Wood made it a tradition to present each departing Flying M E guest with a memento: a Sterling silver medallion which she had made at Hoot Newman's Silver Shop in Reno. The medallion was designed with the M E brand in the center, and each guest's initials and the year of their "graduation" was etched around the perimeter. Janice Goodhue loaned the authors Nathaniel Goodhue's medallion. We are especially grateful, as it is the only one we've discovered in our research.

(Photo David Bazemore)

CHAPTER 37

The Cowboy and the Lady

"A gay young divorcée, she won me..."

—Lyrics by Jack Watt,
Tumbling DW wrangler, early 1940s

Although it sounds like the makings of a Hollywood movie, romances and marriages between Eastern ladies and Nevada cowboys truly happened. Inez Robb summed it up best for *The American Weekly* in 1944:

> RENO, Nevada. Out here in the great open spaces where men are men and the wimmen aim to keep 'em that way, the colorful story of the Cowboy and the Lady is very familiar. There are three possible endings to the inevitable romances between the lady tenderfeet and the cowhands:
>
> No. 1 is the rare and happy ending, about 1 out of every 100.
>
> No. 2 is the transitory marriage lasting from 24 hours to a year before the party of the first part gets fed up with the party in the Stetson hat, the tight-fittin' britches and the wingtip boots.
>
> No. 3 results in marriage until such time as the innocent ol' Cowboy has mulcted the Lady of every penny in her possession, including the cattle or dude ranch she inevitably buys her lanky lover along the banks of the Truckee River or in the beautiful Washoe Valley.[1]

The cowboy and the lady
(Authors' Collection)

Well, during my time wrangling dudes at the Flying M E, I can honestly say that I observed romances between cowboys and lady dudes that fit into all three of Inez Robb's categories. I can also modestly say that more than one attractive and wealthy divorcée made a pass at me. There were offers to buy me a ranch—in Washoe Valley, in Colorado—heck, wherever I wanted. There were offers of marriage—"Marry me and come live in Acapulco. You can keep the Caddy convertible." There were offers of a grander lifestyle—"But you'll have to wear a suit and tuxedo." I had too much pride and self-confidence to play the gigolo. Living off a woman's money was not my idea of independence.

Look at Frank Polk, a hero to us younger cowboys; getting mixed up with those wealthy women caused him nothing but grief. Even after *two* divorces from the wealthy Joan Kaufman Biddle Wintersteen Polk Ladd, Frank took off *again* in '48 when he married a "cute little trick" (his words) by the name of Wanda Remington. I don't know how long their marriage lasted. (See Frank Polk's story in "Landing the Flying M E Wrangler Job.')

My Lady

In late April 1949, Joan Allison was ready to come back to the ranch and resume helping Emmy with the hostess duties. She had been recuperating at her mother's apartment in San

George H. L. Peet and Joan Allison in front of the newly-painted, newly-moved bunkhouse, circa 1949.
(Authors' Collection)

Francisco after her miscarriage in early March. Her mother, Lucy Dodsworth Allison, and George H. L. Peet drove Joan back to the ranch. The ranch was full, but Emmy got George and Lucy accommodations at the Bundy ranch down the road.

Joan and I would be sharing the "rustic bunkhouse" in its new location. We had lots of catching up to do, but first everyone wanted to tour the bunkhouse.

The inside was unchanged: a good-sized cabin sparsely furnished with a double bed, one bedside table, a reading lamp, a bureau, and a small chest of drawers—everything a single cowboy needed, but still no private bathroom. However, now one was only a few steps away, just inside the side door of the ranch house. That sure beat walking two hundred yards. Emmy told Joanie and me that she'd make a budget available so we could fix up the bunkhouse to our liking.

After dinner, Joan and I excused ourselves and drove into Carson City to the Melody Lane, a relatively quiet place where you could talk or listen to music. We were anxious to talk about our relationship.

First I welcomed Joanie home with a toast and a kiss. We were both relieved that she was back on her feet and in good health. Then I brought up the subject of our relationship. "Since I'm the senior member of this team—by eleven months—allow me to recap our ten month relationship.

"We met last July and got to know a little something about each other.

"Last fall we began dating—with Emmy's blessing—after you decided to stay on as Emmy's assistant hostess. Our dating led to a beautiful, intimate relationship.

"In December, we learned you were pregnant and, after very serious deliberation, decided to try getting an abortion. You wanted to pursue a medical career, and I wasn't convinced getting married was the right solution for either of us.

Divorce seekers share stories atop the poolhouse at the Flying M E. (Photo Valerie Vondermuhll, Courtesy George A. Vondermuhll Jr.)

"In January, when we were living together in Reno, the whole scene—the apartment, the neighborhood, your pregnancy—depressed you.

"Then, in early March, after the miscarriage, you became even more depressed. We were both sad over the loss of the baby and confused about our future.

"While we've been apart these last two months, I've given our relationship a lot of thought. We agree that we have absolutely nothing in common, but I still care a lot for you. Maybe I even love you.

"I'm really not sure where we should go from here. If medical school is still important to you, with its six to eight years of study, and if owning my own ranch someday is still important to me, then we should really call it quits right now.

"That might not be what you wanted to hear— I don't know. I'm just trying to be realistic. I've said my piece. Now it's your turn."

There was a long pause, and then Joanie began.

"Bill, remember in San Francisco, we said there was no big rush to decide anything. We said I should return to the ranch and see what happens. Can't we do that?"

"Sure. We both need time. There's something else I haven't told you. I've been weighing the pros and cons of pursuing a career in the entertainment industry. How's that for a major change?"

"That's a surprise. What gave you that idea?"

"When Norman Tokar and Terry Robinson were here, we talked a lot, and I asked them a lot of questions about directing and writing. Then I had that brief gig on KOH radio as John Friendly. Anyway, I've decided to look into it. We'll see. But getting back to you and me, let's take our time deciding what we should do."

Temptations at the Ranch

A night or two later, Joanie surprised me when out of the blue she asked, "Is it true you were

The Greenleaf kids are back in the saddle. (Authors' Collection)

having an affair with Ethel Roosevelt when I was in San Francisco?"

"Hell, no. We became very good friends, that's all. Where did you hear that?"

"I overheard the help talking last night. Maybe they were just speculating. They clammed up as soon as I entered the kitchen. It's taken me awhile, but I'm beginning to know the workings of the backstage scene around here. Like little Audrey. Remember little Audrey last fall? Young, cute, and, if I remember correctly, a bit of a wild one and, of course, getting a divorce. Was I naïve. It never occurred to me that you probably had sex with her. So I have to ask, did you?"

"Honest answer? Yes. You and I weren't married."

"Okay, the answer is yes. I also remember being embarrassed about my innocence in the face of your casual ease. You told of how she hopped up on the bar one night—it must have been a place

other than one of those frequented by Emmy's crowd—and stripped off her clothes. I couldn't believe it. I was envious, no doubt. Then one day Audrey was gone. There was usually one 'Audrey' in the kitchen for general help. She would be of the six-week variety working her way to her divorce."

"Why all the questions now?" I asked.

"To clear the air, I guess. If we're seriously considering marriage, doesn't that make us engaged?"

"I guess it could. Okay, consider us engaged!"

"Okay, in that case, promise me no fooling around. Is that fair?"

"Okay."

• • •

The summer of '49 was every bit as busy as '48. The main difference was we didn't have any college kids like Colin Greenley and Bud Henry. My "adopted children" Ricky and Gail Greenleaf

Emmy doing accounts in her "diggin's," 1948. (Photo Valerie Vondermuhll, Courtesy George A. Vondermuhll Jr.)

Dachshunds Rule!

were here. They were great kids.

We did have one new guest development, at least new to me since I'd been at the ranch. A Mrs. Caroline Burns gave up after five weeks and went back to her husband in Maine. She was miserable from the start: depressed one minute, bravely resolved the next. The phone calls were endless, and the mailman's arrival was always a cause for drama. ("I got a letter today and he still loves me!" "There was no letter today. Oh, what does it mean!") The guests and staff were glad to see her leave, and Emmy made a note in her file, "Suggest Mrs. Burns stay somewhere else when she comes back again for that divorce."

Roped In

On July 22, 1949, Joanie and I were married in Fallon, Nevada, some sixty miles northeast of Carson City. A Justice of the Peace conducted the ceremony, and his wife was our witness. On the way to Fallon, we swung by the Stewart Indian school south of Carson so I could buy a silver and turquoise wedding ring. After the ceremony, we drove up to Virginia City and had drinks at the Brass Rail Saloon and dinner at the Bonanza Inn.

Penna Hinton was working for Pat Hart at the Brass Rail as his blackjack dealer and also tended bar now and then. Rumor had it they had a romance going.

Our marriage was much like an elopement. We hadn't told a soul, and it was all over in no time. Most people at the ranch thought we were already married. Emmy and Allie were pleased when they got the word. Emmy was not comfortable with our "living together" in the bunkhouse.

For my money, I had married the most beautiful woman in the world.

Some chores are more fun than others.
(Photo Valerie Vondermuhll, Courtesy George A. Vondermuhll Jr.)

Ranch Life Goes On

Ranch life went on as usual. Joanie helped Emmy and Allie with the hostess duties and spent a lot of time at the office desk in Emmy's room. It was neat now compared to the mess it had been prior to Joanie's involvement. Keeping track of the guests' phone calls was still an archaic system. The only phone was in the office. When guests used the phone they were supposed to write on a little pad their name, who they called, when and where, and the operator-supplied time and charges. They were supposed to put the slip of paper on a spindle on the desk. I'm sure you can guess the rest of this story. It was a huge headache for Joan and Emmy sorting out the monthly telephone bill.

• • •

Sundays were generally the day off for the help. Edie, the cook, sure earned it. She would work non-stop fixing breakfast and lunch, get in a little

Pickup Picnic

Bill and Allie
(Photo Valerie Vondermuhll, Courtesy George A. Vondermuhll Jr.)

(Courtesy R. C. Greenleaf)

nap, and then prepare dinner. She fed the guests and the help. That's a lot of meals. Sunday night was Edie's night to howl. She always went into Reno to play bingo. Most guests went out to dinner on Sunday nights with Emmy to one of her favorite restaurants.

On Sundays, there was no riding. The wrangler and the horses needed a change of pace, too. This cowboy enjoyed three hobbies: oil painting, photography and reading. The few oils I did at the ranch were likened to Charles Russell, a huge compliment in my book, but I never pursued painting seriously. Penna Hinton and a couple of the other riders gave me a very fine Zeiss Ikon 35 mm camera, and in no time I was hooked. One night at the Old Corner Bar, I met John Nulty, another photography buff. John was with the Warren Engine Company No. 1, Carson City's volunteer fire department. He had a small darkroom in the fire station and taught me how to develop my own film. (Many of the photos in this book credited to "Authors' Collection" were developed with John Nulty's help in the Carson City fire station darkroom. Today John Nulty's highly-prized photos of northern Nevada are archived in the Nevada State Library and Archives in Carson City.) I've always been a history buff, so reading was also one of my favorite pastimes.

Joanie and I went into Reno now and then to see Lena Geiser at the Round Up Bar and to get a bowl of Ramona's chili at the Roaring Camp. One night I introduced Joan to Frank Polk, the "whittlin' cowboy." Frank stuttered when he was sober, but get a few drinks in him and his speech was smooth as glass.

• • •

In the fall of '49, we had some new guests for dinner, Father Riley, priest for the Nevada State prison, and his young nephew, John, who was visiting from Ireland. Emmy wasn't deeply religious, but for some reason Father Riley and young John became her friends and were our dinner guests almost every night.

Father Riley was far from the staid priest. He had a great sense of humor and amused the guests with his stories. Young John had a thick Irish brogue. You could cut it with a knife. He, too, kept the guests entertained.

• • •

Jimmy Murray and I were friends "from the git go." We ate a lot of meals together early on, while Emmy decided whether my upbringing and manners made me fit company for the dinner table.

Jimmy was the first wrangler at the Flying M E, and when he had his stroke Emmy, bless her heart, promised to take care of him and has ever since. Jimmy had a son living in Half Moon Bay on the California coast but, for whatever reason, he never came to visit his father. So one day I said, "Jimmy, what say we pay your son a visit? Half Moon Bay is only a five hour drive. I'm sure Emmy will let us have the time off."

A few days later we visited his son, who managed a small farm in Half Moon Bay. They had a good time talking about family and friends. The son apologized for his lack of communication and support since Jimmy's stroke. But that was it. No offer to take care of his dad. However, had he offered, Jimmy would have turned him down. Jimmy had no intention of deserting Emmy.

Close Call

At one point, I came dangerously close to scuttling my two month marriage over another woman. Cindy Forester, a vivacious, attractive, English brunette, was a regular rider. She was a fashion model in New York prior to marrying a wealthy Mr. Forester.

One warm afternoon during a conversation with Cindy out by the pool, I couldn't help but notice a few strands of dark pubic hairs peeking out from the crotch of her bathing suit. I wondered if it was intentional to attract my attention. I also wondered if that elegance and style she radiated out of bed turned into uninhibited sexuality in bed.

That evening I escorted several guests, including Cindy, to the Old Corner Bar. Joan had decided to stay home and read. She was getting "sick and tired" of the late nights. While the others were gambling, Cindy and I were alone at the bar, and she propositioned me in the most surprising way. "Bill, are you available tonight? Before you answer, you know I have a private entrance to my room."

"Cindy," I replied, "You're a beautiful woman and I'm very flattered by your invitation. But I'm a married man." I was saved from a more expansive explanation when the other guests joined us at the bar.

Around midnight, as I drove the group home, I got to thinking and kept asking myself should I join Cindy in her fireplace room? What would happen if Joanie found out? I hate to admit it but lust almost won out. After checking the bunkhouse and finding Joan fast asleep, I circled back to Cindy's Dutch-door entrance to the fireplace room on the ground floor of the ranch house. Then I stopped. (If I capitulate to Cindy's alluring invitation, it'll be easy to capitulate to others, and that's the end of my marriage.) So I turned around and tip-toed back to the bunkhouse. Many times over the years I've wondered what I missed. Cindy almost caught me in a barriers-down moment.

• • •

In November of '49, Joanie and I journeyed to San Francisco for the wedding of her mother, Lucy Dodsworth Allison, to George H. L. Peet. Lucy was convinced she had stolen George away from

Nathalie Morgan—and George saw it that way, too. Who wants to think of himself as the discarded one? The Peets moved into a beautiful house in the Seacliff district of San Francisco with great views of the Bay.

• • •

Joan Allison drew most of the caricatures you see in this book. She drew them on a tracing pad, either sitting on the bed or at a kneehole desk in one of the guest rooms. Her final caricature at the Flying M E was of herself at work. Joan inherited her artistic talent from her father, John Allison, a fine oil painter. She was employed by the art department at the J. C. Penney advertising division in New York—right out of high school and with no formal schooling.

With due apologies to all

Joan Allison

(Caricature by Joan Allison)

Decision Time— ## Or No Place for a Married Man

It was time for some serious decisions. Joanie and I had many discussions after her return to the ranch, weighing the pros and cons of our future together. The more we talked, the more we realized we were not that much different than other newlyweds. We had experienced a difficult start, what with the pregnancy and the miscarriage. We had weathered some perilous moments of near-infidelity on my part.

In mid-November 1949, we made a decision.

Joanie confessed she was having second thoughts about a career in medicine. Her father, of the old school, pooh-poohed college for women. Her mother wasn't encouraging this route either.

As for me, I decided to confess my "close and almost tryst" with Cindy Forester and admitted that the temptations thrust upon a man at a dude ranch for divorcées was no place for a married man. Maybe that was reason enough for us to move on. Joan surprised me with her response.

"You've just confirmed my suspicions. I was pretty sure Cindy had her eye on you. Let's give Emmy notice tomorrow. Our marriage is bound to fail if we stay here."

Emmy and Allie couldn't have been more understanding. While they both said how much they'd miss Joan and me and how hard we'd be to replace, Emmy alluded to her own husband's straying years earlier. "I know all to well, my dears, why your decision is a sound one." It was still hurtful for her to speak about the incident that occurred years ago in the Tumbling DW days when her husband, Dore, left her for a divorcée whom he had met at the ranch.

On December 1, 1949, we said our goodbyes at the ranch. I put Lucy Dodsworth Allison Peet, now my mother-in-law, and Joanie on the train to Englewood, New Jersey. Then I drove up to Montana for a visit with my brother, before head-

ing east to God only knows what the future would hold.

I was really going to miss the Flying M E: dear Emmy and Allie; that old curmudgeon Jimmy Murray; Edie, the cook, with her cigarette holder and ashes dangling over the food; our Washoe Valley neighbors—especially would-be rodeo announcer Johnnie Jackson and Washoe Pines wrangler Lyle Hardin; trips to beautiful Lake Tahoe and Glenbrook; the familiar sounds of the little V & T chugging past the ranch daily; and all our favorite watering holes and their proprietors whom I'd gotten to know so well—Jinny and Halvor Smedsrud at the Bonanza Inn, Ella Broderick at the Old Corner in Carson, Pat Hart's

big smile and bigger drinks at the Brass Rail, Lena Geiser at the Round Up Bar in Reno. I'd miss the ever-changing cast of interesting characters who stayed at the ranch, and the kids—little Ricky and Gail Greenleaf. And especially—Zorro. I would miss Zorro and would miss being in the saddle. Would I ever ride again, I wondered.

To me, life was one adventure after another, and wanderlust had been in my blood since I was fourteen. I was ready for the future.

So what is the ending to *my* Cowboy and the Lady story? I'm happy to say it was No. 1—the rare and happy ending.

And the Cowboy and his Lady rode off happily into the Eastern sunrise.

Contrary to the popular myth, not all divorcées cast their wedding rings into the Truckee River. Many Flying M E graduates gave their rings to Emmy. One evening, the guests, aided and abetted by Allie, convinced Emmy to let them see her collection of rings, which she kept attached to a gold chain. (Photo Valerie Vondermuhll, Courtesy George A. Vondermuhll Jr.)

Afterword

Flying M E—Final Years

In 1961, Emily Pentz Wood retired and moved into the Greeno Hotel at 108 E. Proctor Street in Carson City.

On September 5, 1963, at about seven o'clock in the evening, the Flying M E came to a fiery end when smoke began to pour out of the hundred year-old building. Suddenly, with a loud roar, the main ranch house exploded into flames. The *Nevada Appeal* reported on September 6, 1963:

> Fire destroyed a page of Nevada history last night when the historical Flying M E Ranch burned to the ground. All that is left of the famous ranch which housed many prominent women who established residence for divorce in Nevada is a memory and the words written on now-faded newspaper pages.
>
> Only a five-car garage and horse barn near the main ranch house were untouched by flames as firemen waged a futile battle against the flames that roared through the once plush quarters of the main building at the 'dude' ranch.
>
> Firemen from four volunteer departments in the Washoe Valley, between Carson City and Reno, and from the state division of forestry, fought the raging blaze.
>
> There were no reports of injury. One estimate placed the damage at more than $100,000. The cause had not been determined.
>
> Mrs. Romeo Bandera, who lives a quarter of a mile to the west of the ME said she saw smoke pouring from the attic of the nine-suite ranch just before 7 p.m.
>
> The Flying M E was the second historic Washoe Valley structure destroyed by fire this summer. Flames burned the old Franktown School, which was being restored as a historic site....
>
> The Flying M E was under lease to William Moss and Ken Robertson at the time of the fire. The ranch has lately been used only as a riding stable. The property is now owned by the Millboss Corp.[1]

Volunteer firemen from Carson City Warren Engine Co. No.1 helped battle the blaze that destroyed the historical Flying M E ranch in Washoe Valley on September 5, 1963. (Photo by Sue Morrow for the *Nevada Appeal*)

Emmy Wood, far right, at the Fireside Bar Inn, Greeno Hotel, 1960s. (Courtesy Nadine Prior)

Emmy Wood, Greeno Hotel lobby, 1960s. (Courtesy Nadine Prior)

Emily Pentz Wood, legendary owner of the Flying M E, dressed for court, 1947.
(Photo Valerie Vondermuhll, Courtesy George A. Vondermuhll Jr.)

Rumor has it that many of Emmy's possessions were pilfered and sold in Reno while the ranch house was unoccupied. There is also an unsubstantiated rumor that the fire was set by an arsonist.

On May 19, 1965, Emmy sold the Flying M E property to Dorothy C. Silvey of Ormsby County, Nevada.[2]

On August 8, 1966, Emily Pentz Wood, owner-operator of the Flying M E ranch for close to a quarter of a century, died in the Carson-Tahoe Hospital in Carson City. Emmy had fallen and fractured her hip a week earlier and apparently was unable to withstand the shock and complications from the injury. A capacity crowd attended a memorial service held at Lone Mountain Cemetery in Carson City. A marble headstone marks Emmy's grave under a pine tree, although it is also said that a close friend scattered her ashes over Washoe Valley.

Friends Remember Emmy

There's a little story about how I happened to meet Emmy. It was about two in the morning and I was on the way back from Reno to Carson when I had a flat tire on the old highway in front of the Bowers Mansion. There wasn't a jack in the car and I couldn't get anyone to come and help me. So I started walkin'. I came to the Flying M E and climbed over the fence and walked through the corrals. I'd never been there before and didn't know how to navigate the driveway.

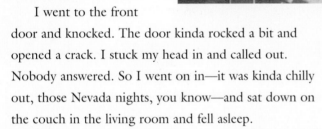

I went to the front door and knocked. The door kinda rocked a bit and opened a crack. I stuck my head in and called out. Nobody answered. So I went on in—it was kinda chilly out, those Nevada nights, you know—and sat down on the couch in the living room and fell asleep.

The next morning, I was awakened by a maid bringing me coffee and breakfast on a silver tray. She assumed I'd been out with one of the guests and had dozed off.

About a week later, I was in Hunter's Lodge in Carson and Emmy was there. She was sittin' at the bar and looked at me and kinda smiled. 'I understand you're the phantom of the couch!' she said. From then on, we had a great friendship.   —*Joe Page*

She wore the monogram "M E" on the left-hand pocket of her western shirts and she epitomized the hospitality for which the West—and this area—was noted in her time.   —*Basil Woon*

Emmy called people "dear" and her room at the ranch "my diggins." She never got up before noon. Edie, the cook, always addressed her as "Mrs. Wood." Everyday at noon, Edie would knock on Emmy's door, "Mrs. Wood, it's noon. Your coffee is served."
        —*Bill McGee*

Working in the office as I did, I saw the notes Emmy made on the guests' cards. "Bad news." "Nut!" "Trouble. Moved them to Pyramid Lake and the Drackerts." "Did Mrs. X return to hubby? Yes!"
        —*Joan Allison*

As the frequent driver in the evening, Emmy always told me, "You go into town with six guests; you return with six guests." Also, "Only two drinks for the driver, Bill."   —*Bill McGee*

I remember a bracelet Emmy showed me. It was gold with large links and many, many wedding bands were fitted on it. There must have been hundreds of precious stones—diamonds, rubies, emeralds and sapphires. Emmy never wore it; that wouldn't have been her style. She told me the rings were given to her by former guests. They just didn't want to keep them afterwards. You never cast off your wedding ring while doing your six weeks. It was a bad omen. But when you descended the courthouse steps, off it came. Whatever happened to that bracelet?
        —*Joan Allison*

The following tribute to Emily Pentz Wood was written by Basil Woon, author, journalist, and good friend. It has been condensed and reprinted here in the hope that it may help perpetuate the memory of a truly great woman of the Silver State.

IN MEMORIAM
EMILY PENTZ WOOD
1895 - 1966

Emily Laurence Pentz was born in New York City on November 27, 1895, the daughter of Mr. and Mrs. Frank Rozat Pentz. She was educated in New York and at Ely Court, a private school outside Greenwich, Conn. She was married to Theodore C. Wood, Jr., of a New York family dating back beyond colonial days to when the city was a Dutch outpost.

To the many who have come here in recent years Emily Wood might possibly have been known (if they knew her at all; her last years were lived in modest retirement at the Hotel Greeno) as merely a woman who had founded and owned the most famous "dude ranch" in the West. She was far, far more than that.

At the news of her passing, grief came to homes and tears were shed in places far removed from her adopted state, as well as here, where she lived. Many who were in faraway places—London, Paris, New York, Boston, Philadelphia, Chicago, Florida and California—felt personally bereft. And cowboys on the range paid silent tribute to the memory of their friend.

Friendship. That was the abiding theme of Emmy's life. And as Lord Bryon said, 'What is friendship but love without wings?' The quality of friendship Emmy gave remained permanently in the hearts even of those who knew her briefly. It was this quality, I think, that fashioned her greatness as a woman.

Emmy was, in a way difficult to describe, a compound of the down-to-earth virtues. Perhaps above all she had a genuine understanding of other people's troubles, and in her chosen career many were loaded on her shoulders. She had instinctive kindness, innate sympathy for those bereft or abandoned—and not only sympathy but practical help for the misunderstood, the less-endowed and for those many she met who were succumbing to despair.

Though she accepted the burden of other people's woes she never at any time gave voice to her own. The sum of her character was a warm sort of integrity. Emmy was many things to many people. "She's more of a mother to me than my own mother," a young girl told me. "She understands me better than any of my wives," a tormented stockbroker said. "I've only known her a fortnight and already she's like a sister,"—this from an English girl, castoff bride of one of America's famous perennial bridegrooms.

I first met Emily Wood about 1947 in Virginia City. Later after I had moved to Nevada I was returning one winter from New York and found myself in an Elko hospital with pneumonia. Discharged, I was met in Reno by my daughter, who said at once, "Emmy says you're to come to the ranch and I'm to bring you." So I spent a winter—one of many visits—at the Flying M E.

So it was to the Flying M E that I was taken that January of '57, weak and still hardly convalescent, and it was there I was privileged to witness the compassionate side of Emmy Wood. I saw deserted women arrive, tears still drying on their checks, some of them with the world crashing about them after fifteen or twenty years of marriage; some disillusioned after only a few years. Some guiltless, some guilty, some wealthy (in money if in little else), some beautiful and young, some raddled and old, some with so little money that Emmy offered them secretly special rates if they would "help her out." Helping her out involved nothing menial; generally it meant shepherding the flock to Reno or Carson City to see the sights, or to church on Sunday.

Emmy believed in people. Yes, she believed in them in spite of the business she was in. Determinedly, she saw the good side in everyone. I remember one man, posing as a wealthy dilettante, who decamped owing Emmy for two months' room and board. "Poor man," said Emmy. "I expect he has his own troubles."

Emmy was always breaking something, her shoulder, an arm, a leg, a kneecap and, finally, a hip, which caused her untimely death (after all, 70 is not really old today). I was, as I have said, ill in her home, but Emmy never made reference to it and was solicitous that I had rest and good food.

Emily Wood brought elegance to the dude ranch business, but much more than that she brought a quality of human understanding. Sometimes her guest-book read like the Social Register or "Who's Who"—Mrs. Franklin Delano Roosevelt, Sr. and Clark Gable were among those who stayed there merely because they loved Emmy—but neither money nor social position meant much for her. Manners, however, meant a lot. Of a celebrated and wealthy writer she said, "He's a boor, my dear, I don't think I shall have him here again"; of a gnarled and sun-blackened rancher, whose only school had been nature itself, she said, "He's a gentleman. He's always welcome here."

Most of the divorcées came to her shattered, miserable, despairing. Before many days Emmy somehow had given them new hope and a better outlook on life.

Emmy was the same to everyone. She met cowboy, divorcée, servant, lawyer, merchant, the casual friend on a night out, on terms of a completely natural equality. She loved everyone and everything—people, trees, flowers, dogs, horses, the mountains, the desert, the sun, the snow, even the wind—which sometimes piled up snowdrifts outside her door. Her staff adored her.

Besides her resident guests (during most of the year every guest-room was taken) dozens of locals dropped in—highway cops, lawyers, judges, fellow ranchers, gamblers, and cowboys.

When Emmy so suddenly left us it was discovered that, so far as anyone knew, she had no living blood relatives. But of course, she had a host of devoted friends who began telephoning from everywhere when they read the AP report.

Her many friends did feel something had to be done to perpetuate Emmy's memory after we who loved her are gone. The "Emily Pentz Wood Memorial Fund for Medical Research" was established at the Carson-Tahoe Hospital—to supply a badly-needed lack at the hospital where "Pollyanna" breathed her last. Contributions to this fund are being received at the hospital, 1201 Mountain Street, Carson City, Nevada.

Such a memorial, it seems to me, is small enough tribute to a truly great woman, the most understanding, the most sympathetic, and the most tolerant friend I and many, many others ever had, and who was, besides, one of Nevada's most useful citizens.[3]

On April 9, 1968, Dorothy Silvey Tesso sold the Flying M E property to Silvey Transportation Inc., a California corporation in Newark, California. On April 1, 1971, Silvey Transportation, now a Nevada Corporation, sold the Flying M E ranch to D.B. and Elaine Azevedo, longtime ranchers in the Elko, Nevada area.[4]

Today the Flying M E ranch is owned by Norman and Rhonda Azevedo, son and daughter-in-law of D.B. and Elaine Azevedo. Norman fondly remembers riding horses at the ranch in his childhood days.

The Azevedos are keenly interested in preserving the history of the historic Flying M E. They have built their home on the site of the old ranch house and in the style of a gentleman's farm in Virginia. The "M E" brand is proudly displayed above the main gate, and appears on the wrought iron railing surrounding the veranda and on stair railings inside the house. The five-car garage and stables are the only structures remaining from before the fire in 1963. During construction, workers uncovered silverware, dinner plates, bottles, horseshoes, and other artifacts from the property's historic days. The Flying M E was featured on an episode of the House & Garden Television series, "If Walls Could Talk".[5]

Almost all the evidence of Washoe Valley's past has been erased by time and man. Only a few ranches, one or two nineteenth century houses, and some old piles of ruins remain to testify to the lively days when Washoe Valley was. Modern developments have sprung up in the "new" Washoe City and in the southwest end of the valley. As Emmy once said, "They call that progress."

New Washoe City along the east shore of Washoe Lake, 1972
(Courtesy Nevada Historical Society)

The Flying M E today
(Courtesy Norman and Rhonda Azevedo)

Postscript

After "riding off into the Eastern sunrise" with my wife, Joan, we spent some time in her hometown of Englewood, New Jersey, then returned west and settled in the San Francisco Bay Area.

Shortly thereafter, I was hired to develop a new import division for a San Francisco-based world trade company. It was a great job with excellent long-range opportunities. I loved the world travel and the buy-sell merchant activities.

Joan and I kept in touch with writer Terry Robinson and actor-director Norman Tokar. We visited Terry in New York and were impressed with her television series writing credits which put her alongside Paddy Chayefsky, Nathaniel Hawthorne, Gore Vidal, and Billy Wilder, to name just a few. We visited Norman in Hollywood on the set of "My Favorite Husband" starring Joan Caulfield and Barry Nelson. Terry and Norman both encouraged me to pursue my interest in the entertainment field, and offered to help where they could. So in 1957, I decided to give it a go.

By now we had four children: Lucy, Betsy, Billy and Kathy. My family responsibilities ruled out most of the entry-level positions in the creative areas of the entertainment business, so I zeroed in on sales and marketing jobs.

My first job in the business was selling television programming to sponsors and stations for ITC (Independent Television Corporation). After three years of constant travel, I moved into the station representation field, and, still later, rose through the ranks to TV station general manager.

In 1971, I founded my own consulting company in the radio, TV and cable business, BMC (Broadcast Marketing Company).

By the time I retired in 1990, I had spent thirty-two very satisfying years in the business.

Why go into all this detail? Not to impress, as it might seem, but to make a few points. I've been lucky, and know it. Joan and I were married for twenty-two years and have four great children. My mother-in-law, Lucy Dodsworth Allison Peet, was a wonderful "Nanny" to our children. (She and George H. L. Peet remained married for twelve years. Then George left Lucy to marry an even-wealthier woman in Arizona.)

Reno, Carson City, Virginia City and Lake Tahoe were very special places in the decades of the 1940s, '50s and '60s, and I was lucky to know them then. They say you can never go back, but, in spite of Nevada's explosive growth and urban sprawl, it still calls me back on a regular basis.

So this postscript is to prove that a cowboy can change horses in mid-stream and adjust to city life. My transition was made easy by an understanding lady dude. My beautiful second wife, Sandra, another lady dude, has put up with me for almost twenty years. She is not only my friend and partner, she is also my co-author, publicist, and—to call a spade a spade—is still trying to get me to kick the corral dust off my boots.

However, hardly a day goes by that I don't wonder—what if I had stayed with cowboyin'?

—W. L. M.

Part III—Gettin' Untied

A. The Nevada Divorce Trade
B. The Lawyers
C. The Stringers
D. Six Minutes In Court

(Postcard courtesy of Susan Countner)

Nevada divorce seekers passin' time on the poolhouse deck at the Flying M E in 1947.
(Photo Valerie Vondermuhll, Courtesy George A. Vondermuhll Jr.)

A. The Nevada Divorce Trade

Cornelius Vanderbilt Jr. obtained so many Reno divorces, he was considered a local.

Nevada Legislature Creates 1931 Boom In Divorce and Gaming

The year 1931, in which the United States hit the depth of the Depression, became a boom year for the Reno economy. Not only did Nevada shave its residence requirement for divorce from three months to six weeks, but the 1931 legislature also returned legalized gambling to Reno after a twenty-year hiatus, giving bored divorcés something to do.

On March 20, 1931, the *Nevada State Journal* headlines shouted out the big news in boldface type on page one:

GAMING, DIVORCE BILLS SIGNED!

Balzar Adds Signature to Complete Passage of More Liberal Measures Through Machinery of Law Making . . . Preparations Underway to Attract Sporting Crowds as Establishments Enlarged... Travel and Publicity Freedom Lure for Decree Seekers.

Governor Fred B. Balzar yesterday afternoon signed the six-weeks divorce act and another much-discussed measure, the so-called "wide-open" gambling bill.

The gambling bill, signalizing Nevada's return to frontier days when poker, roulette, and faro bank games flourished in crowded mining camps, becomes effective immediately.

The six-weeks divorce measure, designed to keep Nevada and Reno foremost in the business of severing unsuccessful marriages, will become effective May 1.

Governor Balzar's only comment in announcing his action was: "Yes, I've signed them both." The two bills reached his office yesterday, and were signed a short time later.

Crowds of men flocked to the city's largest gambling resort, and dice and card games did a flourishing business on their inaugural eve of legal standing.

Reports were rife among members of the sporting fraternity to the effect that large and elaborate casinos were being planned for location either in or near Reno.

Las Vegas was reported as the proposed site for a large race track and gambling establishment to be established by Agua Caliente capital. Similar rumors, none of which had been openly verified, were heard from other sections of Nevada.

Meanwhile a number of court adjustments are to greet the new divorce act when it becomes officially effective May 1, 1931. Under the new law divorce seekers may spend six weeks anywhere within Nevada's borders and file suit for divorce in any district court within the state regardless of county.

This is widely at variance with the old 90-day act, which required continuous residence within the judicial district or county in which the action was to be tried. Divorce seekers now will be privileged to tour about the state during their stay pending the consummation of the litigation.

Divorce machinery is to be oiled up even more thoroughly, however, making "mass production" of decrees more than a mere possibility.

Under the new law complaints may be filed setting forth the allegation merely in the words off the statute without the necessity of stating particulars in regard to family quarrels, etc.

Freedom from publicity is assured by the Heidtman "gag law" which makes it mandatory for courts to hear divorce litigation behind closed doors and to have all court records sealed upon completion of the hearings. The bill was given final approval yesterday when the assembly receded on its amendment which would have removed the mandatory provision.

Another act, which yesterday afternoon had not completely passed through legislative action, was introduced by Senator Heidtman, requiring that corroborative resident witnesses must appear in all divorce cases and actually establish that the litigant had remained in the state for the required six weeks period. This bill was passed by both houses last night.

The divorce and gambling acts, objects of chief interest, have been controversial subjects of discussion for several months in Nevada cities.

A movement for a referendum vote on the gambling bill has been threatened by women's organizations, while the divorce act has been subjected to much criticism.

Reno residents point out that under its "travel" provision much of that city's business may be lost to other sections of the state. Attorneys are declared to be the chief beneficiaries under the bill and they were known to have been actively supporting it.

Reno attorneys appeared in Carson City yesterday in support of the Heidtman bill which assures secrecy to the divorce actions. They also were understood to have been behind the move to keep the law from becoming effective until May 1, so as to prevent a sudden exodus from Reno by those already in the county sufficiently long to apply for decrees under the new residence provision.

In 1931, Nevada law allowed for nine legal grounds for a divorce: impotency, adultery, desertion, conviction of a felony, habitual drunkenness, neglect to provide the common necessities of life, insanity, living apart for three years, and extreme cruelty entirely mental in nature. The most popular ground was mental cruelty and it could cover a wide variety of complaints, even something like "She talks to me when I'm trying to read" or "He interrupts me when I'm trying to write." And plaintiffs did not have to prove their charges.

In other states at that time, it wasn't so easy to get a divorce. In New York, for example, the waiting period was one year, and if you charged your spouse with adultery, you had to prove it. That was good business for the private eyes, but embarrassing for otherwise decent individuals. In California, the grounds for divorce were a little easier, but the waiting period was still one year.

So Nevada's divorce boom exploded with the new 1931 legislation, and thousands of divorce seekers came

running to Reno to "Get Reno-vated"—a term coined by Walter Winchell.

Nevada Divorce Timeline

Year	Residency Requirement
1871	6 months
1914	12 months
1915	6 months
1927	3 months
1931	6 weeks

Three Sensational Divorce Cases

Reno's divorce boom started rumbling right along with the dynamite in the early mining days of the Comstock, when migrant fortune-hunters often left old lives—and wives—behind. In 1871, state courts formally established a six-month residency period and allowed divorces without proof of adultery.

Nevada's reputation as a haven for those seeking to sever the bonds of matrimony grew out of three sensational divorce cases in the first two decades of the twentieth century—those of Lord John Russell, an English nobleman; Mrs. William Ellis Corey, the wife of a famous American industrialist; and Mary Pickford, a noted Hollywood actress.

Lord John Russell Divorce Case. The first widely publicized Nevada divorce case involved Lord John Francis Stanley Russell, age 35, a member of the House of Lords in England, and Mollie Cooke Somerville, described as "over 18." In the fall of 1899, the couple spent the required six months of Nevada residency in solitude at Glenbrook on the eastern shore of Lake Tahoe. On April 14, 1900, they divorced their respective spouses in Genoa, Douglas County. The following day they traveled to Reno to be married in a quiet ceremony.

Upon returning to England, Lady Russell filed a divorce suit on the grounds of bigamy. England did not recognize a Nevada divorce, and Russell was sentenced to three months in prison in London.

Upon his release, he married Mollie a second time.

(Photos Nevada Historical Soociety)

He announced his disgust with his treatment in England and said he intended to give up his citizenship, move back to Nevada, and become a rancher. But the marriage to Mollie did not last. Russell went on to marry a Countess Arnim, and he remained in England and was eventually reinstated in the House of Lords.

The Russell divorce brought international publicity to Nevada.

William Ellis Corey Divorce Case. The next big divorce case involved Laura B. Corey, married to William Ellis Corey, president of United States Steel. The Corey marriage seemed a stable one until William fell in love, in 1903, with a California actress and singer, Mabelle

Gilman. William and Mabelle were seen together at parties and traveled together to Europe, sharing a stateroom. With a scandal in the making, Laura Corey came to Reno in 1905, and obtained a divorce in 1906, with a settlement of $1 million. Less than a year later, William Corey married Mabelle. William gave up the presidency of U. S. Steel, and the new Coreys moved to Paris. Mabelle divorced William in Paris in 1923.

Again, the Corey divorce created publicity for Nevada. The reaction of some Nevada residents was to impose tighter residency laws, but others wanted the business. The six-month requirement remained.

Mary Pickford Divorce Case. Hollywood discovered Nevada in 1920, when actress Mary Pickford came to divorce her film-star husband, Owen Moore. Pickford stayed on the Campbell Ranch near Minden, a small community south of Carson City, using her legal name, Gladys Moore, to avoid publici-

ty. She stayed only sixteen days, however, before having the divorce granted. Then she returned to California and married actor Douglas Fairbanks.

Nevada Attorney General Leonard Fowler challenged the divorce because Pickford failed to meet the residency requirement of six months. He took the case to the Nevada Supreme Court. Pickford's attorney, Patrick McCarran, later a U.S. Senator from Nevada, found a loophole in the law, that said the attorney general had no authority to represent the state in a divorce proceeding, and won the case.

The sensational case was followed by the entire country. Mary Pickford's image went from that of a sweet child to a full-grown woman with marital problems. However, the marriage to Douglas Fairbanks did not last, and Mary never quite lived down her suspected part in what may have been an evasion of Nevada law.

The publicity fallout from the Pickford case was enormous, and from then on Reno was a national byword for divorce. Movies and songs were written about it, and Walter Winchell coined the divorce term, "Reno-vation," for the change that divorcés went through while in Reno.

Other high profile divorce cases followed: Jack Dempsey, Sinclair Lewis, Barbara Hutton, the Maharaja of Indore, and many Vanderbilts, Roosevelts, and Mrs. Tommie Manvilles, to name just a few. In 1933, Carole Lombard divorced William Powell in Carson City. Cornelius Vanderbilt Jr. was said to have obtain so many divorces in Reno he was considered a local resident.

Why all the celebrities, socialites, and famous people? It took someone of wealth to come for six months and live in idleness. So Reno got a reputation for catering to the wealthy.

Las Vegas Gets in the Act. It was the Clark Gable-Ria Langham Gable divorce in 1939 that launched Las Vegas into the divorce business. John Cahlan, editor of the *Las Vegas Review-Journal,* Florence Jones, a reporter, and the local Chamber of Commerce agreed to keep the divorce proceeding quiet until it was final in exchange for a big story that would publicize the divorce and the town.

Ria Langham cooperated and posed for publicity pictures at casinos and Lake Mead. She enjoyed the attention. Las Vegas liked it even better, since the city was desperately trying any gimmick that might lead to a national dateline. For six weeks she was Las Vegas' first citizen.

A record number of divorces, 738, were granted in Las Vegas in 1939, including a new high in the month of the Gable divorce, and then again two months later. Everyone, it seemed, wanted to get a divorce where the Gables had gotten theirs: Las Vegas.

In July 1939, the first haven for Las Vegas

divorces— the Boulderado Dude Ranch (formerly the Kyle Ranch)—opened, and others soon followed. Las Vegas began to creep up on her northern sister, Reno, and was granting half the state's divorces by 1962.[1]

• • •

The divorce trade was already a major facet of Reno's economy before the Pickford divorce scandal in the early twenties, and it became increasingly so as the decade passed. The legislation which accomplished this was passed in the 1931 legislative session, with later charges that financier George Wingfield had contrived to get the law changed in order to generate business for his new Riverside Hotel in Reno. The mayor of Reno, E. E. Roberts, as well as other business and community leaders, were also strong supporters.

Moralists criticized the state and spoke of threats to family life, but the main concern in Reno was whether the expected increase in volume would make up for the shorter time the divorce-seekers would remain there.

As was the case in 1927, the only real opposition to the new 1931 six-week bill came from those concerned about the economic impact. Would the six-weeks law draw a sufficient volume of trade to compensate for the shorter stay? Arkansas and Idaho had meanwhile gone to a ninety-day residency, so Governor Fred Balzar signed the bill on March 19, 1931, after the two houses of the Legislature worked out some minor differences. There were also some concerns that the shorter period would draw a lower class of temporary resident, but supporters of the bill maintained that those with moderate incomes should have the same opportunities as the wealthy.

On December 21, 1942, the Supreme Court of the United States upheld the validity of Nevada's liberal divorce laws. In a six-to-two decision, the court held that legal separations won in the courts of one state shall be recognized throughout the country, regardless of the conflicting divorce laws of any other state.

Harry B. Swanson, prominent Reno lawyer, has written extensively on divorce in Nevada. He had this to say on the 1948 case that opened the post-war floodgates to Nevada divorces:

> This landmark case, *Sherrer vs Sherrer*, opened the door to six-week divorces between consenting parties. It guaranteed that one spouse could come to Nevada for six weeks and the other could file an answer without ever making a personal appearance

before a judge and the divorce would be granted and could not be later contested.

In the late 1940s, '50s, and '60s, however, most states had very strict standards. New York, for instance, would grant divorces only in cases involving adultery, and Californians were forced to wait one year. Now, most states have modified their divorce laws and have gone to no-fault divorce.

(See Appendix B, "The Lawyers," for an interview with Harry B. Swanson.)

Nevada's Marriage and Divorce Trends

A survey of records in Nevada's seventeen counties for the years 1949-1951 revealed that marriages outran divorces by more than four-to-one.

There were only 4,459 divorces granted in Reno during 1951, 1,443 less than in 1949. There were 22,105 marriages during 1951; 1,330 more than in 1949.

The all-time Washoe County records (as of 1952) in the two departments were 28,874 marriages and 11,060 divorces, both marks set in 1946.

WASHOE COUNTY MARRIAGES AND DIVORCES (Circa 1945-1952)		
YEAR	MARRIAGES	DIVORCES
1945	18,751	8,590
1946	28,874	11,060
1947	26,874	7,164
1948	24,245	6,068
1949	20,775	5,902
1950	22,048	4,599
1951	22,105	4,459
1952	21,881	4,713

Extracted from Biennial Report of the Nevada State Board of Health: Nevada Vital Statistics, compiled by Mona Reno, Nevada State Data Center, Nevada State Library and Archives.

Lawyers and judges have advanced various reasons for the decline in Nevada's divorce trade. Some said there were just as many husbands and wives agreeing to disagree as ever, but that they had found other easier places in the early 1950s to make their separations legal—such as Sun Valley in Idaho, Mexico, the Virgin Islands or Florida. Others said there just weren't as many couples splitting since most of the maladjusted marriages of World War II had ended.

Reno had the greatest number of Nevada marriages and divorces in 1952: 20,358 and 4,493 respectively. But Las Vegas was not far behind, with 18,298 marriages and 3,472 divorces. All of the other fifteen counties put together accounted for only 3,402 marriages and 1,429 divorces.

Nevada Marriage Boom. In 1927, the California legislature passed what was known as the "anti-gin marriage" law. It required a minimum waiting period of three days between issuance of a license and performance of the ceremony.

Almost overnight, the Washoe County marriage rate skyrocketed, as impatient Californians began to look toward Reno as a quickie wedding center.

During the 56-year period from the time the first marriage license was issued in 1871 through the year preceding the 1927 California law, Washoe County issued a total of only 12,319 licenses—an average of about 220 a year.

Then came the 1927 boom, and the total for the next 25 years jumped to 337,681, or an average of more than 13,500 yearly.

Although the anti-gin marriage measure finally was erased from the California books in 1943, Washoe County's marriage wealth was not threatened, for in place of California's anti-gin marriage law went a pre-marital examination law.[2]

Observations. The explosive growth in Clark County's population since 1985 (see table at botttom of this page) no doubt accounts for much of the increase in marriage licenses and, to a lesser degree, for the increase in divorces as well.

Washoe's District Judges Performed Average of 37 Marriages Per Day In '48

During 1948, the district judges at the Washoe County Courthouse performed 13,597 weddings, for an average of more than 37 per day including Sundays and holidays.

At an average of five minutes per wedding, that means the district judges during 1948 spent almost one fourth of their time in the court house performing marriage ceremonies.

The fees charged the bridegrooms averaged about $10. The fees were frequently shared with the witnesses, or given to the churches, but that was up to the person who received the fee.

Tops in the marrying business was Judge A. J. Maestretti who racked up a total of 6,340—more than any other district judge had done in any of the previous four years. Second in line was Judge William McKnight with 5,076.

The marrying business "top ten" included four judges, one Justice of the Peace, and five ministers in 1948.

Judge Maestretti	6,340
Judge McKnight	5,076
Laurance Layman	2,762
Judge Brown	1,865
Rev. Edward L. Mills	1,565
C. G. Powning*	1,149
Rev. Brewster Adams	837
Rev. Donald Fleming	674
Rev. Gideon Emigh	498
Rev. C. A. Crosby	449

Source: *Nevada State Journal*, Jan. 29, 1949
*Acting Justice of the Peace for the first four months of 1948

SELECTIVE TRENDS (Circa 1960-2000)

	MARRIAGE			DIVORCE		
Years	State	Washoe County	Clark County	State	Washoe County	Clark County
1960*	62,456	22,235	29,017	8,502	4,024	3,538
1967	86,412	28,378	42,341	9,587	3,605	5,046
1975	101,559	33,032	49,341	10,542	3,020	6,166
1980	108,190	32,250	56,936	13,853	3,916	8,383
1985	106,507	32,758	59,417	13,318	4,504	7,502
1990	120,619	31,580	74,868	13,095	2,813	8,032
2000	134,908	19,281	106,997	14,804	2,425	10,208

Extracted from Biennial Report of the Nevada State Board of Health: Nevada Vital Statistics, compiled by Mona Reno, Nevada State Data Center, Nevada State Library and Archives.
* 1960-1961 fiscal year. Note: 1970 data not available as of this writing.

Newsworthy Divorce Trends. Divorce and marriage helped put Reno on the map. The following newspaper excerpts highlight the evolution of divorce.

New York *Daily News*, August 24-26, 1967—Panicked by a Sept. 1 deadline that may mean the end of quickie Mexican divorces, marriage dropouts trying to avoid "Divorce, New York Style" are making a run on Juarez, Mexico, to get their decrees. As the deadline gets closer, the run is turning into a stampede.

New York's new divorce law is worse than confusing, cumbersome, inept, and badly drawn—criticisms hurled at it by nearly every reputable lawyer who had studied it.

There may be a new divorce law on the books, but for the rich of New York it will be the same old story—an out-of-state divorce, because they can afford it; and for the poor the same deadend—no escape from a marriage that has become unholy deadlock because it costs too much.

New York Times, February 13, 1972—Barbara Streisand and Elliott Gould took "the Dominican route" last July and early this month George C. Scott of "Patton" fame and his actress-wife Colleen Dewhurst did the same. Both couples took advantage of recently liberalized divorce laws that have made the Dominican Republic one of the two new "divorce capitals" of the Western Hemisphere—the other being Haiti, its neighbor on the island of Hispaniola.

In the Streisand-Gould divorce, Gould flew to Santo Domingo, the Dominican capital, and within 24 hours had a mutual consent decree. In the Dewhurst-Scott action, the actress was the partner appearing, getting a decree virtually overnight. In between, more than 1,700 other couples have dissolved their marriages on the island—in the quickie fashion of those former Mexican divorces.

Mexico, the former divorce "capital"—anxious to shed that image—passed reform legislation last March shutting down the divorce mills of Juarez and Caliente. Into the breach—at the persistent prod-ding of several Juarez-wise lawyers—stepped first Haiti (in February) and then the Dominican Republic (in June). Tourist-shy, they hoped to snare what is reported to have been a $50-million-a-year "industry" in Mexico that drew some 18,000 Americans annually. About 75,000 Americans, all told, had terminated marriages in Mexico—among them Elizabeth Taylor, Mia Farrow, Lauren Bacall, Sheila MacRae, Rod Steiger, Franklin Roosevelt Jr. and Huntington Hartford.

Reno Evening-Gazette, March 6, 1979—Wives watch out! The days of alimony being the exclusive right of former wives and disabled men may have ended Monday with a 6-3 decision by the U.S. Supreme Court.

The nation's highest court said it is unconstitutional to grant alimony payments to wives but not to former husbands, and that decision may require a turnaround in Nevada's alimony law.

State divorce laws allow a court to grant alimony to the wife, but require that a husband be disabled or unable to provide for himself before he can receive any payments from his former spouse.

Reno Gazette-Journal, May 26, 1991—A senate panel voted Friday to keep Nevada's "divorce capital" reputation alive, killing a bill to make Nevadans wait 60 days instead of 24-hours for a "quickie divorce."

The Judiciary Committee voted 5-2 against SB537, which allowed the waiting period to be shortened only if a judge finds an emergency exists or the divorcing couple has already gone through at least three counseling sessions.

Reno News & Review, October 4, 1995—Do-It-Yourself Divorce.

For around $20, you can buy a "divorce kit" from Office Max and similar retailers, and the Reno-area Yellow Pages list a surprising number of legal/divorce service centers. Among them, Nevada Business Services boasts a "24-48 hour turnaround" with its divorce kit.

B. The Lawyers

*It was said that matches are made in Heaven,
lighted on Earth, and put out in Reno.*

In his 1941 book, *Reno*, Max Miller, speaking in broad generalities, perpetuated a number of myths about the divorce business:

Myth #1. It is a fact that nine of the ten women who come to Reno for a divorce are doing so under order of their husbands. Nine of the ten women—so the Reno lawyers tell us—do not want what they are sent to get. But the axe has fallen. The expense account is furnished. And the women, for the sake of their own pride, must do the rest.

Myth #2. A good Reno lawyer has to be both a doctor and a father confessor.

Myth #3. A dozen of the 180 lawyers in town have 90 percent of the business.

Myth #4. Of Reno's horde of lawyers, 90 percent are having one hell of a time trying to make a living. This town is still so overstocked in struggling lawyers that a few so-called "train-meeting" shysters do promise to hand out divorces for fifty dollars a throw.

Research has dispelled some of Max Miller's myths:

• In 1948, the Reno phonebook listed 130 lawyers, excluding the 15 law firm listings.

• With rare exception, all attorneys in Reno participated in the migratory divorce business. It was quick and easy (in most cases), lucrative, and, if nothing else, it paid the overhead.

• An estimated 20 percent of the Reno attorneys handled 80% of the divorce cases.

• Reno was probably the only town where a lawyer, or his or her secretary, might meet a client at the train. Many clients were met by a dude ranch owner or hotel representative. Other clients hired a taxi to take them where they were going.

Upon their arrival in Reno, a client's first stop was frequently at their attorney's office. Here the client was briefed on crucial details, such as the importance of

being present in the State of Nevada on each and every day of their six weeks' residency.

Most well-to-do clients already had their Reno lawyer and accommodations arranged for them by their East Coast lawyer. However, if a client needed accommodations, the lawyer might help here. For a client of modest means, the lawyer might recommend a boarding house or motel. For the more affluent client, the lawyer might suggest a hotel like the Riverside or one of the exclusive divorce ranches outside of town.

If a client needed to work during their six weeks, the lawyer might help them find employment, usually as a waitress, a shill in a casino, or, if a man, in construction.

Having settled the important matters between client and lawyer, the attorney might offer to show the client around town, or take them sightseeing sometime during the six weeks.

Interviews with Reno Attorneys

Three of Reno's most distinguished attorneys of the 1940s to 1960s era will tell the rest of this lawyer story—and hopefully dispel a myth or two along the way. (See Bibliography)

An Interview with Harry B. Swanson, Esq.

by the Authors

Harry B. Swanson. Born (1928) and raised in Reno, Nevada. University of Nevada, B.A.; University of California, Hastings College of Law, San Francisco (with honors). JAG officer, USAF, Korean war. The son of prominent Reno attorney Harry Swanson, Harry B. Swanson practiced law in Reno from 1956 to 1990. He served three terms in the Nevada Legislature and was editor of the Nevada State Bar Journal. He authored numerous articles, notes and comments in legal periodicals including the American Bar Association Journal. He has lectured on Migratory Divorce Law together with Continuing Legal Education in divorce law. Swanson is an avid international hunter and fisherman, and has served as past State Chairman and National Trustee of Ducks Unlimited. He came in from a fishing trip to meet the authors at his Reno office for this interview.

Harry B. Swanson, Esq.
(Courtesy Harry B. Swanson, © Kelly Wheeler, Portrait Design, Inc.)

Did you ever go down to the train station to look for clients?

Absolutely not. And I never saw that happen. I had my secretary go to the train to meet clients. I didn't.

What years did your father and you practice in Reno?

My father, Harry Swanson, practiced from the early 1920s until 1966. I started in 1956 and retired in 1990.

I went with my father to the dude ranches to visit with his clients or the management. Just a kid going with his dad. The guest ranches around Reno were really quite nice. They catered to the very wealthy people who came here. They entertained their clients. Took them on horseback rides. Escorted them around to the nightclubs. Had absolutely excellent food. Accommodations were outstanding. Made their guests feel as if it was a vacation. You could be critical of that by saying, 'You're getting a divorce and it's a vacation?' But these people had already settled their problems. In most cases, with their husbands. Most of the time the wife came out because the husband couldn't get away from his business. But they had settled their problems and there was a property settlement agreement outlining everything. Essentially a domestic contract. So why not come out and have fun? And they did.

According to the 1948 telephone directory, there were 130 lawyers in Reno. How many of these were active in divorce practice?

Lots of lawyers practiced in the divorce field. That's not to say that they handled the high-class divorce cases, like I did. There were a lot of lawyers who practiced in the divorce field who would take cases, but they would handle other

matters which would be more lucrative for them.

Would you agree with the statement, "A good divorce lawyer has to be a father confessor, an escort around town, even a love interest to the average woman coming to Reno for divorce?"

I was not. The way I handled my cases, it would be best to say that I was all business. My function was to essentially handle the divorce in a very competent, legal manner, which I did. Oh, I'm sure there were a few upset ladies who attempted to use me to express their solace and their chagrin at losing their husbands. But I remember it happened only very rarely. I think by the time the first appointment was over, the lady knew what my function was.

I'm sure there were young, buck lawyers that liked the divorce practice because of the ladies they got to meet— and bed—if the truth were known. Would you not agree with that? Men are men, and some women are glad of it.

Well, (long pause), I suppose a lot of that went on. But I can tell you this, it didn't go on with me. I'm not trying to be righteous. I like the female species. But I always felt that it was business.

If you handled a hundred divorce cases over a period of time, would at least half of them be happy to end the relationship?

Absolutely. More than half. It was kind of a myth that all divorcées came to Reno crushed and crying. A lot of them had their next husband picked out. Some of them even brought them with them.

Did you have to work to develop relationships with the Eastern law firms so that referrals came your way?

I had written an article for the American Bar Association Journal in my last year of law school on the subject of migratory divorce. It was exceedingly well-received. I also lectured extensively in continuing legal education on divorce law. Somehow or other it evolved.

You must have inherited some pretty nice contacts from your father?

I'm sure that I inherited from him much of the contacts that he had in the East. Repeat business. If you do a good job for people, what goes around comes around.

If you were to take 100 cases from out-of-state clients, would you say at least half of them were referrals from other attorneys?

Yes.

More than that?

The good ones—the ones I call high-class—almost all were referred by out-of-state lawyers. The husband and wife became involved in divorce litigation or negotiation in their home state—New York, for example—and normally things would be pretty much settled by the lawyers in New York between the husband and the wife by the time they were referred to me. Then I would handle it, so to speak, as a case that was over with, essentially pretty friendly on both sides. That's the way it was with those high-class divorce cases, what we called Park Avenue Bluebloods or Social Register types.

What was your impression of the number of men who came to Nevada for a divorce versus women?

Very few men came to Reno if it was a high-class case. But a lot of hard-working people came to Nevada for a divorce, and they just came without any referral at all. They'd just show up. They'd get a tip from a cab driver or simply walk into a lawyer's office unannounced. I had a lot of that.

What was the Reno bar recommending as the average fee for an uncomplicated divorce?

In the 1950s, the recommended fee was $350. In the 1930s, the Bar-recommended fee was $250, but there was no maximum. There were always the rumored extraordinary fees—usually uncheckable.

Did you ever have Eastern lawyers propose that they would send you a client if you would split your fee with them?

Oh, sure.

My understanding is that they made their money off the client back there, and you were supposed to be able to charge whatever you could out here and not have to share it with them. But there were some that would try and get you to share.

Oh, yes. You bet.

As I understand it, the Bar recommends a fee but each lawyer maintains the right to set their own fee. How did the discounters work?

There were two lawyers in Reno, Morrissett and McCluskey, who handled a good deal of divorce business, but they had a poor reputation in the Bar primarily because they handled cases below the Bar-recommended fee. The Bar was recommending a fee of $350 for an uncontested divorce case in the 1950s. These gentlemen were handling divorces for the more modest folk for $100-$150 per case.

Mac McCluskey was a friend of mine and we got along fine. I just ignored the fact that he was

handling these cases. The way Mac would do it was to take these cases for these low fees. Friday was "law and motion" day in Storey County, the only day that court was open in Storey County at that time. Mac had a van and he would take four or five clients and their resident witnesses and go up to Virginia City and handle them one after another in front of the court. The reason he went to Virginia City was that the fee for filing a complaint, best I recall, was $10. In Washoe County it was $35.

Morrissett did not go to Virginia City, as I recall, but he handled a lot of divorce cases and his fees were very, very nominal compared to what the Bar recommended.

Wouldn't these clients be the working stiffs who came to town broke and had to get a job?

That's what they were. These were people who had had it with their spouses. They lived primarily in California. California had the interlocutory divorce law where you got an interlocutory divorce decree and had to wait a year to get the final decree. So the cocktail waitress in the Mark Hopkins Hotel in San Francisco, for example, gets an interlocutory decree of divorce, falls in love with some guy, wants to marry him, and she can't. So she comes to Reno for six weeks and gets tied up with McCluskey or Morrissett. Pays them a fee of $100 and goes to work here as a cocktail waitress to pay her way. That's the way it worked with a lot of these cases.

Would you say a lot of men, too? In that income bracket, it wouldn't be hard for them to quit a construction job, let's say, and come here and find similar work.

Oh, yes, there were these men, too. If you worked in construction in San Francisco, you could work in construction in Reno, too.

When I started practicing law in 1956, McCluskey and Morrissett were very active and were for many years until the divorce business faded away.

Did these lawyers leave town then and look for work elsewhere?

No. Mac McCluskey was very well-to-do. I don't think Morrissett was as well off, but he wasn't a pauper by a long shot.

I can tell you this about this list of lawyers (referring to "A Selective List of Reno Lawyers of the Late 1940s, 1950s and 1960s"). My father told me when I started practicing law, "Son, the

Harry B. Swanson trout fishing in Tierra del Fuego, Argentina (Courtesy Harry B. Swanson)

A Selective List of Reno Lawyers of the Late 1940s, 1950s and 1960s Who Represented Prominent Clients Coming to Nevada for a Divorce

Morgan Anglim, John S. Belford, F. R. Breen, Douglas Busey, William Cashill, Thomas Craven, Kenneth P. Dillon, John Squire Drendel, William Forman, Clel Georgetta, Morley Griswold, John Halley, Prince Archer Hawkins, Robert Ziemer Hawkins, Harlan Heward, John T. McLaughlin, Miles N. Pike, Bryce Rhodes, Sidney W. Robinson, David P. Sinai, John S. Sinai, Lloyd V. Smith, George Springmeyer, Sallie Springmeyer, Lester D. Summerfield, Harry Swanson, Harry B. Swanson, George L. Vargas, Virgil H. Wedge*, William Woodburn.

*Virgil Wedge's mentor was Senator Pat McCarran, who helped Wedge through law school in Washington, D. C. When Wedge got out of law school and returned to Nevada, he and McCarran created a law firm, McCarran & Wedge. McCarran, a prominent senator in Washington, didn't practice law, but he had to be a terrific "spinmaster" for Wedge and his high-class divorce clients.   —David P. Sinai, Esq.

Other attorneys during the same era who represented clients of modest means who generally had to work for a living when coming to Nevada for a divorce: Howard Browne, Sidney Fox, W. C. McCluskey, E. J. Morrissett.

—Compiled by the authors with the assistance of Harry B. Swanson.

best thing you can do is to memorize the names of all the lawyers in Reno. If you see them on the street, say hello, be friendly. That's the way you get referrals from the lawyers."

When I first started practicing law, I'd see this lawyer on the street, say, John Belford, and I'd say, "Hi, John. If you have any cases you don't want to handle, refer them over to me!" I'm talking about civil cases. Next thing you know, John would send over a collection case.

I did a lot of work in other fields, too, such as real estate law and other phases of the law. I had more business than I could handle. That's how I happen to know all these lawyers. They were all good guys. I liked them.

I've always defined myself as a high-class lawyer. I was a good lawyer and did a good job for my clients. I have no question about that.

Divorces on the Comstock, 1947 and 1948

In 1947, according to the *Virginia City News*, (Jan. 14, 1949), there were 666 divorce actions filed in the county clerk's office in Storey County. In 1948, there were 680 divorce actions, three of which were civil suits. Lawyers who handled the cases in 1947 were: William C. McCluskey, 563; Robert E. Berry, 62; Franklyn Koehler, 23; Charlotte Hunter, 9; Donal Richards, 3; J. T. Rutherford, 2; Norman Samuelson, 2; Arthur Lasher, 2.

Rumored Extraordinary Fees Barbara Hutton reportedly arrived in Reno on March 30, 1935, and hired the law firm of Thatcher and Woodburn for an estimated fee of $15,000 to $20,000. Big money in those days.

William Woodburn was rumored to have received a $50,000 fee for Rita Hayworth's divorce from Prince Aly Khan in 1953.

An Interview with David P. Sinai, Esq.

by the Authors

David P. Sinai, Esq.
(Courtesy David P. Sinai))

David P. Sinai, Esq. Born (1923) and raised in Reno, Nevada. University of Nevada; University of California Hastings College of Law, San Francisco. U. S. Navy, World War II. The son of prominent Reno attorney John S. Sinai, David P. Sinai passed the Bar in 1949 and joined his father's practice. Together they practiced law as Sinai & Sinai until his father's death in 1973. Their firm represented many prominent and famous clients during the period when Reno was the divorce capital of the world. Today David Sinai is the senior member of Sinai, Schroeder, Mooney, Boetsch, Bradley & Pace in Reno.

Do you have a favorite client story?

I'm reminded of a funny story. I got a call from an Iowa lawyer asking me to meet his client that he was sending out. I met her at the bus station and, there she was, sitting there, carrying a bird cage with a bird in it that she had brought all the way cross-country on the bus from Iowa. I talked to her awhile, and then drove her to one of the less expensive guest houses. She didn't have much money. That's the last I heard of her.

What happened was a cab driver told her our firm was too expensive and why didn't she go to a lawyer who's only going to charge $125 bucks? So that's where she went.

About a month later, I was walking through Harolds Club, and here is this gal dealing cards like an old pro. I don't know how the hell she learned in four weeks, but she did. I talked to her for a few minutes, and that's when she told me she had another lawyer.

When other lawyers sent someone to you, did they expect you to kick back some of your fee to them?

Yes. Most of them wanted a referral fee. It was perfectly proper. When a lawyer said they're sending someone out and wanted to be included as counsel, you knew indirectly that they expected a referral fee. No one frowned on it. It was just part of the cost. It didn't come out of the client's pocket.

According to the newspaper clippings file at the Washoe County library, Albert Schnitzer was disbarred in the 1960s for advertising Reno's liberal divorce laws in the New York papers. His copy supposedly read: "Come to Reno and Git a Divorce!" Why the disbarment?

The Bar Association frowned on its members advertising their services in such a blatant and distasteful manner.

Storey County Courthouse, Virginia City.
(Courtesy of Special Collections Department, University of Nevada, Reno Library)

Clel Georgetta, Esq.,

Excerpts from his Unpublished Diaries, 1948 and 1949

Clel Evan Georgetta, Esq.
(Authors' Collection)

Clel Evan Georgetta practiced law in Reno from 1933 to 1967, and was instrumental in passing the six-week divorce residency requirement in 1931. Georgetta stated that in his thirty-four years as an attorney, he lost only eleven cases. Throughout his life, Georgetta kept a daily diary. The entries pertaining to his divorce clients are brutally honest and often humorous.

This evening I put pressure on Joe Haller to clean up the Hall case tomorrow. He demanded two changes in the agreement. So I called Mrs. Hall. She said 'yes' to one, 'no' to the other. I called Haller. He called Mr. Hall, then called me back and said, 'Approved. We will make the changes in the morning and go to court.' An hour later, Mrs. Hall called me and said she had changed her mind. It is 'No!' to both changes. I called Haller. I groaned and he groaned and said, 'I'll call you tomorrow.' Mr. Hall said 'No!' and made a counteroffer to three points. Mrs. Hall said, 'No, but let me think it over until Monday.' So goes the practice of law.   *–CG, Friday-Saturday, 23-24, January 1948*

Yesterday I liberated three marriage prisoners, Mr. Hink at 9:40 a.m., Mrs. Jackson at 1:30 p.m., and Mrs. Worden at 2:00 p.m. For a change, the man was the nervous one.   *– CG. Thursday, 4 March 1948*

A new client, Mrs. Ferris, was sent to me by my new contact, Mr. Miller, in New York. She is paying a fee of $430 for plaintiff's attorney (one-third or $145 goes to Miller and $285 to me).

Mrs. Ferris is at Hotel Riverside but desires to move to a ranch. I drove her to Donner Trail Ranch, then to the Silver Saddle, and then to the Lazy A Ranch, just so she could see each place and decide which she prefers. Then we went up to the Christmas Tree to eat a good steak. While there, I introduced her to several people including Eddie Questa, Vice President of the First National Bank. He said he would

call her tomorrow for lunch.
          –CG, Monday, 26 April 1948

So far I have not done a thing for my client, Mrs. Ferris, at the Silver Saddle. So this seemed a good time to perform a "duty." I called her. "So sorry, she had a date." Half an hour later, Mrs. Ferris called me and said her date is "off." While we were eating dinner at Sierra Villa, who should show up but Eddie Questa, Vice President of the First National Bank. It seems Mrs. Ferris had a date this evening with him and broke it. She has gone out with him for nine nights in a row.
          –CG, Tuesday, 25 May 1948

Good Lord, here comes Mrs. Lee—again! For many weeks I have enjoyed the peace and quiet of a law practice without "crazy clients." Mrs. 'True Love' has passed out of my life, Mrs. 'Lust' calls me seldom, and Mrs. Lee had made up with her husband and had quit calling me at twelve, one, two, even three-thirty a.m. as well as almost every morning at 8:15 when I'm usually in the bathtub.

This evening I went to the office with a definite plan to do certain work. At ten p.m. the telephone rang and like a fool I answered. There was the whiney voice of Lucille Lee in tears. But this time she was angry at me and now she cannot get a lawyer to represent her. She has had four and has called five others these last few days. No one will take her case. They all know she is a neurotic who will drive them insane with telephone calls and then when they have the stage all set to get her a settlement or go to trial, she will change her mind and go back to Harold Lee.

Over and over and over again she told me the same story and talked for one solid hour and twenty-five minutes. If no one comes to her rescue she may lose her house. So I told her when I get back from Denver I will represent her provided (1) she will stick by her guns and go through with it, (2) she will follow my advice, and (3) she will not pester me with telephone calls.   *–CG, Wednesday, 9 June 1948*

Do these women really fall in love with me? I am certainly not an attractive man. Oh, I may be passable, and I may be rather entertaining at times. One thing I have observed—nearly every woman who has ever said she has fallen in love with me really did need a husband. In fact, very worthy of note is that the rich ones who already have security do not fall in love with me. What does that prove?   *–CG, Thursday, 20 January 1949*

My secretary said to me today, 'Guess what? We now have 21 divorce cases pending, 7 of them are women and 14 are men. Why?' I wonder. Usually it is just the reverse because even when it is the man who wants a divorce he cannot leave his job for six weeks so he continues to work and sends his idle wife to Reno to put in the required six weeks to establish a domicile. Furthermore, a free trip to Reno and a six weeks' vacation 'far away' has sold many a woman on the idea of consenting to a divorce instead of fighting her husband's demand for freedom.

-CG, Monday, 9 August 1948

A visit with Joe Mutnick [in New York] yesterday straightened out a lot of misunderstandings we have had in the past regarding fees. We reached an agreement. Hereafter he will charge the client whatever he can get for services performed in New Jersey. He will tell the client—and I am free to tell the client—that my fee for the work done in Nevada is $250 plus costs of $60 plus defense attorney fee of $25 or more. Out of my $250, I will send Joe one-third of the $250 or $84 as a forwarding fee. Concerning which the client will know nothing.

I recall that in one case, Mutnick sent me a client and a fee of $150. The client came to my office and said, "Mr. Georgetta, at the house where I'm living, there are people paying only $250. Why must I pay you $750?" I was not free to tell the client my fee was only $150.

Joe sends many cases to Florida which he could send to Reno. Perhaps now he will send more my way.

– CG, Saturday, 17 September, 1949

My client and her sister are staying at a place where management does nothing to entertain them. So today I picked them up and up over the winding Geiger Grade we went to Virginia City. They were truly awed by the majestic mountains, frightened by the dangerous road, and interested by the romance of old Virginia City. After a drink at the Bucket of Blood Saloon, we drove down the mountain to Carson City, on up over the Sierras to Lake Tahoe, around to Cal-Neva Lodge, and back over Mount Rose to the Christmas Tree where we ate dinner. Ah, those broiled steaks! The best I know of in any place in any land. A great day for the ladies.

-CG, Sunday, 6 November 1949 [1]

A Little Divorce Humor

From the *Nevada State Journal*, November 23, 1947:

DONALD DUCK GETS DIVORCE IN RENO

Donald Duck was divorced yesterday. Betty C. Duck obtained a divorce here on grounds of mental cruelty from Donald W. Duck, a former resident of San Francisco, now in Guam as a civilian worker. Custody of a duckling...er... son, Barry, aged four, was awarded to Mrs. Duck.

• • •

Overheard at the Washoe County Courthouse between two lawyers:

"How are you doing? How's it going?"

"Fine! I'm handling a major—really major—New York divorce case. But I'm afraid reconciliation is rearing its ugly head."

Migratory Divorce Fades Away

Harry B. Swanson was a student at the Hastings College of Law at San Francisco when he authored his visionary paper in 1952, *Migratory Divorce: Sherrer vs. Sherrer and the Future*. From pages 15 and 24:

It cannot be disputed that our society is changing in favor of more liberal divorce laws. Divorce has come to be almost commonplace; one scarcely loses an iota of his good standing in society merely because he or she is a divorcée. This fact hardly commends the strict divorce laws and nonrecognition of migratory divorces...It may be that education will ultimately be the answer to the deplorable divorce situation....

Whatever view the individual adopts, whether in favor of recognition or nonrecognition of migratory divorce, it is obvious that the two views are virtually irreconcilable, neither giving way to the other. The court is confronted on the one side by arguments as to the predominating interest of the state of the true domicile and the accompanying sociological interest in discouraging easy divorces. In contra-distinction to the latter, there is the predominant interest in favor of certainty in the matter of marriage, legitimacy of children, and divorce.

At the present time, the trend in the Supreme Court is definitely in favor of liberalization and a greater degree of certainty in the field of migratory divorce. One may reasonably predict that the Court is not likely to retreat to a more conservative position, one which would impede the certainty which has already been achieved by the decisions of *Sherrer v. Sherrer* and *Johnson v. Muelberger.* If anything, the *Sherrer* and *Johnson* cases will be extended, greater effect being given to the full faith and credit clause in the matter of additional recognition of migratory divorce.[2]

Harry B. Swanson: "I always felt a part of an evolution because I could see what was happening, I could see it was coming—that the divorce business in Nevada would cease to exist. On a migratory basis, I could absolutely see it coming because there were so many changes in the attitudes of the politicians and the attitudes of the religious authorities. I don't think the religious authorities ever wanted to let go. They never wanted to make divorce easy.

"However, after all, people demand those things, and the politicians had to honor these demands, and ultimately you could see each state, as time went on, would change its divorce laws. Pretty soon, the business in Nevada started evaporating because, why come here? In due course, it did evaporate. Our reputation didn't."[3]

Will Nevada Gaming Also Fade Away?

Some Nevadans predict the state is passing through the same kind of historical evolution with legalized gambling now that it has already gone through with divorce. In both "legislated industries" or trades, Nevada developed her frontier traditions to economic advantage. The migratory divorce business ended when the rest of the nation essentially caught up with Nevada. That appears to be happening now with legalized gambling.

C. The Stringers

The constant traffic of high society and celebrities coming to Reno for a divorce in the 1940s and 1950s was a journalist's dream. Normally, the Reno press ignored these divorce stories—so many well-known people got divorced in Reno it was hardly considered newsworthy. However, the big city news agencies hired freelance correspondents—stringers as they were called—and sent them off to Reno to sniff out the stories and wire them to their publications.

William Banks "Bill" Berry (1903-1999) came to Reno in 1928. He launched a freelance news service and hooked up with International News Service, United Press International, Associated Press Photo, and major U.S. dailies. From 1941 to 1964, he was a stringer for the New York *Daily News*, covering the Reno divorce scene. His copy grabbed page one bylines, due to his celebrity coverage of Reno as "The Divorce Capital of the World."

Berry developed a reputation as "Reno's super sleuth for gossip." A smart, savvy reporter, Berry usually got his story, which wasn't always easy. He and the other stringers had to struggle with the likes of an Emmy Wood, who protected the privacy of her dude ranch guests. But there might always

Clark Bigler (left), stringer for the Sacramento Bee, *and Bill Berry,* New York Daily News *correspondent, calling in a "hot" story*
(Photo Don Dondero)

be someone at a dude ranch or hotel who might wither under a reporter's persistence and divulge a famous name. It was said that Berry had Reno wired, and if there was anything a newswriter needed to know, all he had to do was call Berry.

One of Berry's biggest stories was in 1941, when he broke the news that millionairess Gloria Vanderbilt was in Reno to divorce Pat DeCicco in order to marry the famed conductor Leopold Stokowski. Berry learned that Vanderbilt had checked into the Riverside Hotel and intended to secretly meet her future husband at the train station in Truckee, in order to avoid reporters. She left her rented car prominently parked in front of the Riverside, to fool the reporters, and then drove off to Truckee in the middle of the night in a snowstorm in another car.

But when she arrived at the Truckee station to meet the 4 a.m. train, Bill Berry was waiting for her. The train arrived, and Stokowski stepped off, wearing the hat he wore for disguise. Berry grabbed the famous conductor's hand to shake it. Stokowski thought Berry was a railroad employee and tried to hand him his luggage until Berry announced, "I represent the New York *Daily News*. Welcome to Truckee, the back door to Reno!"

Berry got wind of another story through a local telephone operator. In 1956, Arthur Miller was staying at the Pyramid Lake Ranch to get a divorce, and would use a party line to call a number in Los Angeles and have the operator there reverse the charges. He did this often. A Reno operator told Berry, and Berry decided to take a casual walk along the Pyramid Lake beach with his Great Dane, Duke. With Duke at his side, Berry met Miller and convinced him to divulge the name behind the mysterious unlisted phone number. It was Marilyn Monroe.[1]

Guy Shipler Jr. (1913-1996) came to northern Nevada after a long and successful career in New York as an editor at *Business Week* and a staff writer at *Newsweek* and *Time* magazine, where he wrote in virtually every department from Business to Religion. In Nevada, Shipler wrote weekly political columns for several Nevada newspapers, and served as a stringer for Time, Inc. (publisher of *Time, Life, Sports Illustrated, People,* and *Fortune*). Shipler was known as the freelance correspondent with "all the important strings."

A stringer's best friend was a publicity photographer, and none was more intrepid than Don Dondero (1920-2003). In *Dateline: Reno,* Dondero writes, "The Riverside Hotel began to boom in the mid-1940s, and the Mapes Hotel opened in 1948. A Reno dateline meant excitement and show-biz pizzazz to the rest of the country." Some say Dondero's biggest photographic coup may have been in the Nelson Rockefeller divorce story in 1962.

Stringers at Work:
The Nelson Rockefeller Divorce Story

Other Rockefellers had come to Reno for a divorce. There was Edith Rockefeller McCormick, the daughter of Standard Oil magnate John D. Rockefeller, to divorce Harold McCormick, the son of harvester king Cyrus McCormick. In 1943, Edith's niece, Mrs. Abby Rockefeller Milton, granddaughter of John D. Rockefeller, came to divorce David M. Milton, wealthy New York broker. In 1954, Mrs. Barbara "Bobo" Rockefeller came to divorce Winthrop Rockefeller. Then, in 1962, Mrs. Mary Todhunter Clark Rockefeller came to divorce then-Governor Nelson Rockefeller.

From the files of Guy Shipler Jr., let's follow Shipler, Bill Berry and Don Dondero as they cover—or try to cover—the six weeks' residency and divorce of Mrs. Nelson Rockefeller in Reno:

February 2, 1962, Shipler in Carson City to Time, Inc. in Los Angeles

For Newsfront (requested): Sorry, but a Kremlin-like security has been clamped around Mrs. Rockefeller and no one at all has been able to get any pictures. My day-long campout at the Donner Trail Ranch with a photographer produced no film.

A "press conference" at her attorney's office in Reno this afternoon produced a two-sentence statement which was handed to the press without comment. It reads in full:

"Attorney William K. Woodburn has announced that Mrs. Nelson Rockefeller has established residence

Mary Rockefeller leaving Washoe County Courthouse.
(Drackert Collection, Courtesy of Special Collections Department, University of Nevada, Reno Library)

in Nevada and will, in due course, seek a divorce from Governor Rockefeller. No further statements or comments on this subject can or will be made."

The Reno divorce business has lately been rather light on the high society or big name level because of the recent popularity of quick, overnight Alabama divorces. Maybe the presence of Mrs. Rockefeller will change things. It is by all odds the biggest Reno divorce story in a decade since a distant relative, Bobo Rockefeller, was in town for hers. Again, apologies for the lack of pictures. —*Regards, Guy Shipler Jr.*

February 4, 1962, Shipler in Carson City to Time, Inc. in Los Angeles

For Press (suggested): The arrival here of Mrs. Nelson Rockefeller last week provides the biggest divorce story in a decade for Reno.

But by Reno standards the story never should have broken. Normally, the security regulations are so tight that it is nearly impossible for the press to locate a big name during the six weeks he or she is here. The bigger the name, the more elaborate—and effective—are the precautions.

What those of us in the business dreaded most when we heard that Mrs. Rockefeller was probably coming to Reno for a divorce—how would we take even the first step of finding out where she was staying? And, if we found her, the interviews, pictures, breakfast menus and other demands would come to us only through great luck or greater bribery—and, greatest of all, the luck to find someone to bribe effectively.

But the first part of this case didn't follow the script at all. By midnight of the day she arrived, we all not only knew definitely that Mrs. Rockefeller was here, we knew how she got here, and at roughly what time. Most incredible of all, we knew definitely exactly where she was staying. At that point security clamped down tight, but it was too late to prevent Mrs. Rockefeller from being hounded to a point where she dared not venture out.

Why did it happen? Does Mrs. R. really want publicity? Does her lawyer? Does the Donner Trail Ranch?

According to one story, still unchecked, attorney William Woodburn tipped Bill Berry. If this is true, it would indicate that there was a deliberate reason; i.e., Mary Rockefeller wanted it known. Normally a lawyer is a divorcee's greatest protector from the public if she wants it that way and nothing will shake him.

Another theory is that Harry and Joan Drackert, operators of the Donner Trail Ranch, couldn't resist the temptation to capitalize publicity-wise on their famous guest. But they have been in the business a long time, and if this is true, they have committed a cardinal sin in the Reno divorce business.

Betty de la Montanya, former owner of the Washoe Pines guest ranch, was furious when asked about this. "The very reason for a dude ranch is to protect people from this kind of thing."

Whatever the reason, certainly Mrs. Rockefeller's stay is not going to be pleasant. Unless Don Dondero, the photographer who Saturday got a picture of her, succeeded in driving her indoors for good, other photographers are going to be after her and will get their own scoops.

The Dondero feat, incidentally, is a story in its own right, since he just took a fantastically long shot and came up with the only picture taken so far of Mrs. Rockefeller in Reno. *—Regards, Guy Shipler Jr.*

March 2, 1962, Shipler in Carson City to Time, Inc. in Los Angeles

For People (suggested): Mrs. Mary Rockefeller has just completed the fourth week of her required six-week stay. Although she still avoids the press and photographers like the plague, she has lately come out of

seclusion to engage in considerable sightseeing and dining out at top Reno restaurants. She often drives the white station wagon owned by Harry Drackert, operator of Donner Trail Ranch, where she is staying. She goes daily to the post office at Verdi and usually stops to chat with the locals, some of whom she now calls by their names. She has several times shopped at a western clothing store and wears western clothing all the time. She is so tall that her Levis end way above her ankle. No one in the store will give any inquiring reporters the time of day regarding Mrs. R.

—Regards, Guy Shipler Jr.

March 5, 1962, Shipler in Carson City to Time, Inc. in Beverly Hills

For Newsfront (suggested): A Reno photographer got seven pictures of Mrs. Nelson Rockefeller leaving Trinity Episcopal Church Sunday, most of them trying to dodge the camera, but one candid. These are only pix taken of her since one on horseback taken the second day after her arrival at Donner Trail Ranch. They have been offered to me for a *Life* exclusive. Note that if used this week, pix would be in issue hitting the stands just about the time she is due to get her divorce, which would be March 15 or 16.

—Regards, Guy Shipler Jr.

March 6, 1962, Time, Inc. in New York to Shipler at JS Bar Ranch in Carson City

For Nation This Week need pix. If possible, Mrs. Rockefeller and ranch owner nightclubbing. If she's impossible to shoot, please send whatever is available of her stay in Reno.   *—H. Time Inc.*

March 6, 1962, Shipler in Carson City to Time, Inc. in Los Angeles

For Nation: Only pix taken of Mrs. Rockefeller since one on horseback when she first arrived have been offered to me for Time, Inc. exclusive. Taken by same photographer, they show her leaving Trinity Church and getting in her car (trying to hide) on Sunday. Will send these tomorrow night if unable to get any others as per your request.

—Regards, Guy Shipler Jr.

March 6, 1962, Time, Inc. in New York to Shipler at JS Bar Ranch in Carson City

Nation scheduling story on activities of Mrs. Rockefeller in Reno. Understand she has come out of her seclusion and is seen in public with owner of the ranch at which she is staying, that she has been going to night clubs and buying western clothes. Can you confirm and give any and all details. Need overnight if possible. —*P. Time Inc.*

March 7, 1962, Shipler in Carson City to Time, Inc. in Los Angeles

For Nation (requested): Mary Rockefeller still shies away from the press with as much determination and vigilance as ever. Friends and relatives have come to stay with her at the ranch in shifts during her residency here. One friend is an associate editor of the *Ladies Home Journal.* Asked by someone at the ranch if she was going to do a story about Mrs. Rockefeller, the friend was shocked. "Oh, no," she exclaimed. "We are old friends." Moaned one local reporter here who has been hounded by New York newspapers for stories about Mrs. R.: "What a deal. This friend is one of the luckiest newswriters in the world and she probably won't do a thing with it."

Mrs. Rockefeller has made a fine, positive impression on the people who have come to know her during her stay. When she warms up to people she has gotten to know, she turns out to be completely natural and unaffected—qualities highly appreciated in this area which has a healthy dislike of phoniness and snobbishness. (It's felt most "dudes" from the East are likely to be phonies and snobs.)

People like her so much that they have generated a feeling of over-protectiveness toward her. Grumbled one reporter, "I'll be glad when she gets out of here and I can get back to covering something that doesn't ruin my reputation."

The security will doubtless really clamp down on the day of her divorce. She may be whisked off almost anywhere in the state for the actual hearing (it can be in any state district court, not necessarily in Reno). The hearing can be closed and the proceedings sealed so that no terms of the agreements are known. If I learn any more from my cowboy friend out at the ranch who is a wrangler, will file an add on Thursday. —*Regards, Guy Shipler Jr.*

March 7, 1962, Shipler in Carson City to Time, Inc. in New York

Herewith seven negatives of Mrs. Nelson Rockefeller, taken last Sunday as she emerged from Trinity Episcopal Church in Reno, and one of her on horseback, taken the second day after her arrival at Donner Trail Ranch. CREDIT: Don Dondero (on all pictures). —*Regards, Guy Shipler Jr.*

March 8, 1962, Shipler in Carson City to Time, Inc. in Los Angeles

For Nation (requested): Wrangler source at Donner Trail has evidently been brainwashed by Mrs. Rockefeller's charm. He so far has kept mum except to confirm that she does indeed ride an English saddle, and that she is a great gal.

Some people here claim the "great gal" bit is a role designed to gain sympathy for her, and that her dodging of the press is an effective way to get publicity.

Striking evidence to give some weight to this view lies in the way the normally watertight Reno security system has operated in this case. Mrs. R could have slipped into Nevada and hidden out so no one could find her. This is a vast state; she didn't have to spend her six weeks in Reno. Even if we knew she was here, we would still be hard-pressed to know when she would get her divorce because that would depend on her arrival date.

As it was, every newsman here knew her arrival date the day she arrived and—most incredible of all—where she was staying. It would take a nearly impossible combination of breaks for all these things to become known accidentally. And she is still at Donner Trail Ranch. If it were important to hide, she would have been whisked out of there in the middle of the first or second night of her stay.

Although I'm betting now that the normal impenetrable security will surround the time and place of her divorce, it will be interesting to see whether or not it is allowed to leak in advance. —*Regards, Guy Shipler Jr.*

March 9, 1962, Time, Inc. in New York to Shipler at JS Bar Ranch in Carson City

For Nation This Week: Please advise soonest name and any other information of friend with Mrs. Rockefeller in Dondero church pix. —*H. Time Inc.*

March 10, 1962, Shipler in Carson City to Time, Inc. in New York

For Nation (requested): Other woman is Mrs. Harry A. (Grace) Frans, who is also at Donner Trail for a divorce. Sorry, but unable to learn where she is from except "someplace back East."

—*Regards, Guy Shipler Jr.*

Don Dondero's office at the time of the Rockefeller divorce. From left, an AP staff photographer, Life *stringer Guy Shipler at the typewriter, and Dwight Dyer, AP staffer.* (Photo Don Dondero)

March 14, 1962, Time, Inc. in Beverly Hills to Shipler at JS Bar Ranch in Carson City

For Rockefeller divorce proceedings, realize problems but hire best local photographer to shoot if you can pin point location.   –*S. Time Inc.*

March 14, 1962, Time, Inc. in New York to Shipler at JS Bar Ranch in Carson City

Please flag us when Mary Rockefeller divorce takes place, giving grounds, how many minutes in court, what courthouse.   –*J. Time Inc.*

March 15, 1962, Shipler in Carson City to Time, Inc. in Beverly Hills

It now appears that Mrs. Rockefeller will get divorce tomorrow at Washoe County Court House in Reno. Have photographer bird-dogging, and some other lines out in this area in case there is a change of venue to Carson City or Virginia City. Chances of pix look fair, but for backstop suggest you get hold of

church pictures taken last week.–*Regards, Guy Shipler Jr.*

March 16, 1962, Shipler in Reno to Time, Inc. in Los Angeles

For Newsfront (requested): Washoe County Court House, Reno—One of the best yardsticks of the impact of the divorce today of Gov. Nelson Rockefeller by his wife, Mary, in Reno was the play the story got in the *Reno Evening-Gazette*. It ran all of seven inches under a three-column UPI picture of Mrs. Rockefeller with her two sons and a two-column head ("Mrs. Rockefeller Obtains Divorce in Reno Court").

None of this may sound like much. But it is nearly unique, since the Reno press normally all but ignores any divorce, no matter how famous the people involved, grudgingly giving a stick or two on page twelve. So many well-known people get divorces here that it is considered scarcely newsworthy. Only the political implications made this one any different.

It is of more than passing significance that news-

"The quality of this picture isn't even marginal—it's just plain bad—but it's one of the hottest news photos I ever shot," *said Don Dondero of this photo of Mary Rockefeller and her sister, shot through a dirty windshield.* (Photo Don Dondero)

men and photographers were able to record this event, and it follows a pattern unusual for Reno divorces. Mary Rockefeller could have come to Nevada and hidden out so that no one could have found her. Knowing exactly the day she arrived meant that it was possible for us to know exactly when she could get her divorce. Also, while here, it was possible for us to get an occasional picture and for newsmen to pick up odds and ends on how she was spending her time.

The Reno divorce security system is so tight that it could have prevented all this—providing she wanted it that way. But a little leakage and a shunning of direct contact with the press, plus her being so personally charming, could have the effect of emphasizing that Nelson Rockefeller was an SOB of the first order. And he couldn't protest this without looking even worse.

—Regards, Guy Shipler Jr.

March 16, 1962, Shipler in Reno to Time, Inc. in New York

Eleven negatives shot on assignment of Mrs.

Rockefeller at Washoe County Court House in Reno before and after divorce to be put aboard United Jet Flight eight oh six. Arrive Idlewild at six forty Saturday morning collect.   *—Regards, Guy Shipler Jr.*

March 17, 1962, Shipler in Reno to Time, Inc. in New York

Add to Mary Rockefeller: Good authority here says part of the terms of divorce settlement are as follows: Mary gets apartment at 812 Fifth Ave., Nelson gets home at Seal Harbor, Maine, both get use of Washington apartment and of the family home at Tarrytown.

Other odds and ends: Dillon, attorney for Rockefeller, is rumored to have received a $5,000 fee for his part in representing the governor yesterday— a job whose normal fee commands $25 or $50. No word on Woodburn's fee, but understand he got $50,000 for Hayworth divorce (that's uncheckable).

—Regards, Guy Shipler Jr.[2]

D. Six Minutes in Court

The average divorce hearing for an uncontested Reno divorce lasted less than six minutes, and went something like the following scenario:

A battery of press people were on hand for the day's proceedings at the Washoe County Courthouse. The famed courthouse had been the site of thousands of divorces for everyone from Hollywood stars, East Coast socialites, to Mr. and Mrs. Ordinary Citizen. Today the press was gathered to report the case of New York socialite, Mrs. Simpson, the plaintiff, vs. Mr. Simpson, the defendant, both of the Hamptons on Long Island (names and places are fictional).

Mrs. Simpson was descended was an impeccable New York family, and had come out properly as a debutante. It was at the debutante ball that she met Mr. Simpson. Following their chaperoned dating and a suitable period of engagement, they were married at a ceremony attended by a Who's Who of New York society.

Now Mrs. Simpson was in Reno to divorce her husband of twenty years. Most of the divorces granted at the Washoe County Courthouse were granted on the grounds of mental cruelty; or in legal lingo, "The defendant treated the plaintiff with extreme cruelty, entirely mental in character, which caused the plaintiff great unhappiness and injured his or her general health."

Mrs. Simpson was early for her rendezvous with marital freedom. At three minutes to nine, she calmly and with dignity walked up the courthouse steps, accompanied by her attorney and Mrs. Emily Pentz

Graduation Day—free at last!
(Courtesy of Special Collections Department, University of Nevada, Reno Library)

Wood. Mrs. Wood was an important key: Not only was she the owner of the Flying M E, where Mrs. Simpson "did her time" for six weeks to become a legal resident of Nevada, Mrs. Wood was also the witness to the fact that Mrs. Simpson had been in Nevada every one of the forty-two days required. Witnessing was serious business. Swearing falsely in regard to someone's residence was among the most serious crimes in Nevada, with the penalty of up to fourteen years in prison.

Dressed smartly in a navy wool suit, hat and gloves, Mrs. Simpson made no attempt to avoid the photographers on the courthouse steps. Tipped off in advance, newsmen on hand included correspondents and photographers from the New York and San Francisco papers.

The bailiff unlocked a courtroom and let the party in. Soon after, the attorney representing the defendant arrived. Last to arrive was a court reporter.

All rose when the judge entered the chambers. Mrs. Simpson's attorney filed Case No. XXX,XXX, a two-page complaint charging "extreme cruelty." Mr. Simpson's attorney then filed the defendant's reply which he had sworn to under oath before a New York notary four weeks earlier. It said with utmost simplicity, "The defendant denies each and every, all and singular, allegations."

Once the hearing got under way, it lasted less than six minutes, about average for the most common type of uncontested Reno divorce.

Certain questions had to be asked about the plaintiff's place of residence because only permanent residents of Nevada can be granted divorces:

"Your honor, May we have a private hearing and request the records be sealed?" Mrs. Simpson's attorney asked the judge.

"That will be the order of the court."

Mrs. Wood was called at once as a witness and sworn in.

"Do you know this lady?" Mrs. Simpson's attorney turned and indicated Mrs. Simpson.

"Yes, I do."

"She is Mrs. Simpson, the plaintiff?"

"Yes."

"When did you meet Mrs. Simpson?"

"At my ranch, the Flying M E, exactly six weeks ago today."

"And she has lived at the Flying M E since that time?"

"She has."

"You have either seen Mrs. Simpson in Nevada each and every day of the past six weeks or you know that she was here all of that time?"

"I do."

"Are you in any way related to the plaintiff?"

"We are not related."

Mrs. Simpson was then directed to take the stand.

"Do you swear to tell the truth, the whole truth, and nothing but the truth, so help you, God?"

"I do."

"Where do you reside?"

"The Flying M E ranch, Highway 395, Franktown, Nevada."

"When did you come to Nevada?"

"Six weeks ago today."

"Have you any other home or place of legal residence?"

"No."

"When you arrived, was it your intention to live here indefinitely and make Nevada your home?"

"Yes."

"Has that intention abided with you until the present day?"

"Yes."

"Is it still your present intention?"

"Yes."

Allegation and denial were read and there was some conversation about the property settlement. Then the judge said, "This marriage is forever declared at an end."

When Mrs. Simpson emerged from the courtroom, she made a wrong turn which took her to the Marriage Bureau—the next stop for many Reno divorcées. She was pursued down the courthouse steps by the newsmen and photographers. Knowing she'd make all the New York papers, she decided to smile—just a little—

The Divorce Seekers' Day in Court

Emily Pentz Wood, proprietor of the Flying M E, dressed smartly for court. Mrs. Wood would be the residence witness and testify in court that her guests had been in Nevada every one of the forty-two days required. Swearing falsely in regard to someone's residence was a serious crime in Nevada, with a penalty of up to fourteen years in prison.

The day's divorce seekers emerge from the ranch house with solemn resolve as the time draws nearer to ending their matrimonial ties. Not all divorcés were shattered or depressed; many had their next husbands or wives picked out. Some brought their future spouses with them— known as "the Spare" in Reno divorce jargon.

Court day was often the only day a divorce ranch guest would don a dress or suit. Western wear was acceptable in all but the most formal of occasions.

(Photos Valerie Vondermuhll Courtesy George A. Vondermuhll Jr.)

which caught her in a more flattering light.

All the testimony about setting up a permanent residence might generally be considered perjury—but the State of Nevada has always recognized a person's inalienable right to change his or her mind.

Within an hour after her divorce, Mrs. Simpson—having just sworn she planned to stay in Nevada—was whisked off to the Reno airport for the short hop to San Francisco. There she would board a United Airlines Mainliner headed straight back to New York.[1]

Clockwise from right, Although Emily Pentz Wood has made this trip to court many times to testify for her guests, she is still reminded of her own painful divorce not that long ago, when her husband, Dore Wood, fell for a reputedly wealthy divorcée who was staying at the Tumbling DW; Dee Allen, from Newport, Rhode Island and Emmy Wood; Dee Allen and Emmy Wood descending the courthouse steps. Their next stop would be the "Widow's" Corner Bar at the Riverside Hotel for a drink, and to collect the other ranch guests who came into town to shop, or for appointments; Joan Drackert, right, manager of the Donner Trail Ranch, frequently acted as a residence witness and accompanied a guest to court to obtain a divorce decree.

(Drackert Collection, Courtesy of Special Collections Department, University of Nevada, Reno Library)

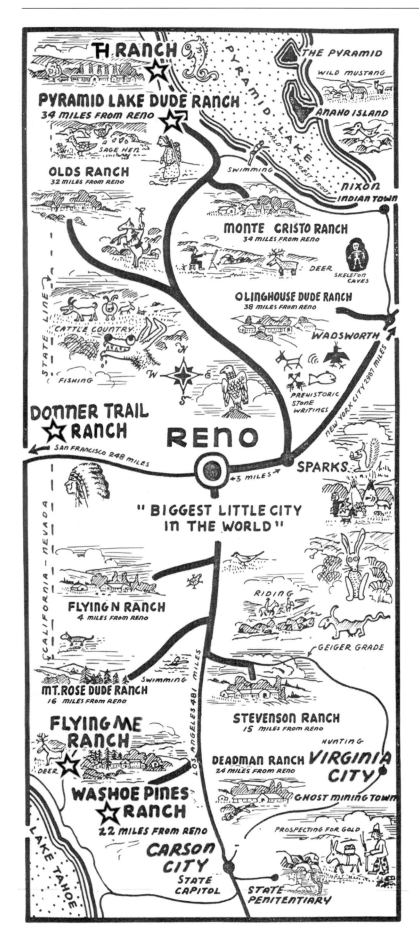

Northern Nevada Dude-Divorce Ranches Circa 1930-1960

This map includes the approximate locations for 12 of the 38 dude-divorce ranches mentioned in this book (Chapter 6 plus Appendices E - I). The starred ranches were considered the leading dude-divorce ranch operations of the era, even though not all of them were in business for the full thirty years.

Part IV—Other Leading Nevada Dude-Divorce Ranches

Circa 1930-1960

TH Ranch, circa 1930s
(Courtesy Jack and Grace Horgan, and Christine Carter)

E. H Ranch

Nevada's First Dude Ranch

The beginning of dude ranching in Nevada was the idea of a Reno Baptist minister. In 1929, the Reverend Brewster Adams returned home to Nevada after visiting Eatons' Ranch in Wolf, Wyoming. Adams suggested to an acquaintance, Neill Hakes West, that Nevada should have a dude ranch similar to Eatons' Ranch. West owned a horse ranch in Sutcliffe by Pyramid Lake about thirty miles from Reno. He decided to act on Adams' suggestion and built ten small cabins on his ranch. He charged guests $35 per week, which included the cabin, two meals a day and the use of a horse. Thus, the TH Ranch became the first ranch in Nevada catering to dudes.

TH Ranch, circa 1920s (Courtesy Nevada Historical Society)

History

The following brief history is taken from Knach and Stewart's *As Long As The River Shall Run*:

Various people as far back as the mid-1800s settled on the land now occupied by the TH Ranch. Some were squatters; others were rightful title holders.

In 1859, the Pyramid Lake Indian Reservation was established under the auspices of agent Frederick Dodge. It was founded by executive order and required neither negotiations with the Paiute Indian tribe nor the approval of Congress. It was vaguely described but its boundaries were not recorded on any map.

In 1865, Eugene Monroe was hired to survey the boundaries of the Pyramid Lake Indian Reservation and to make a sketch map recording those boundaries. By 1873, there was still no copy of the map in the Reservation office and no surveyor's marks on the land, so it was impossible to tell if anyone was encroaching. In 1889, a second survey was completed, which was the final one until the 1940s, when minor sections were remapped.

White settlers, stockmen, and ranch operators inhabited the Reservation until they controlled almost all of the land suited for farms and ranches. State and Federal officials did little to uphold the integrity of reservation lands, and trespassers and squatters refused to move.

To quote Knach and Stewart, "There in Hardscrabble Creek Canyon, where Numaga and Captain Jim had previously lived, the Whiteheads took the land and water and forced these Indians to abandon their holding." (In Basil Woon's *None of the Comforts of Home*, a reference is found to the effect that John Wesley Whitehead may have originally homesteaded the land in 1864.)

In 1892, Senator William Stewart wrote to a Reno attorney advising him to tell a Mr. Calligan (who at this point held the Whitehead ranch) that he would use his best endeavors to get Calligan's and others' lands similarly situated released.

These few names have been noted as having "occupied" the land, but they left no record of having legally owned it.

On June 7, 1924, Nevada Senator Key Pittman's bill was passed to allow the white occupants of land on the Pyramid Lake Indian Reservation to purchase this land from the government. Patrick L. Flanigan occupied the land at that time and promptly purchased what was then known as the Hardscrabble Ranch. During Flanigan's ownership, when he wanted to take up more parcels of land, a favored device of his was to claim only the spring; thus he would own only a small amount of land but control a large area.[1]

TH Ranch, rodeo, circa 1927 (Courtesy Nevada Historical Society)

Ownership sequence of the Hardscrabble Ranch, later the TH Ranch:

🐄 John Newmarker took up some parts of the ranch from the State of Nevada, as recorded June 30, 1898.

🐄 Robert C. Turrittin took up some parts of the ranch from the United States of America, as recorded on August 27, 1917 and September 26, 1917.

🐄 Robert C. Turrittin transferred title to Pyramid Land and Stock Company, owned by Patrick L. Flanigan, as recorded December 4, 1917. (P. L. Flanigan was one of Nevada's most influential pioneers. He started as a sheepherder and became the largest wool producer in the state, building his herd to 60,000 sheep. In addition, he owned 5,000 head of cattle and controlled 60,000 acres of Washoe County land. Among his other achievements, he was an influential politician, having served both in the state assembly and senate.)

🐄 Pyramid Land and Stock Company transferred title to Sierra Nevada Livestock Company, as recorded September 19, 1924. (Both of the preceding were holdings of P. L. Flanigan.)

🐄 Sierra Nevada Livestock Company trans-

ferred title to Neill Hakes West, as recorded January 6, 1927. West bought a herd of cattle and the TH brand from Tom Hill, who owned a ranch midway between Reno and Fernley. West changed the ranch name from Hardscrabble Ranch to TH Ranch. Neill Hakes West died on the ranch on May 17, 1950, and title passed to his wife, Augusta West.

🐄 Augusta West transferred title to the Matley family, as recorded April 2, 1952.

🐄 The Matley family transferred title to Howard Alfred Peigh, as recorded November 20, 1961. Peigh built a modern luxury home on the hill north of the old ranch buildings. It was a two-story building with a magnificent view of Pyramid Lake and the surrounding hills. This home burned down sometime during his ownership. All that remains today are a concrete pad with a tall chimney, a 15,000 gallon redwood tank, a generator house, and a bench used as a skeet shooting base.

🐄 H. A. Peigh transferred title to Michael F. Lintner, as recorded July 28, 1970.

🐄 Michael F. Lintner transferred title to the Edward J. Horgan Family Trust (Jack and Grace Horgan), as recorded June 5, 1980. Jack and Grace Horgan were able to obtain the TH brand when they acquired the ranch.[2]

The deeded property of the TH Ranch forms a highly irregular shape since there are ten separate parcels that total approximately 1,347 acres. The main portion of the ranch consists of 961 acres, which is a finger of land that protrudes from the Bureau of Land Management (BLM) land on the west side into the Pyramid Lake Indian Reservation toward the east. Beside the main portion, there are nine other parcels which vary from twenty acres to sixty-four acres each. These are all off the Reservation and surrounded by BLM ground. Each of these nine parcels contains at least one good spring.

There is a large degree of variation in terrain characteristics, ranging from fairly level meadow areas to hillside plateaus, steep canyons and high, rocky mountain tops. Elevations range from 4,200 feet at the entry gate at the east end of the property to about 5,400 feet at the westerly side of the main portion of the 961 acres. The drainage slope, upon which are numerous springs and contributing canyons, all with an easterly direction, produces Hardscrabble Creek.[3]

The TH Takes In Dudes

In the 1920s, Reno was already on its way to becoming a divorce colony. In the early '20s, the residency requirement was six months; in 1927, it was changed to three months; then in 1931, it was reduced to six weeks.

When the TH started taking in dudes in 1929, most of its guests came for recreation, not divorce. Among the guests in those early days were Charles Jones, president of the Richfield Oil Company, and Mrs. Jones; J. Darrel Chase, president of Associated Oil Company, and Mrs. Chase; Edgar D. Turner, president of Sherman and Clay of San Francisco, and Mrs. Turner; Mr. and Mrs. Drew Pearson; and Henry Morgenthau Sr., former Ambassador to Turkey, and Mrs. Morgenthau. The first divorce dude was Ethel Andrews Murphy, later the wife of Supreme Court Justice Harlan.

Then Cornelius Vanderbilt Jr. came to the TH to establish his Nevada residency for a divorce. Due to his prominence and fortune, his attorneys advised him to own property while in Nevada, so that his residency would not be in question. Vanderbilt reportedly bought a parcel of land on the TH Ranch from Neill Hakes West and occupied some of his time by supervising construction of a stone cabin. After obtaining his divorce, the property would revert back to West. The cabin burned down, but a stone wall and fireplace ruin remain today.

By 1932, nearly all the guests at the TH were

there for divorces. One such guest was Augusta L'Hommedieu Hines. Augusta was the great, great granddaughter of Captain L'Hommedieu, the first captain of the USS *Constitution*, "Old Ironsides." She came to the TH to divorce Jackson Hines, who was being held and accused of murder. "Gussie" caught the eye of Neill Hakes, and they married after her divorce from Hines was final. (Hines was eventually exonerated for killing his previous wife's rapist.) Like many husband and wife ranch owners, Gussie worked by her husband's side and managed the dude business part of the ranch. She also had an aptitude for machines and did all the mechanical work around the ranch.

The TH took in dudes until 1942, when the war and rationing made it too difficult to continue. Neill Hakes died on the ranch in 1950. Augusta sold the ranch in 1952 and moved to La Jolla, California to live out the rest of her years.

Activities and Attractions. Riding, roundups, swimming, ranch parties, rodeos, fishing and horseback picnics.

Accommodations and Rates. In 1929, a small cabin, two meals a day, and the use of a saddle horse were $35 a week. Neill Edward West, the grandson of Neill Hakes West, described the cabins: "My dad, Chaska West, and I stayed in one of those cabins for a time after the dude ranch business closed. Just a little one room cabin with a wood stove in it. You'd build a fire and go to bed. There was no water, nothing. You'd go outside to get a drink of water or use the john."

TH Stories

One day, one of the former owners of the TH drove into the yard with his team and buckboard. As he got out of the buckboard, he stuck the switch he was using for a buggy whip into the ground. The switch flourished and grew into the black walnut tree so prominent in the yard today.

—Harry Drackert, operator, Pyramid Lake Ranch

Neill Hakes West owned a horse-drawn stagecoach, which he used to meet guests at the Southern Pacific Railroad Station in Sutcliffe, about two miles from the ranch. One Fourth of July, an Indian band was on the stagecoach going to the ranch for a celebration and rodeo. The driver had been celebrating a

TH Ranch—The First Dude Ranch in Nevada

Clockwise from above left: Neill Hakes West (on horseback and sitting) built ten small cabins on his horse ranch in Sutcliffe in 1929 and began taking in dudes; Chaska West (son of Neill Hakes West) sitting on the fence at the TH, circa 1930s; Arriving dudes were met by stagecoach at the S. P. Railroad Station in Sutcliffe

and were "attacked" by Indians on the drive to the ranch; a bunkhouse, circa 1927; rodeos were staged to entertain the dudes; branding in a dusty corral; the view of Pyramid Lake from the TH.

(Chaska West and bunkhouse, courtesy of Nevada Historical Society; other photos courtesy of Jack and Grace Horgan, and Christine Carter)

great deal and took a corner too fast, scattering the band around the ranch.   *—Earl Crain*

My grandfather had a stagecoach. When a bunch of dudes arrived in Sutcliffe on the train, he'd hook up the stagecoach, alert the Indians to put on a pow-wow, drive the stagecoach down to the train, and pick up the dudes and all their luggage. Back up the road, the Indians would "attack." They'd get a bottle of booze, which was hidden under the sagebrush. Of course, my grandfather made the booze. This was during Prohibition and he had a little still.

—Neill Edward West

It seems that Neill and his wife, Augusta, had a disagreement as to how many cattle were on the ranch. Mrs. West took a position in the yard and requested that the cattle be driven by her while she counted them. What Mrs. West didn't know was that the cattle were driven past her, then down the road and around the hill behind her, to be counted again as they passed before her a second time. *—Gardner Sheehan, wrangler*

Probably the most tantalizing story about the TH was related by Mrs. West herself, who vouched for its veracity:

Patrick L. Flanigan ran into financial difficulties, and the Hardscrabble Ranch, along with his other ranches, were put in the hands of a bank which installed 'French Louis' as caretaker. During World War I, 'Frenchie' bought a lot of Liberty Bonds and cached them, along with $10,000 in gold and a picture of his sister, somewhere on the ranch. The cache could not have been far from the house because when he wished to show visitors the picture of his sister, he would be gone only a few minutes. One cold, stormy day, Frenchie drove to the Pyramid Lake post office in a Model T Ford and had trouble re-starting the car. He cranked and cranked until he was dripping with perspiration. Finally he got the car started and drove home. The result: he caught a terrible cold and died within the week of pneumonia. No one since has discovered where Frenchie hid his gold and it is probably still there! All of the owners, since Frenchie died, swear that it was never found. Some disbelieve the story.

—Augusta West to Basil Woon

Another treasure never found was two five-gallon wooden kegs of moonshine buried in the front garden during Prohibition. My grandfather got word that the Prohibitionists were coming and buried his kegs in the front yard. Story is they were never found.

—Neill Edward West

When the movie, *The Iron Horse*, was made near Pyramid Lake in 1924, Neill Hakes West furnished all of the western equipment, horses, riders, Indians, and stagecoaches, and was a technical advisor to director John Ford. West also furnished the horses used in the 1936 musical, *Rose-Marie*, starring Jeanette MacDonald and Nelson Eddy, and filmed at Lake Tahoe.

An article appeared in the *Reno Evening Gazette*, August 26, 1922, to the effect that the stage-coach owned by Neill West was once owned by Hank Monk, a stagecoach driver of considerable repute in early Nevada. It was also noted in the same paper on September 6, 1922, that West won the stagecoach race of the Nevada Roundup on September 2 and 3, 1922.

Interviews

In the fall of 2002, the authors interviewed Neill Edward West, the grandson of Neill Hakes West, and Jack and Grace Horgan, the current owners of the TH. The interviews cleared up some historical facts about the TH.

An Interview with Neill Edward West
New Washoe City, Nevada, September 11, 2002.

Neill Edward West's grandfather owned and operated the TH from 1927 to 1950. Neill Edward's father, Chaska West, was a well-known cowboy around Lake Tahoe in the 1940s. Neill Edward was particularly interested in setting the record straight about his grandfather's life.

Neill, when and where were you born?
I was born in Reno in 1933 at a house my dad built on Vassar Street, half a block from So. Virginia. Today's there's a Finarama fish shop there.

The TH has such an important place in Nevada's dude ranching history. Tell us what you remember about your grandfather and the TH.
I'll tell you, there's been so much wrong information passed around about my grandfather. If you're going to write about him, please get it right.

That's why we're here, to check the facts for ourselves. Give us some examples of wrong information about your grandfather.

Well, my grandfather never had a partner in the ranch. He did not raise Arabian horses. He did not sell out before he died. Furthermore, I don't like to see my grandfather portrayed as just a dude rancher. That was only a ten-to-fifteen year period in his eighty year life.

As for the rumor that Cornelius Vanderbilt Jr. bought land on the TH to build a stone cabin, as far as I know he never bought a building site on the ranch from my grandfather. Cornelius didn't like the cabins my grandfather had to offer, so he built himself a stone cabin on the TH property, but he never actually bought the site. Also, Cornelius was never a partner of my grandfather, in spite of what he wrote in his book, *Ranches and Ranch Life in America.*

We read that your grandfather's wife, Augusta L'Hommedieu Hines West, was his partner.

She probably came the closest to being my grandfather's partner. Augusta came out here for a divorce and stayed at the TH. She had some money. My grandfather had the ranch, the cabins, and the horses. He raised horses, that was his business. Raising work horses, not Arabians. He brought a purebred Clydesdale stud over from England to breed work horses. And he was also selling remount horses to the U. S. Army.

Grandfather had a Bureau of Land Management permit that came with the ranch for 500 head of cattle. However, he didn't have the money to buy the cattle. But Augusta did. She put up the dough to buy the cattle. So it was a business arrangement. She became his partner when he married her. He had no outside partners.

Where did the TH brand come from?

It came with the cattle my grandfather bought from Tom Hill. Tom's ranch folded up and my grandfather bought all the cattle and the TH irons. The TH was the cattle iron; the Quartercircle A-J was the horse iron. I still have these irons.

Tell us more about your grandfather.

I know that before my grandfather bought the TH, there were several people who squatted there, lived there, but never owned it. By the time my grandfather owned the TH in the late 1920s, the railroad ran three, maybe four miles away

from the ranch, right by Sutcliffe.

How would you like to see your grandfather portrayed in history?

First and foremost, my grandfather was a horseman. He loved horses and raised them all his life. It just happened that he was also the first rancher in Nevada to take in dudes. But that was for a very short period of time, only ten-to-fifteen years. And he wasn't a cattleman. To my grandfather, a horse was worth as much money—if not more—than a cow in those days.

How many head of horses would he normally be running?

Around 300.

Were most of them saddle horses?

A combination. He was breeding a good, heavy horse that could be used either for work or for saddle. He liked Pinto horses because they sold well. My dad, Chaska, used to get a lot of the horses from the ranch for his stables at the Lake.

My grandfather also ran a construction company in Reno with horses. His home ranch was on the corner of California and So. Virginia, out in the country then. That was where my dad, Chaska, was born and raised. Grandfather built the original road from Reno to Truckee, which was through Dog Valley. He built it with horses and scrapers. Ever been over Dog Valley Road? It's amazing how they built that without a bulldozer. Just horses. I suppose they blasted a lot of the stuff with dynamite. Then they came in with horses and scrapers and hauled it out. It was solid rock.

Was your grandfather involved with your dad's stable business at Lake Tahoe?

No, he was never involved in the stable business at Tahoe, or in the dude business at Donner Lake, like this says he was (pointing to an excerpt from a book).

How many children did your grandfather have?

You should note that my grandfather was married four times before he bought the TH Ranch and married Augusta. He had five children that I know of. Two boys, three girls. One boy was my dad, Chaska. I never met my uncle, the other boy, and don't even know his name. He's buried at Mountain View Cemetery, and the name on the tombstone says "Butch." The girls were Juanita, Winona and Louella. In Indian, Juanita is "oldest daughter" and Chaska is "oldest son."

We think Reverend Brewster Adams gave your grand-

father some good advice about taking in dudes.

I guess so, but I don't like to see my grandfather portrayed as only a dude rancher. Adams was the family minister for years and years. He performed at least one of my grandfather's five marriages, and he married my mother and father, Marguerite and Chaska.

Let's talk about your father, Chaska. You know, I knew him in 1947, when I worked at Lake Tahoe one summer for Bob Scates. Your dad was a well-known, popular figure around Tahoe. Everyone liked Chaska. He was about my dad's age, and we all looked up to him. Tell me more about his life. How did he acquire his cowboy skills?

Dad was born in Reno in 1895, in the house at California and So. Virginia streets. He never finished school. He climbed out the school bathroom window in the eighth grade and quit—or so he told me. Dad was always a cowboy. If he wasn't riding horses, he was driving them.

He probably worked for your grandfather at the TH.

Not very much. He was pretty much on his own from the time he was a little kid. I don't know too much, because he never really talked about that. I know he was married and divorced once before my mother.

Dad met my mother when she came here for a divorce. They got married, and he took her out to his homestead by Red Rock, called Rye Patch. Red Rock is north of Reno on the way to Cold Springs and the California border. Dad took mom out there—which she did not appreciate. There was an outdoor john, a well outside where you pumped your own water, and a water drip cooler to keep meat and butter in. It wasn't long before they moved to town. Dad built the place on Vassar Street where I was born.

Chaska rode for your grandfather in several of the annual Pony Express reenactment rides and won it a couple times.

I know he got one gold medal for the fastest time in one ride. Dad weighed maybe 125 pounds if he was wringin' wet! I never knew him to wear a bigger Levi than a size 29. He would buy a 29, bring it home, and throw them in the horse trough overnight. The next day, he'd pick them up and dry them out.

Speaking of which, look at this advertisement for Pony Express riders: "Wanted. Young, skinny, wiry fellows, not over 18. Must be expert riders, willing to risk death daily. Orphans preferred. Wages $25 a week." How did Chaska

get into the stable business at Tahoe?

My dad started a stable at Lake Tahoe at Lake Forest about 1921, maybe '22. About 1933 or '34, he moved the stables to King's Beach, Tahoe Vista. They were called the Brockway Riding Livery.

The hotel there was called Brockway Hot Springs.

Yes, that's right, but it's been torn down, and there are condominiums now.

I enjoyed your dad a lot. He and Bob Scates were a couple of old pros.

When those two got together it was a wild time. Bob Scates could be a wild one, all right. One summer night, he pulled in at our house at the Lake drunker than a skunk. I guess he decided to sleep it off at our house rather than drive home around the Lake. Anyway, he crawled into bed— with my mother. You should have heard the screams!

The last time I saw your dad was the end of the '47 season. He was driving the pickup and was our flag man to slow down the cars coming over Mount Rose. You were probably with us. We brought the horses down to Reno and turned them out in the pasture. I got in the pickup, and your dad dropped me at the Nevada Hotel. I never saw him again.

Neill, a personal question. It sounds like you and your grandfather had a close relationship. Did he ever talk to you about taking over the TH someday?

Yes, of course, many, many times. But I was in high school then, still a kid. Living four miles up a canyon from Sutcliffe—I didn't think then I wanted to live my life being so remote. Today I have an acre here in New Washoe City with a great view of Slide Mountain. I've been here for twenty years.

• • •

An Interview wih Jack and Grace Horgan
TH Ranch, Sutcliffe, Nevada, September 11, 2002

Jack and Grace Horgan are the current owners of the TH Ranch. Their roots run deep in Nevada; both of their mothers were born in Virginia City. Jack and Grace met after college and were married in 1940. Now in their eighties, they are a handsome couple and still cut trim figures in their Western wear.

Why did you decide to buy the TH Ranch?

[Jack] When I was in high school, I would come

Jack and Grace Horgan (Courtesy Jack and Grace Horgan)

out here on the weekends for the rodeos. A lot of people born and raised in Reno had never heard of this place. But Grace and I knew it pretty well. About the time Grace and I were looking for a few acres, we heard this place was up for sale. I suggested we take a look. We both thought, "Oh, no, that place is too big for us. We can't handle that." [Grace] But when we saw the ranch again, well, nothing else would do. We had to have it. We started out looking for a few acres—and ended up with more than a thousand!

It's pretty remote here. Who helps you take care of the ranch?

No one, really. We don't have livestock so we really don't need much help.

You don't have a telephone here, not to mention e-mail and things like that.

[Jack] We have a cell phone, but to use it we have to go a mile out of the canyon to make a call or check for messages.

[Grace] That's what we love about it here. On Mondays, we go into town, usually Sparks or Reno. Jack goes to his Rotary luncheon, and I meet a friend or my granddaughter. Then we do a weekly shopping.

Far right, Neill Edward West presenting the original TH and Quartercircle A-J branding irons to Grace and Jack Horgan, 2002. (Courtesy Jack and Grace Horgan)

Jack, someone told us you still ride everyday.

Yes, I do, although my routine's changed a bit. Six years ago a horse fell with me, and I broke my hip. So now I can't swing my leg up. I made a depression in the corral where I make the horse stand, and then I can get up on him. But if I get off somewhere along my ride, well then, I've got to look for a rock.

Tell us about the couple who visited you in 1992.

This couple wrote to us asking if they could visit the ranch. They were married in Reno in 1942 by the Reverend Brewster Adams. Adams was the one who talked Neill West into taking in dudes at the TH in the late '20s, so Adams must have recommended the TH to this couple, because they spent their honeymoon here. Anyway, they revisited the ranch in 1992, when they were celebrating their fiftieth anniversary!

Will one of your three sons take over the ranch someday?

All three of our sons and their families want the TH to stay in the family. So it will be turned over to them someday, when they retire.

Postscript

Today the TH Ranch in Hardscrabble Canyon is still very remote. Even seekers of solitude would find its location too far off the beaten path. Only one of the small guest cabins built in 1929 by Neill Hakes West remains. Certainly the dudes who made the trip "out West" to the TH Ranch and Pyramid Lake in the 1920s and '30s can only be described as very adventurous.

While the TH will factually maintain its place in history as "Nevada's First Dude Ranch," the authors hope to have left the reader with a more accurate portrayal of Neill Hakes West—foremost a horseman.

This chapter ends on a nice note. Following our interviews in the fall of 2002, Neill Edward West paid a visit to Jack and Grace Horgan at the TH Ranch. West presented the Horgans with the original TH and Quartercircle A-J branding irons—with the hope that the irons will remain with the historic property for generations to come.

Pyramid Lake Ranch dudes on a trail ride. The lake and Anaho Island in backtround.
(Drackert Collection, Courtesy of Special Collections Department, University of Nevada, Reno Library)

F. Pyramid Lake Ranch

Harry and Joan Drackert were one of the few truly successful cowboy-dude teams in northern Nevada.

The Pyramid Lake Ranch was one of Nevada's leading guest ranches in the post-World War II era. Its desert lakeside setting was uniquely different from other dude ranches in the west.

Pyramid Lake is the largest surviving remnant of a great prehistoric ocean which once covered most of Nevada, as well as much of Idaho and Utah. It is a cool, freshwater lake fed by the Truckee River, which drains from Lake Tahoe. Around the lake there is little vegetation and hardly any habitation.

The ranch was on an old California-Oregon trail, built on the site of an emigrant post where the forty-niners watered their cattle and oxen. Later, the site became a Pony Express and stagecoach stop.

Pyramid Lake Ranch ad from
The Nevada Magazine, *July 1947*

ty miles broad. It broke upon our eyes like the ocean. We camped opposite a very remarkable rock on the lake which attracted our attention. It rose, according to our estimate about 600 feet above the water and presented a pretty exact outline of the Pyramid of Cheops. This suggested a name and I called it "Pyramid Lake."[1]

James Sutcliffe. The original site resident was James Sutcliffe, who reportedly established a remount station for army convoys traveling in the 1860s and '70s between Fort Bidwell, Oregon and Fort Churchill, on the Carson River, when Indian troubles were rife. Sutcliffe subsequently homesteaded the ranch so that when, much later, Congress approved the Pyramid Lake Indian Reservation, Sutcliffe's homestead and one other, the Whitney's, were excluded, and so remained small "islands" within the reservation.

In 1863, the United States Government declared Pyramid Lake and about 500 square miles of territory surrounding it to be a Paiute Indian Reservation. The property on the lake shore was exempt, however, through the laws which granted squatters full title to land which they had held for fifty years or more.

History

Captain John C. Frémont and his expedition were probably the first non-Indians to see Pyramid Lake. Frémont described his first dramatic encounter with the lake on January 14, 1844:

> Beyond a defile between mountains and filling up the lower space was a sheet of green water some twen-

Captain John Frémont at Pyramid Lake.
(Courtesy of Nevada Historical Society)

Olds Ranch. Sutcliffe leased the site to "Ma" Olds in 1927. She operated the ranch as a resort during the late 1920s and early '30s. A memorial to Ma still exists in the form of a huge fireplace which she built herself.

Following Ma Olds, John Albert "Al" Marshall II became the owner-manager in the 1930s. He built more cabins, refurnished the older premises, and reportedly experienced considerable success. Then Wayne and Bernie Cutlip took over the management. Now the ranch frequently accommodated guests seeking a six weeks' Nevada divorce. (Wayne Cutlip was also a rodeo cowboy, as well as a wrangler for Hollywood Western movies.)

Sage Ranch. In 1936, Alva LaSalle Kitselman, better known to his friends and family as "Beau," bought the ranch for $67,000. Beau's father was a wealthy steel man of Muncie, Indiana. Beau's mother was the former Leslie Curtis, a prominent newspaperwoman and the author of *Reno Reveries*, the first nationally circulated book about Reno, published about 1910.

Beau's mother, now Leslie Kitselman Figueroa, and sister, Marjorie Kitselman Rautzahn, claimed they were deeded the ranch from Beau in 1940. They incorporated the ranch as The Sage, Inc., and leased it to the Pyramid Lake Ranch, Inc., headed by Walter L. Pattridge. In 1946, Harry Drackert subleased the ranch from the Pyramid Lake Ranch, Inc.

On November 26, 1947, Beau Kitselman filed suit to regain possession of the ranch from his mother and sister which he claimed he gave away while under a yoga spell. *Nevada State Journal*, November, 26-27, 1947:

> Beau Kitselman claimed yesterday on the witness stand that his mother and sister got the ranch away from him while he was practicing yoga and sitting cross-legged in a dark room at his ranch until he fell into periods of unconsciousness.
>
> The defendants, on the other hand, are seeking to show that Beau is an able business man, an accomplished mathematician, and musician, and fully capable of taking care of business transactions, even when he gives away ranches.
>
> He testified that he had studied Hindu philosophy prior to making the agreement with his mother and sister, and that the philosophy made him incapable of questioning anyone's word.
>
> Since then, he says, he has returned to a western outlook which has brought about a desire to get back his former possessions.

The yoga posture, coupled with an effort to suspend breathing, probably was incompetently learned by him, Mr. Kitselman confessed.

Drackert Years, 1946-1956

Harry Drackert. Harry Drackert was born in Pony, Montana on December 23, 1904. By the age of sixteen, he was working the local rodeo circuit. After graduating from Gallatin County High School in Montana, he joined the national rodeo circuit and earned the title "All-Around Champion Cowboy" at Madison Square Garden in New York City.

Drackert soon gained a reputation for working well with both horses and people, and eventually went to work for the Elkhorn Dude Ranch near West Yellowstone, Montana. Later, he tried a stint as a cowboy in Hollywood and, although he didn't become a star, he did work as a wrangler for several Western movie productions.

In 1931, Harry quit the rodeo circuit and moved to northern Nevada, where he entered the stable business as a riding instructor. By 1940, he was operating Drackert's Stables at Brockway, Lake Tahoe.

During World War II, he worked in the shipyards in San Francisco. Late in the war, he returned to Reno and

Joan and Harry Drackert, a successful cowboy-dude team. (Drackert Collection, Courtesy of Special Collections Department, University of Nevada, Reno Library)

briefly managed the Mount Rose Lodge, before subleasing the Pyramid Lake Ranch in 1946.

Joan Drackert. Joan Abry was born at Morelands, the Abry family farm in Talbot County, Maryland, in 1914. As a teenager, she spent her summers in Evergreen, Colorado, where she learned to ride horses and fell in love with the West.

By 1940, Joan had moved to New York City, where she became a fashion model for the Powers Agency. Along the way she learned to fly and became an expert trapshooter.

During World War II, she worked at the Quartermasters' Depot in Bellemead, New Jersey, where she met and married Major Robert Deeley.

In 1946, Joan came to Reno to get a divorce, with $300 in her pocket. While establishing her six weeks' residency, she needed to work and got a job at the Mount Rose Lodge, where she met Harry Drackert. "The first night, the owner was called away, and she was left alone. All the calamities of the business came down on her—a maid who was stealing jewelry, a husband who turned up threatening to commit suicide, unpaid bills and uncontrolled tantrums. She has never been really surprised by anything since."[2]

Joan liked Reno and decided to stay on after her divorce was final. In 1947, she worked as a ranch hostess for Jack Fugitt, owner of the Donner Trail Ranch.

Then in 1949, Joan Abry Deeley went to work for Harry Drackert as the ranch hostess at the Pyramid Lake Ranch. The couple were married in 1950. Harry and Joan Drackert would enjoy a long and successful run of dude ranch management spanning forty years, and were one of the few truly successful cowboy-dude teams in Northern Nevada.

Location. Pyramid Lake Ranch was thirty-four miles north of Reno at Sutcliffe, Nevada, 900 feet from the shores of Pyramid Lake, and surrounded by large shade trees and purple mountain ranges. The ranch was one of the few parcels of land within the Pyramid Lake Indian Reservation not owned by the Paiute Tribe.

Harry Drackert acquired the right to run a guest ranch for the ranch's owner, based, as Harry put it, "on a pledge and a handshake." Harry ran the ranch from 1946-1956—with Joan joining him in 1949. They hosted guests who came to establish their six weeks' Nevada residency, and Harry raised thoroughbred and quarter horses for both racing and ranch use. They also ran a small bar on the ranch—the only one between Sparks

and Gerlach—and a modest gift shop, the Indian Trading Post.

Activities and Attractions. Riding, pack trips, hunting and fishing, boating, swimming in temperate lake water, flying instruction, fifteen miles of sandy beaches, ranch parties and barbeques.

Pyramid Lake is famous for two kinds of fish: the Lahontan cutthroat trout and the *cui-ui* (pronounced coo'ee-oo'ee. The Paiute language is spoken, not written.). The cui-ui is a sucker fish living in the depths of the lake and comes up once a year, in April, to spawn in the Truckee River. It tastes something like mackerel and is said to have existed since prehistoric days when most of the western United States was still under water. The lake is shaped like a harp, thirty-one miles on its longest axis, with the narrow end south. It is almost eleven miles across at the wide end.

The noted writer A. J. Liebling described the lake's water as having "the soothing quality of a cool solution of boric acid, while in the mouth it tastes like Alka-Seltzer gone flat. It thus affords the greatest double-action hangover cure known to man, and were it possible to transport sufferers from their beds of pain to the lakeside before their affliction subsided, Pyramid might become one of the great spas of the world."

Guest Relations. The Pyramid Lake Ranch was ranked as one of the four top Nevada dude ranches for more than a quarter of a century. Many famous and notable guests untied their matrimonial bonds at Pyramid Lake, including playwright Arthur Miller and writers A. J. Liebling and Saul Bellow. One brochure promised divorce seekers, "Troubles are soon forgotten—you will meet congenial companions—swim, ride, rest—or dash into Reno for a taste of city life. Ship your trunks and luggage direct to Sutcliffe, the Southern Pacific Railroad station at the Ranch. Yes—the Ranch and Reno are both in Washoe County."

When A. J. Liebling came to Nevada in 1949 to get a divorce, he described his arrival in Reno and his introduction to the Pyramid Lake Ranch with humor and irony, and in what can only be described as "vintage Liebling":

> Two nights in the Biggest Little City in the World had indicated to me that if I stayed there I might not last the distance. I had counted on doing a bit of writing while in limbo, and so far it had all been on American Express checks. I explained my

A. J. Liebling described the lake's water as having "the soothing quality of a cool solution of boric acid, while in the mouth it tastes like Alka-Seltzer gone flat. It thus affords the greatest double-action hangover cure known to man...."
(Drackert Collection, Courtesy of Special Collections Department, University of Nevada, Reno Library)

apprehensions to my Nevada attorney, and he, grasping the fact that his fee might depend on my leaving Reno quickly, advised "a ranch."

The judge and I (my attorney was addressed as Judge, as are half the members of the Nevada bar) were talking in the apple-green corner bar of the Riverside Hotel, where he often held consultations....He introduced me to a fellow named Harry Drackert, who, he said, had been the national bronc-riding champion back in the twenties—both Harry's and the century's. Mr. Drackert, it developed, conducted a guest ranch on the western side of Pyramid Lake, about thirty miles from town, and it was from his lips that I had my first inkling of the lake's scenic glories.

All the guests at the ranch were people who, like me, had decided to become residents of Nevada, although they might change their minds six weeks later, after obtaining a divorce. Mr. Drackert said that practically all the other guests were women, but after looking me over he added that he didn't think they'd make enough of a run at me to keep me from working. Most of them had children to wrangle, he explained; a ranch was an ideal place to run children, who, if kept in Reno, might become addicted to faro or bingo.

Out by the lake, I could commune with nature

and get a lot of work done. There were dude horses, if I cared to ride—which I didn't—and if I wanted to swim, there was a pool as well as the lake. There was also a bar, but no roulette wheel. The last point was the clincher. I told him I would be out the next afternoon, which would give me twenty-four hours to collect my thoughts and possessions.

Once we had struck a bargain, Drackert began telling me some of the disadvantages of dude wrangling. One was the daily *corvée* of bringing a detail of the women in to shop and have their hair done, which accounted for his presence in Reno. All the women didn't come in every day, of course. The ones who wanted to go to town signed up on the previous evening. He would load eight or ten head in a station wagon, he said, and take off in the morning in plenty of time to get them to Reno before lunch, but if he made even a trivial detour of twenty or twenty-five miles to buy alfalfa or look over a quarter-horse colt, they would complain. "If they would only show some interest in what I'm doing, they'd be interested," he said. "But they're so blasé you can't do nothing for them"

Arriving at the Riverside Hotel, which was the general rendezvous for dude-ranch people, he would turn the women loose unhobbled, and they would scatter on varied and mysterious missions, having been instructed to return at four-thirty, which they interpreted as five-forty-five. They would leave Harry with time on his hands, even though he had to load laundry or provisions for the ranch, or perhaps go over to the Washoe County Courthouse and testify that a guest had not left the State of Nevada overnight since signing his register. (Swearing falsely—with special regard to one's residence—is among the most serious crimes in the Nevada code.)

It wasn't until the next day that I learned that the lake was on an Indian reservation, of which the ranch had once been a small part. Wallie Warren told me about it while he was driving me out there; he was a friend of Harry's and had some business at the ranch. I could have waited for the station wagon and ridden

Pyramid Lake Ranch

Clockwise from top: A stagecoach ride entertained the dudes; the Pyramid Lake Ranch entrance stood close to the road, behind a lawn and trees, unusual vegetation around the desert lake; rows of one-room cabins were set around the swimming pool; the ranch had once been a small part of the Paiute Indian Reservation; the Indian Trading Post sold Native American jewelry and baskets.
(Drackert Collection, Courtesy of Special Collections Department, University of Nevada, Reno Library)

out with the shoppers, but I felt suddenly shy. It had occurred to me that I was in the position of a lone Turkish child entering an Armenian orphanage. I represented the enemy.

My first view of Harry's place had rather dismayed me; it looked comfortable enough but hardly seemed the spot to cultivate detachment. The main house stood fairly close to the road, behind an old established lawn with flower beds and trees. (Vegetation of this sort is possible around Pyramid Lake only on land that has long been under irrigation; the stand of trees made the ranch a conspicuous landmark.) Behind the house were company streets of one-room cabins with porches, set around a swimming pool, and children of all ages, whom I took to be the unhappy offshoots of broken homes, careened whooping through all the interstices between the buildings. I knew the mothers would do nothing to increase the children's sense of insecurity during this tragic interlude in the little beasts' struggle toward adjustment, and there wasn't a chance that they would shut up of their own accord.

I could picture myself seated on a hut porch typewriting with all the privacy of a street portrait artist at the Greenwich Village art festival. The mothers themselves looked all right—very all right, some of them, in shorts and halter things—but they would not be particularly conducive to concentration, either.

Joan Drackert, Harry's wife and hostess, had saved the day by suggesting a room in a second ranch house, high up on the side of a hill. The approach to it was protected by a railroad embankment and a deep gully, which one crossed on a shaky plank. In front of this house was a big empty corral and, nearer, a green lawn with fruit trees around it, and I proposed to set up my typewriter on a table under one of them.

Liebling recalls the impression he made on the lady dudes:

I was determining that my entrance among those offended women should be as diffident as possible, with a minimum of brash verbiage, and one eye always on the nearest exit. This proved an error, for my fellow-boarders turned out to be a civil lot. They sensibly declined, however, to let my presence restrain them from talking about their husbands. Not one woman complained of having been brutalized. Each, according to her tale, had simply tired of being a nursemaid and protector. The repudiation of this

role evidently entailed a certain sense of guilt. None of them could figure how the poor devil she had left was going to get along without her.

Once I knew what was wanted, I tried to cultivate a decisive manner, but I had made my mistake at the outset and the first impression proved ineradicable. My cringing amiability reminded them of their husbands. At dinner the first evening, I heard a woman behind me say, "I can always tell their ages by the backs of their necks." I turtled my head between my shoulders and dined from a slight crouch from then on. I was looking forward to an escape to the bar. It was the only bar between Sparks, a suburb of Reno, thirty miles south, and Gerlach, ninety miles to the north. The bar, however, presented unanticipated difficulties of its own. I have never been reluctant to buy a lady a drink, but there were thirty-eight ladies in residence at the ranch, and this offered a problem in economics.[3]

Accommodations and Rates. The ranch cabins could accommodate sixty guests. Rates in 1936 ranged from $33 to $46 per week per person and included room, meals, and daily transportation to Reno for shopping or appointments. Experienced residence witness was included.

Final Years

In 1956, the Drackert lease at Pyramid Lake Ranch expired. In 1957, Harry Drackert circulated a Prospectus to a select list of investors soliciting funds to buy the ranch. The Prospectus read in part:

PRESENT OPPORTUNITY
HIGHLY FLEETING

Because of certain privileged opportunities which I enjoy, I can arrange the purchase of Pyramid Lake Ranch with immediate possession, but this situation cannot last; other operators have their eye on the area and immediate options should be obtained pending an accurate appraisal.

Harry was unable to generate sufficient funds to purchase the ranch, so he executed a lease for the Donner Trail Ranch property in 1959.[4] (See "Donner Trail Ranch" for the continuing guest ranch saga of Harry and Joan Drackert.)

Clockwise from top right: Pyramid Lake as seen from the north shore; dudes in the recreation room; divorcées relaxing in the living room; right to left: A. J. Liebling and Lucille Spectorsky being congratulated by Lucius Beebe, Chuck Clegg and Katie Hillyer following their wedding at the old Nevada Brewery in Six Mile Canyon; the bar at Pyramid Lake Ranch—the only one between Sparks, thirty miles south, and Gerlach, ninety miles north. (Photo of A. J. Liebling wedding courtesy of Peter Kraemer; other photos from the Drackert Collection, Courtesy of Special Collections Department, University of Nevada, Reno Library)

"The bar (at the Pyramid Lake Ranch), however, presented unanticipated difficulties of its own. I have never been reluctant to buy a lady a drink, but there were thirty-eight ladies in residence at the ranch, and this offered a problem in economics." —*A. J. Liebling* (Drackert Collection, Courtesy of Special Collections Department, University of Nevada, Reno Library)

G. Donner Trail Ranch

Thank you again for the wonderful divorce!

The Donner Trail Ranch was the last of the luxury dude ranches in northern Nevada. It was named in honor of the Donner Party, pioneers who met their tragic end stranded in a Sierra snowstorm more than one hundred and fifty years ago.

History

The main ranch building dated back to the Civil War era, when it was known as the Merrill Ranch (or Inn) and served as a tavern and hotel for stagecoach passengers.

In 1945, the ranch came under the ownership of John "Jack" Fugitt. He moved the spacious ranch building back from the Truckee River bank, remodeled and expanded it, and developed it into an exclusive guest ranch.

In 1956, Fugitt sold the Donner Trail Ranch to a group of promoters who re-named it the Truckee River Country Club.

Donner Trail Ranch, dude and wrangler (Drackert Collection, Courtesy of Special Collections Department, University of Nevada, Reno Library)

Drackert Years, 1959-1970

In 1959, having lost their lease at the Pyramid Lake Ranch, Harry and Joan Drackert leased the Truckee River Country Club from the Baxter Realty Company of Los Angeles and New York, and changed its name back to the Donner Trail Ranch. The Drackerts would successfully operate the Donner Trail from 1959-1970.

To Harry Drackert, the divorce trade was a cash crop in the summertime. As he had at Pyramid Lake, he raised horses at Donner Trail for racing and for use by the guests. Joan was the ranch hostess. By the 1960s, the 3,000-acre ranch was the biggest and only working divorce ranch remaining in northern Nevada.

Location. The Donner Trail Ranch was ten miles west of Reno on the Truckee River in the Sierra foothills. It was just outside the small town of Verdi (Nevadans pronounce it "Verd-eye").

Robert Wernick aptly described the Donner Trail Ranch in "The Last of the Divorce Ranches":

The Donner Trail Ranch looks just like a dozen other ranches in this corner of Nevada —the usual sprawling frame building and red-roofed barn, the usual horses at pasture, sagebrush hills leading up to pine-covered mountains, empty blue sky....The ride out to the ranch, that first taste of the open Nevada air, is always a little disconcerting. Sierra pines, the muted, silvery grays and greens of the sagebrush—it all looks drab and stark and hostile to someone raised in the East. Even the animals are different: A magpie eviscerating a runover jackrabbit flies off with a harsh screak {*sic*} as the car passes.[1]

Activities and Attractions. The Drackerts offered their guests a gracious introduction to "the West," with opportunities for horseback riding, hiking, pack trips into the Sierras, hunting, skiing, excursions to Pyramid Lake, Lake Tahoe, and Reno—or simply quiet rest and reflection, as some guests preferred.

Donner Trail Ranch

Above, Old Merrill Ranch and Hotel buildings near Verdi, circa 1900. The main building formed a portion of the Donner Trail Ranch; left and below, Donner Trail Ranch, summer and winter scenes.

(Drackert Collection, Courtesy of Special Collections Department, University of Nevada, Reno Library)

Actor Gary Cooper (right) and Harry Drackert graduated a year apart from Gallitan County High School in Pony, Montana. They remained lifelong friends. When Drackert came to Hollywood in the 1930s, Cooper recommended him for a job on the Lashie Ranch (now Griffith Park), where Drackert met many movie people. Although Drackert didn't become a star, he did work as a wrangler for many Western movie productions.

Other photos: Donner Trail dudes enjoying the great outdoors around Verdi.

Inside at the Donner Trail

Clockwise from top left: Joan Drackert, a former Powers model, wore Western and Indian garb with style; Joan by the Christmas tree; the main ranch house decorated for Christmas; a guest room with a view; another view of the ranch living room.

(Drackert Collection, Courtesy of Special Collections Department, University of Nevada, Reno Library)

Harry Drackert described a typical evening at the ranch: "Joan, who manages the 'inside' part of the ranch, keeps everyone occupied. As 7 p.m. approaches, guests file into the living room in preparation for dinner, and small talk takes command. Despite the sophistication of the guests, the evening activities are mostly prosaic—Scrabble, Monopoly, and bridge."

Guest Relations. The Donner Trail Ranch catered to a moneyed clientele who wanted privacy, status, and believed no Reno divorce was complete without spending days riding horseback and socializing with other prospective divorcés, while waiting to be "Reno-vated." Famous guests who appeared on the ranch register included Johnny "Tarzan" Weissmuller (five hours after getting his divorce from San Francisco socialite Beryel [*sic*] Scott, Weissmuller married blonde golf star Allene Gates), former Ziegfeld girl Dorothy Mackaill (who managed to be there during the big snowstorm of January '49), William M. Davey (the husband of silent screen star Gloria Swanson), socialite Dolly Fritz McMasters (later Mrs. Newton Cope), and Mrs. Nelson Rockefeller (the Mary Rockefeller-Governor Nelson Rockefeller divorce in 1962 was possibly Reno's last highly-publicized divorce case).

Harry Drackert described the routine most guests followed when they arrived at the ranch: "For a few days, they follow me around the ranch. After they get acquainted, I hardly ever see them."

Drackert added, "Most guests who come here for a divorce aren't the usual depressed types depicted in movies and television. The hard part is over. They've already decided to come to Nevada to get a divorce. Most get out and enjoy the area."

Single men from the local scene were often invited out to the ranch for dinner. Reno attorney Clel Georgetta:

I was invited to one of those splendid dinner parties at Donner Trail Ranch to add one more stranger to the crowd that would celebrate some- one's "graduation." These dinner parties are always a cross-section of the idle rich and this evening was no exception. I met a successful author, Mr. James Michener, who wrote "Tales of the South Pacific."

Shortly after arriving, there fastened onto me a dowager bedecked in jewels of many kinds and large sizes. Mrs. F. W., of New York, London, Paris, and almost any other place. She told me she received her divorce about a month ago but remained at Donner

Trail because she likes the place and finds life interest- ing in Reno. She had to buy her freedom from her last husband, "The Rat." Now she is looking for a man who will truly appreciate her for her charms, as well as her riches. As I looked at the hard lines in her face and the dyed hair that has been dipped many times, I thought, "Well, madam, it will have to be some other man than me." —*CG, Sunday, 15 August 1948* [2]

Accommodations and Rates. Rates at the Donner Trail ranged from $130 to $150 per week in 1970. The sprawling white house and annex had some twenty-two rooms for guests. The rooms were furnished in rather a Spartan style but had a splendid view of the mountains and an orchard. Each room had a bed, a table, a cup- board, a chest of drawers. The main ranch house was comfortable and had a great fireplace with Indian rugs on the floor and Indian arrowheads on the walls.

Ranch Staff and Services. Some eight men and women worked at the ranch at a variety of jobs ranging from cook to wrangler. Transportation into Reno was provid- ed for those on "essential" trips. Harry Drackert defined "essential" as the beauty parlor, the lawyer, the court house, and the airport. "If they wanted to go into town and play the slots, they had to find their own way," he was known to say.

Dude Wranglers and Horses. Drackert claimed to have "the best horses in the county at the Donner Trail Ranch, bar none." He ran about 60 head, including some 25 for guest riding. Occasionally guests would bring their own horse if it looked like it would be an extended stay.

Robert Wernick described the wranglers at the Donner Trail:

Chris is lean and rangy, and he drawls and lopes around. "That big black horse glares at me," an English guest tells him. "I think he hates me." "Oh, no, he don't," says Chris. "I had a long visit with him last night and he told me, 'I go for that Limey.'"....

Hugh Marchbanks is a little long in the teeth now, but he is still spry and graceful, and his pale- blue eyes are candid and mischievous. The wrinkles around the eyes come from all the staring into the sun after wild horses or spooked steers, but the creases in his neck come from turning to stare at pretty women for 40 years. "Hello, beautiful," he greets the new arrival. "I'm a dancer, a prancer and a gay romancer. I'm fifty-four now, but I can do anything I ever did, only not quite so often. Yes, I'm wild, my whole family was wild. Why they had to hobble my mother before she'd let me nurse." They know it's a line, but they love it.[3]

(As I write this, I can't help but wonder if these wranglers ever heard the story of my fiasco in 1947 with Jack Fugitt at the Donner Trail Ranch. The wranglers have me to thank for not having to milk six cows twice a day!)

Final Years

In 1970, the Drackerts' lease was abruptly terminated in mid-season, when the owners decided to subdivide the property. The main ranch building was demolished and most of the land sold and subdivided. The Drackerts sold their livestock, stored their furnishings, and moved into Reno.

During forty years of marriage, Harry and Joan Drackert successfully managed three dude ranches: Pyramid Lake Ranch (1946-56), Donner Trail Ranch (1959-70), and Silver Circle Ranch (1971-76). Joan also managed Indian Territory, a retail Indian crafts store in Reno that sold items made by Nevada Indians, especially members of the Pyramid Lake Paiute Tribe.

Joan's charm and skill as a hostess is reflected in the letters she received from appreciative guests and friends who were grateful for her moral support in turning an often painful experience into a restful vacation.

In addition to his horse breeding and racing interests, Harry was a director of the Reno Rodeo Association from its inception, and was president of the Association until 1968. He was also one of the first members of Reno's private Prospectors' Club.

Joan and Harry Drackert were among the last, if not the last, of the survivors of the dude-guest ranches in the Reno area that catered to the six-weekers. Changing attitudes about divorce and more liberal laws in other states gradually put an end to the dude ranches in Nevada.

Bill Berry, the widely known news reporter of splashy Reno divorce cases, lamented, "I can remember a day when fifteen or twenty ranches catered exclusively to divorcées. The name, Reno, used to have color and glamour as a divorce center. But...the glamour is gone." [4]

The Drackerts spent their retirement years as Reno suburbanites living in Huffaker Hills, and worrying about the encroaching new apartment buildings rising outside their development. Harry Drackert passed away on December 26, 1990, and Joan died the following year on October 2, 1991.

The success of the Drackerts, one of the most successful cowboy-dude relationships, may be best summed up in this line from a letter sent by a grateful guest, "Joan and Harry, Thank you *again* for the wonderful divorce!"[5]

H. Washoe Pines Ranch

Serving Time at The Pines

At first glance, little has changed at Washoe Pines since its heyday as a guest ranch in the 1940s and 1950s. The main ranch house, a large log cabin where cowboy artist and author Will James lived and worked in the 1920s, is virtually unchanged, as are several of the guest log cabins nestled amongst the rustling pines. Nevada divorce historian Mella Rothwell Harmon surmises, "Add to this rustic setting a handsome wrangler and you can imagine what effect Washoe Pines would have on a housewife from Schenectady."

History

The Washoe Pines has had a long and colorful succession of owners:

🐾 August 20, 1914, Charles A. Stout bought the property from the sheriff, who had attached it for debts. [1]

🐾 May 1915, Stout sold it to  Dan C. Wheeler, who had a half-interest in the Myron C. Lake ranch near Reno in 1876, and raised cattle and sheep.[2] Wheeler died October 14, 1915, and his wife, Amelia, took over as president of the Wheeler Corporation.

🐾 January 24, 1923, Mrs. Wheeler conveyed nineteen acres of land in the pines along the edge of the hills to cowboy author and artist, Will James, and his wife, Alice.[3]

🐾 January 26, 1925, Will and Alice James sold the property to Ralph and Florence Elsman.[4] The James' moved to Montana, where Will purchased the Rocking R Ranch fifty miles south of Billings in the Pryor Mountains.[5]

🐾 September 13, 1935, Ralph Elsman and wife sold

Washoe Pines log cabin ranch house, built for cowboy artist and author Will James in the 1920s
(Authors' Collection)

the ranch to Enid C. Blackmer, a single woman.[6] Ms. Blackmer was listed as the Washoe Pines manager in the 1936 Nevada Dude Ranch Association brochure.

🐾 April 3, 1939, Enid C. Blackmer Van Law sold the ranch to Deborah Hull, a single woman. Enid and Carlos Van Law went to live in Bolivia.[7]

🐾 March 14, 1946, Deborah Hull Foster and Ken G. Foster sold the ranch to Walter H. Barner, President, and Drucilla Mason Barner, Secretary, Washoe Pines, Inc., a Nevada corporation.[8]

🐾 August 7, 1950, Charlotte White acquired all of the stock in Washoe Pines, Inc., in a liquidation sale. In 1954, Charlotte White hired Betty and Lyle Hardin, newlyweds, to run the ranch.[9]

🐾 August 2, 1955, Charlotte White sold the ranch to Elizabeth Silverthorne Hardin, wife of Washoe Pines wrangler Lyle Hardin. They were the last owners to run dudes at the Washoe Pines Guest Ranch.[10]

🐾 September 27, 1961, Elizabeth Silverthorne De La Montanya, formerly Elizabeth Silverthorne Hardin and formerly Elizabeth S. Cathles, and now a single woman, sold the property to Dr. Richard G. and Maya Miller.[11] The Millers first came to Nevada in 1941. After World War II, Dr. Miller was the director of the Nevada State Museum in Carson City (1946 and 1947). The Millers used a large portion of their Washoe Pines property to establish the Foresta Institute, a summer camp for the study of ecology.

Cowboy-lean, Clark Gable-handsome, Will and his classically lovely wife, Alice, turned heads wherever they went. Below right: Alice James cut a natty figure in cowgirl garb, circa 1930s; below center and left: Though Will James gave up bronc-busting for brush and pencil, his memories of the cowboy life kept his drawings action-packed. (Courtesy Will James Art Company)

Will James, Washoe Pines' Most Famous Resident

Cowboy artist and author Will James may well be the Washoe Pines' most famous resident. In 1914, James served one year in the Nevada State Prison on charges of cattle theft (rustling). (Stealing cattle was a hanging offense in some states in the Old West, although not everyone in Nevada thought it should be. H. M. Yerington, who was long active in Nevada political affairs, wrote to a friend, "Being a cattle thief don't disqualify a man for anything political he may want in this state. Really, from instances I have known…it adds to a man's standing in the community.") While serving his time, James made a composite sketch illustrating his resolve to turn over a new leaf.

Following his parole from prison, Will and his wife, Alice, settled in the Washoe Valley, on nineteen acres of land that would become the Washoe Pines Ranch. They built a small log and stone cabin in the hillside of their property. Then Alice's family reportedly built the couple a large and comfortable log cabin (which would later be used as the main ranch house for the Washoe Pines Guest Ranch).

The small log cabin in the hillside became Will James' studio and gave him an environment which nurtured his writing and drawing talent. In this peaceful and private retreat, the author-illustrator wrote two of his best-known books, *Cowboys North and South* and *Smoky, The Cowhorse*, and sketched some of his finest action illustrations.

His resolve to turn over a new leaf came true. Just twelve years after being released from prison, Will James was famous internationally as a cowboy artist and author.

Although the couple lived only a few years on their Washoe Pines property, these years turned out to be their happiest. Fame and fortune brought their share of unhappiness, and the couple drifted apart. The talented Will James died in 1942 at the age of fifty.

Alice James would marry Johnny Ross, and together they would build the Christmas Tree, a successful mountain eatery on the Mount Rose Highway.

The original sketch made by Will James in prison is preserved in the Special Collections Department of the University of Nevada, Reno Library. Will James' name is inscribed in the Nevada Writers' Hall of Fame in Reno, and the Will James Society is dedicated to preserving the memory and works of Will James.

Serving Time at The Pines

Location. The Washoe Pines Guest Ranch, popularly known as "The Pines," is located in Washoe Valley, twenty-two miles south of Reno, at the foot of the Sierras.

Activities. Horseback riding, swimming, fishing, hunting, pack trips, picnics, barbecues, and all winter sports, in season. There were also trips to Virginia City, Pyramid Lake and Lake Tahoe.

Guests. Washoe Pines was a rustic and secluded retreat for divorcés doing their "six-week time." The Pines reportedly attracted a somewhat younger crowd, but society came to the Pines, too, as did Hollywood's Myrna Loy and Gypsy Rose Lee.

An old plaque in the log cabin lodge recites the words to a song by soon-to-be divorcées (to the tune of "O Tannenbaum"). The first verse goes like this:

> *O Washoe Pines, O Washoe Pines*
> *We are so glad to leave you.*
> *You are indeed a marvelous jail*
> *But one cannot make love by mail.*
> *O Washoe Pines, O Washoe Pines*
> *We are so glad to leave you.*

Accommodations and Rates. The main ranch house (the former home of Will and Alice James) was a large log cabin with a living room, dining room, bar, kitchen, and ranch office. The interior walls were covered with knotty pine, and the ceilings were low, with heavy wood beams. The living room featured a large stone fireplace with "W P" prominently displayed on the wrought iron fire screen. Conversations usually centered on the pine coffee table with the ranch brand, "W P", carved in the middle and surrounded by a circle broken in half—symbolizing a wedding ring broken in two.

Scattered about the shady grounds were a dozen or more comfortable log cabins for guests, most with private baths. The outdoor setting included pastures and stables for the horses, as well as a large swimming pool, reported to be the first in Nevada, and a wishing well.

The one and two room guest cabins had names like "Washoe" and "Paiute." Knotty pine walls, low ceilings, and small and very basic bathrooms may have come as a surprise to Park Avenue socialites, but great views of Washoe Lake, the sound of wind rushing through the giant pine trees, and cocktails enjoyed before a warm fire at night certainly made their six-week sojourn an adventure.

Rates ranged from $50 to $75 per week in 1936, depending on the accommodations desired. This included a horse and all meals. The ranch was small, and references were required in order to keep groups as congenial as possible.[12]

THE WOMEN

"Whither, oh, whither shall I fly?"
"To the arms of that cowboy up at the dude ranch?"
–Countess de Lage to Miriam, *The Women*

In 1929, when Clare Boothe came to Reno to get a divorce from husband George Tuttle Brokaw, the residency requirement was three months. Boothe was staying at the Riverside Hotel in town, but she had ample time to visit friends and relax at Washoe Pines. As the story goes, Boothe particularly noted the Pines' rustic setting as well as the "chattering females."

Clare sensed she was destined for something more than being a Fifth Avenue matron. Upon returning to New York, her professional career as a writer and editor took off at *Vogue* and *Vanity Fair*. In 1935, she married Henry R. Luce, world renowned Time-Life publisher.

In 1936, Boothe's play, *The Women*, opened on Broadway. A satire on the idleness of Park Avenue wealthy wives and divorcées, the play included a scene in Act II which took place in "a Reno hotel room." When the play was adapted for the big screen in 1939, the Reno hotel room became "a dude ranch outside of Reno." Washoe Pines, with its rustic setting, log cabins and "chattering females," was believed to be the inspiration for this classic scene in the film version

Cowboy-Dude Relationships

In the late 1940s, when this writer was the dude wrangler at the neighboring Flying M E, Lyle Hardin was the wrangler at the Washoe Pines. Lyle had worked for previous Pines owners, Walt and Drucilla Barner and Charlotte White, before teaming up with Elizabeth "Betty" Silverthorne as the cowboy-dude operators of the ranch in the 1950s.

Like socialite Charlotte White before her, Betty Silverthorne came to the Pines to get a divorce. Betty liked Nevada so much she wanted to stay, so she proceeded to buy the Pines ranch from Charlotte White.

Lyle met Betty when she was "serving time at the Pines."

Lyle and I became good friends. He was a good hand with a horse, and we used to join forces on occasion for the ride up to Little Valley.

Journalist Robert Wernick on cowboy-dude relationships:

For almost half a century now, the divorcées and cowboys have been intermingling. You never know, meeting a leathery old codger in a Reno bar, whether he will tell you a tale of a blizzard he was caught in once that froze his legs off, or rather a tale about this girl, a real cute one, and they were saying good-bye at the station and 'a-kissin' and 'a-sobbin', and the train pulled out, and by gosh he was still holding her mink coat, and he didn't know if she had left it to him as a souvenir or if she'd send the cops after him if he kept it. What would you do, pardner?

To women just breaking loose from the sad and sissified husbands so prevalent today in the East, meeting lanky, Gary Cooperish men engaged in the Neolithic occupation of herding animals may be overwhelming. It is easy to flirt with them, flirtations often lead to love affairs, and on occasion a love affair leads to a marriage. Here, however, the cultural gap is apt to prove too wide for bridging. You cannot transplant a cowboy to Park Avenue; he will trip over the furniture, he will sulk and shrivel in the confining city.

The number of such marriages that succeed can be counted on the fingers of one hand. There was one that made page one of the tabloids a dozen years or so ago, and to the amazement of all seemed to thrive year after year. Between the wife's money and the husband's unfailing good humor they lived happily. But the wife found a new outlet for her feelings in the campaign of Barry Goldwater, the cowboy developed ulcers, and soon he was back in Reno, charming the young female blackjack dealers with the old blarneying cowboy charm: "I traded in my forty-year-old wife for two twenty-year-old girls. But then I found out I wasn't wired for 220."[13]

Sad to say, Betty and Lyle's relationship didn't last either, and they split blankets after a few years. Lyle stayed on at the Pines working for the Millers in the early '60s, and then moved up to Virginia City to pursue his interest in painting. His obituary read simply: "Lyle Hardin was born September 8, 1911 in Frankclay,

*Washoe Pines wrangler
Lyle Hardin, left,
and cowboy friend*

Washoe Pines silver charm

Washoe Pines, picnic tables

Washoe Pines trail ride

*Washoe Pines pool and wishing well. The Pines
attracted divorcées with small children because of the
individual cabin accommodations.*

*Washoe Pines guest Patricia Cramer, center, and Lyle Hardin, right,
taking a break at a nearby Washoe Valley ruin.*

(Photos and charm, courtesy of Patricia Cramer)

This detail of the pine coffee table in the living room of the main ranch house featured a carved "WP" surrounded by a broken circle, symbolic of a busted marriage. (Authors' Collection)

Missouri and moved to Nevada in 1940. He lived on cattle ranches in New Mexico, Oregon, Nebraska and Nevada. He was an Army veteran of World War II, a cowboy and an artist. A resident of Dayton since 1974, he died Saturday, September 13, 1980 in a Reno hospital at the age of 69. Burial took place in Ironton, Missouri."14

Postscript

In 1961, Dr. Richard and Maya Miller purchased The Pines and turned it into a private residence. As onetime U.S. Senate candidate Maya Miller said, "I wasn't equipped to take care of all those women!" Part of the property houses the Foresta Institute, a summer camp founded by the Millers for the study of ecology.

A Reno journalist writing about divorce ranches in the "good old days," summed up the status of Washoe Pines with these words:

Today, the Washoe Pines is a quiet family homestead, with a small Christmas tree farm just below the

lodge and several of the old cabins rented out year-round. Groups can also rent the lodge for workshops, weddings and other functions.

But the ranch isn't the nest of "chattering ladies" (as the old song says) that it used to be. The old swimming pool is now empty, a picturesque well is overgrown, and many of the cabins are no longer used.15

However, the memory of the Pines' most famous resident, Will James, lives on. Collectors of Western art seek out his drawings, and children still love reading *Smoky, The Cowhorse.* The Will James Society was formed in 1992 and is dedicated to preserving the memory and works of Will James. The Society holds annual gatherings to celebrate the cowboy artist and author's life and works, and is one of the primary catalysts behind a growing interest in Will James, his work, his life, and his heritage as a working cowboy. (For more information, contact: Will James Society, P.O. Box 20382, Billings, Montana 59104.)

Dr. Richard Miller, a Will James fan, reminisced, "I still have a sheaf of drawings I made on book pages at school when I was growing up—waiting for each new Will James book."

I. More Nevada Dude-Divorce Ranches

Northern Nevada

In addition to the five leading northern Nevada dude-divorce ranches featured in previous sections, thirteen more are profiled in this section in alphabetical order.

Many of the smaller, so-called dude ranches on the outskirts of Reno, especially those that operated in the 1930s and 1940s, more closely resembled a boarding house than the genuine rural setting of an authentic Nevada divorce ranch. However, if they qualified for membership and appeared in the 1936 Nevada Dude Ranch Association (NDRA) brochure, they're included here. Many of these operations were swallowed up by the city's urban sprawl of the 1950s and '60s.

Following the thirteen profiles is a list of other Nevada dude-divorce ranch "possibles."

By the 1960s, Las Vegas was receiving the lion's share of the divorce business, and the divorce or dude ranches around Reno were beginning to close. The last of these, the Silver Circle and Whitney ranches, shut down in the 1970s.

The following profiles are based in part on information from the 1936 Nevada Dude Ranch Association brochure and Basil Woon's *None of the Comforts of Home, But Oh Those Cowboys.*

An asterisk (*) after the ranch name indicates membership in the 1936 NDRA.

YOU WILL FIND
RECREATION, REJUVENATION and
RENO-VATION at the...

Palomino Ranch

Reno's Finest Guest Ranch
2½ Miles South On Virginia Rd.
OPEN THE YEAR ROUND
Air Conditioned
RIDING HORSES — COMPLETE RANCH ACTIVITIES — SUN PATIO
MEALS SERVED RANCH STYLE
ADJACENT TO MINERAL POOL & GOLF COURSE
Mailing Address: In the Heart of the Skiing, Hunting & Fishing Country   Phone Reno
MARIE & MILTON STEARNS   TRANSPORTATION SERVICE
RENO, NEVADA   **8789**

Big Canyon Ranch
North Washoe County, at the north end of Pyramid Lake, about six miles up the canyon.

Big Canyon Ranch began as a combination cattle-dude ranch, and evolved into a straight dude ranch as ownership changed hands. Hiram "Hi" West, the brother of Neill Hakes West of the TH Ranch in Sutcliffe, married Mae Barnum, heiress to the Barnum & Bailey fortune, and bought the Big Canyon Ranch in the late 1920s. Hiram West then sold Big Canyon to Beverly and Francesca Blackmer, who ran it as a dude ranch from about 1934 to 1938. The ranch house burned down and was rebuilt by the Blackmers into a mansion that looked like it might have been imported from Narragansett. The Blackmers sold Big Canyon to a gentleman from New York named Kennedy who, it was said, was convinced Hitler was going to win the war and wanted to get as far away as possible from the Eastern seaboard when the Fuehrer landed. Kennedy leased Big Canyon to cattleman Joe Capurro, and later sold it to Harry Richman, the nightclub owner and singer famed in Prohibition days. Richman had lost his voice in the East and, loving an active life in the open air, moved to Nevada where, after several years, his voice came back. Richman used to walk into the Riverside Hotel in Reno dressed in the role of a gentleman rancher. The Riverside's owner, Lou Wertheimer, said that when Richman was in town he arranged to be paged on the loud speaker every hour. Richman denied this.

Activities include riding, roundups, fishing, hunting trips in season, swimming, hiking, ranch parties, and horseback picnics.

No information on accommodations or rates was available as of this writing.

Hi West was buried on top of Tule Mountain. A number of stalwarts of the region held a service on the peak, and Johnnie Matley, the rancher, who owned a resonant tenor voice, sang the *Requiem*. A brass plate was placed in a boulder to mark the spot where Hi was buried, but it has since disappeared.

Mae Barnum raised Belgian police dogs. When she died she left instructions in her will that they were to be turned loose on the mountain. This was done and, according to local belief, the dogs proved animal experts wrong and mated with the coyotes, which on Tule Mountain are notably larger and darker in color than other coyotes in Nevada.

Dead Man's Ranch *
Located in a canyon 22 miles south of Reno

Bud and Lois McPherson, a cowboy-dude team, reportedly started this dude operation. Louise W. Exton was the owner-manager in 1936.

Dead Man's Ranch was a small ranch which took only a limited number of guests. Activities included riding, swimming, pack trips, and complete relaxation. A flat rate of $45 per week included room and board, and use of saddle horses. The ranch was open year round and references were required.

Flying N Ranch *
5 miles southwest of Reno
at the foot of the Sierra mountains

The Flying N Ranch was one of the oldest stock ranches in the valley, with several hundred acres of rolling pastureland. In 1936, the ranch was run as a cattle ranch catering to dudes by Buck Nielsen and his wife.

Activities included riding well-broken horses, picnics, sightseeing trips, and rodeos. The nearby Sierra mountain range offered good hunting and fishing.

Limited to six guests, accommodations were newly equipped and had been completely modernized by 1936, with electric lights, telephones, bathrooms, and an adequate hot water supply.

The rate was $40 per week and included room, meals, use of horses and transportation. The ranch was open year round.

Lazy A Guest Ranch
Southwest Washoe County, at the foot of Mount Rose, about ten miles from Reno, off the scenic Mt. Rose Highway at 14403 So. Virginia Street

Al Peigh, who developed, bought and sold many Nevada ranch properties before World War II, built the Lazy A dude ranch in the 1920s. Peigh later sold the Lazy A to Mr. and Mrs. B. J. Winne, an old Nevada family. "Bert" Winne and her son Lee ran the operation.

Activities included riding, swimming and sunbathing, ranch parties, hiking, horseback picnics, cards, scrabble, and checkers. In winter, many guests took advantage of the excellent skiing at the nearby Sierra resorts.

While the ranch had many group activities, a guest could enjoy complete privacy, one of the features that helped make guest ranches popular. Mrs. Winne believed that while many divorcés came with the idea of being left alone, usually after a week they became more relaxed and joined in with the rest of the guests. Comradeship and participation in various activities usually helped to take their minds off their problems.

Mrs. Winne told the story of a rich heiress who arrived at the Lazy A with three automobiles, a trailer, two black servants, a chauffeur and his son, a handy man, a small baby, a nurse, a girlfriend who was expecting, and two horses of her own. Upon leaving the ranch, she hired a whole boxcar to ship the horses back east, along with a ton of Nevada oats. "They're used to Nevada oats," she explained. "I want them to have what they've become used to."

Accommodations were a small attractive main ranch house with six cabins, plus a stable with good riding stock. Rates averaged $100 per week in 1962.[1]

Lazy Me Ranch
In Washoe County, south of Reno

Caleb Whitbeck built the Lazy Me, in partnership with Cornelius Vanderbilt Jr. in the 1920s, about the time Al Peigh was building the Lazy A. In his book, *Ranches and Ranch Life in America*, Cornelius Vanderbilt Jr. described the Lazy Me operation:

Lazy Me, circa 1930s (Courtesy of Nevada Historical Society)

I had my Lazy Me spread just south of Reno. I dressed it up in typical public relations fashion. Our competitors were many, and they advertised all over the country. But I advertised in only two publications—*Town Topics* in New York and *The Beverly Hills Script*, both catering to snob appeal.

In those days, cross-country flying was just beginning to be known. I was in Reno when young Lindbergh arrived on a barnstorming tour some weeks after his successful Atlantic solo flight. Even in Reno he was looked upon as something of a freak—this young "lone eagle," as he was then called.

When Amelia Earhart visited Reno, we offered her accommodations at the Lazy Me, where she stayed during her visit. Her stay, incidentally, brought us great acclaim also. So I decided to invite some of my Hollywood friends, such as Douglas Fairbanks Sr., Charlie Chaplin, Will Rogers, Tom Mix, Gary Cooper, and Clark Gable, to visit us. We gave them free accommodations for one week, and we put on our own rodeos which they attended and at which many of them performed.

We used to dress up a couple of wranglers in ten-gallon hats and put them on the box of the Rolls-Royce and Packard town cars we bought each year at the sale of old White House cars used yearly by Presidents of the United States in Washington, D.C. We had these cars meet the trains every day at the Southern Pacific Railroad Station, and later, when people began to fly in the old eight- and ten-passenger planes, they met them at the old airport. The other dude ranches in the neighborhood soon followed suit. The Monte Cristo went us one better and drew up in an old stagecoach in front of the Pullman entrance of the Southern Pacific depot. In this way, we both secured a goodly share of the dude ranch trade.

When the above marketing program began to peter out, Vanderbilt devised a new plan which became known as the "Package Ranch Divorce":

For $795, we gave anyone who came to the Lazy Me Guest Ranch six weeks room and board, a horse to ride,

Monte Cristo Ranch, circa 1927
(Courtesy of Nevada Historical Society)

Monte Cristo Dude Ranch. Left to right: Ike Blundell, Phyllis Blundell and Bud Blundell. Bud and Phyllis, a cowboy-dude marriage, turned the Monte Cristo into a dude ranch in 1930. (Photo from a Christmas card.)
(Courtesy of Nevada Historical Society)

Monte Cristo Dude Ranch in its first year as a dude ranch, circa 1930. Left to right, Bud Blundell and Lige Langston shoeing horses.
(Courtesy of Nevada Historical Society)

a trip to Reno twice a week in our station wagon, a free package of cigarettes per diem, and a free bottle of any liquor they asked for once a week.

This plan was immediately publicized in the newspapers and we were flooded with reservation requests from all over the country. So popular became the Lazy Me Ranch that we were forced to build twenty double tent cottages, enlarge our main house, and build much larger dining-room and kitchen facilities.

This gave us accommodations for about fifty to sixty guests and our income, of course, shot up commensurately. Also, we were doing a land-office business with the lawyers of own choice, providing the guests had "open-and-shut" cases and did not require further legal services. Other dude ranchers became very jealous of our success, and a hue and cry arose, so much so that the Bar Association in Reno forced us to withdraw our plan. But

we had already received worldwide publicity. At the height of our popularity we had as many as seventy-six guests for every three-month period.

Vanderbilt chronicled the sad end to his successful dude ranch operation in these words:

What happened to the Lazy Me is now a part of the history of dude ranching in the West. One day my ranch foreman came to tell me that our water supply from one of the ponds we used above the ranch in the high Sierras was mighty near exhaustion. He figured at best, unless we received some rain, we could not last much more than ninety days. Meanwhile I had signed a contract to go to Europe on a series of newspaper interviews. While I was over there, I received a cable from my Reno attorney advising me he had received a phenomenal offer for the ranch and all its property. We took it, and that was the end of my Lazy Me guest ranch operation.[2]

Monte Cristo Ranch *

North Washoe County, overlooking Pyramid Lake, 6 miles off the old Sutcliffe-Reno stage road, and about 34 miles from Reno

The Monte Cristo had been a real Western cattle ranch since 1899, and was known as the old Blundell Ranch on Rodeo Creek. Brothers "Bud" (Ivan) and "Ike" (Ira) Blundell had been running a small cow out-fit since the death of their father. In 1930, Bud and Phyllis Blundell, a successful cowboy-dude marriage combination, built the usual row of small unconnected cabins that were the trademark of the early dude ranch-es. They filled the old ranch house with leather furni-ture, and made money with their operation. The view from the ranch overlooked the magnificent Pyramid Lake-Sand Desert spread. (Bud and Phyllis were later divorced.) Subsequent owners-managers were Edith Warfield McCormack and, in 1936, Lois Thomas Reiners.

Activities included pack trips through the moun-tainous ranges at 5,800 feet above sea level, plus riding, roping, round ups, fishing, swimming, and sightseeing trips to nearby places.

When Theodore and Emily Wood arrived in Nevada in the 1930s, they stayed at the Monte Cristo Ranch. The Monte Cristo was a genuine dude ranch then, catering chiefly to "six-weekers" taking advantage of Nevada's recently-enacted six weeks divorce law. It was also a real working ranch, with cows and cowboys, and the dudes were expected to help in ranch chores. Accommodations were on the Spartan side: "chuck," to be charitable, was filling; the nightly thrill was a thirty-four-mile ride into Reno, where gambling had just been made legal.

The ranch had a number of wranglers over the years, including Gardner Sheehan, "Maverick" and Jimmy Murray, the latter an ex-jockey who would become the first wrangler for Theodore and Emmy Wood's Tumbling DW ranch in Washoe Valley.

The Monte Cristo had a couple of historic relics on the property. One of the original stakes of the Indian reservation formed a cornerstone for the ranch. There were a number of ore wagons around the ranch, report-edly used in a clandestine mine which was supplying sil-ver to the South during the Civil War.

Rates for cabins or ranch house rooms were $35-$50 per week in 1936. Everything was included.

Mount Rose Lodge *

On the eastern slope of majestic Mt. Rose in the High Sierras, eight miles south of Reno, then west on the beauti-ful Mt. Rose Highway for another twelve miles

The Mount Rose Lodge was a popular dude ranch built by Lemar Washington and managed by Joe Schlederer and his wife. The ranch was later remodeled by new owner John S. Sinai, a prominent Reno attorney, and then leased to John ("Jack") and Helen Morrow. Still later, the Lodge became a restaurant and bar run by Walt and Nell Daly.

Activities included riding, pack trips, target practice, stream trout fishing, seasonal deer and game bird hunt-ing. The ranch was within easy access to golf, tennis, swimming, and skiing (in season).

Situated in the pines, the ranch was lovely and cool all summer. It was ideal for both vacationers and those wishing to establish residence in Nevada at a ranch maintaining an atmosphere of the Old West.

Accommodations consisted of a main house, cot-tages and cabins. There were telephones, electric lights, bathrooms with hot and cold running water, and health-ful, well-balanced meals.

Rates in 1936 were $30-$40 per week and included room, meals, saddle horse, regular trips to Reno, and one sightseeing trip weekly to interesting points around Nevada.

Olds Ranch *

North Washoe County, 32 miles north of Reno

"Ma" Olds, with a husband crippled in a Virginia City mine disaster and three children to raise, filed on the ranch in 1909, then built a house. The ranch was reportedly sold to a dude named Marion Dennett some-time during the 1920s. Ma had three girls and a boy. Edson B. Olds, Ma's son, bought the ranch back from Dennett in 1932 and ran it as a combination cattle-dude ranch until 1937.

Activities included gathering cattle, pack trips, swimming, and car trips to interesting places about the area.

Accommodations were in an attractive and com-fortable ranch house, and were limited to about six guests. Rates in 1936 were $50 per week for two in a double room; $30 per week single. Rates included room, board and a saddle horse. The ranch was open year round.

At an elevation of 5,000 feet, the climate was cool in summer. There were beautiful views of Tule Peak rising in the north at 8,722 feet.

According to Ma Olds, they raised "cows, horses, turkeys, chickens, sheep, goats, children, and dudes." About once a month during her tenure, they would journey to Reno in the combination buggy-cart she had fashioned to take her produce to market.

On the marketing trips to Reno, before she acquired a second-hand Model T, Ma would stay the night at Twenty Mile, which was a stage stop almost at the junction of the county road with the highway. The Twenty Mile stop, like all stage stops in those days, harbored a couple of girls upstairs. "I got plenty of gossip every time I stopped at Twenty Mile," said Ma.

In a conversation with Basil Woon many years later, Ma elaborated on conditions between 1909 to 1925:

> It was a bit far to take the children to school— it took two days to get to Reno in the buggy—so I applied to the State to let me start a school at the ranch. They said we had to have seven children— that was the law. Well, I looked around and found three other kids living on ranches down the valley, but we were still one child short. So I looked my husband straight in the eye—and told him what was needed!

A short time later, Ma Olds was teaching school at the ranch.

Among those who stayed at the Olds Ranch when Edson ran it were Mr. and Mrs. Alfred E. Brush, who became owners of the well-known Brush Ranch in Carson City. They had met previously when both were dudes at the Monte Cristo Ranch.

Olinghouse Dude Ranch *
38 miles northeast of Reno on U.S. 40 (later U.S. 80), several miles off the highway, near Wadsworth

In 1936, the owner was Mrs. Margaret L. Marsh.

Activities included riding, fishing in Truckee River or Pyramid Lake, swimming in the lake or nearby hot pools, beautiful walks and hikes, and Western rodeos once a week. Elevation 6,000 feet.

Accommodations were for 18-20 guests and consisted of a main ranch house of six rooms with baths,

and six double cabins with outside warm showers and toilets.

Rates in 1936 were $25-$30 per week and included room, board and saddle horse. Open year round.

Quail Canyon Ranch
North Washoe County, on the old Pyramid Lake highway near the Indian Reservation gate, and about 34 miles from Reno

Quail Canyon Ranch, formerly known as the Benoist Ranch, was a combination cattle-dude ranch. Two of the better-known entrepreneurs-owners were women. Edith Warfield McCormack, reportedly a cousin of the Warfield who married the Duke of Windsor, bought the ranch and moved it up the canyon, where she operated it as a dude ranch until it burned down. Then she took over the management of the Monte Cristo Ranch, seven miles further up the canyon. Mrs. Adine Haviland Stix bought the Quail Canyon and rebuilt the burned-out ranch house.

Activities included riding, roundups, pack trips, and sightseeing car trips to interesting nearby places.

Accommodations were for 6-8 guests. In 1936, rates for room and board, plus a saddle horse, were $30-$50 per week.

In 1956, playwright Arthur Miller visited Quail Canyon Ranch. Miller was staying at the Pyramid Lake Ranch for a divorce. At Quail Canyon Ranch, he met a young woman who had come from the East to get a divorce, as well as two cowboys, who inspired his story of *The Misfits*. In 1960, Mrs. Adine Haviland Stix rented the ranch to the film company shooting *The Misfits* for scenes at Guido's ranch.

Silver Circle Guest Ranch
About 6 miles south of central Reno on Holcomb Lane

In 1971, after losing their lease on the Donner Trail Ranch, neither Harry nor Joan Drackert were ready to retire. They heard the Silver Circle was for sale, and bid on it. They didn't expect to get the ranch, but did, and found themselves in business again, with the Cal-Neva's Warren Nelson and his wife. (See Appendix sections on Pyramid Lake Ranch and Donner Trail Ranch).

The Drackerts emphasized things to do in the Reno area. Many guests skied, rode horses, fished, and enjoyed the desert and Lake Tahoe. In the summer, there was swimming in the ranch pool.

The Silver Circle was a working ranch, in addition

to providing room and board in a home-like atmosphere for their guests. References were exchanged, and walk-ins were not accepted. The number of guests was limited to about 20. The Drackerts used mailing lists and referrals from several Washington, D.C. and New York lawyers for attracting guests. They also enjoyed a fair amount of repeat business.

In 1974, the Drackerts established the Indian Territory store at 130 N. Virginia Street, where they sold quality Indian jewelry, baskets, pottery, and Navajo rugs.

In 1976, the Drackerts sold the Silver Circle Guest Ranch and continued to operate the Indian Territory store until 1986, when they finally retired.

In the early 1970s, rates were competitive with Reno's best hotels.[3]

Stevenson Ranch *

15 miles southeast of Reno, off SR 341, the Comstock Highway to historic Virginia City

W. H. Stevenson and Janet Harlan Stevenson were the proprietors in 1936.

Activities included riding, picnics, transportation to and from town, trips to Lake Tahoe, Virginia City, Pyramid Lake and other points of interest in Nevada and California. Pack trips were at a slight additional cost. Fishing, swimming, deer hunting, and skiing were available in season. Rodeos in Reno and nearby towns were available during summer.

Stevenson Ranch was in a secluded canyon surrounded by mountains and open rangeland, ideal for riding and pack trips.

Accommodations were double and single rooms with adjoining baths in the main ranch house, and separate cabins.

Rates in 1936 were $40-$50 per week and included room, meals, and maid service. Special rates for children. Open year round. References were requested.

Whitney Guest Ranch

Washoe County, south of Reno on Del Monte Lane about 4 miles from the city center

Owned and operated by Mrs. L. M. Whitney, activities included swimming and an evening social hour under an apple tree. Sometimes the entire group would go out together to dinner or a show. "It was not a party place, but I wouldn't say it was snobbish," said Mrs. Whitney.

Mrs. Whitney dropped horseback riding as an activity because of the high cost and insurance problems. "Only one in twenty was really interested and they just wanted to say they had ridden a horse." Riding stables were available on nearby Moana Lane.

Earlier, when the ranch still maintained its own stable, a man arrived for a divorce. Apparently he was impressed with ranch living, for in succeeding years he returned for two more divorces. The guest was also an avid horseman. On his third trip he brought his own horse, a Tennessee Walker. He would then leave his horse at the ranch.

The Whitney catered to the upper-classes, mostly from New England and Washington, D.C. A number of their guests came from foreign countries such as France, China, Canada, North Africa.

Shunning the "Old West" trimmings, the cottages were carpeted wall-to-wall and were completely furnished. A maid was available for those who didn't want to do housework. Owners, such as Mrs. Whitney, said they would not have traded their way of life for any other. They felt that it was most rewarding.

Accommodations were in the main ranch house and seven cottages. By 1962, the rates averaged $100 per week, and no longer included horseback riding. The guests also did their own cooking in the cottages.

Postscript

Guest ranches catering to the divorce business experienced a rapid decline in numbers in the 1960s and '70s. By 1970, there were only two guest ranches in northern Nevada, the Silver Circle Guest Ranch and the Whitney Ranch, and they were finding more and more guests came for a Western vacation rather than for a divorce. The Whitney Ranch was the last of the divorce ranches in the immediate Reno, area due to zoning restrictions and spreading development.[4]

Based on archival research at the Nevada Historical Society in Reno during 2001-2002, and on telephone directory research in the 1947-1953 directories, there were no dude or guest ranches in southern Nevada during the late 1940s and early 1950s. Bear in mind that Nevada had a single directory, 3/4-inch thick, for the entire state, which included both White and Yellow Page listings for the years the authors were researching.

However, the Nevada Historical Society informed us in 2003 that they had just uncovered several old brochures on dude ranches, including one for the Boulderado Ranch in Las Vegas.

Southern Nevada

The highly-publicized Clark Gable-Ria Langham divorce in 1939 drew national media attention to Las Vegas. Everyone, it seemed, wanted to get a divorce where the Gables had gotten theirs. In July 1939, Las Vegas' first haven for prospective divorcés, the Boulderado Ranch, opened, and others soon followed.[5]

Boulderado Ranch

In the 1940s, the Boulderado Ranch was under the supervision of Mr. and Mrs. E. L. Losee. It was located 2-1/2 miles northwest of Las Vegas, Nevada, 30 miles from world-famous Boulder Dam. It was one of the oldest ranches in Nevada—originally a camp site on the "Old Mormon Trail."

Activities included horseback riding, campfire suppers, hay rides, quail and duck hunting on the ranch in season, fishing on Lake Mead, golf, and sightseeing trips to many places of interest, such as Death Valley and Zion and Bryce Canyons. The Boulderado was ten minutes from downtown Las Vegas night clubs, bars and casinos.

Accommodations were for a dozen guests in the main ranch house and separate cottages. The main ranch house was built on the lines of the Old South. The cottages, for from one to four guests, were all equipped with private baths, with a few exceptions.

Boulderado Ranch was for two types of vacationers: the person looking for amusement and entertainment and the guest seeking seclusion and complete rest and relaxation.

Other Nevada Dude-Divorce Ranch "Possibles"

In addition to the thirteen preceding profiles for northern Nevada, the following listings were found in the statewide Nevada Telephone Directory Yellow Pages under "Dude Ranches" for two or more years between 1947-1953. Most were no doubt more like boarding houses, but due to insufficient information, they're included here. Readers are encouraged to call or write the authors to share additional information on these or any other Nevada dude ranch operations that existed between 1926-1972.

Dude or Guest Ranch	Reno or Area Address
Alamo Ranch	Lakeside Drive, 3 minutes from downtown Reno
Beatrice Kay Guest Ranch	Peckham Lane
Biltmore Guest Ranch	So. Virginia Road, 3 miles south of Reno
Brookline Rancho	Holcomb Lane
Circle W Ranch	15 miles south of Reno
The Countryside Guest Ranch	Holcomb Lane, 6-1/2 miles south of Reno
Del Monte Guest Ranch *	So. Virginia Road, 3-1/2 miles south of Reno
Henry Weisenfeld Ranch	So. Virginia Road
Lakeview Guest Ranch	Reno-Carson Highway
Lone Star Ranch **	So. Virginia Road
Palomino Ranch	So. Virginia Road, 2-1/2 miles south of Reno
Randalls Ranch	Baker Lane
Stardust Guest Ranch	Dickerson Road, west of Reno
Swinging H Bar Ranch	9 miles north of Carson City
Thisisit Ranch	So. Virginia Road
Town & Country Guest House	So. Virginia Road
Triangle D Ranch	So. Verdi Road
Valley Ranch	So. Virginia Road, 7 miles south of Reno
Windy Acres Guest Ranch	Old Virginia Road, 6 miles from Reno
Willow Hill Guest Ranch	Wedekind Road, 2 miles north of the Reno Arch

* Formerly the Lake Ranch, owned and operated by Reno founder, Myron Lake.
** Owned by Washoe County Assessor J. L. Hash
Source: Nevada Telephone Directory Yellow Pages, "Dude Ranches" listings for two or more years between 1947-1953.

Ads from the Nevada Telephone Directory Yellow Pages, circa 1947-1953
(Courtesy Nevada Historical Society)

In 1898, Howard Eaton launched his first pack trip into Yellowstone Park, from the Custer Trail Ranch in the Badlands of North Dakota. The above photo was taken in the 1920s during a pack trip into Yellowstone from Eatons' Ranch in Wolf, Wyoming. (Courtesy Eatons' Ranch)

J. Origins of Dude Ranching

The big cattle drives out of Texas to the Great Plains and Rocky Mountain West after the Civil War, which made a folk hero out of the cowboy, slowed to a crawl after the disastrous winter of 1886-87. Continuous snowstorms, blizzards, and bitter cold killed thousands of cattle and crimped the glory days of the open range cattle industry. The cattle business continued but it was far less spectacular and successful, and the big outfits' profits were sporadic for many years.

A few visionary ranchers, like the Eaton brothers, began to diversify and, in the process, gave shape to an emerging dude ranching industry. Following is a condensed history of the origins of dude ranching, excerpted with permission from *Dude Ranching, A Complete History* by Lawrence A. Borne.

Howard Eaton, The Founder of Dude Ranching

Dude ranching started before all the national parks in the West except Yellowstone National Park. The early pioneers saw the wildness of the West as something beautiful and intriguing that should be preserved. It was valuable for its own sake and could be enjoyable to others who would travel far to see it.

A number of claims have been made about which ranch was the first to accept paying guests, but it has generally been conceded that the Eaton brothers' Custer Trail Ranch in the Dakota Territory was the first dude ranch with respect to the way the industry finally developed.

Main gate, Eatons' Ranch, Wolf, Wyoming (Courtesy Eatons' Ranch)

Three pioneers of dude ranching: (from left) brothers Alden, Willis and Howard Eaton, shown at their ranch at Wolf Creek, Wyoming. (Courtesy Joel H. Bernstein Collection)

Custer Trail Ranch, Badlands of North Dakota

The story of Eatons' Ranch began in Pittsburgh, Pennsylvania with two men, Howard Eaton and A. C. Huidekoper. Howard Eaton, born in 1851, was one of nine children, and at the age of seventeen he went to Omaha to see the West and work there for awhile. He returned home the following year, traveled to various places, and in 1879 returned to the West, this time to the Dakota Badlands. He made his living hunting wild game and selling the meat to the Northern Pacific Railway. Howard soon settled near Medora and took over a cabin abandoned by the Bismarck and Fort Keogh Stage Company. Howard named his place the Custer Trail Ranch because George Armstrong Custer had apparently camped nearby prior to the Battle of the Little Big Horn in 1876. Alden and Willis Eaton would soon join their brother in the start-up operation.

Meanwhile, A. C. Huidekoper, a member of a prominent Dutch family in Pennsylvania and an acquaintance of the Eaton brothers, was persuaded to join them in the Custer Trail Cattle Company in 1882. Huidekoper supplied money to purchase the stock, and the Eatons did the work. The profits were to be split

equally. Howard Eaton purchased 1,000 mother cows and Huidekoper purchased a carload of purebred Shorthorn bulls and some railroad land. Expectations were high for the future.

The Eaton brothers, like other East Coast transplants, raved about their newfound paradise and wrote letters to their Eastern friends describing the wonderful country. One of these letters, written by Howard Eaton and published in a New York newspaper, led to the westward migration of the most famous dude of all—Theodore Roosevelt. Roosevelt read Eaton's letter and decided to go west in 1883. Although Roosevelt's first love was for the outdoors, he soon became interested in raising cattle. For him, ranching was an excuse to be outdoors and do what he enjoyed: riding, hunting, and camping. Within a few months, Roosevelt owned the Maltese Cross Ranch near the Custer Trail Ranch and visited the Eaton brothers frequently.

Another visitor to the Custer Trail Ranch was Owen Wister. Wister would later write the best-selling novel, *The Virginian*, and is often credited with creating the character of the romantic cowboy.

The Eatons, like most ranchers, were very generous and soon became the hosts for hundreds of people eager to hunt or experience ranch life. They were pleased to have guests but costs were overwhelming; fortunately, some of their visitors offered to pay enough to cover their expenses. Although the practice was contrary to the code of ranching hospitality, the Eatons did take their first paying guest in 1882, Bert Rumsey of Buffalo, New York. A guest book was purchased, and the Custer Trail Ranch was accepting dudes. Howard even led the first of his many pack trips to Yellowstone Park the following year.

Howard, Willis, and Alden were learning that dude ranching held some surprises. They were still primarily stockmen, however, and suffered greatly when a fire started by Indians got out of control and destroyed most of their property. They persevered and were soon building up their cattle herds just as hundreds of other ranchers were doing in the 1880s. Then the harsh winter of 1886-87 hit the Custer Trail Cattle Company. At the roundup that year, an accurate count was made, and the partners learned they had about the same number of cattle as when they had started the business several years earlier.

At this point, the Eaton brothers and Huidekoper ended their partnership amicably and the Custer Trail Ranch continued to raise horses and cattle. The Eatons were still concerned about their visitors; although a few people had paid, the Eatons counted 2,200 free meals they had given guests in just one year. They decided to charge ten dollars per week for each guest, but this did not keep people away. Paying guests continued coming through the 1880s and became a regular feature at the Eatons' ranch in 1891. Dudes were a permanent factor in their ranch operation from this point on. Their business did not boom immediately, but many guests returned East with glowing accounts of the free, open life, hunting and adventure, and good fellowship.

It was fortunate that Easterners were seeking this outdoor life, for economic necessity was making more people look at dude ranching in a different light. The winter of 1886-87 was probably the worst disaster that hit the cattle business, but the Panic of 1893 also hurt Westerners and recovery from it was not rapid.

Howard Eaton took charge among the brothers, for he enjoyed taking the dudes on hunting and scenic trips. As he did so, he tried to learn what they enjoyed most about the West and what additional things he could do to please them. In 1898, he launched his first large pack trip into Yellowstone Park with forty guests (all men); he took lots of saddle and pack horses, tents, a wagon, a cook, horse wrangler, teamster, guides, and other workers.

Meanwhile, the Eaton brothers were making some changes. As noted earlier, they had made the dude business a regular part of the Dakota ranch by 1891. However, changes were coming to the Dakotas. Thousands of dry land farmers were moving in and putting pressure on the ranchers to move out. Rangeland was disappearing fast in the Badlands and the Eatons were being pushed out of North Dakota.

In 1903, some men offered cash for the Custer Trail Ranch, so the brothers sold out and turned toward Wyoming. Eventually other ranchers were also forced out, so the Eatons apparently made the right choice in leaving when they did.

They were now looking for a new ranch that had several desirable characteristics: good horseback riding, both mountain trails and level country; a high enough altitude for comfortable summer weather but low enough so the winters weren't too miserable; a spot reasonably secluded from towns and the intrusions of passersby, but not too far from the railway that brought supplies and guests; abundant natural feed for the horses and an unfailing water supply; some fishing and hunting nearby; and open country for pack trips away from settlements. They found what they wanted at an elevation of 4,500 feet along Wolf Creek in the foothills of the Big Horn Mountains, just eighteen miles from Sheridan, Wyoming.

Eatons' Ranch, Wolf, Wyoming

In 1904, the three brothers made their move. They sent out a brochure to "announce to their friends and patrons, and to the public, their change of location from the Badlands of North Dakota to the Big Horn Mountain region of Wyoming."

They had decided not to take any guests that first year because they did not have the cabins or other buildings ready, but they did not count on the tenacity of the dudes. Seventy of them arrived that first summer of 1904. They slept in tents or on the ground, ate off ironing boards or anything else that would hold a plate, filled kerosene lamps, helped with beds and dishes, cleaned the cabins as soon as the builders finished constructing them—and, of course, paid for the privilege. This dogged loyalty is significant, for it shows how early some Easterners had become absolutely dedicated to their ranch vacations and how this dedication could ensure the continuation of some ranches for years or even decades.

Howard Eaton was an incredibly genial host.

Big Bill Eaton, ropin' (Courtesy Eatons' Ranch)

Patty Eaton
(Courtesy Joel H. Bernstein
Collection)

Clearly he had found the best of all possible ways of life—he was doing exactly what he wanted to do and was able to make a living at it. Hundreds of guests journeyed to Wolf, Wyoming during a season that lasted from June 1 to mid-October, enjoying excellent food, good service, and magnificent scenery.

Howard, Willis, and Alden Eaton's concern about their guests was always appreciated. Of course, another factor that aided Eatons' Ranch was the association of the brothers with Theodore Roosevelt who was then president when they moved to Wyoming and were getting firmly established there.

By 1917, Eatons' Ranch comprised over 7,000 acres of land, 500 horses, hundreds of cattle, and accommodations for 125 guests. It was the largest dude ranch in the country.

After the death of Howard in 1922, Willis took charge of the guests while brother Alden assumed management of the other facets of the ranch operation. In 1929, death claimed the second of the Eaton brothers, Willis, who suffered a heart attack. Alden and his son, Big Bill, continued to operate the ranch at Wolf, as well as the Bar Eleven Ranch in Wyoming that they had purchased to supply good grazing country for their horses.

In 1928, the Eatons also acquired the Rimrock Ranch in Arizona, east of Prescott and south of Flagstaff. They saw the growing interest in the Southwest and bought this ranch so they could offer ranch vacations to their guests throughout the year. Big Bill Eaton managed the Rimrock Ranch until it was sold in 1939, as it proved difficult to manage two ranches so far apart.

The history of the Eaton brothers shows that they had thoroughly analyzed their business and what was needed for a successful dude ranch operation. They also chose their site well. Eatons' Ranch in Wolf, Wyoming has operated in the same location for nearly one hundred years.

Postscript

The authors asked Jeff Way, General Manager of Eatons' Ranch and a fifth generation Eaton, to summarize the chain of ranch management following the deaths of Howard (1922) and Willis (1929):

> After the deaths of Howard and Willis, it was Alden and his son, Big Bill Eaton (my great-grandfather), who ran the ranch. Big Bill's daughter, Nancy, married Tommy Ferguson (my grandfather). As Big Bill became older and less active, Tommy and Nancy, operated the ranch.
>
> Following Tommy Ferguson's death in 1983, Frank Eaton and Tommy's son, Bill Ferguson (my father), were in charge.
>
> I became the general manager of the ranch in 1996, in charge of all day-to-day operations. I am Big Bill and Patty Eaton's great-grandson, and Tommy and Nancy Ferguson's grandson—so I am a fifth generation Eaton.

Jeff Way also confirmed that the family still owns and operates the Bar Eleven Ranch, located between Arvada and Gillette, Wyoming. What an amazing and successful family story.

Eatons' Ranch Yesterday and Today...

Clockwise from top left: Loading up; aerial of horses in the corral; horses at the picket; ready for the morning ride; a dude family on vacation; inside the main ranch house; ranch cabin interior. (Courtesy Eatons' Ranch)

Other Pioneer Western Dude Ranchers

Space limitations preclude profiling all the other ranchers who helped pioneer dude ranching in the West. Each has a fascinating story and interested readers are urged to check the Bibliography for more information on the history of dude ranching. The books may be found in some libraries or often on amazon.com as an out-of-print book. However, a few ranchers must be singled out for their contributions. They are listed here by state:

Montana

Dick Randall, OTO Ranch, Gardiner
Paul Van Cleve Family, Lazy K Bar Ranch, Big Timber
Ernest and Grace Miller, Elkhorn Ranch, Bozeman

Wyoming

Charles C. Moore, CM Ranch, Dubois
Larry Larom, Valley Ranch, Cody
William Wells, Gros Ventres Lodge, Jackson Hole

Colorado

John G. Holzworth Sr., Holzworth's Neversummer Ranch, Grand Lake Region
Henry Lehman, Lehman Ranch, Granby
James Ferguson, Bar Lazy J Ranch, Marshall

New Mexico

W. J. Gourley, Vermejo Park Ranch, Taos-Santa Fe

Arizona

Faraway Ranch, Douglas
Kay El Bar Guest Ranch, Wickenburg
Tanque Verde Ranch, Tucson

Observations

While dude ranches have grown more elaborate everywhere, the trend is most noticeable in Arizona and New Mexico. One of the reasons for this is the phenomenal urban sprawl, especially near Tucson. Spots chosen as guest ranch sites were remote from that city when it was relatively small, but many of the ranches became surrounded by the rapidly growing town. Once an area became crowded, subdivided, and incorporated, horseback riding and other ranch activities became nearly impossible, so the ranch became a resort.

However, urban sprawl is not the sole factor for the metamorphosis from ranch to resort in the Southwest.

The long season of sunshine draws the "sun seekers" to these ranches—golfers, swimmers, tennis players, and those who just want to escape foul weather.

Dude Ranch Associations Today

There are several state dude ranch associations in the western United States and Canada. As of this writing, the principal organization, The Dude Ranchers' Association (DRA), includes 116 member ranches in 12 western states, and 5 in Canada.

For more information on these associations and their member ranches, please see the Notes section.[1]

Clockwise from left: Dick and Dora Randall, OTO Ranch; Four Van Cleve generations, circa 1940. From left, Paul IV (Tack), Paul Jr., Paul Sr., and Paul III (Spike) of the Lazy K Bar.; Ernie Miller, Elkhorn Ranch; The Turner's Triangle X Ranch in Wyoming was the setting for the filming of the movie Spencer's Mountain, *in which Henry Fonda (right) starred. Others are (from left), Weldon Richardson, Louise Turner, Harold T. Mapes, and Donald Turner; Larry Larom, Valley Ranch, speaking with Charlie Moore, CM Ranch (on his right)* (Courtesy Joel H. Bernstein Collection)

Rocky Mountain High

(Waunita Hot Springs Ranch, Colorado Dude & Guest Ranch Association)

Cowgirls (Courtesy: Photos by Dude Ranchers'
Association & jeff@jagphotoinc.com © 2002)

Notes

Chapter 2: Reno—Timeout

1. William L. McGee has authored *Bluejacket Odyssey, 1942-1946: Guadalcanal to Bikini, Naval Armed Guard in the Pacific*, a memoir within a Pacific War history which chronicles his four-year hitch in the U.S. Naval Armed Guard during World War II. (Santa Barbara: BMC Publications, rev. ed. 2000)

2. Washoe County Library, clippings file, *Nevada State Journal*, 1947 (rest of date missing).

3. Until 1942, Reno's attitude towards commercialized vice was the more commercial, the better. Prostitution was legal and every brothel in the city was licensed. The red-light district was compact and neat, with all the houses being located in two long, low buildings that ran the length of a city block. The buildings faced each other across a tree-shaded courtyard, and 75 girls worked 24 hours a day in three eight-hour shifts. Each girl had a two-room apartment with a kitchen and a bedroom. According to the prostitutes, it was the best set-up west of the Mississippi. When off duty, they gambled in the downtown clubs, or sat in the shade in front of their houses and read. The whole thing was known as "The Stockade." One end of it was fenced off, and the other end blocked by a tavern so that the girls couldn't make a show of themselves in public. From *Men*, "The Raw Side of Reno," October 1952.

4. Certain nuances in the shape, size, and style of the cowboy hat provided information as to the wearer's background and geographical base. With an adjustment to the brim and the creases, a cowboy could indicate that he was from Montana in the Northwest, the plains of Texas, the Rocky Mountain range, or the deserts of the Southwest.

Chapter 3: Tahoe Dude Wrangler

1. Carol Van Etten, *Tahoe City Yesterdays*, p. 82.

2. Ibid., Tahoe City, pp. 8-10, 27, 42-43, 52, 60, 94, 97-98; Tahoe Inn, pp. 70-72, 74-66; and Tahoe Tavern, pp. 12-14.

Chapter 4: Tahoe Hunting Guide

1. Packsaddles are designed to support the load on a pack animal's back. Panniers consist of two baskets or box-like compartments with leather straps that can be draped over the crosstrees of a packsaddle so one compartment hangs on each side.

2. A wire stretcher is a tool comprised of rope, clamps and a series of pulleys used to stretch wire when building or repairing fences. Hunters need to treat their booty with special care from the moment it is shot. For example: immediate and careful gutting, immediate removal of all hair near exposed flesh, and prompt skinning are essential. Hunters should also be careful not to cut into the musk glands on the lower belly, and be sure to remove all fat from game animals as it grows rancid quickly.

Chapter 6: The Flying M E

1. Washoe County Recorder, Book 119, p. 349.

2. Myra Sauer Ratay, *Pioneers of the Ponderosa*, pp. 138-141.

3. Washoe County Recorder, Book 143, p. 91.

4. Ratay, *Pioneers of the Ponderosa*, pp. 3, 17-18, 135-36.

5. Robert Wernick, "Last of the Divorce Ranches," *The Saturday Evening Post*, January 17, 1965, pp. 30-34. Another excellent article on the subject of Reno divorces by Robert Wernick is "Where you went if you *really* had to get unhitched," *Smithsonian*, June 1996, pp. 64-73.

6. Lawrence Borne, *Dude Ranching: A Complete History*, p. 117.

7. Written at the Monte Cristo Ranch by an unknown poet.

Chapter 7:
Eleanor Roosevelt Vacations at the Tumbling DW

1. *Nevada State Journal*, July 10, 1943. (Note: The date on the page may have been misprinted as July 10, 1943; the actual issue date is July 11, 1943.)

2. Author note: In the same issue, the column adjacent to "My Day" carried a UP analysis headlined, "Japs May Risk Much to Halt U.S. Offensive." This referred to U.S. operations in the Central Solomons and New Guinea—a not-so-subtle reminder that the author was there experiencing his first enemy action off Guadalcanal as a seventeen year old Navy man. –W.L.M.

3. *Nevada State Journal*, July 10, 1943. (Note: The date on the page may have been misprinted as July 10, 1943; the actual issue date is July 11, 1943.)

4. Eleanor Roosevelt's "My Day" columns have been collected in two volumes: *Eleanor Roosevelt's My Day, Her acclaimed columns 1936-1945*, Vol. 1, edited by Rochelle Chadakoff with an introduction by Martha Gellhorn; *Eleanor Roosevelt's My Day, The post-war years, her acclaimed columns, 1945-1952*, Vol. 2, edited by David Emblidge with an introduction by Pamela C. Harriman (New York: Pharos Books, 1989). Mimeographed copies are also available from the Franklin D. Roosevelt Library, 4079 Albany Post Road, Hyde Park, NY 12538.

Chapter 10: Valerie Vondermuhll, Letters Home

1. One of the "former *Life* people" Valerie refers to was probably Roger Butterfield, a nationally-known magazine writer and former editor of *Life*. Butterfield had been spending each summer and most of fall in Virginia City since 1945, when he came to Nevada for a divorce and to re-marry. His book, *The American Past,* had just been published by Simon & Schuster in 1947. William and Virginia Pedroli owned the neighboring ranch to the Flying M E. William was descended from Swiss stock, as were a number of Washoe Valley ranchers. See "Eleanor Roosevelt Vacations at the Tumbling DW" and "Washoe Valley Neighbors" for more about the Pedrolis.

2. Two of the children were Ricky and Gail Greenleaf. They were staying at the ranch with their mother, Ann Greenleaf. See "Autumn Leaves as Greenleafs Arrive" for more about the Greenleaf family.

Chapter 15: Virginia & Truckee Railroad

1. "V & T History" includes condensed excerpts from Myra Sauer Ratay's *Pioneers of the Ponderosa*, pp. 159-174. A granddaughter of one of the early Washoe Valley pioneers, about whom she writes, Ms. Ratay was born in Washoe Valley on the Twaddle Ranch, next door to Bowers Mansion. She grew up listening to her father tell exciting stories about people and early days in Washoe Valley, and gained an intimate knowledge of the settings for the events she describes.

2. *Reno Reporter,* May 19, 1949.

3. Lucius Beebe and Charles Clegg, *Virginia & Truckee: A Story of Virginia City and Comstock Times*, pp. 60-61.

4. Unpublished Diaries of Clel Georgetta, 1948 and 1949. Special Collections Department, University of Nevada, Reno Library.

5. Beebe and Clegg, *Virginia & Truckee: A Story of Virginia City and Comstock Times,* pp. 54, 57, 61, 67.

6. "V & T Reborn" was updated by Judie Fisher-Crowley, Executive Director, NNRF, on 09/27/03.

Chapter 16: Lucius Beebe and Charles Clegg

1. Andria Daley-Taylor, "Boardwalk Bons Vivants," *Nevada Magazine,* November/December 1992, pp. 20-37. Ms. Daley-Taylor is the former chairman of the Comstock Historic District Commission, and an advisor to the National Trust for Historic Preservation, and lived in the Piper-Beebe House in Virginia City. She is currently writing a biography of Lucius Beebe and Charles Clegg, and recently completed a history of the Civil War in the American West.

2. Hobo lore has it the originals carried hoes with them for field work; hence the name "hoe boy," later shortened to "hobo."

3. Daley-Taylor, "Boardwalk Bons Vivants," *Nevada Magazine,* November/December 1992, pp. 20-37.

4. *San Francisco Chronicle,* February 13, 1966 and February 17, 1991.

5. Sources for "Writers of the Comstock":

Andria Daley-Taylor, "Girls of the Golden West," *Comstock Women.*

Nevada State Journal, November 9, 1947.

Reno Reporter, September 12, 15, 22, 1949, October 6, 1949, and January 26, 1950.

Virginia City News, September 3, 17, 24, 1949, and October 8, 1949.

Chapter 17: Cal-Neva Lodge

1. Barbara Land and Myrick Land, *A Short History of Reno,* pp. 59-61.

2. Wayne Kling, *The Rise and Fall of the Biggest Little City,* pp. 57, 106-7.

Chapter 20: Clark Gable

1. Sources for "The Making of *The Misfits*":

Arthur Miller and Serge Toubiana, *The Misfits: Story of a*

Shoot. This book includes two hundred exclusive photographs by the world-famous Magnum photographic agency; a revealing interview with playwright Arthur Miller; and an essay recounting the tragic and triumphant story of the film and its stars.

A. J. Liebling, *A Reporter At Large, Dateline: Pyramid Lake, Nevada.*

Guy Louis Rocha, "Myths and 'The Misfits'", Nevada State Archives, Myth #60.

Warren G. Harris, *Clark Gable, A Biography.*

Cheryll Glotfelty, "Old Folks in the New West: Surviving Change and Staying Fit in 'The Misfits'," *Western American Literature*, Spring 2002.

Anthony Amaral, "The Last Machismo in the West," *Nevada Magazine*, Volume 38, Number 1 (January/February/March 1978).

Basil Woon, *None of the Comforts of Home, But Oh, Those Cowboys.*

Chapter 23:
Favorite Watering Holes—and Sights Along the Way

1. *The following sources provided additional information for this chapter:*

Carson City: *Carson Review*, October 26, 1973; *Nevada Appeal*, February 21, 1977.

Genoa: Genoa Bar brochure.

Virginia City: *Virginia City News*, April 3, April 17, May 22, October 1, November 12, 1948; April 15, April 22, May 6, October 1, 1949; *Reno Reporter*, March 4, 1948; *The Genoa-Carson Valley Book*, Nancy Miluck, Editor, and R. M. Smith; Andria Daley-Taylor, "Boardwalk Bons Vivants," *Nevada Magazine*, November/December 1992, p. 23.

Reno: Mapes Hotel: *Nevada State Journal*, December 17 and 18, 1947; *Reno Reporter*, November 21, 1947 and January 1, 1948; Wayne Kling, *The Rise of the Biggest Little City*, pp. 101-103. Riverside Hotel: Kling, *The Rise of the Biggest Little City*, pp. 140-142.

Pyramid Lake: John Charles Frémont, *Report of the Exploring Expedition to the Rocky Mountains.*

Mount Rose Highway and Lake Tahoe: Wayne Kling, *The Rise of the Biggest Little City*, pp. 21-22, 107.

Chapter 29: Cowboyin' Mishap

1. Dr. Ernest W. Mack became a pioneer in the specialty of neurosurgery, and wrote one of the first papers on the subject of ruptured intervertebral discs and the lumbar spine.

He believed that surgery was always the last option. In retirement, he authored a fascinating biography, *Keep the Faith, The Biography Of A Nevada Brain Surgeon And Avid Fisherman.*

Chapter 31: Washoe Valley Neighbors

1. Myra Sauer Ratay, *Pioneers of the Ponderosa*, p. 143.

2. Ibid., p. 143

3. Sources for the Bundy Ranch:

Basil Woon, "Gus Bundy Ranch in Washoe Valley Combines Industry with Artistry," *Nevada State Journal*, December 20, 1953.

Nevada State Journal, October 22, 1967.

Nevada Appeal, March 25, 1973.

Reno Gazette-Journal, June 17, 1984.

4. Sources for the Winters Ranch:

Correspondence with Mr. and Mrs. JohnD Winters, 2003.

Winters (CA) Express, Centennial Edition, October 8, 1998.

Datin, *Nevada Appeal*, October 30, 1977.

Myra Sauer Ratay, *Pioneers of the Ponderosa*, pp. 293-328.

5. Myra Sauer Ratay, *Pioneers of the Ponderosa*, pp. 217-239. It is interesting to note that various records show Eilley's first name spelled Ellison, Alisen, and Alson. An article in the *Nevada State Journal*, December 26, 1948, says the Bowers silver was marked "A. B. S" suggesting her name was spelled Alisen or Alson. However, in a Bible which belonged to the Bowers, under "Marriages" is this record: "L. S. Bowers to Ellison Cowan" (*Nevada State Journal*, January 16, 1949). The authors will use the spelling Alisen.

Chapter 32: The Gambler and the Lady

1. Barbara Land and Myrick Land, *A Short History of Reno.*

2. *New York American*, March 1931.

3. *Reno Reporter*, October 13, 1949.

4. Charles Renshaw Jr., "The Gambler and the Lady," *The American Weekly*, January 22, 1950, p. 4.

5. *Virginia City Legend*, August 26, 1971.

6. Newspaper name and date missing.

Chapter 33:
Equestrienne Socialite Arrives Incognito

1. Delano Forums, *The Roosevelt Dynasty*, Part 3.

2. Max Dorian, *The Du Ponts, From Gunpowder to Nylon.*

Chapter 34: Yerington Rodeo

1. Prices taken from a Parker's advertisement in the *Nevada State Journal*, 1949.

2. As of this writing, the national finals for the Professional Rodeo Cowboys Association (PRCA) are held in Las Vegas, Nevada.

Chapter 36: Eastern Gentleman Weds Western Lady

1. *War Stories: Veterans Remember WW II*, edited by R. T. King (Reno: University of Nevada, Oral History Program, 1995).

Chapter 37: The Cowboy and the Lady

1. Inez Robb, "Out of this World—In Reno," *The American Weekly*, Chapter 8, June 25, 1944.

Afterword

1. As of this writing, the authors have found no property transfer records from Emily Pentz Wood to a Millboss Corporation, a William Moss, or a Ken Robertson.

2. Washoe County Recorder, Book 91, pp. 154-65.

3. Basil Woon's tribute to Emily Pentz Wood was first published in the *Nevada Appeal*, August 28, 1966, and subsequently reprinted as a memorial booklet. The Carson-Tahoe Hospital Foundation's current address is P.O. Box 2168, Carson City, Nevada 89702. Tel: 775/883-3308.

4. Washoe County Recorder, Book 316, pp. 244-45, and Book 533, pp. 191-92.

5. House & Garden Television (HGTV), "If Walls Could Talk," Episode WCT-706, February 24, 2002.

Appendix A: The Nevada Divorce Trade

1. Excerpted and condensed from interviews with Guy Louis Rocha, Assistant Administrator for Archives and Records, Nevada State Library and Archives; and Phillip Earl, former Curator of History, Nevada Historical Society.

   Other sources:

   "Behind Nevada's Divorce Laws," by Phillip Earl, *Nevadan*, May 3, 1961.

   Reno Gazette-Journal, November 10, 1996.

   Nevada Appeal, December 21, 1992.

2. As of the early 1990s, California no longer requires a pre-marital examination and blood test. Furthermore, the California marriage license can be used immediately.

Appendix B: The Lawyers

1. Unpublished Diaries of Clel Georgetta, 1948 and 1949. Special Collections Department, University of Nevada, Reno Library.

2. Harry B. Swanson, *Migratory Divorce: Sherrer vs. Sherrer and the Future*. This article first appeared in Volume IV, Fall Issue, 1952, Hastings Law Journal, of the Hastings College of Law University of California at San Francisco, California, and was reprinted in the July 1953 issue of The Nevada State Bar Journal, Volume 18, (No. 3).

3. "The Nevada Experience: The Reno Cure," #203. KNPB, Ch. 5, PBS, Reno.

Appendix C: The Stringers

1. Sources for the Vanderbilt and Miller-Monroe story:

   Mark McLaughlin, Bill Berry biographer.

   Barbara Land and Myrick Land, *A Short History of Reno.*

   It must be noted that, in addition to covering the Reno divorce scene, Bill Berry was passionate about skiing and the ski industry in the Sierra Nevada mountains. Berry is a member of the U. S. Ski Hall of Fame; Historian Emeritus of the U.S. Ski Association and the Far West Ski Association; has won numerous ski journalism awards; and is an honorary lifetime member of the North American Ski Journalists Association (NASJA).

2. Guy Shipler Jr. Papers, Special Collections, Nevada State Library and Archives.

Appendix D: Six Minutes in Court

1. Sources for "Six Minutes in Court":

   Guy Shipler Jr. Papers, Special Collections, Nevada State Library and Archives.

   Jane Rule, *Desert of the Heart.*

Appendix E: TH Ranch

1. This brief history is taken from Martha C. Knach & Omer C. Stewart, *As Long As The River Shall Run.*

2. Washoe County Recorder.

3. This property description is from the appraisal report of William M. White to Michael Lintner, May 17, 1978.

Appendix F: Pyramid Lake Ranch

1. John Charles Frémont, *Report of the Exploring Expedition to the Rocky Mountains.*

2. Robert Wernick, "Last of the Divorce Ranches," *The Saturday Evening Post,* July 17, 1965.

3. Excerpted from "The Lake of the Cui-ui Eaters," a series of four articles on Pyramid Lake by A. J. Liebling, originally published in *The New Yorker* in 1955. During Liebling's stay at Pyramid Lake in 1949, he became interested in the ongoing dispute between the Paiute Indians and the non-Indian squatters on lands within the reservation. In 1953, he returned to Pyramid Lake Ranch with his second wife, Lucille. This nearly two-month stay was no doubt used to gather most of the material for what became "The Lake of the Cui-ui Eaters." The four articles have been brought together in *A. J. Liebling, A Reporter at Large, Dateline: Pyramid Lake, Nevada.* Edited, with an update, by Elmer R. Rusco, (Reno & Las Vegas: University of Nevada Press, 2000).

   Liebling also wrote "The Mustang Buzzers," a two-part series published in *The New Yorker* in 1954. The series' subject is the wild horse roundups on the Smoke Creek Desert, north of Pyramid Lake. See "Clark Gable" for more about wild horse roundups.

4. Data on the Drackerts are in part from the Drackert Papers, Special Collections Department, University of Nevada, Reno Library. (See Susan Searcy's, "A Guide to the Papers of Harry and Joan Drackert," 1991.) Information on the previous owners of the Pyramid Lake Ranch can be found in the papers of Mary Bean, also at the University of Nevada, Reno Library.

Appendix G: Donner Trail Ranch

1. Robert Wernick, "Last of the Divorce Ranches," *The Saturday Evening Post,* July 17, 1965, pp. 30-31.

2. Unpublished Diaries of Clel Georgetta, 1948 and 1949. Special Collections Department, University of Nevada, Reno Library.

3. Wernick, "Last of the Divorce Ranches," *The Saturday Evening Post,* July 17, 1965, p. 32.

4. *Nevada State Journal,* July 8, 1965.

5. Data on the Drackerts are in part from the Drackert Papers, Special Collections Department, University of Nevada, Reno Library. (See Susan Searcy's, "A Guide to the Papers of Harry and Joan Drackert," 1991.) For more

biographical information on the Drackerts, see Appendix section, "Pyramid Lake Ranch."

Appendix H: Washoe Pines Ranch

1. Myra Sauer Ratay, *Pioneers of the Ponderosa,* p. 88.

2. Washoe County Recorder, Book 45, p. 473.

3. Ibid., Book 64, p. 110.

4. Ibid., Book 67, p. 588.

5. Carolyn Zieg Cunningham, "Tempestuous Life of Will James," *Montana Magazine,* Spring 1981.

6. Washoe County Recorder, Book 99, pp. 595-96.

7. Ibid., Book 99, pp. 595-96.

8. Ibid., Book 178, pp. 396-98; Book 187, pp. 69; and Book 227, p. 28-29.

9. Ibid., Book 259, pp. 291-93.

10. Ibid., Book 390, pp. 570-73.

11. Ibid., Book 599, p. 248.

12. Northern Nevada Dude Ranch Association brochure, 1936.

13. Robert Wernick, "Last of the Divorce Ranches," *The Saturday Evening Post,* July 17, 1965, p. 34.

14. *Reno Evening Gazette,* September 15, 1980.

15. Heidi Hart, *Reno News and Review,* October 4, 1995.

Appendix I: More Nevada Dude-Divorce Ranches

1. *Reno Evening Gazette,* April 16, 1962.

2. Cornelius Vanderbilt Jr., *Ranches and Ranch Life in America,* pp. 251-53.

3. *Reno Evening-Gazette,* February 23, 1972.

4. *Reno Evening-Gazette,* April 16, 1962 and February 23, 1972.

5. Guy Louis Rocha, "Gable vs. Gable," *Nevada Magazine,* November/December 1981.

Appendix J: Origins of Dude Ranching

1. The Dude Ranchers' Association (DRA) celebrated its seventy-seventh anniversary in 2003. The DRA was formed in September 1926, as some ranchers began to realize that their mutual problems relating to transportation, forestry regulations, game laws, insurance, and other items required an organization. According to several sources, Ernest Miller, of the Elkhorn Ranch in Montana, convinced Max Goodsill, general passenger agent of the

Northern Pacific, of the value of an organization. Larry Larom, of the Valley Ranch in Wyoming, was also a prime mover in getting the Association off the ground.

DRA members were very conscious of their unique background and character, and paid special attention to the way they functioned. They were especially concerned about not taking transient trade, as such a move might cause government officials to classify them as public places. This could subject the ranches to various hotel laws and force them to accept anyone who wished to stay. Numerous ranchers, especially those who had operated for many years, disliked this possibility, since they still regarded the dudes as personal guests in their homes and wanted to be able to choose these visitors.

The Association requires that its members receive advance reservations with deposits; do not cater to transient trade; offer the American Plan with rates on a weekly basis; do not have bars; do not use billboards for advertising; and must offer horseback riding.

The Dude Ranchers' Association and its three affiliated state associations may be reached at:

The Dude Ranchers' Association, P.O. Box 2307, Cody, WY 82414, Tel: 307/587-2339, Fax 307/587-2776, info@duderanch.org, www.duderanch.org.

Arizona DRA, P.O. Box 603, Cortaro, AZ 85652, www.azdra.com, 13 ranches listed.

Montana DRA, 1627 W. Main, Ste. 434, Bozeman, MT 59715, office@montanadra.com, www.montanadra.com.

Wyoming DRA, P.O. Box 618, Dubois, WY 82513, Tel: 307/455-2084, www.wyomingduderanchers.com.

The Colorado Dude & Guest Ranch Association's (CDGRA) first brochure was printed in 1936 and listed 11 ranches. Since then, membership has varied from a high of 50 ranches in 1972, to 36 in 2002. The CDGRA has operated somewhat differently from the DRA, although the two organizations cooperate with each other.
The CDGRA does regularly publish a list of its members, with descriptions and the rates of its member ranches, and aggressively distributes these through state agencies, travel bureaus, and the airlines.

The CDGRA requires that members use the word *ranch* in their names and that they foster and promote "western atmosphere." They also must solicit weekly or longer visits; have at least 50 percent of their business on the American Plan; and offer a resident, supervised horse program.

Of the eleven ranches listed in 1936, four are still operating some seventy years later: Bar Lazy J Ranch (then Buckhorn Lodge), Drowsy Water Ranch, Smille's F Slash Ranch (later C Lazy U Ranch), and Wind River Ranch.

The Colorado Dude & Guest Ranch Association may be reached at: Colorado Dude & Guest Ranch Association, P.O. Box 2120, Granby, CO 80446, Tel: 970/887-3128, www.coloradoranch.com.

Bibliography

Interviews by the Authors

Azevedo, Norman and Rhonda. Carson City, Nev., May 2001.

Bechdolt, Bernadette (Mrs. William). Tahoe City, Calif., May 17-18, 2002.

Bechdolt, William. Tape. Tahoe City, Calif., September 18, 1997.

Bliss, William W. Tape. Glenbrook, Nev., May 26, September 27, and October 15, 2002.

Champlin, Charles. Telephone tape. Los Angeles, Calif., July 6, 2002.

Conrad, Barnaby. Santa Barbara, Calif., May 30, 2003.

Cramer, Patricia. Santa Barbara, Calif., November 25, 2002.

Goodhue, Janice (Mrs. Nathaniel). Tape. Reno, Nev., May 24, July 22, 2002; March 4, April 17, 2003.

Green, Anthonie (Mrs. J. Elton). Telephone tape. Grass Valley, Calif., June 9, 2002.

Greenleaf, Richard C. Telephone tape. Ambler, Pa., July 17, 2002.

Hencken, Gail Greenleaf. Telephone tape. Maitland, Fla., July 18, 2002.

Hinton, Kit. Santa Barbara, Calif., February 6, 2003.

Hinton, Dirck L. Telephone. Sparks, Nev., January 2003.

Horgan, Jack and Grace. Tape. TH Ranch, Sutcliffe, Nev., September 11, 2002.

Humphreys, Noreen I. K. Carson City, Nev., October 2002.

La Grange, Jack. Telephone. Fall River Mills, Calif., October 26, 2002.

McClary, Penny (Mrs. Eric). Washoe Pines Ranch, Franktown, Nev., October 27, 2002.

Miller, Dr. Richard. Telephone. Tucson, Az., October 2002.

Miller, Maya. Washoe Pines Ranch, Franktown, Nev., May 2002.

Morrow, Sue. Carson City, Nev., October 2002.

Murphy, Gerri. Tape. Carson City, Nev., October 27, 2002.

Myrick, David F. Tape. Santa Barbara, Calif., April 5, 2002.

Nappe, Tina Bundy. Tape. Reno, Nev., October 11, 2002.

Page, Joe. Tape. Virginia City, Nev., May 20, 2002.

Parker, Harry. Reno, Nev., October 22, 2002.

Patton, Paul Scates and Judy. Tape. Tahoe City, Calif., September 22, 2002.

Paulsen, Albert and Alice. Tape. Glenbrook, Nev., September 21, 2002.

Payette, Gail Hinton. Telephone. Eugene, Ore., February 3, 2003.

Prior, Nadine. Carson City, Nev., May, October 2002.

Schneider, Deborah Tokar. Telephone interview. Windham, N.H., June 21, 2002.

Scott, Patti (Mrs. E. B.), Telephone tape. Pebble Beach, Calif., August 26, 2002.

Shontz, Rebecca. Tape. Tahoe City, Calif., August 28, 2002.

Sinai, Esq., David P. Telephone tape. San Diego, Calif., May 11, 2002.

Swanson, Esq., Harry B. Tape. Reno, Nev., May 25, 2002.

Van Etten, Carol. Tahoe City and Homewood, Calif., May 2002.

Vondermuhll Jr., George A. Telephone. Bloomfield, Conn., April 2002.

Wagner, Joan Allison Borg McGee. Tape. Napa, Calif., July 23, 1993; Tahoe City, Calif., May 17-18, 2002.

Walsh, Jill. Santa Monica, Calif., July 7, 2002.

West, Neill E. Tape. New Washoe City, Nev., September 11, 2002.

Winters, JohnD and Kay. Telephone. Dayton, Nev., February 23, 2003.

Archives and Special Collections

The following archives, libraries and museums have been generous in sharing their knowledge and their history files:

University of Nevada, Reno. Special Collections Department, Robert E. Blesse, Director:

Bartlett, George. *Papers*. Collection NC1253.

Bliss, William. *The Bliss Papers*.

Drackert, Harry and Joan. *A Guide to the Papers of Harry and Joan Drackert*. Collection No. 91-49.

Georgetta, Clel. *Unpublished Diaries of Clel Georgetta, 1948 and 1949*.

Reno Chamber of Commerce, 1930. *Reno, Land of Charm.*

Nevada Historical Society, Reno. Eric Moody, Curator of Manuscripts; Lee Philip Brumbaugh, Curator of Photography; Phillip Earl, former Curator of History, (retired).

Nevada State Historic Preservation Office, Carson City. Ronald M. James, Nevada State Historic Preservation Officer; Mella Rothwell Harmon, National Register Coordinator.

Nevada State Library and Archives, Carson City. Guy Louis Rocha, Assistant Administrator for Archives and Records; Jeffrey M. Kintop, State Archives Manager; Baylen B. Limasa, Rick Rasmussen, Micrographics and Imaging Program; Joyce Cox, Head of Public Service and Reference; Mona Reno, State Data Center Librarian.

Nevada State Museum, Carson City. Bob Nylen, Curator of History.

Nevada State Railroad Museum, Carson City. Jane O'Cain, Curator of History/Collections Mgr.

North Lake Tahoe Historical Society, Tahoe City, Calif. Sara Larson, Director of Museums.

Washoe County Library, Reno.

Washoe County Recorder, Reno.

Jackson Hole Historical Society and Museum. Jackson, Wyoming.

Books

Abbott, E. C. *We Pointed Them North: Recollections of a Cowpuncher.* Norman: University of Oklahoma Press, 1955.

A Century of Memories: The Historic Photo Album of Carson City. Foreword by Jeff Ackerman. Vancouver, Wash.: Pediment Publishing, 2000.

Adams, Andy. *The Log of a Cowboy, A Narrative of the Old Trail Days.* Lincoln: University of Nebraska Press, 1964.

Alexander, E. P. *Iron Horses, American Locomotives, 1829-1900.* New York: Bonanza Books, 1941.

Angel, Myron, ed. *History of Nevada, 1881.* Oakland, Calif.: Thompson and West, 1881; reissued with introduction by David F. Myrick, 1958.

Bancroft, Hubert Howe. *History of California,* San Francisco, 1884-90.

———. *History of Nevada, Colorado and Wyoming,* San Francisco, 1890.

Bard, Floyd C. *Dude Wrangler, Hunter, Line Rider.* Denver: Sage Books, 1964.

Bartlett, George A. *Is Marriage Necessary?* New York: Penguin Books, Inc., 1947, rev. ed.

———. Men, *Women and Conflict.* London: G. P. Putnam's Sons, 1931.

Beebe, Lucius. *The Central Pacific and the Southern Pacific Railroads.* Berkeley: Howell-North Publications, 1963.

Beebe, Lucius, and Charles Clegg. *Legends of the Comstock Lode.* Stanford: Stanford University Press, 1954.

———. *Steamcars to the Comstock.* Berkeley: Howell-North, 1957.

———. *U. S. West, the Saga of Wells Fargo.* E. P. Dutton & Co., 1949.

———. *Virginia & Truckee: A Story of Virginia City and Comstock Times.* Oakland, Calif.: Grahame Hardy, 1949; Eighth Edition, Carson City: Nevada State Railroad Museum, 1991.

Bernstein, Joel H. *Families That Take In Friends: An Informal History of Dude Ranching.* Stevensville, Mont.: Stoneydale Press Publishing Company, 1982.

Borne, Lawrence R. *Dude Ranching: A Complete History.* Albuquerque: University of New Mexico Press, 1983.

Bourne, Russell. *Americans on the Move: A History of Waterways, Railways, and Highways.* Golden: Fulcrum Publishing, 1995.

Brewer, William H. *Up and Down California in 1860-1864.* Edited by Francis P. Farquhar. Berkeley: University of California Press, 1974.

Brooker, Angela M. *Nevada's Waters, Lifeline For a Thirsty World.* Reno: Nevada Historical Society, (n.d.).

Brown, Dee. *Hear That Lonesome Whistle Blow.* New York: Touchtone, 1977.

Burt, Nathaniel. *First Families, The Making of an American Aristocracy.* Boston-Toronto: Little, Brown and Company, 1970.

Burt, Struthers. *The Diary of a Dude-Wrangler.* New York: Charles Scribner's Sons, 1924.

Carhart, Arthur. *Hi Stranger! A Complete Guide to Dude Ranches.* Chicago: Ziff-Davis, 1949.

Chapman, Arthur. *The Pony Express.* New York: Putnam, 1932.

Cheney, Roberta, and Clyde Erskine. *Music, Saddles and Flapjacks: Dudes at the OTO Ranch.* Missoula, Mont.: Mountain Press Publishing Co., 1978.

Clark, Badger. *Sun and Saddle Leather.* Boston: Chapman and Grimes, n.d.

Collier, Peter with David Horowitz. *The Roosevelts: An American Saga.* New York: Simon & Schuster, 1994.

Cowles, Virginia. *The Astors.* New York: Alfred A. Knopf, 1979.

Dahlgren, Carl. *Adolph Sutro: A Brief Story of a Brilliant Life.* San Francisco: Press of San Francisco, 1895.

De Nevi, Don. *America's Fighting Railroads.* Missoula: Pictorial Histories Publishing, 1996.

Degler, Carl. *At Odds: Women and the Family in America from the Revolution to the Present.* New York: Oxford University Press, 1980.

De Quille, Dan [William Wright]. *The Big Bonanza.* 1876. Reprint, New York: Alfred A. Knopf, 1947.

Dondero, Don, with Jean Stoess. *Dateline: Reno, Photography by D. Dondero.* Reno, 1991.

Dorian, Max. *The du Ponts: From Gunpowder to Nylon.* Boston: Little, Brown and Company, 1962.

Downs, James F. *The Two Worlds of the Washo.* New York: Holt, Rinehart and Winston, 1966.

Earl, Phillip I. *This Was Nevada: Volume II, The Comstock Lode.* Reno: Nevada Historical Society, 2000.

Elleson, Robert W. *First Impressions: The Trail Through Carson Valley, 1848-1852.* Minden: Hot Springs Mountain Press, 2001.

Elliott, Russell R. *History of Nevada.* Lincoln: University of Nebraska Press, 1973.

Farquhar, Francis P. *History of the Sierra Nevada.* Berkeley: University of California Press, 1966.

Farr, Lillian, Dorothy Fordham, Bert Troelsen. The Ponderosa Area. Edited by John Corbett. Sparks, Nev.: Western Printing and Publishing Co., 1964.

Frantz, Joe B., and Julian E. Choate Jr. *The American Cowboy: The Myth and the Reality.* Norman: University of Oklahoma Press, 1968.

Frazier, Don. *The Will James Books.* Missoula: The Mountain Press Publishing Co., 1998.

Frémont, John Charles. *Report of the Exploring Expedition to the Rocky Mountains.* Ann Arbor: University Microfilms, 1966.

Furlong, Charles Wellington. *Let 'er Buck.* New York: G. P. Putnam's Sons, n.d.

Goin, Peter, and C. Elizabeth Raymond, Robert E. Blesse. *Stopping Time: A Rephotographic Survey of Lake Tahoe.* Albuquerque: University of New Mexico Press, 1992.

Goldman, Marion S. *Gold Diggers and Silver Miners.* Ann Arbor, Michigan: University of Michigan Press, 1981.

Graham, Otis L., and Meghan Robinson Wander (Contributor). *Franklin D. Roosevelt: His Life and Times: An Encyclopedic View.* New York: Da Capo Press, Inc., 1985.

Green, Michael S., and Gary E. Elliot. *Nevada Readings and Perspectives.* Reno: Nevada Historical Society, 1997.

Halem, Lynne Carol. *Divorce Reform.* New York: The Free Press, 1980.

Halem, Lynne, and Nelson Blake. *The Road to Reno: A History of Divorce in the United States.* New York: McMillan, 1962.

Harris, Warren G. *Clark Gable: A Biography.* New York: Harmony Books, 2002.

Haussamen, Florence, and Mary Anne Guitar. *The Divorce Handbook.* New York: G. P. Putnam's Sons, 1960.

Hoopes, Gene. *Tales of a Dude Wrangler.* San Antonio: Naylor Co., 1963.

Holbrook, Stewart H. *The Story of American Railroads.* New York: Crown Publishers, 1947.

Hollon, W. Eugene. *Great Days of the Overland Stage.* New York: American Heritage, 1957.

Hough, Emerson. *The Story of the Cowboy.* New York: D. Appleton-Century Co., n.d.

Hulse, James W. *Forty Years in the Wilderness: Impressions of Nevada, 1940-1980.* Reno: University of Nevada Press, 1986.

————. *The Nevada Adventure, A History.* Reno: University of Nevada Press, 1990.

Hungerford, Edward. *Wells Fargo: Advancing the American Frontier.* New York: Random House, 1949.

Jackson, Nancy J. "Dude Ranches in Nevada." In *Nevada Towns and Tales.* Las Vegas: Nevada Publications, Stanley W. Paher, ed., 1981.

James, George Wharton. *Lake Tahoe: Lake of the Sky.* Las Vegas: Nevada Publications, 1992. A new edition of the 1915 classic.

James, Ronald M. *The Roar and the Silence: A History of Virginia City and the Comstock Lode.* Reno: University of Nevada Press, 1998.

James, Ronald M. and C. Elizabeth Raymond, editors. *Comstock Women: The Making of a Mining Community.* Reno: University of Nevada Press, 1998.

James, Will. *Lone Cowboy: My Life Story.* New York: Charles Scribner's Sons, 1930; Missoula: Mountain Press Publishing Co., 1996.

————. *Smoky: The Cowhorse.* New York: Charles Scribner's Sons, 1926; Missoula: Mountain Press Publishing Co., 2001.

Jeffers, Barbara J. *Sandy Bowers' Widow: The Biography of Allison Eilley Bowers.* Reno: Barringer Historical Books, 1993.

Jones, Mary Somerville. *An Historical Geography of the Changing Divorce Law in the United States.* New York: Garland Publishing, Inc., 1987.

Kavaler, Lucy. *The Astors: A Family Chronicle of Pomp and Power.* New York: Dodd, Mead & Company, 1966.

Kessler, Sheila. *The American Way of Divorce.* Chicago: Nelson-Hall, 1975.

King, R.T., Editor. *War Stories.* Reno: University of Nevada Oral History Program, 1995.

Klein, Rochelle. *City Slickers on a Dude Ranch.* New York: Comet Press Books, 1959.

Kling, Wayne. *The Rise of the Biggest Little City.* Reno: University of Nevada Press, 2000.

Knack, Martha C., and Omer C. Stewart. *As Long as the River Shall Run: An Ethnohistory of the Pyramid Lake Indian Reservation.* Berkeley: University of California Press, 1984; Reno: University of Nevada Press, 1999.

Land, Barbara and Myrick Land. *A Short History of Reno.* Reno: University of Nevada Press, 1995.

Laxalt, Robert. *Nevada: A Bicentennial History.* New York: W. W. Norton, 1977.

————. *Nevada, A History.* Reno: University of Nevada Press, 1977.

Lewis, Oscar. *Silver Kings: The Lives and Times of Mackay, Fair, Flood, and O'Brien, Lords of the Nevada Comstock.* New York: Alfred A. Knopf, 1947. Reprint, Reno: University of Nevada Press, 1986.

Liebling, A. J. *A Reporter At Large, Dateline: Pyramid Lake, Nevada.* Reno: University of Nevada Press, 2000.

Lord, Eliot. *Comstock Mining and Miners.* 1883. Reprint, San Diego: Howell-North, 1959.

McCague, James. *Moguls and Iron Men: The Story of the First Transcontinental Railroad.* New York: Harper & Row, 1964.

McGlashan, C. F. *History of the Donner Party.* Stanford: Stanford University Press, 1975.

McKeon, Owen F. *Railroads and Steamers of Lake Tahoe.* South Lake Tahoe: Lake Tahoe Historical Society, 1984.

McLane, Alvin R. *Pyramid Lake: A Bibliography.* Reno: Camp Nevada, 1975.

Meschery, Joanne. *Truckee: An Illustrated History of the Town and its Surroundings.* Truckee: Rookingstone Press, 1978.

Miller, Arthur, and Serge Toubiana. *The Misfits, Story of a Shoot.* London: Phaidon Press Limited, 2000.

Miller, Max. *Reno.* New York: Dodd, Mead & Co., 1941.

Miluck, Nancy, Editor. *The Genoa-Carson Valley Book.* Vol. 5. Genoa: Dragon Enterprises, 2001.

Mintz, Steven, and Susan Kellogg. *Domestic Revolutions: A Social History of American Family Life.* New York: The Free Press, 1988.

Moody, Ralph. *The Old Trails West.* New York: Thomas Y. Crowell Co., 1963.

———. *Riders of the Pony Express.* Boston: Houghton-Mifflin Co., 1958.

Morris, Sylvia Jukes. *Rage for Fame: The Ascent of Clare Boothe Luce.* New York: Random House, 1997.

Myrick, David F. *Railroads of Nevada and Eastern California.* Vol. 1, *The Northern Roads;* Vol. 2, *The Southern Roads.* Berkeley: Howell-North, 1962, 1963.

O'Neill, William L. *Divorce in the Progressive Era.* New Haven: Yale University Press, 1967.

Paher, Stanley W. *Nevada Ghost Towns & Mining Camps: Illustrated Atlas.* Las Vegas: Nevada Publications, 1970.

Paher, Stanley W., Editor. *Fort Churchill: Nevada Military Outpost of the 1860's.* Las Vegas: Nevada Publications, 1981.

———. *Nevada Towns and Tales.* Las Vegas: Nevada Publications, 1981.

Paine, Swift. *Eilley Orrum: Queen of the Comstock.* Palo Alto: Pacific Books, 1949.

Pascoe, Peggy. *Relations of Rescue: The Search for Female Moral Authority in the American West, 1874-1939.* New York: Oxford University Press, 1990.

Polk's Reno City Directory, 1950, including Washoe County and Carson City. San Francisco: R. L. Polk and Company, 1950.

Pringle, Henry. *Theodore Roosevelt: A Biography.* New York: Harcourt, Brace & Co., 1931.

Prosor, Larry. *Lake Tahoe: A Photo Essay of the Lake Tahoe Region.* Truckee: Fine Line Productions, 1988.

Ratay, Myra Sauer. *Pioneers of the Ponderosa: How Washoe Valley Rescued the Comstock.* Sparks: Western Printing and Publishing Co., 1973.

Reed, Waller H. *Population of Nevada: Counties and Communities, 1860-1980.* Reno: Nevada Historical Society, 1983-84.

Reynolds, William and Ritch Rand. *The Cowboy Hat Book.* Salt Lake City: Gibbs, Smith Publisher, 1995.

Riley, Glenda. *Divorce: An American Tradition.* New York: Oxford University Press, 1991.

———. *The Female Frontier: A Comparative View of Women on the Prairies and the Plains.* Lawrence: University Press of Kansas, 1988.

Rollins, Philip Ashton. *The Cowboy.* New York: Charles Scribner's Sons, 1936. Revised and enlarged edition by Norman: University of Oklahoma Press, 1997.

Roosevelt, Eleanor. *Eleanor Roosevelt's My Day, Her Acclaimed Columns, 1936-1945.* Vol. 1. Edited by Rochelle Chadakoff with an Introduction by Martha Gellhorn. New York: Pharos Books, 1989.

Rowley, William D. *Reno: Hub of the Washoe Country.* Woodland Hills, Calif.: Windsor Publications, 1984.

Rule, Jane. *Desert of the Heart.* Los Angeles: Talonbooks, 1964.

Saylor, David J. *Jackson Hole, Wyoming: In the Shadow of the Tetons.* Norman: University of Oklahoma Press, 1970.

Scott, Edward B. *Saga of Lake Tahoe.* Vols. 1 and 2. Crystal Bay: Sierra-Tahoe Publishing Co., 1957 and 1973.

Shamberger, Hugh. *The Story of the Water Supply for the Comstock.* Geological Survey Professional Paper 779. Washington, D. C.: U. S. Geological Survey, Government Printing Office, 1965.

Shipler, Guy. *Nevada: Golden Challenge in the Silver State.* Windsor Publications, Inc., 1990.

Skolnick, Jerome H. *House of Cards: The Legalization and Control of Casino Gambling.* Boston: Little, Brown and Company, 1978.

Smith, Lawrence B. *Dude Ranches and Ponies.* New York: Coward-McCann, 1936.

Smith, Raymond M. *Untold Tales of Carson, Eagle and Smith Valleys, Nevada,* Vol. 3. Minden: Silver State Printing, 1996.

Social Register New York 1948. Vol. 62, No. 1. New York City: Social Register Association, November 1947.

Social Register New York 1949. Vol. 63, No. 1. New York City: Social Register Association, November 1948.

Steinberg, Alfred. *Mrs. R: The Life of Eleanor Roosevelt.* New York: G. P. Putnams's Sons, 1958.

Stewart, Robert E. Jr., and Mary Frances Stewart. *Adolph Sutro: A Biography.* Berkeley: Howell-North, 1962.

Storer, Tracy I. and Robert L. Usinger. *Sierra Nevada Natural History.* Berkeley: University of California Press, 1963.

Summerfield, Mary Winslow. "Refuge for Restless Hearts." In *Nevada Towns and Tales.* Las Vegas: Nevada Publications, Stanley W. Paher, ed., 1981.

Thompson, Thomas H., and Albert A. West. *History of Placer County, California.* Oakland, 1882.

———. *History of Nevada County, California.* 1880. Republished, Berkeley: Howell-North Books, 1970.

Twain, Mark [Samuel Langhorne Clemens]. *Mark Twain in Virginia City, Nevada.* Las Vegas: Nevada Publications, 1985.

———. *Roughing It.* 1871. Reprint, New York: Harper and Brothers Publishers, 1913.

Van Cleve, Spike. *A Day Late and A Dollar Short.* Kansas City: Lowell Press, 1982.

———. *Forty Years' Gatherin's.* Kansas City: Lowell Press, 1977.

Van Etten, Carol. *Tahoe City Yesterdays.* Tahoe City: Sierra Maritime Publications, 1987.

Vanderbilt Jr., Cornelius. *Ranches and Ranch Life in America.* New York: Crown Publishers, 1968.

Webster, Paul. *The Mighty Sierra.* New York: Weathervane Books, 1974.

Wheeler, Sessions S. *The Desert Lake: The Story of Nevada's Pyramid Lake.* Caldwell: The Caxton Printers, 1967.

Wheeler, Sessions S. with William W. Bliss. *Tahoe Heritage: The Bliss Family of Glenbrook, Nevada.* Reno: University of Nevada Press, 1992.

Wilson, Dutch. *Let Me Tell You: Stories of a California Cowboy.* Los Olivos: The Los Olivos Press, 1993.

Winnemucca Hopkins, Sarah. *Life Among the Piutes: Their Wrongs and Claims.* Boston: Cupples, Upham & Co., 1883. Reprint, Reno: University of Nevada Press, 1994.

Wister, Owen. *The Virginian: Horseman of the Plains.* New York: Signet/Penguin, 1902/1979.

Woon, Basil. *In Memoriam, Emily Pentz Wood, 1895-1966.* Pahokee, Fla.: Lake Shore Press Inc., 1966.

———. *None of the Comforts of Home: But Oh, Those Cowboys.* Reno: Federated Features, 1967.

Wren, Thomas. *A History of the State of Nevada: Its Resources and People.* New York, Chicago: The Lewis Publishing Company, 1904.

Zauner, Phyllis. *Lake Tahoe.* Tahoe Paradise, Calif.: Zanel Publications, 1982.

Newspapers

News items are listed separately where they are referenced in the text. The run of dates for most newspapers was generally 1940-1990.

Auburn Journal

Carson City Daily Appeal

Carson City Daily State Register

Carson City Nevada Appeal

Daily Sparks Tribune

Fallon Lahontan Valley News

Gardnerville Record-Courier

Gold Hill Daily News

Grass Valley Union

Humboldt Sun

Las Vegas Review-Journal

Las Vegas Sun

New York American

New York Daily News

New York Times

North Lake Tahoe Bonanza

Reno Evening Gazette

Reno Gazette-Journal

Reno Nevada State Journal

Reno Reporter
    (continued by: *Nevada Independent* and *Reno Reporter*)

Sacramento Bee

San Francisco Chronicle

San Rafael (Calif.) Independent Journal

Virginia City Comstock Chronicle

Virginia City Legend

Virginia City News

Virginia City Territorial Enterprise

Yerington Mason Valley News

Periodicals

Amaral, Anthony. "The Last Machismo in the West." *Nevada Magazine* 38, no. 1 (January/February/March 1978): 18-21.

———. "Movie Cowboy: An American Hero!" *Nevada Magazine* 35, no.1 (Spring 1975): 18-23.

Clancy, Gwendolyn. "In Search of Will James." *Nevada Magazine* (September/October 1990).

Clausen, John. "The Reno Quickie," *Reno Magazine,* May 1979, 25-26.

Cunningham, Carolyn Zieg. "The Tempestuous Life of Will James," *Montana Magazine,* Spring 1981, 18-22.

Cowboys North and South, Official Publication of the Will James Society.

Daley-Taylor, Andria. "Boardwalk Bons Vivants." *Nevada Magazine* 52, no. 6 (November/December 1992): 20-24, 35-37.

Edwards, Jerome. "Mary Pickford's Divorce." *Nevada Historical Society Quarterly* (Fall 1976).

Glotfelty, Cheryll. "Old Folks in the New West: Surviving Change and Staying Fit in 'The Misfits'." *Western American Literature* (Spring 2002): 26-49.

Hage, Bud. "History of Hats and Boots" from "Cowboy Chic." *Nevada Magazine* 39, no. 3 (July/August 1979): 24-28.

Harmon, Mella Rothwell. "Getting Renovated: Reno Divorces in the 1930s." *Nevada Historical Society Quarterly* 42, no. 1 (Spring 1999): 46-68.

Hart, Heidi. "Divorce Depot. Reno: Still Splitsville After All These Years." *Reno News and Review* 1, no. 33 (October 4, 1995): 9-11.

Horton, Susan. "The Six-Week Cure." *Nevada Magazine* (November/December 1981): 27-28.

Jensen, Katharine. "Donner Trail Days." *Nevada Magazine* (March/April 2000): 20-22, 80.

Land, Barbara, and Myrick Land. "Reno Divorce Days." *Nevada Magazine* 56, no. 1. (January/February 1996).

Liebling, A. J. "The Mustang Buzzers." *The New Yorker* (April 3, 1954 and April 10, 1954): 81-91.

McLaughlin, Mark. "Divorce Nevada Style." Parts 1-3. *North Tahoe Truckee This Week*. (June 23, June 30, and July 7, 1999): 14, 22, 28.

"Mechanics of a Reno Divorce are Simple and Swift." *Life* (June 21, 1937): 34-40.

Renshaw Jr., Charles. "The Gambler & the Lady." *The American Weekly*, January 22, 1950, 4.

Robb, Inez. "Out of This World in Reno: Fantastic Story of Life, Liberty and the Pursuit of Alimony in the Dizzy Divorce Capitol Where Law and License Never Clash." Parts 2-8 and 10. *The American Weekly*, May 14-July 9, 1944.

Rocha, Guy Louis. "Gable vs. Gable." *Nevada Magazine* (November/December 1981): 29-30.

Swanson, Harry B. "Migratory Divorce: Sherrer vs. Sherrer and the Future." *Hastings College of Law Journal* 4 (1952).

Wernick, Robert. "Where You Went If You Really Had To Get Unhitched." *Smithsonian* 27, no. 3 (June 1996): 64-73.

_____. "Last of the Divorce Ranches." *The Saturday Evening Post* (July 17, 1965): 30-34.

Unpublished Sources

Ford, Bonnie L. "Women, Marriage, and Divorce in California, 1849-1872." Ph.D. diss., University of California, Davis, 1985.

Harmon, Mella Rothwell. "Divorce and Economic Opportunity in Reno, Nevada During the Great Depression." Unpublished Master's thesis, University of Nevada, Reno, 1998.

Watson, Anita J. "Tarnished Silver: Popular Image and Business Reality of Divorce in 1900-1939." Unpublished Master's thesis, University of Nevada, Reno, 1989.

Other Sources

Calhoun, James. W. "Building the Mine Exhibit and Becoming Museum Director," Oral History Program, University of Nevada, 1987. Conducted and edited by R. T. King. pp 77-81.

Delano Forums, "The Roosevelt Dynasty Article, Part 3." www.delanoye.org/forums

Guild, Clark J. "Memoirs of Careers with Nevada Bench and Bar." Oral History Program, University of Nevada, Reno, 1967.

Mosconi, Joseph P. "Reflection on Life in Truckee, Verdi and Reno, 1900-1960." Oral History Program, University of Nevada, Reno, 1987.

"Nevada Dude Ranch Association," Reno: Chamber of Commerce (1936).

Rocha, Guy Louis. "Historical Myth a Month." Nevada State Library and Archives. http://dmla.clan.lib.nv.us/docs/nsla/archives/myth.

Myth #9 & 100, A Capital Name: Kit Carson and Carson City

Myth #21, Marilyn Monroe: Mystery and Myth;

Myth #38, Levi's 501 Jeans: A Riveting Story in Early Reno

Myth #42, The First Hotel Built in the World After World War II?

Myth #44, Carson City's Jack's Bar: "A Saloon Since 1859?"

Myth #49, Divorcing Myth From Truth: Mary Pickford's Divorce

Myth #60, Myths and "The Misfits"

Myth #68, Getting "Reno-Vated": The Ring of Truth

Myth #72, Stepping Up To The Bar: Female Attorneys in Nevada

"The Nevada Experience: The Reno Cure." #203, Channel 5, KNPB, Reno, PBS.

Index

BMC PUBLICATIONS "History In The First Person"

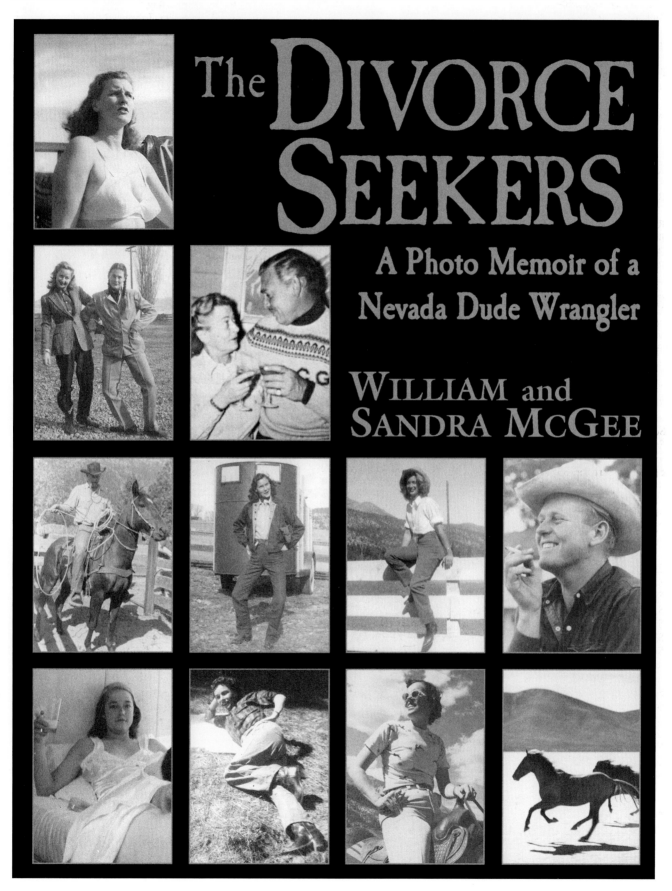

The DIVORCE SEEKERS

A Photo Memoir of a Nevada Dude Wrangler

WILLIAM and SANDRA McGEE

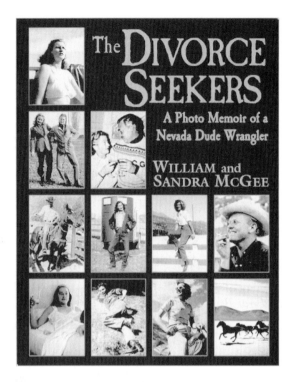

THE DIVORCE SEEKERS
A Photo Memoir of a Nevada Dude Wrangler

William and Sandra McGee

$49.95, Hardcover, 444 pages, 502 b/w illus., plus maps, appendices, notes, bibliography, index, 8-1/2 x 11, ISBN 0-9701678-1-4, 2004.

Bill McGee is one of the few dude wranglers "still above ground" (as he puts it) who lived and worked on a leading Nevada dude ranch during the post-World War II era....Bill tells it like it really was on a dude ranch when Reno was the "Divorce Capital of the World."
—From the Foreword by William W. Bliss

It was 1947...the heyday of the Nevada six weeks divorce when Reno was *the* place to go. Montana cowboy Bill McGee recalls his years wrangling dudes at the Flying M E, an exclusive dude ranch, twenty-one miles south of Reno, catering to wealthy Easterners and the occasional titled European or Hollywood celebrity seeking a quick "Cure" from their matrimonial bonds.

In Part I, McGee enters Montana State on the G. I. Bill, but is soon lured away by a job wrangling horses in Yellowstone National Park in Wyoming. Flat broke, after losing all his earnings at Jackson's Cowboy Bar, he ships his footlocker and saddle freight collect and hitchhikes his way to Reno, Nevada, hiring on as a hunting guide at pristine Lake Tahoe. A chance conversation at the Round Up bar—Reno's unofficial hiring hall for cowboys—puts him in the right place at the right time for his next job: wrangling dudes at the famous Flying M E.

In Part II, McGee profiles the changing cast of characters he met at the ranch. His stories are laced with humor, romance and intrigue, and peppered with names like Astor, du Pont, Roosevelt, and Gable. He recounts how he and the guests passed their time—from "private" riding lessons to bar-hopping in the saloons of Virginia City. One is struck by the number of Eastern dudes who came out West for "just six weeks," fell in love with the wide open spaces—or a cowboy—and stayed.

Part III briefly examines the business of the migratory divorce trade. Two of Reno's leading attorneys are interviewed, and explain Nevada's lenient divorce laws of the era, and how they helped to establish the relatively easy, uncontested grounds for a divorce in most states today. The reader tags along with the press as they cover the high profile Nelson Rockefeller divorce. Part IV profiles Nevada's first ranch to take in dudes, plus other leading Nevada dude-divorce ranches of the era, and concludes with a brief history of the origins of dude ranching in the West.

Bill and his co-author/wife, Sandra, have collected more than 500 black-and-white photographs (most never before published), providing readers with an up-close glimpse into this brief but fascinating era in Nevada history.

Other Books by William L. McGee

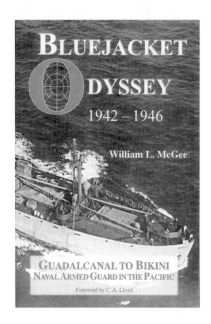

BLUEJACKET ODYSSEY 1942-1946
Guadalcanal to Bikini
Naval Armed Guard in the Pacific

$35.00, Softcover, 546 pages, 250 photos and illustrations, plus appendices, bibliography and index, 6 x 9, ISBN 0-9701678-0-6, revised edition 2000. Foreword by C. A. Lloyd, Chairman, USN Armed Guard Veterans of WWII.

Your book brought tears to my eyes. A "must read" for all veterans, and their descendants, too. —Charles C. Espy, Lt. (jg), USNR, *SS Thomas Nelson*

Montana cowboy, William McGee, joined the U.S. Navy in 1942 on his seventeenth birthday. He was assigned to the Naval Armed Guard, the Navy branch that protected Merchant Marine ships and their valuable cargo and crew from enemy attacks and sabotage. McGee's "Kid's Cruise" threw him in the middle of air attacks at Guadalcanal, torpedoing in the South Pacific, carried him through the war in the Western Pacific, and ended with the atomic bomb tests at Bikini. Drawing on his own daily shipboard journal, three years of interviews with former shipmates, records and declassified documents from the National Archives, and exhaustive research, McGee has produced an engrossing book that has the inimitable mark of one that has been there. He tells an honest, factual story that takes the reader for a ride through the war zones on four merchant ships and the heavy cruiser *Fall River*.

Amphibious Operations in the South Pacific in WWII Series

This series provides both the history buff and casual reader of WWII history with a close-up look at amphibious operations in the South Pacific.

THE AMPHIBIANS ARE COMING!
Emergence of the 'Gator Navy and its Revolutionary Landing Craft
Volume I

$29.95, Softcover, 308 pages, 110 photos and illustrations, plus appendices, notes, bibliography and index, 6 x 9, ISBN 0-9701678-6-5, 2000.

Bill McGee has not only done exhaustive research into how the amphibious forces were built, he has added the words of the men who took the theory of the amphibious doctrine and the new machines to sea. His dedicated work will surely help keep the day-to-day naval record of the "Greatest Generation" from being lost.
— John Lorelli, author of
To Foreign Shores–U. S. Amphibious Operations in World War II

A compelling story of "green" crews, "green" officers, "green" dragons, and "green" camouflage. You'll find yourself chuckling and nodding in the affirmative as you recall your own moments of terror, mind-numbing boredom and outrageous pranks. I guarantee you'll have renewed respect for the guy you see in the mirror every morning. — Howard Clarkson, USS LCI National Association

The first in the series titled, *Amphibious Operations in the South Pacific in WWII, The Amphibians Are Coming!* is a biographical history of the revolutionary WWII landing craft and the brave men who manned them. McGee's careful research, hundreds of interviews, and a point-blank writing style combine to capture the very essence of the amphibians' assignments in the WWII 'Gator Navy. Includes a brief history of amphibious warfare, from the Revolutionary War to the 1942 Guadalcanal and North Africa campaigns. Profiles the famed "Green Dragons," the high-speed destroyer transports that filled a pressing Marine Corps need for ship-to-shore delivery prior to the availability of the new landing craft. Focuses on the "Earlybird" Flotilla Five LCTs, LSTs and LCIs, from design and construction, to on-the-job warfare training in the Southern Solomons—in preparation for their first invasion of enemy-held territory, Operation TOENAILS.

THE SOLOMONS CAMPAIGNS
1942-1943
From Guadalcanal to Bougainville–Pacific War Turning Point
Volume II

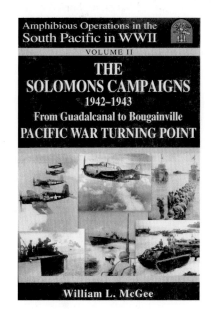

$39.95, Softcover, 688 pages, 352 photos and illustrations, maps and charts, plus appendices, notes, bibliography and index, 6 x 9, ISBN 0-9701678-7-3, 2002.

Enough gripping drama, heroism, and heartbreak in McGee's almost encyclopedic work to supply Hollywood with material for a century. –Marine Corps League

A thoroughgoing historical record and analysis that historians and scholars will find invaluable. –Library Journal

The follow-up to *The Amphibians Are Coming!*, this second volume covers all the Solomons Campaigns and tells the story of America's first offensive after Pearl Harbor. Part I, "The Southern Solomons Campaigns," is excerpted from Volumes IV and V of distinguished naval historian Samuel Loring Morison's *History of United States Naval Operations in World War II*, and covers the bloody six-month struggle for Guadalcanal. Part II, "The Central Solomons Campaigns," chronicles the amphibious operations in the New Georgia Islands group, including the five separate landings at Rendova, Segi Point, Viru Harbor, Wickham Anchorage, and Rice Anchorage. Part III, "The Northern Solomons Campaigns," recounts the seizure of the Treasury Islands, the Choiseul Diversion, the Bougainville campaign, and sums up the many valuable lessons learned during the Solomons Campaigns—most becoming doctrine in later Pacific campaigns.

For Reviews and more Testimonials, visit www.BMCpublications.com
To order direct from the publisher, please see Order Form on next page.

BMC PUBLICATIONS "History In The First Person"

ORDER FORM

If you are unable to obtain a BMC title through your local bookstore or Amazon.com, you may place your order directly with BMC. Please complete this Order Form and mail it along with your check payable to BMC Publications to:

BMC Publications
1397 St. James Drive
St. Helena, CA 94574

QTY	Title	Price	Total
	The Divorce Seekers	$49.95	$
	Bluejacket Odyssey 1942-1946	$35.00	$
	The Amphibians Are Coming! Volume I	$29.95	$
	The Solomons Campaigns, Volume II	$39.95	$
	The Amphibians Are Coming! Volume I and The Solomons Campaigns, Volume II Order both volumes and save 20%	$55.95	$
	SUB TOTAL		$
	California residents include 7.75% sales tax		$
	Shipping and handling for first title		$ 5.00
	S&H per each additional title, $2.00		$
	TOTAL		$

Please ship to:

Name _____

Address _____

City _____ State _____ Zip _____

Daytime Phone ( ) _____ (if there's a question about your order)

❏ I would like the author(s) to sign my book(s).

All domestic orders shipped via U.S. Media Mail. Please allow 14 days for delivery.

BMC Publications, 1397 St. James Drive, St. Helena, CA 94574
email: BMCpublications@aol.com
www.BMCpublications.com
Tel: 707-967-8322

THANK YOU FOR YOUR ORDER